D1706781

THE TRANSFORMATION OF THE CLASSICAL HERITAGE
Peter Brown, General Editor

The Barbarian Plain

The Barbarian Plain

Saint Sergius between Rome and Iran

Elizabeth Key Fowden

UNIVERSITY OF CALIFORNIA PRESS
Berkeley   Los Angeles   London

Title page image: Rusafa. Aerial view from north.

University of California Press
Berkeley and Los Angeles, California

University of California Press, Ltd.
London, England

© 1999 by the Regents of the University of California

Library of Congress Cataloging-in-Publication Data

Fowden, Elizabeth Key, 1964–
    The barbarian plain : Saint Sergius between Rome and
Iran / Elizabeth Key Fowden.
        p.   cm. — (The transformation of the classical
heritage ; 28)
    Includes bibliographical references and index.
    ISBN 0-520-21685-7 (alk. paper)
    1. Sargis, Saint, 4th cent—Cult.   2. Rusfa (Extinct
city)—Church history.   3. Syria—Church history.
4. Iraq—Church history.   I. Title.   II. Series.
BR1720.S23F68   1999
270.2'092—dc21
    [B]   99-22672
                                                        CIP

Manufactured in the United States of America
08   07   06   05   04   03   02   01   00   99
10   9   8   7   6   5   4   3   2   1

The paper used in this publication meets the minimum
requirements of ANSI/NISO z39.48-1992 (R 1997)
(*Permanence of Paper*).

In memory of my father
R. E. Key

grandfathers
R. W. Key
K. W. Crusius

and godfather
P. O. A. Sherrard

City built on a high mountain, which cannot be taken!
Fortress of our country, by which the whole region is protected!

Beautiful name, Sergius, which is beloved to all ears,
and whose story is the favorite and the pride of the populace.

JACOB OF SARUG (D. 521), *MIMRA ON THE VICTORIOUS SERGIUS AND BACCHUS* 117–118, TR. ANDREW PALMER

CONTENTS

ILLUSTRATIONS

PREFACE

My interest in the cultural landscape of Syria grew out of a visit to southeastern Turkey and northern Syria in 1989, after a year spent in Greece. Looking down on the Euphrates from Samosata, not yet inundated, I was struck by the diversity of the landscapes and communities that the river would pass before dissipating itself in the marshes of southern Iraq. The idea of using the cult of Saint Sergius as a way into these overlapping communities arose, gradually, after my study of Syrian epigraphy with Glen Bowersock in 1991.

While writing this book, I have been kept in good company by three groups of people, variously enmeshed with Syria. Each, I believe, has left its impression. They resist chronological classification, so I shall begin with the representatives of the French tradition of scholarship in Mandate Syria—René Dussaud, Jean Sauvaget, Daniel Schlumberger, Henri Seyrig—who set the standard for fusing literary, archeological, architectural, and topographical evidence in historical enquiry, broadly writ. The second presence here is Princeton University, both as the sponsor of the Princeton Archaeological Expedition to Syria at the beginning of the twentieth century, and as the academic institution in whose Prentice, Firestone, and Jones-Palmer libraries much of this book's framework was laid. At Princeton, conversations with Glen Bowersock, Ted Champlin, Danny Ćurčić, Oleg Grabar, and especially my supervisor, Peter Brown, were always stimulating, even if the sediment stirred settled into new shapes only once I was back at my home in northern Euboea.

Unlike the first two, the third presence reaches back much further than a century, back, at least, to King Abgar of Edessa. This is the Syrian Orthodox community of Aleppo, guided by its excellent metropolitan Mor Yohanna Grigorios Ibrahim. Five months with the Aleppo community taught me much about historical memory and community identity, as I waded through the torrential winter floods to sing Syriac morning hymns with the children at S. George's under the zealous leadership of Malfono Abrohom Nuro; read S. Ephrem with the metropolitan before his daily stream of petitioners began to flow; and traveled in convoy to the jubilant consecration in Qamishli of the new archbishop and patriarchal vicar for the eastern United States. For their generosity and interest, I warmly thank Metropolitan Yohanna and the Syrian Orthodox community of Aleppo.

One of the great pleasures of this project has been the glimpse it has allowed me into the world of Syriac scholarship. I was fortunate to begin Syriac with John Marks at Princeton in his last year before retirement. None of the Syriac literature concerned with S. Sergius has been previously studied, and I owe much gratitude to Sebastian Brock and Andrew Palmer, to whom I several times turned with questions relating to these texts. For matters Arabic (as well as countless others), I have benefited from Garth Fowden's enthusiasm for both that language and S. Sergius. Where not otherwise attributed, translations from Arabic are his. al-Isfahani's *Kitab al-aghani* served as the leitmotif of our stay in Aleppo, and some of the labor exerted there has borne fruit in this book.

The German archeologists and architectural historians involved with Rusafa have been exceptionally generous in their response to my work. I would like to thank their leader, Thilo Ulbert, as well as Gunnar Brands and Stephan Westphalen. I am also indebted to Jonathan Rae and George 'Arab of the International Center for Agricultural Research in Dry Areas, with whom we spent invaluable hours in the north Syrian steppe. I am grateful to Glen Bowersock, Peter Brown, Ted Champlin, Garth Fowden, and James Howard-Johnston for reading and commenting on the entire typescript at various stages; as well as to Tom Sinclair and Joel Walker, who commented on an earlier draft of chapter 2, and to Gunnar Brands and Thilo Ulbert, who did the same for earlier drafts of chapter 3 and the end of chapter 5. None of these should be held responsible for authorial error or gamble.

Limni, Euboea, Greece
21 December 1998

ACKNOWLEDGMENTS

I have been able to travel and conduct research in Syria, Turkey, Jordan, and Palestine thanks to the Robert F. Goheen Prize in Classical Studies of the Woodrow Wilson National Fellowships Foundation, as well as travel grants from the Association of Princeton Graduate Alumni, the Department of Classics, the Group for the Study of Late Antiquity, and the Seeger Fellowship Fund of the Program of Hellenic Studies, all at Princeton University. A Mellon Fellowship in the Humanities and a Dissertation Grant from the National Endowment for the Humanities allowed me two free years for the completion of my dissertation. Subsequently, I was able to spend five months in Syria thanks to the Olivia James Travelling Fellowship of the American Institute of Archaeology, and enjoyed a full year as the Gennadeion Fellow at the American School of Classical Studies at Athens, working out the implications of my fieldwork and writing the final chapter on S. Sergius in Islamic Syria. Finally, thanks to a research fellowship at the Centre for Greek and Roman Antiquity at the National Research Foundation in Athens, I have had the opportunity to be part of an academic community engaged in exemplary interpretation of material evidence in its physical and literary context. I would like to express my gratitude in particular to Miltiades Hatzopoulos, Louisa Loukopoulou, and Athanasios Rizakis

For permission to illustrate objects or reproduce photographs I am obliged to the Walters Art Gallery, Baltimore, Maryland (fig. 1); the Trustees of the British Museum (fig. 3); the Ninth Ephoria of Byzantine Antiquities, Thessaloniki (fig. 4); the Museum of Art and Archaeology, University of Missouri–Columbia (fig. 6a); Janet Zacos (fig. 6c); the Royal Ontario Museum (fig. 6d); Verlag Philipp von Zabern (figs. 8, 9, 12, and 15); Richard

Anderson, courtesy of Dumbarton Oaks (fig. 13); Domos Publications, Athens (fig. 14); Thilo Ulbert, courtesy of Deutsches Archäologisches Institut Damaskus (fig. 16).

Sources for the photographs are R. Mouterde and A. Poidebard, *Limes de Chalcis* (Paris, 1945), pl. LXXIV (title page image); K. Weitzmann, *The Monastery of Saint Catherine at Mount Sinai: The Icons, 1: From the Sixth to the Tenth Century* (Princeton, N.J., 1976), pl. XII (fig. 2); J. Meischner, *AA* (1993), pl. 1 (fig. 5); C. Mondésert, *Syria* 37 (1960), fig. 4 (fig. 6b); G. Zacos and A. Veglery, *Byzantine Lead Seals* (Basel, 1972), no. 2975 (fig. 6c); G. Vikan, *DOP* 38 (1984), fig. 10 (fig. 6d); P. Ronzevalle, *CRAI* 1904, fig. 1 (fig. 7); J. Kollwitz, *AA* (1957): 70, fig. 2 (fig. 10); author (fig. 11).

NOTE ON TRANSLITERATION

In my transliterations of Syriac and Arabic I have kept diacritics to a minimum. Syriac and Arabic titles are transliterated where that form is well known; otherwise, they are cited in the established Latin or English translation. Where available, translations of the oriental sources are included in the bibliography. Greek authors and sources are given their conventional Latin spelling and titles.

In cases where both ancient and modern names are known for a site, both appear, in that order, on first occurrence in the text, but only the ancient name appears subsequently. Map 3 uses modern names, cross-referenced in the index where possible, since the majority of the Hawranian sites I discuss are known only by their Arabic names.

ABBREVIATIONS

Abbreviations follow the conventions of *Prosopography of the Later Roman Empire*, ed. A. H. M. Jones, J. R. Martindale, J. Morris et al., and F. R. Adrados, *Diccionario Griego-Español*; for periodicals, see *L'Année philologique*. Note also the following:

AAS	*Annales archéologiques syriennes* (Damascus)
ACOec.	*Acta conciliorum oecumenicorum,* ed. E. Schwartz (Strasbourg, 1914–)
Acta Sanct.	*Acta Sanctorum* (Antwerp 1643–)
AMS	*Acta martyrum et sanctorum,* ed. P. Bedjan (Paris, 1890–97)
BAFIC	I. Shahîd, *Byzantium and the Arabs in the Fifth Century* (Washington, D.C., 1989)
BAFOC	I. Shahîd, *Byzantium and the Arabs in the Fourth Century* (Washington, D.C., 1984)
BA-IAS	*Bulletin of the Anglo-Israeli Archaeological Society* (London)
BASIC	I. Shahîd, *Byzantium and the Arabs in the Sixth Century* (Washington, D.C., 1995–)
BHG	*Bibliotheca hagiographica graeca,* ed. F. Halkin (Brussels, 1957)
BHO	*Bibliotheca hagiographica orientalis,* ed. P. Peeters (Brussels, 1910)
Bib.Sanct.	*Bibliotheca Sanctorum* (Rome, 1961–69)
BIFAO	*Bulletin de l'Institut français d'archéologie orientale* (Cairo)
BMGS	*Byzantine and Modern Greek Studies* (Birmingham)
BRL	*Bulletin of the John Rylands Library* (Manchester)
BSOAS	*Bulletin of the School of Oriental and African Studies* (London)
Bull.	*Bulletin épigraphique* (Paris)
CArch	*Cahiers archéologiques* (Paris)

CHIran	*The Cambridge History of Iran*, ed. W. B. Fisher et al. (Cambridge, 1968–91)
Chron 1234	*Chronicum ad annum Christi 1234 pertinens*, ed. J.-B. Chabot (Louvain, 1920), and tr. (Louvain, 1937)
CIG	*Corpus inscriptionum graecarum* (Berlin, 1828–77)
CIL	*Corpus inscriptionum latinarum* (Berlin 1863–)
CIMRM	*Corpus inscriptionum et monumentorum religionis mithriacae*, ed. M. J. Vermaseren (The Hague, 1956–60)
CSEL	*Corpus scriptorum ecclesiasticorum latinorum*
DACL	*Dictionnaire d'archéologie chrétienne et de liturgie* (Paris, 1907–53)
DaM	*Damaszener Mitteilungen* (Mainz)
DCAE	*Δελτίον τῆς Χριστιανικῆς Ἀρχαιολογικῆς Ἑταιρείας* (Athens)
DHGE	*Dictionnaire de l'histoire et de la géographie ecclésiastiques* (Paris 1912–)
Dict. de théologie	*Dictionnaire de théologie catholique* (Paris, 1909–50)
EI[1]	*The Encyclopaedia of Islam*[1], ed. M. Th. Houtsma et al. (Leiden, 1913–38)
EI[2]	*The Encyclopaedia of Islam*[2], ed. H. A. R. Gibb et al. (Leiden, 1960–)
Gatier, *Inscriptions*	P.-L. Gatier, *Inscriptions de la Jordanie*, vol. 2: *Région centrale (Amman, Hesban, Madaba, Main, Dhiban)* (Paris, 1986)
Hist.Ahud.	*History of Ahudemmeh*, ed. F. Nau, *PO* 3.1.7–51
IEJ	*Israel Exploration Journal* (Jerusalem)
IGLS	*Inscriptions grecques et latines de la Syrie*, ed. L. Jalabert, R. Mouterde et al. (Paris, 1929–)
JA	*Journal asiatique* (Paris)
JECS	*Journal of Early Christian Studies* (Baltimore)
JRAS	*Journal of the Royal Asiatic Society* (London)
MDOG	*Mitteilungen der Deutschen Orient-Gesellschaft zu Berlin* (Berlin)
MGH, SRM	*Monumenta germaniae historica, Scriptores rerum Merovingicarum*
MHR	*Mediterranean Historical Review* (Tel Aviv)
MUSJ	*Mélanges de l'Université Saint-Joseph* (Beirut)
NJKA	*Neue Jahrbücher für das klassische Altertum*
Nouvelles archives	*Nouvelles archives des missions scientifiques et littéraires* (Paris)
OC	*Oriens christianus* (Wiesbaden)
OCP	*Orientalia christiana periodica* (Rome)
PAES	*Princeton University Archaeological Expedition to Syria in 1904–1905 and 1909* (Leiden, 1907–22)

PEQ	*Palestine Exploration Quarterly* (London)
PG	*Patrologia graeca,* ed. J. P. Migne (Paris, 1857–66)
PL	*Patrologia latina,* ed. J. P. Migne (Paris, 1844–64)
PLRE	*The Prosopography of the Later Roman Empire,* ed. A. H. M. Jones (vol. 1), J. R. Martindale (vols. 1–3) and J. Morris (vol. 1) (Cambridge, 1971–92)
PO	*Patrologia orientalis,* ed. R. Graffin and F. Nau et al. (Paris, 1907–)
P-OChr	*Proche-orient chrétienne* (Jerusalem)
Prentice, *Greek and Latin Inscriptions*	W. K. Prentice, *Greek and Latin Inscriptions,* Publications of an American Archaeological Expedition to Syria in 1899–1900, part 3 (New York, 1908)
PSAS	*Proceedings of the Seminar for Arabian Studies* (Cambridge)
RAC	*Reallexikon für Antike und Christentum* (Stuttgart, 1950–)
RE	*Real-Encyclopädie der klassischen Altertumswissenschaft,* ed. A. Pauly, G. Wissowa, and W. Kroll (Stuttgart, 1893–1980)
REArm	*Revue des études arméniennes* (Paris)
RSO	*Rivista degli studi orientali* (Rome)
SC	*Sources chrétiennes* (Paris)
SEG	*Supplementum epigraphicum graecum* (Leiden, 1923–)
Waddington, *Inscriptions*	W. H. Waddington, *Inscriptions grecques et latines de la Syrie (Paris, 1870)*
ZDMG	*Zeitschrift der Deutschen Morgenländischen Gesellschaft* (Leipzig)
ZDP-V	*Zeitschrift des Deutschen Palästina-Vereins* (Weisbaden)

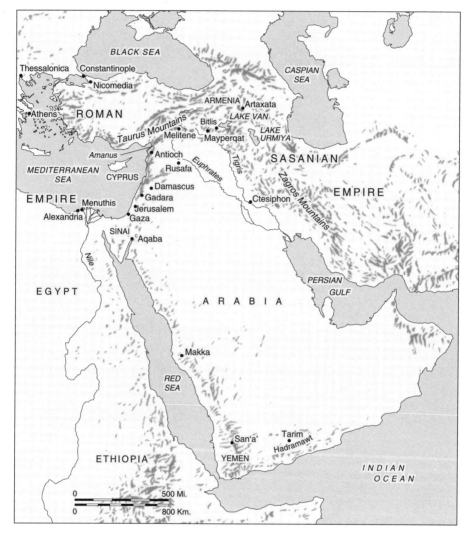

Map 1. The eastern Mediterranean world in late antiquity.

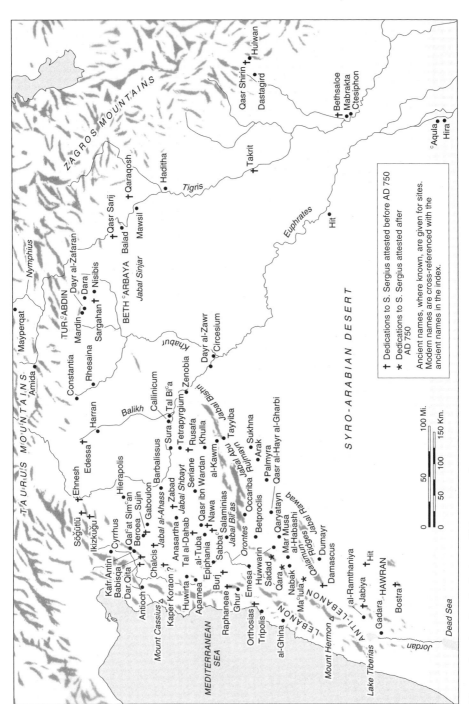

Map 2. Sergius sites in Syria and Mesopotamia.

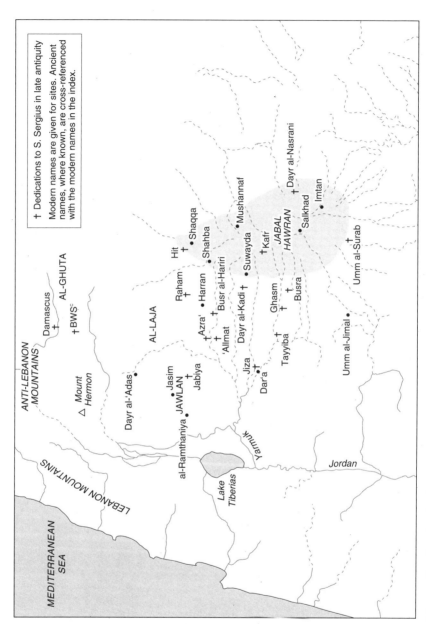

Map 3. Sergius sites in the Hawran.

Introduction

In the sixth century A.D., the Greek-speaking world knew the Syrian steppe that spread out around Rusafa as the "Barbarian Plain."[1] Rusafa was situated in the frontier zone between the great late antique empires of Rome and Sasanian Iran, a geographical position that gave the fortified settlement political and cultural importance for the Romans, for the Iranians, and for their Arab allies who inhabited the region. All these parties sought in varying ways, from military invasion to more subtle cultural penetration, to stake claims to this crucial region. It was at Rusafa in the Barbarian Plain that the cult of S. Sergius was sown and gradually took root in the region's diverse communities. The widespread dissemination of reverence for the martyr offers a rare opportunity to view the overlapping of the cultural traditions that flourished in late antique Syria and Mesopotamia.

Viewed on the ground, Rusafa occupies the near-center of Syria and Mesopotamia combined. But on the mental maps of the region's diverse inhabitants and visitors, Rusafa's position varied. To a wandering monk from Constantinople, Rusafa belonged to the "Persian desert"; to a Western pilgrim, it lay in "Saracen country" just beyond the Holy Land's eastern limit; the orbit of influence claimed by a Nestorian monastery east of the Euphrates extended as far west as Rusafa; while for the Arabs of the Banu Ghassan, the fortress-shrine marked the northeasternmost reach of their territory.

The Barbarian Plain is a space within the much greater plain that is Syria-Mesopotamia, an enormous, variegated area that owes what unity it possesses to the mountains around it—from the hills of Palestine to the

---

1. τὸ Βαρβαρικὸν Πεδίον. Proc., *BP* 2.5.29; Theoph. Sim., *Hist.* 5.13.3; Evagr., *HE* 6.21; *Vita Gulanducht* 24–26. For further discussion, see pp. 65–66.

Amanus on the west, the Taurus on the north, and the Zagros on the east. To the south the plain blurs into the Syro-Arabian desert. The mountains, which form an arch around the plain, did not act as impenetrable barriers, since trade and transhumance linked Syria and Mesopotamia with lands beyond.[2] The mountains' abruptness could impose an obstacle, but a more significant determinant of a mountain's permeability was the cultural character of those who dwelt in or around it. The great Zagros range stretches from the Persian Gulf to the Caspian Sea and divides the Syro-Mesopotamian plain from the harsher Iranian plateau, the stronghold of a more homogeneous Iranian culture than ever flourished in the plain below. Just below the Caspian Sea, the Zagros links up with the Taurus range, which reaches as far as southwestern Anatolia. The Taurus, abrupt but not impervious, rises high above the Syro-Mesopotamian plain. At the plain's northwesterly limit, the Orontes river flows out to the Mediterranean between Amanus and Mount Cassius. Caught between the sea and the mountains, the westward-looking coastal plain was married to the Mediterranean world and to some extent alienated from the experience of Syria and Mesopotamia east of the mountains.

Bounded on the west by this mountain belt, the high Syro-Mesopotamian plain is always much more elevated, at ca. 500 m, than the Mediterranean coastal plain. Its altitude, its isolation from the sea's temperate influence and its exposure to the Syro-Arabian desert to the south combine to create an extreme continental climate, in which temperatures may vary dramatically according to season, but also within twenty-four hours. Most of the Syro-Mesopotamian plain is best described as steppe, often treeless. Its seasonal grasses and bushes can be surprisingly abundant after rains, which, in turn, determine the movements of pastoralists with their flocks. Steppeland differs from desert in potential. For practical purposes, the steppe is defined here as potentially cultivable arid land. The desert too sprouts grasses, but thanks to occasional wells, springs, and seasonal rains, the steppe can, in places, support cultivation. The Syro-Mesopotamian steppe is crossed by a network of ridges—Qalamun, Abu Rujmayn, Bishri—extending northeast from the Anti-Lebanon mountains to the Euphrates. The north Syrian steppe undulates eastward toward Mesopotamia with little interruption, save salt marshes, basalt outcrops, and scattered tells. Low ridges and wadis punctuate the gravel- and stone-covered south Syrian steppe, which merges with the great Syro-Arabian desert.

Because of its size and diversity, the Syro-Mesopotamian plain could not

2. For particularly memorable evocations of the cultural unity of Syria-Mesopotamia in late antiquity, see Garsoïan, *CHIran*, 3: 568–75, and Brown, *Religion and Society*, 101–5. See also Howard-Johnston in *Byzantine and Early Islamic Near East*, ed. Cameron, 3: 157–226, for a study of the Sasanian empire that emphasizes the role of geography in its political institutions.

be dominated by one group of its inhabitants. Instead, pastoralists, farmers, craftsmen, merchants, monks, and soldiers were joined in a network of symbioses. The eastern, northern, and western fringes were densely populated in many places, and their inhabitants, especially in the eastern half, were very diverse. They included Zoroastrians, Jews, polytheists, and Christians of Nestorian, Chalcedonian, and non-Chalcedonian ("monophysite") allegiance. Many of both the permanent and of the less permanent inhabitants of Syria and Mesopotamia were mobile by vocation—pastoralists, semi-pastoralists, merchants, teachers, students, and pilgrims.

Seen from the outside, life in the more arid regions of the steppe, and even more so in the desert, is restless. Settled populations often view the steppe as an obstacle, a sterile, alien territory. Much of this impression derives from ignorance of the landscape. Knowledge of the steppe's variety and potential was the basic tool of pastoralists, and this knowledge had to be both detailed and local, but at the same time command the grander patterns of the steppe. Because movement in the steppe, whether for seasonal migration, commercial interests, warfare, or pilgrimage, frequently took one through lonely expanses, great importance was assumed by points of convergence, especially round water sources. In the great Syro-Mesopotamian spaces, these fixed places were flash points where all forms of human interaction—social, economic, political, and religious—tended to concentrate.

Within this landscape, the political frontier between the Roman and Iranian empires acted as an artificial divide. In order to maintain their territorial claims, both empires turned to military alliances with the Arab inhabitants of the region and to the construction of fortifications. It is in part the intention of this study to demonstrate how from the point of view of Romans, Iranians, and Arabs alike, divine defense went hand in hand with arms and walls, a fact of late antique history often overlooked or ignored. If one of the historian's goals ought to be to "attempt to ascertain contemporary thinking and values and then look at how these were realized in practice," we cannot afford to project onto our evidence a separation of religious belief and political or military action.[3] Unless we take seriously the widely held belief in the power of saints and their relics to influence the political and military history of the frontier zone, any attempt to explain developments in the region and their broader impact will be one-dimensional.

Procopius names towers and fortresses throughout the Roman empire that bore the names of saints.[4] In Roman Syria, it was not uncommon for

---

3. The quotation is from Isaac in *Byzantine and Early Islamic Near East,* ed. Cameron, 3: 150.

4. See Proc., *Aed.* 4.4, for fortresses dedicated to S. Sabianus and S. Stephen in Epirus Nova, one to S. Sabianus and two to S. Donatus in Epirus Vetus; ibid. 4.11, to S. Trajan, S. Julian, and S. Theodore in Thrace; ibid. 5.7, to S. Cyril in Scythia.

military architecture to be placed under the protection of Christian saints. For instance, between Chalcis / Qinnasrin and Emesa / Homs, three fortified posts (μητᾶτα) dating from the late fifth and sixth centuries were associated with holy patrons: the archangel Michael and the centurion Longinus at Burj ("tower" in Arabic); S. Longinus along with S. Theodore and S. George at Ghur; and, finally, the martyr Sergius, dedicatee of a metaton at Raphanaea / Rafniya, a vital station in a pass through the Anti-Lebanon.[5] At another Burj, near Dumayr, northeast of Damascus, an inscription relates that the Ghassanid phylarch al-Mundhir dedicated a tower to S. Julian.[6] Saints Longinus, Theodore, George, Sergius, and Julian all distinguished themselves as soldier-martyrs, and all earned respectable followings in the Roman East.[7] What was unusual about the soldier-martyr Sergius was the breadth of his appeal: by the sixth century, his reputation had spread beyond Roman territory into Iran, as well as among the Arab tribes between the two empires. S. Sergius seems to have been politically color-blind. S. George also attracted devotees in the Sasanian empire. But although the soldier saints George and Sergius were sometimes confused, it was S. Sergius and not S. George who was chosen by political leaders in the region as a means of affirming their authority. Vital to this development was the fact that in hagiographical tradition, S. Sergius had been executed during the Great Persecution at the fort of Rusafa near the middle Euphrates.

This study of the cult of S. Sergius in Syria and Mesopotamia focuses on the nature of the cult in the frontier zone in late antiquity. It by no means aspires to be a comprehensive account of the Sergius cult wherever and whenever it took root, which would take us as far east as Mongolia in geographical space,[8] and in time right up to the present day, inasmuch as together with George and Thecla, Sergius remains one of the most revered saints in the Middle East among both Christian and Muslims. *The Barbarian Plain* consists of six chapters. In the first, an examination of the *Passio* and artistic images of S. Sergius attempts to reconstruct the rise of the martyr's cult at Rusafa in the fifth century. With S. Sergius established at Rusafa, chapter 2 takes a broader view of the increasing interest in martyrs in connection with frontier defense—the particular example chosen to illustrate this development is Bishop Marutha's cult of Iranian martyrs at Mayperqat. This provides the necessary context for the buildup of S. Sergius's cult at Rusafa. The third chapter discusses the historical and archeological evidence for the Sergius cult at Rusafa: the strategic importance of the site at

5. For references and discussion, see pp. 113–14 below.

6. Waddington, *Inscriptions*, no. 2562c. On al-Mundhir's tower, see Shahîd, *BASIC*, 1: 495–50, 524–26.

7. On the cult of military saints, see Delehaye, *Légendes grecques*, and Orselli, *Santitá militare*.

8. For the easternmost appearance of S. Sergius, see Mingana, *BRL* 9 (1925): 297–371.

Rome's eastern limit; Rusafa's place in trade and transhumance patterns; and its significance as a pilgrimage center. With the growth of pilgrimage, the Sergius cult spread outward from the site of his martyrdom, and chapter 4 traces the material and literary evidence for the saint's popularity in Syria and Mesopotamia. In chapter 5, the leaders of Rome, Iran, and the Arab tribes that dwelt between them take center stage, and the discussion focuses on their attempts to tap into the martyr's popularity and influence in Syria and Mesopotamia for their own political ends. The final chapter is concerned with the Sergius cult after the Islamic conquests, joining together disparate evidence to reconstruct a picture, not only of the continuity of Christian cult, but also of the symbiosis achieved by Christian and Muslim followers of S. Sergius.

"Barbarian Plain" is, of course, an outsider's label. It is useful, though, since in the name itself the steppe is fused with its inhabitants. While much of this book focuses on the empires of Rome and Iran, in whose frontier zone the cult of S. Sergius flourished, one of the most important factors that emerges is the role of architecture and fixed points, such as Rusafa, in the lives of the pastoralists and semi-pastoralists who inhabited the frontier zone. This study is offered as one step toward the history of what Fergus Millar has called "the marginal zone between the steppe and the cultivable land."[9]

9. Millar, *Roman Near East*, 333.

ONE

Portraits of a Martyr

Not long before 431, Bishop Alexander of Hierapolis / Manbij in northern Syria invested three hundred pounds of gold to build a church in the middle of the Syrian steppe, a region he himself described as a wilderness. The church rose up within the walls of the fortress called Rusafa and was dedicated to the martyr Sergius. This event is the first evidence we can comfortably associate with S. Sergius and his cult—before the church's construction, there is silence in the sources. Afterward, the cult gained impetus and the *Passio* of SS. Sergius and Bacchus was written down. Gradually, the cult of S. Sergius established itself as a prominent feature in the cultural landscape of late antique Syria and Mesopotamia. Rusafa, located about 30 kilometers south of a bend in the middle Euphrates, lay at the eastern limit of the Roman empire, at the western limit of the Iranian empire, and near the center of the Syro-Mesopotamian world. The shrine attracted a wide range of patrons, including the Roman emperor Justinian, the Iranian king of kings Khusrau II, and the Ghassanid phylarch al-Mundhir. Already in the fifth century, the martyr's influence had begun to radiate outward from Rusafa across Syria and Mesopotamia. It was to extend as far afield as the foothills of the Zagros Mountains, Armenia, Egypt, and Gaul. But S. Sergius's prominence in fifth- through seventh-century Syria and Mesopotamia remained closely linked to his principal shrine's location in a region where diverse cultures mingled and two great powers, Rome and Iran, confronted each other.

The *Passio* of SS. Sergius and Bacchus relates the martyrdom of both saints and the miracles worked by S. Sergius after his death. Hagiography is a notorious minefield for the historian, and we would be wise to approach the *Passio* from the perspective of the fifth-century world it reflects—that is, of the time of its composition. Anachronism and confusion in the *Passio* reflect the quality of the author's information and should be seen within the framework of his purpose, which was to describe the crowning of a martyr. In such a work, accounts of events might be historically inaccurate, but it did not matter as long as they fulfilled their purpose of setting the symbolic scene in which the current of God's redemptive grace could flow through the miracle-working saint to his followers. This *Passio* seems to have done just that. The course of history is influenced as much, if not more, by what is perceived to have happened in the past as by what can perhaps be documented from written sources. What is of concern to the historian of the cult of S. Sergius is the martyr's posthumous reputation. Whether or not there was a soldier named Sergius who was martyred outside Rusafa, and whether this was at the command of the emperor Galerius, Maximinus Daia, or even Julian, was more or less irrelevant to the cult's later development. From at least the early fifth century onward, Sergius was believed in the hearts of the faithful to have been martyred at Rusafa sometime in the distant past, in the Age of Persecution when martyrs were made. Reading the *Passio* from a fifth-century perspective, the story ceases to be a frustrating puzzle that no philological or archeological sleuth will ever be able to put right and becomes instead a precious portrait of a martyr cult in its early stages.

THE *PASSIO* OF SS. SERGIUS AND BACCHUS

With this said by way of introduction, the *Passio* of SS. Sergius and Bacchus now deserves to be retold.[1] Sergius was *primicerius scholae gentilium,* that is, the highest-ranking junior officer in the horse guard, a regiment originally

---

1. The account is preserved in the original Greek, ed. van den Gheyn, *AB* 14 (1895): 373–95 (cited below as *Pass. gr.*); a Syriac translation of the original Greek, ed. Bedjan, *AMS* 3: 283–322 (cited below as *Pass. syr.*); a Latin translation of the original Greek, ed. Byeus, *Acta sanct. Oct.* 3: 863–70; and the Metaphrastic version, a recasting of the Greek original in a more literary style, ed. Byeus, *Acta sanct. Oct.* 3: 871–82. On this later redaction, see Høgel, *Metaphrasis,* 18–21. The Syriac translation retains many Latin military terms from *Pass. gr.* and occasionally substitutes Syriac toponyms. The *Chronicle of Seert* 12.253–54 (Scher) preserves in Arabic a much-distilled version of the *Passio,* as does the Coptic redaction of the *Arab Jacobite Synaxarion* for 1 Oct. (Bacchus) and 7 Oct. (Sergius). The Coptic redaction cannot be dated precisely, but its debt to the *Passio* is clear in the narrative outline, despite certain innovations that are otherwise unattested. For the Arabic redactions, see Graf, *Geschichte der christlichen arabischen Literatur,* 1: 152. The *Armenian Synaxarion of Ter Israel* for 7 Oct. also contains a much-abbreviated version of the *Passio.* This thirteenth-century synaxarion is based on a tradition of translations of saints' lives extending back in some cases as far as the fifth century: see the introductory comments in *PO* 5.3.350–53. Boswell, *Same-Sex Unions,* 375–90, provides a somewhat inaccurate English translation of *Pass. gr.,* in which, for example, *schola gentilium* is rendered as "school of the Gentiles" and Sergius (always referred to as Serge) and Bacchus are called "directors of our school" (and, in conjunction with this mistranslation, see ibid., 377 n. 12, on discrimination against homosexual teachers in schools, evoking the literary parallel of Lillian Hellman's play *The Children's Hour* [1934]).

composed of non-Romans. He was highly favored at the court of an emperor whom the texts call Maximianus, renowned for his persecution of Christians.[2] Sergius was a friend of the emperor and, according to the Syriac account, his kinsman. Together with Bacchus, by analogy the *secundocerius*, he enjoyed great freedom of speech before the throne.[3] Sergius and Bacchus were also Christians, whose faith had not interfered with their worldly prosperity until envious colleagues used it against them. Once, when the two officers were absent from Maximianus's side, they were denounced for their impiety toward the gods and proselytism among the ranks. To find out the truth, Maximianus ordered the pair to accompany him and his assembled soldiers to a temple of Zeus for a sacrifice. As he was partaking of the sacrificial meat there, the emperor looked around but did not see Sergius and Bacchus, who were discovered outside the temple singing hymns against idolatry. Maximianus had the two soldiers brought inside and ordered them to sacrifice and partake in the ritual meal. Reciting Psalm 135 against senseless images, Sergius and Bacchus refused. At once they were stripped of their belts, cloaks, and golden torques (*maniakia*), their symbols of power, and dressed instead in women's garments. Heavy chains were clamped around their necks, and in this fashion they were paraded through the city to the palace, where Maximianus pressed them about their betrayal of him and the gods of Rome. Again the officers responded with a recitation of Christian doctrine. Furious, Maximianus ordered their entire

2. For the identity of the emperor, see below.

3. *Pass. syr.*, p. 285. After Bacchus's execution, Sergius mourns the loss of his "brother," and Bacchus, who appears to Sergius that night, likewise addresses Sergius as "brother" (*Pass. gr.* 9, 20, and *Pass. syr.*, p. 307). Both the Greek and Syriac emphasize that Sergius and Bacchus were joined not by a familial but a spiritual relationship (*Pass. gr.* 2; *Pass. syr.*, p. 285). Yet the Piacenza Pilgrim (ca. 570) understood Bacchus to be Sergius's actual brother (*Itinerarium*, 191). It was perhaps from the Pilgrim's account that Devreesse acquired the erroneous view that they were literally brothers (*Patriarcat*, 284). Boswell, *Same-Sex Unions*, 17–25, discusses a wide range of ancient and modern meanings given to the term "brother" and concludes that Sergius and Bacchus did not call each other brother because they were biologically related, adding "so the appellation 'brother' must be understood as reflective of ancient usage in erotic subcultures or as reflecting biblical usage (particularly in Greek versions). Either way, it would have distinctly erotic connotations" (151). Boswell does not seem to notice that the *Passio*'s author also attaches the appellation to the monks who retrieve Bacchus's body only a few lines before the new martyr addresses Sergius as his brother (*Pass. gr.* 19; *Pass. syr.*, p. 306). Severus of Antioch, who in his homily on S. Sergius draws heavily on the *Passio*, also emphasizes the similarities between the two young men and would surely have alluded to a blood relation had tradition recalled one (Sev. Ant., *Hom. cath.* 57, pp. 85–86; see discussion below). Although Boswell acknowledges that the term "brother" could be employed simply to describe fellow Christians (23), his commentary ignores this usage. In general, Boswell is not much concerned with the historical background of the cult of Sergius and Bacchus (see, e.g., his rendering of the name of the well-known castrum Sura [Σοῦρα] as Souros and Syrum, both inaccurate), but rather with the saintly pair's appearance from the tenth century onward.

bodies to be bound in chains and had them sent to the empire's edge, to Antiochus, *dux* of the province of Augusta Euphratensis, who owed his position to Sergius's recommendation. Maximinus sent with them a letter in which he instructed Antiochus that if Sergius and Bacchus repented, they were to be restored to their former status and would enjoy even greater privileges. For refusal, they would pay with their lives.

The first night they stayed at an inn twelve miles from the unnamed location of their fall from grace. They traveled from city to city until they arrived "in the frontier zone near where the race of Saracens dwell."[4] In the praetorium at the fortress of Barbalissus / Beth Blash, they were brought before the *dux* Antiochus; but he had no success in undermining their resolve, which had in the meantime been strengthened by angelic visitations. Antiochus had Sergius thrown into prison. Bacchus was left to be tortured. After exhausting several crews of floggers, Bacchus rebutted for one last time Antiochus's arguments against Christianity. He then hearkened to a heavenly voice that called the "athlete and soldier" to receive his eternal reward. The martyr's soul fled from Bacchus's tattered body, which was left to the dogs outside the fortress walls. Antiochus rose from the judgment seat and went to dinner. Outside the walls, wild animals circled around Bacchus's corpse, but contrary to nature, guarded it until nightfall, when monks emerged from nearby caves to retrieve the body and provide the martyr with a fitting burial. That night Bacchus, now received into the heavenly ranks and dressed again as a soldier, appeared to Sergius in a dream with consolation and encouragement.

The next day, Antiochus offered Sergius another opportunity to sacrifice, which Sergius again loquaciously refused. Antiochus then had him taken to the fortress of Sura / Shura, where, at another praetorium, the *dux* conducted yet another futile inquisition, after which Sergius was made to put on shoes spiked inside with long nails and forced to run nine miles in front of the ducal chariot to the next fortress, Tetrapyrgium / Magdla d-mayya. Upon arrival, the *dux* went in for a meal and sent Sergius to the military prison. During the night an angel healed Sergius's feet. The next morning Sergius appeared before the tribunal unaided by even a crutch, provoking Antiochus to accuse him of sorcery. Still mindful of his former debt to Sergius, Antiochus again in vain offered him a chance to repent. Then he remounted his chariot and drove toward the fortress of Rusafa with Sergius leading the way, singing hymns. At Rusafa, Sergius made his final refusal, Antiochus thereupon condemned him to death by the sword, and the public executioner led him away from the tribunal. A great crowd of men, women, and children gathered to witness the execution and were moved by

---

4. *Pass. gr.* 13: ἐν τοῖς λιμίτοις πλησιοχώροις οὖσι τῷ τῶν Σαρακηνῶν ἔθνει; and cf. *Pass. syr.*, pp. 298–99: "limiton, a desert place."

the youth of the condemned officer. Animals abandoned their folds[5] and harmlessly added their inarticulate cries to the general mourning. After a final prayer, Sergius crossed himself and knelt. His head was cut off and a heavenly voice welcomed him to join the army of angels, ranks of patriarchs, and choirs of apostles and prophets.

To protect the holy site from contamination by unbelievers, a chasm appeared where the martyr's blood had been spilled and remained there as a sign of divine intervention. Some witnesses buried Sergius's body at the site of his martyrdom. A long time afterward, zealous Christians from Sura attempted to steal the relics for themselves, but the martyr would not permit himself to be removed from his victory seat and sent a brilliant flare from his grave to alert those within Rusafa's walls to the Surans' clandestine activity. The soldiers garrisoned in Rusafa took this as a sign of brewing hostilities and set out from the walled town fully armed to drive away the offenders. The would-be thieves then asked permission to build a funerary monument at the potent site, and they left a few days afterward.[6] Later, when Christianity had spread across the land, abolishing polytheism, a martyrium was built within the walls and consecrated by fifteen bishops. On the anniversary of Sergius's martyrdom, 7 October, the martyr's relics were transferred to the new site. The *Passio* records that many miracles and cures were worked by the saint at Rusafa, especially at the old monument outside the walls. The martyr displayed the power to cure the sick and possessed and to tame beasts, especially on the anniversary of his death, when wild animals would flock to the site from the desert's furthest reaches, mixing peaceably with the other pilgrims to honor the martyr established there by God's command.

HISTORY IN THE *PASSIO:* THE EMPEROR

The story moves from an impressionistic, often stereotyped setting at the Zeus temple of an unnamed city to an increasingly tangible world of familiar place-names in the Syrian steppe. By the end of the story, fifteen bish-

---

5. *Pass. syr.*, p. 316: "holes."

6. In the Greek it is unclear whether the Surans ask the Rusafans for permission to build the monument or whether the Rusafans ask the Surans to build one. The latter interpretation is preferred by Boswell, *Same-Sex Unions* 389, with n. 77, and Woods, *JECS* 3 (1997): 338 and 365, where, contrary to the Greek that is his source, Woods identifies the Surans as soldiers and describes the building project as a joint effort of Rusafan and Suran soldiers. In this case reference to the Syriac is helpful. At *Pass. syr.*, p. 321, the Syriac translator clearly understood the former interpretation, which I have also adopted on grounds of logic as well as the Syriac evidence: "[T]hose people [i.e., the Surans] who had attempted to steal the holy martyr used persuasion and requested that the Rusafans allow them to be there for a few days in order to build a sepulcher for the veneration of the bones of the blessed one and then to go away."

ops consecrate a specific building at Rusafa—which has recently been identified, with the help of both the literary texts and archeological investigation. Finally, the author testifies that even in his day, more miracles were worked at the original site of the martyr's bones than at the new martyr shrine built within the walls. We move from the mists of oral tradition to the clarifying moment of composition. The number of possible anachronisms suggests that what we have is an accumulation of ideas and historical details, and even of literary motifs, that were felt to be compatible with the basic story of the soldier's martyrdom. Whether this assimilation occurred gradually over a long period of time, or in the mind of a single author is not certain, but the tendency of other more or less contemporary saints' stories to take shape over time makes the former more likely also in the case of our *Passio*.[7]

Because the identity of Sergius's persecutor has been for some time a matter of scholarly comment, a brief look at the historical difficulties posed by the *Passio* cannot be avoided. That way we can hope either finally to lay to rest the temptation to learn anything about the historical Sergius before the fifteen bishops appear at Rusafa or, if it proves impossible to deny the story any historical plausibility, at least arrive at the most probable historical setting for the events described. First of all there is the question, who was the emperor called Maximianus? The *Passio*'s setting is one of general repression of Christianity, so our emperor must be one known to have been involved in persecutions. Was he, then, Galerius Maximianus (caesar 293–305; augustus 305–11) or Maximinus (Maximin) Daia (caesar 305–10; augustus 310–13)? Or was he, as has recently been suggested, the apostate Julian? All three were famous persecutors, and Galerius and Maximinus Daia, at least, were easily and commonly confused. One possible clue might be the title βασιλεῦς used to describe Maximianus in the Greek text. Βασιλεῦς would most naturally denote an augustus, making it unlikely though not impossible that a caesar (such as Galerius on campaign in the East between 293 and 299, or Maximinus Daia at Antioch in 305–6) should be considered.[8] On the other hand, it would be uncharacteristic of this particular text to provide a precise portrait of the imperial college in the late third and early fourth centuries.[9]

---

7. See, e.g., Walter, *REB* 53 (1995): 295–326, on the cult of S. George.

8. It was not unheard of for a caesar to appear as sebastos or augustus already on third-century coins: see Ziegler, *Tyche* 9 (1994): 189. On nonofficial use of basileus through the third century, see Wifstrand, in *Dragma*, 529–39; on the official use of imperator for both augustus and caesar, see Kolb, *Diocletian*, 22 n. 54 and 46 n. 122; also Millar, *Emperor*, 613–15, for the use of basileus in both official documents and literature.

9. This means that little weight can be placed on the term basileus, either to rule out entirely the possibility that Maximianus was in fact a caesar or to suggest, as does Woods, *JECS* 5 (1997): 354, that the persecuting emperor was a sole ruler, since no partner is mentioned.

The choice is not made easier by the texts' silence concerning the site of the accusation against Sergius and Bacchus. The *Passio's* omission of the city's name is suggestive in itself—probably it was too obvious to merit mention, or considered irrelevant. All we are told is that it had a *palatium,* a marketplace, and a temple of Zeus, and that the officers traveled thence city by city, without any indication of time, until they reached the province of Augusta Euphratensis and the fortress of Barbalissus on the Euphrates.[10] The most natural choice is Antioch, whence one traveled some 170 kilometers along the northern Syro-Mesopotamian route via Beroea and Hierapolis to Barbalissus on the Euphrates.[11]

Since the city mentioned in the *Passio* had a *palatium,* Nicomedia should be briefly noted as an alternative, although the journey would obviously have been much longer. If we consider Nicomedia as the first scene of action, then the augustus Galerius becomes a candidate for "Maximianus." According to the existing record of his movements, the caesar Galerius left Syria in 299, following his eastern campaigns, and is not known to have returned.[12] After 299, Galerius fought and ruled primarily in the Balkans, but he could be found occasionally at Nicomedia, where on 24 February 303, Diocletian's edict against Christians was promulgated. The *Passio's* action takes place in an atmosphere of persecution, with anti-Christian proclamations posted in marketplaces, resulting in the torture and execution of nonconformists.[13] However, Galerius's absence from that capital for most of 303–5 leaves only a few brief occasions when the action of the *Passio* could have taken place during his presence at Nicomedia, if we are to identify the text's Maximianus with Galerius as augustus.[14]

The argument in favor of Julian is inspired by discomfort with certain details in the *Passio* that have been thought irreconcilable with a date under the tetrarchy, and by the existence of literary parallels to the *Passio* in historical and hagiographical sources that can be matched with events during

---

10. *Pass. gr.* 13; *Pass. syr.,* p. 298. To my knowledge, there is no evidence to support the assertion that Sergius was martyred "on the Euphrates front where he was stationed against the Persians" (Shahîd, *BASIC,* 1: 953).

11. Mouterde and Poidebard, *Limes,* 27.

12. Barnes, *New Empire,* 61–64.

13. *Pass. gr.* 1, 3; *Pass. syr.,* pp. 284, 286; cf. Eusebius, *HE* 9.3–7.

14. A. H. M. Jones, who accepts the *Passio* as "rhetorical" but "accurate in factual detail," takes "Maximianus" to mean "Galerius as caesar before his proclamation as augustus in 305; for the incident took place in Syria" (*Later Roman Empire,* 54); cf. the date of 303–5, published a decade earlier by Jones as the date of their martyrdom and reprinted in *Roman Economy,* 268 n. 32. However, as stated above, there is no clear evidence that Galerius ever returned to Syria after 299 (Barnes, *New Empire,* 64–66). It should be noted that the *PLRE* entry for Antiochus *dux* of Augusta Euphratensis (*PLRE,* 1: 71, Antiochus 2) relies on Jones's dating of the martyrdom to 303–5 (*Roman Economy,* 268 n. 32) for its dating of Antiochus.

Julian's brief rule.[15] It is possible to reconstruct a context in which the Sergius and Bacchus story might make sense during his reign. Zosimus, for example, records that Julian once paraded soldiers dressed in women's clothing as a punishment for desertion[16] and, indeed, Sergius and Bacchus are accused of desertion by the emperor, who inflicts on them the same punishment. Julian is also known to have sacrificed regularly at the temple of Zeus in Antioch.[17] But none of these parallels is sufficiently distinctive to render an identification with Julian unavoidable. Besides being a rather obvious form of humiliation, dressing delinquent soldiers in women's clothing is a frequently noted punishment for deserters in later Byzantium, as well as in the Sasanian and 'Abbasid empires.[18] It also turns up long before Julian, in the fifth century B.C., in the law code of the Thurii.[19] In the Republican period, one characteristic element in a soldier's attire was the military belt, the *cingulum militiae*. One form of degradation was to remove the *cingulum* and compel the delinquent soldier to stand with his tunic ungirt in public.[20]

Certainly the identification of the text's Maximianus with Julian would relieve the *Passio* of some possible anachronisms regarding the frontier situation, which is discussed below. And it is not utterly impossible (although quite unprovable) that the author had read some lost accounts of Christian soldiers persecuted by Julian, as has been suggested by David Woods.[21] But even if the author had read and borrowed from such accounts, that does not imply that the martyrdom of Sergius that he was narrating also took place under Julian.[22] It remains difficult to explain why it is that Sergius's publicist

15. I would like to thank David Woods for sending me his article "The Emperor Julian and the Passion of Sergius and Bacchus," *JECS* 5 (1997): 335–67. Woods develops in great detail, treated here only briefly, a suggestion made by Franchi de' Cavalieri, *Note agiografiche* 9: 169–200, esp. 194–99.

16. Zos., *Hist. nov.* 3.3.4–5.

17. Jul., *Misop.* 346 B–C.

18. For Byzantine incidents, see Cinnamus, *Epitome* 1.5.11–13; Pachymeres, *De Mich. et Andron. Paleolog.* 3.25; Nicetas Choniates, *Hist.* 6, p. 196; Scylitzes, *Synop. hist.* p. 429.4. Theoph., *Chron.*, A. M. 6080, p. 263, records that, adding insult to injury, Hormisdas had women's garments delivered to his general Bahram Chobin after his defeat by the Romans in 587/8 (589 in other sources). See Scylitzes, *Synop. hist.*, pp. 444–45.9 for the 'Abbasid practice.

19. For the Thurii, see Diodorus Siculus 12.16.1. For more general discussion, see Polites in Λαογραφία 4 (1913–14): 628, with n. 5; Koukoules, Βυζαντινῶν βίος, 3: 198, with n. 9; Guilland in *Byzantinoslavica* 27 (1966): 304–5; and Alan Cameron, *Circus Factions*, 172, with n.4.

20. For numerous examples, see Müller, *NJKA* 17 (1906): 560–68.

21. Woods, *JECS* 5 (1997): 344, 357, 361, 363–64, 366–67, posits that such accounts existed and were subsequently lost.

22. Woods assumes that the *Passio* is a complete fiction. This is a position with a certain pedigree. Without ever arguing his point directly, the influential Bollandist Hippolyte Delehaye several times dismissed the *Passio* of Sergius and Bacchus as devoid of historical value, a fantasy: see, e.g., *AB* 23 (1904): 478; *Mélanges d'hagiographie*, 238; *Origines*, 210; also see

chose to call the tyrannical emperor Maximianus rather than using the—surely sufficiently infamous—name of Julian, if indeed the *Passio* depended so heavily on stories of Julianic persecutions. Woods does not raise this issue, although in a note he draws attention to Christian frustration at Julian's policy of persecution without execution, hence starving the Christians of martyrs. Precisely because of this dearth, and of Julian's lasting reputation as Christianity's enemy par excellence, it would be peculiar for any Julianic heroes to have been transposed to the time of a vague "Maximianus."

Maximinus Daia, to consider the third possible emperor, arrived at Antioch in the late spring of 305, after his proclamation as caesar.[23] In his capacity as caesar in the East, but especially as augustus from 310 to 313, Maximinus pursued a well-publicized anti-Christian campaign with great energy. He directly involved governors and *duces* in the harassment of Christians, a situation that again calls to mind the active role given to the *dux* Antiochus in the *Passio*.[24] A scurrilous confession by two allegedly ex-Christian prostitutes at Damascus was posted in marketplaces around the eastern Empire, rescripts encouraged communities to drive Christians from their midst, and the ancient priesthoods and temples were revamped in the spirit of the buoyant polytheism that Maximinus espoused.[25] It would seem most natural to place the martyrdom of Sergius and Bacchus in the later phase of Maximinus's persecution, when he was augustus between spring 310 and 313. During late 311 and early 312, he was resident at Nicomedia, which cannot be absolutely excluded as the scene of Sergius's and Bacchus's denouncement. But Maximinus's anti-Christian campaign intensified in

---

Delehaye et al., eds., *Martyrologium romanum,* 439. On Delehaye's influential contribution to the study of hagiography, see Peeters, *Oeuvre,* 103–49, and Knowles, *Historical Enterprises,* esp. 25–27. This view has been embraced by Honigmann, *EI*[1], 3: 1265, who nonetheless confirms the accuracy of the *Passio*'s topographical details, and by Barnes, *New Empire,* 186. But Barnes has demoted Antiochus to fictional status following Delehaye's unargued claim that the *Passio* is fictitious. In an attempt to bolster Delehaye's summary judgment, Barnes suggests that "the name 'Antiochus' is an obvious allusion to the Seleucid king of the second century B.C. against whom the Maccabees rebelled" (*New Empire,* 186). But *PLRE,* 1: 71–73, has sixteen entries for Antiochus, not an unusual name in the late antique East. The excavators of Rusafa have continued this uneasy relationship with the *Passio,* which is both a hagiographical text and a mine of historical and topographical information. Kollwitz, the first director of the excavations, claimed on the one hand that "im übrigen sind diese Akten spät und ohne Quellenwert" (*Neue Deutsche Ausgrabungen,* 46), while proceeding, on the other, to exploit the *Passio*'s clues to Rusafa's architectural development. Ulbert, Kollwitz's successor, continued to use the *Passio* as one of several guides to understanding the early phases of architectural development at Rusafa, e.g., in *Actes,* 445.

23. Barnes, *New Empire,* 65–66; Downey, *History of Antioch* 318–23, 644–45.

24. Eusebius, *HE* 8.14.9–10 and *Mart. Pal.* 9.2; cf. Lact., *De mort. persec.* 36.4.

25. For prostitutes: Euseb., *HE* 9.5.1–2; rescripts: Mitchell, *JRS* 78 (1988): 105–24, esp. 111–12; polytheist reform: Nicholson, *JEH* 45 (1994): 3–10, esp. 3–4.

312. During that year the dioceses of Asiana, Pontica, and Oriens are recorded to have sent embassies to Maximinus concerning the Christian blight in their communities, and the emperor responded with a rescript giving carte blanche to the polytheists on 6 April 312.[26] Among the cities requesting the emperor's assistance against the Christians was Antioch, led by its dynamic *curator* Theotecnus.[27] It was a suitable climate for the accusation against Sergius and Bacchus.[28] Maximinus was in Antioch in the summer of 312, before his Armenian campaign that autumn, which would allow for the tradition that Sergius and Bacchus were martyred on the frontier in early October, Sergius on the seventh.[29] But we cannot assume that the festal date necessarily represents the precise date of Sergius's martyrdom.

Further support for postulating the date of 312 under Maximinus Daia is found in the martyrdom's setting. The frontier fortresses that provide the backdrop for the officers' execution are said in the *Passio* to belong to the province of Augusta Euphratensis.[30] This province is attested in the *Laterculus Veronensis,* whose record of the eastern provinces can be fixed between 314/15 and 324.[31] This date, supported by epigraphical and papyrological evidence, dissolves Honigmann's skepticism about the *Passio*'s chronological trustworthiness, which was founded on his belief that Augusta Euphratensis was established in 341.[32] The 314/15–24 date for the *Laterculus Veronensis* would easily accommodate a martyrdom in Augusta Euphratensis in 312.[33]

---

26. Euseb., *HE* 9.7.3–14, translates the original Latin rescript that was posted at Tyre. A fragmentary copy was found at Arycanda in Lycia, which includes also the petition to the emperor by the province of Lycia and Pamphylia (*CIL* 3.12132). Another copy was recently discovered at Colbasa, a Pisidian community also located in the province of Lycia and Pamphylia; see Mitchell, *JRS* 78 (1988): 105–24, for publication and commentary. Eusebius, *HE* 9.2, and Lactantius, *De mort. pers.* 36.3, accuse Maximinus of inspiring the petitions himself.

27. Euseb., *HE* 9.2–3; *PLRE,* 1: 908, Theotecnus 2; see also Mitchell, *JRS* 78 (1988): 114.

28. The claim made by Woods, *JECS* 5 (1997): 352–54, that between 299–312, two Christians could not possibly have risen to the highest echelons of the imperial bodyguard without detection, paints an unjustifiably black-and-white picture of historical realities, which were influenced by the unpredictability and flexibility of both the Christians' and the authorities' attitudes toward cohabitation.

29. The *Chronicle of Seert* 25, p. 292, records that "Maximin" killed Sergius and Bacchus, although earlier in the *Chronicle* the *passio* is recounted with "Maximianus" as the antagonist. There is a long tradition in favor of Maximinus Daia, which includes the early commentators on and editors of the texts: Tillemont, *Mémoires,* 5: 492; Byeus, *Acta sanct. Oct.* 3: 838, 844; and van den Gheyn, *AB* 14 (1895): 375 n. 1; see also Chabot in his edition of Mich. Syr., *Chron.,* 1: 188 n. 3; Honigmann in *RE,* 4A: 1706; Poidebard and Mouterde, *AB* 67 (1949): 110; Halkin, *BHG,* 2: 238; Hoffmann, *Spätrömische Bewegungsheer,* 282 n. 788 (in Antioch).

30. *Pass. gr.* 2, 13.

31. Barnes, *New Empire,* 205.

32. Honigmann in *RE,* 4A: 1698, 1706.

33. Of course, the date of the *Laterculus Veronensis* gives merely a terminus ante quem for the establishment of the provinces it records. A. H. M. Jones, who dates the *Laterculus Veronen-*

As is often the case with toponyms, the Syriac *Passio* does not simply translate the Greek, but incorporates local usage. In the Syriac *Passio*, Antiochus is called the "*dux* of the Euphrates" and the province is named "Phoenicia, in the authority of the western side of the river."[34] These variations resist easy explanation. It is quite likely that the variation derives from the name known to the translator. But the Syriac could also reflect the third-century provincial divisions when the province of Phoenicia stretched at least as far northeast as Palmyra. Temporary reversions to former provincial names, either as part of actual administrative restructuring or as literary slips, are not unknown. For example, even though the province of Augusta Euphratensis existed at least by the second decade of the fourth century, the Nicene signatures of 325 recognize the old third-century divisions of Coele Syria, Phoenicia, Arabia, and Palestine.[35] However we interpret the Syriac text's divergence, the name Augusta Euphratensis in the original Greek corresponds to the provincial nomenclature in 312.

THE HAGIOGRAPHIC MILIEU

Simply to brush aside the historical setting presented in the *Passio* risks forfeiting traces of the background that might aid our understanding of the cult's development. Nonetheless, the fact remains that the stereotypes, vagueness and even confusion of the narrative's early sections exist in large part thanks to the fact that the *Passio* of SS. Sergius and Bacchus belongs to the fermenting hagiographical environment of the fifth and sixth centuries, when accounts of martyrs' trials mutually inspired and reinforced each other.[36] The author of the *martyrion* of S. Athanasius of Clysma, for example, used the story of SS. Sergius and Bacchus as a model for his martyr's ordeal, and even gave Sergius and Bacchus parts to play.[37] In the *martyrion*, Athanasius is a high-ranking officer under Maximianus suspected of Christian sympathies. To test Athanasius, Maximianus sends him to Egypt—not as a humiliated, exiled officer, but as a *procurator*. Athanasius bids farewell to his

---

sis to 312, sees no difficulty in dating the martyrdom in *Augusta Euphratensis* to 303–5 (*Roman Economy*, 265, 268 n. 32).

34. *Pass. syr.*, p. 285, and cf. p. 298. See too Sev. Ant., *Hom. cath.* 57, which relies heavily on the Greek *Passio*. There Severus describes how Sergius and Bacchus were led "to that region in Mesopotamia which the local people call Euphratesia" (p. 90). See below for a discussion of this homily.

35. Barnes, *New Empire*, 224, with n. 58; Jones, *Roman Economy*, 267.

36. On hagiographical *topoi* in the *Passio*, see Byeus, *Acta sanct. Oct.*, 3: 838, and Delehaye, *Légendes hagiographiques*, 27–28.

37. Μαρτύριον τοῦ ἁγίου μεγαλομάρτυρος Ἀθανασίου, ed. Papadopoulos-Kerameus in Ἀνάλεκτα Ἱεροσολυμιτικῆς Σταχυολογίας 5: 360–67.

friends Sergius and Bacchus, members of the *schola gentilium,* and encourages them in their future struggles, which he foresees will take place "in the province of Augusta Euphratesia." The debt of the *martyrion* of Athanasius is straightforward.

A somewhat less clear connection can be discerned in the *Vita* of Victor and Corona, an account with a very complicated history and multiple recensions in Latin, Coptic, Arabic, and Ethiopic. The original Greek *Vita* is not dated, but can be placed in the milieu of fifth- to sixth-century hagiographical writing.[38] Even in the original, the story appears to be confused: Victor is an Italian soldier who refuses to sacrifice to the gods. A *dux* named Sebastianus is assigned to persuade him, Victor is adamant in his refusal and is eventually decapitated. At the end, it is stated that the martyrdom took place in Damascus, a city in Italy, during the reign of the emperor Antoninus. In a Coptic recension, the story becomes more interesting and includes a scene in which the Christian soldier Victor throws his golden chain in the face of the persecuting emperor Diocletian. This gesture also appears in the *Vita* of Gordius, a soldier in Antioch under Maximianus who, like Sergius and Bacchus, is dressed in female clothing as punishment.[39] A millstone is then tied round Gordius's neck and he is thrown into the Orontes River. The exchange of a military torque for a martyr's crown is a potent image and appears as early as the fourth century, in Prudentius's *Peristephanon.*[40] These literary echoes are vexing, since it is not usually possible to date the recensions with much precision, and thereby to retrace the direction of influence, if any, from one account to another. The slow absorption of literary commonplaces must be viewed side by side with more direct literary borrowing.[41] The emperor "Maximianus," the penal role of the *dux,* and the removal of military insignia have all been absorbed into the repertoire of military martyr accounts, but may well have sprung originally from actual events before they sparked the hagiographers' imaginations.

Together with the influence of fifth- and sixth-century hagiographical trends on the *Passio* of SS. Sergius and Bacchus, we must also consider the problem of seeming anachronism within the *Passio.* One possible anach-

38. Delehaye, *AB* 40 (1922): 117–18, 151. For comparison of the Latin recension and a Coptic eulogy on Victor, see Galtier, *BIFAO* 4 (1905): 105–221. The brief account of the *Passio* of SS. Sergius and Bacchus in the Coptic recension of the *Arab Jacobite Synaxarion*, 102–3, 113–14, belongs to this atmosphere, in which many strands of hagiography crossed.

39. Halkin, *AB* 79 (1961): 5–15.

40. Prud., *Perist.* 1.65.

41. On the literary genre of hagiography, the "Epic Passions" and the use of commonplaces, see Delehaye, *Passions des martyrs*, 236–315. See also Garsoïan in *East of Byzantium*, ed. id., Mathews, and Thomson, 151–52, with n. 11, who draws attention to parallels between the trials of SS. Sergius and Bacchus and of S. Gregory of Armenia, as depicted in their *passiones*.

ronism in the *Passio* more serious than the name Augusta Euphratensis is the alleged existence in the early fourth century of the *schola gentilium*. The *Passio*'s representation of Sergius as *primicerius* and Bacchus, by analogy, as the *secundocerius* of the *schola gentilium* would be the earliest attestation of that body, the foreign regiment of the imperial horse guard, otherwise only known to have existed from the reign of Constantine onward.[42] Another possible anachronism is the presence of monks living in caves near the middle Euphrates in the early fourth century.[43] Monasticism had begun to take root in upper Mesopotamia, in the Tur ʿAbdin, in the fourth century, and certainly by the early fifth century a monastic community had gathered round Alexander Akoimetes on the banks of the middle Euphrates.[44] But in its suggestion that monks had taken up residence in caves near Barbalissus by the early fourth century, the *Passio* stands alone.[45] As in the case of the early date suggested by the *Passio* for the *schola gentilium,* we cannot absolutely rule out the *Passio*'s contribution to our knowledge of early fourth-

42. *Pass. gr.* 1, 2; *Pass. syr.* p. 285. See Speidel, *Riding,* 75–76, on the Constantinian reorganization of the horse guard (*scholae*), and Frank, *Scholae,* 54–55, on the definition of *gentiles,* although neither he nor Speidel discusses Jones's argument in *Later Roman Empire,* 613, where with some caution he cites the *Passio* as evidence of the existence of the *schola gentilium* already under Diocletian. See also Byeus, *Acta sanct. Oct.,* 3: 839. Sergius and Bacchus, the earliest attested members by Jones's calculation, bore Roman names either because they were Roman officers set over foreign troops or because, as in the case of many non-Romans serving the East, they had adopted Roman names. Already in Ammianus any distinction had blurred, since most regiments, the *scholae* in particular, were manned by Germans. Jones, *Later Roman Empire,* 613–14 n. 12, cites examples of barbarian tribunes of the *scholae*. On the frequency of German officers in the *scholae,* see Hoffmann, *Spätrömische Bewegungsheer,* 1: 281–85, 299–300; and see Liebeschuetz, *Barbarians and Bishops,* 8, on German officers' preference for Latin names, and 23, on the upward mobility of German soldiers in the *scholae*. Since Sergius is a well-attested Roman name and goes back to the Republican period, Peeters's suggestion, *Tréfonds,* 68, that the name Sergius is a Hellenized version of the Syriac *shraga,* meaning lamp or torch, is unnecessary. However, it does seem that to the Semitic ear, the resemblance between Sarjis and *shraga* or *siraj* (the respective Syriac and Arabic words for "lamp") lent itself to puns: e.g., Jacob of Sarug, *Mimra on the Victorious Sergius and Bacchus,* v. 116 (p. 658 [Bedjan]), and al-Buhturi, *Diwan,* 108. Unfortunately, the *Passio* provides no background information on the martyrs that might suggest their familiarity with the region.

43. *Pass. gr.* 19; *Pass. syr.,* pp. 306.

44. *Vita et institutum piisimi patris nostri Alexandri* 26.31, pp. 677–82. On the historical reliability of the Euphrates episode in the *Vita Alex.,* see Gatier, in *Frontières terrestres,* 435–57; also Brinkmann, *BJ* 99 (1896): 252–54; Peeters, *Tréfonds,* 150.

45. Palmer, *Monk and Mason,* 21–22, 24, 30–31, discusses a possible mid fourth-century foundation date for the monastery of Mor ʿAbay, as well as fourth-century activities of monks in the frontier zone between the Roman and Iranian empires. Excavation of the monastic settlement at Tal Biʿa, near modern Raqqa, has advanced our knowledge of Euphratine monasticism in late antiquity. Graves discovered in the area of the large courtyard south of the church have been dated in the period of the fourth and fifth centuries (Strommenger, *MDOG* 123 [1991]: 10–11).

century asceticism, since it foreshadows conditions known to have existed in the mid fourth century; but it is thin evidence.

Anachronism reflects on the text in which it appears but tells us little or nothing about the events the text purports to describe. It is most likely that the *schola gentilium* did not exist under the tetrarchy; but the author's intrusion of this later entity into Sergius's martyrdom does not allow us to exclude the possibility that Sergius was executed by a tetrarch. It merely convicts the author (or some earlier participant in the development of the oral tradition) of projecting his knowledge of the *scholae,* and perhaps likewise of Euphratine monks, into Sergius's story in order to lend it a certain specificity.[46]

Particularly important from the point of view of the Sergius cult's development in late antique Syria and Mesopotamia is the attention paid in the *Passio* to topography, as Sergius and Bacchus travel from *castrum* to *castrum* along a military road to their martyrdoms. Topographical and archeological details seem correct for both fourth- and fifth-century Syria. The road later called the Strata Diocletiana had been marked with milestones from the time of Vespasian.[47] Generally speaking, the military *castra* that serve as the backdrop for the *Passio's* action were foci of Diocletian's eastern fortification activity, and some existed, it now seems, even earlier.[48] Archeological investigation confirms a Diocletianic date for the forts at Sura, Rusafa, and also Khulla, another fort located some 20 kilometers south of Rusafa, but not mentioned in the *Passio.* Excavation at Tetrapyrgium / Qasr al-Sayla, Sergius's penultimate stop in the *Passio,* has uncovered a Neronian or Flavian military post followed by no material evidence of a fort or other settlement before ca. 320.[49] Here again, it must be understood that the

---

46. Hoffmann, *Spätrömische Bewegungsheer,* 282–83, surveys the anachronisms related to institutions and interprets them as later additions to the *Passio.*

47. For the Vespasianic milestone from Arak attesting to road construction in A.D. 75 between Sura and Palmyra via Rusafa, Tayyiba and Arak, see Seyrig, *Syria* 13 (1932): 270–72; *AE = RA* 1 (1933): 421–22, no. 205, with the discussion by Bowersock, *JRS* 63 (1973): 133–40. For an overview of the Roman presence in the neighborhood of Rusafa from the first to the sixth centuries A.D., see Isaac in *Frontières,* 110 and n. 12. For discussion of the *Strata Diocletiana* from the second to the fourth century, see Bauzou in *Archéologie,* 211–53. See also Konrad, *DaM* 6 (1992): 346, with nn. 166, 167; Mouterde and Poidebard, *Limes,* 131–32; and Honigmann in *RE,* 2A: 1684. Rusafa's place in the frontier zone is discussed further in chapter 3.

48. Konrad, *DaM* 9 (1996): 163–76. For Diocletianic fortification and Rusafa's place in it, see esp. Konrad, *DaM* 6 (1992): 347–50; Bauzou in *Archéologie,* 211–13; Ulbert in *Actes,* 1: 445, and in *Archéologie,* 283–96, esp. 288–91; and Poidebard, *Trace de Rome,* 73–74. Joh. Mal., *Chron.* 12, p. 308, describes Diocletian's erection of milestones marking the military routes along the eastern frontier.

49. I am grateful to the excavator, Michaela Konrad, for correspondence regarding this site. For the publication of the early Roman evidence, see Konrad, *DaM* 9 (1996): 163–76, and

author's inclusion of Tetrapyrgium in Sergius's martyrdom may well have been inspired by his personal knowledge of the region in the fifth century. However, considering the range of imprecision inherent in dating archeological evidence, a date of ca. 320 for the earliest late antique evidence at Tetrapyrgium does not allow us to exclude the possibility that Sergius spent a night in Tetrapyrgium in 312.

Evidence exists also for the presence at this time of troops in the forts mentioned in the *Passio*. Barbalissus had served as a garrison for the Equites Dalmatae Illyriciani since the time of Diocletian.[50] Rusafa appears as a station on this route on Ptolemy's map and the *Tabula Peutingeriana,* which is based in its eastern part on a second-century archetype, as well as in the late fourth-century *Notitia dignitatum,* which records at Rusafa the Equites sagitarii indigenae, locally recruited cavalry.[51] The *Passio* recounts that many years after Sergius's martyrdom, the saint's relics were defended by fully armed soldiers who emerged from within Rusafa's walls. The Syriac adds that the Surans wished, by stealing the relics from Rusafa, to venerate the bones "in a pacified place."[52] If the martyrdom took place in 312, "many years later" would push the date of the attempted grave robbery well into the fourth century, when the martyr's fame had grown sufficiently for his relics to merit theft, and into the period of military organization recorded by the late fourth-century *Notitia dignitatum* for the East. Not long afterward, probably late in the second decade of the fifth century, we are finally on firm ground with the translation of the bones within the walls to the new church built by the bishop of Hierapolis.

From this weighing up of the *Passio*'s details against the historical and topographical situation known from other sources, the following picture emerges. With the establishment of the martyr's bones in a new church inside Rusafa's walls, someone was called upon, or inspired, to write down the martyr's story. The author would have collected all the evidence he could

---

for the late antique material, id., *Resafa,* vol. 5: *Der spätrömische Limes in Syrien.* Also for Tetrapyrgium, see Konrad, *DaM* 6 (1992): 347–50; Poidebard and Mouterde, *AB* 67 (1949): 109–10; and Musil, *Palmyrena,* 263–64. Tetrapyrgium, unlike Rusafa, was not heavily settled in late antiquity. Excavation within the walls at Tetrapyrgium has uncovered a sixth-century monastery similar in plan to that discovered at Tal Bi'a on the Euphrates near Raqqa (*AA* 1993: 730, and 1991: 672). Ceramics at the fortified site of Umm al-Tlala near al-Kawm reveal settlement phases similar to those at Tetrapyrgium, i.e., late first to early third century A.D., followed by fifth- to seventh-century occupation (Majcherek and Taha, *Cahiers de l'Euphrat* 7 [1993] 107).

50. *Not. dig., Oriens* 33.25; Ulbert in *Archéologie,* 284, 286.

51. Ptol., *Geog.* 5.15.24; cf. Ravenna Geographer, *Cosmogr.* 2.15, p. 89.1; *Not. dig., Oriens* 33.27. Kollwitz suggests without good reason that the *equites* at Rusafa were a corps of camel riders (*Neue Deutsche Ausgrabungen,* 46).

52. *Pass. syr.* p. 320.

for the martyr's life and death and life after death, and then he would have been left to flesh out the story himself where it seemed fit. He would have understood the price of time's forgetfulness bemoaned by Prudentius in the *Peristephanon:* "Alas for what is forgotten and lost to knowledge in the silence of olden time! We are denied the facts about these matters, the very tradition is destroyed."[53] Taking a minimalist view of the author's raw material, we can accept that he learned that a soldier (perhaps named Sergius) had been martyred outside Rusafa's walls in the distant past and a cult had grown up focused on the site of the martyrdom. He could certainly have been told that the martyrdom happened during the Great Persecution under the tetrarchs, among whom Maximianus was a common name. Sergius and Bacchus may have suffered along the Strata Diocletiana as the *Passio* relates, with place-names added to bring it up to date for contemporary listeners and readers; or, perhaps the presence of another martyr's bones at Barbalissus served as a catalyst for the idea of linking up the two lives along the military highway.

What all students of the *Passio* must accept is that the author's hand is clearly visible in the story he produced. Therefore, for the purpose of studying the cult's spread, the date of the *Passio*'s composition is crucial. The earliest datable evidence for the use of the written *Passio* is Severus of Antioch's homily on S. Sergius. Severus delivered this sermon at the feast of Sergius at Chalcis / Qinnasrin, celebrated in this case, it seems, on 1 October 514.[54]

---

53. Prud., *Perist.* 1.73–74 (tr. Thomson).

54. Sev. Ant., *Hom. cath.* 57, pp. 83–94. On Severus's background and the place of *Hom. cath.* 57 in his extant work, see Brière, *Introduction,* 55–56. Menologia reveal a variety of dates for the commemoration of SS. Sergius and Bacchus, of which 1 and 7 October are the most common. Neither S. Sergius nor S. Bacchus appears in the *Calendar of Edessa of 411,* dated between 362 and 411, a poor Syriac translation of a Greek calendar. The sources for the Greek are not oriental, a fact that helps explain the absence of SS. Sergius and Bacchus. The *Passio* unambiguously names 7 October as the feast of S. Sergius at Rusafa, and there is nothing to suggest that the date is a later insertion. A late seventh-century non-Chalcedonian menologion in the *Syrian Calendar,* 31–35, records S. Sergius and S. Bacchus on 1 October; a ninth-century non-Chalcedonian menologion in the *Syrian Calendar,* 35–48, is unique in placing the commemoration of both saints on 3 March, 1 September, 1 October (adding that on this day Bacchus was killed), and 7 October (adding that on this day Sergius was killed); a tenth–twelfth-century non-Chalcedonian menologion in the *Syrian Calendar,* 48–53, has S. Sergius and S. Bacchus twice, on 9 December and 1 September; a twelfth-century non-Chalcedonian menologion in the *Syrian Calendar,* 53–56, records the illustrious SS. Sergius and Bacchus on 31 October. The only date consecrated to SS. Sergius and Bacchus in fourteen other non-Chalcedonian menologia dating from the twelfth to the fifteenth centuries in the *Syrian Calendar,* 56 and 63 87, is 7 October. The same date is also recorded for SS. Sergius and Bacchus in the Chalcedonian *Synaxarium ecclesiae Constantinopolitanae,* which was formed in the tenth century. The Coptic redaction of the *Arab Jacobite Synaxarion* commemorates the death of S. Bacchus on 1 October and the death of S. Sergius on 7 October. Some of the manuscripts

As patriarch, Severus spent most of his time in Syria at Antioch, although we know of a few occasions when he preached at churches outside the great city. In another impromptu sermon, delivered at Chalcis on an unspecified date, Severus addresses his audience as an "assembly of the faithful and God-loving" and "the living church of God," which confesses the true Orthodox faith.[55] He also describes Chalcis as the true daughter of Antioch. Clearly, his visit must be seen in the context of his efforts to rally support for his anti-Chalcedonian views in Antioch's hinterland. The sermon's explanatory introduction added by the compiler, James of Edessa, notes that this particular homily was interrupted by a raucous crowd demanding that Severus arbitrate in some unnamed municipal dispute.

Chalcis was also an important camp for the pastoral Arabs of the region, who would have gathered for the feast of the famous martyr.[56] We can imagine how, looking around at the tents of the nomad pilgrims, Severus chose to open his homily with a comparison of the generosity of the people at Chalcis with the hospitality of Abraham, who emerged from his tent to serve the angels at Mamre.[57] After this brief, personalized introduction, Severus retells the story of the two martyrs, and of Sergius's miracles at Rusafa.[58] He concludes his sermon with a cadenza inspired by Sergius's pierced feet: We must be watchful against Satan, the snake who with sleepless eye fixed on our heels lies waiting to push us into the pit of sin by our love of pleasure— such as stuffing one's belly, which Severus warns against early on. On the whole, Severus recycles rather predictable, spoilsport festal themes.[59]

It is apparent from the opening of the sermon that Severus was acquainted with the cult of S. Sergius from the written *Passio,* and had no personal experience of the cult at Rusafa. With great faithfulness Severus follows the sequence of events in the *Passio,* but he tells a punchier story and dwells on certain incidents, such as the dressing up of the two soldiers in women's garments, in order to hold the attention of a lively audience. Both the *Passio* and Severus's homily exploit the symbolic value of clothing and adornment to stress the soldiers' transgression of culturally fixed bound-

---

of this synaxarion also commemorate the consecration of the church of S. Sergius at Rusafa on 15 November, an otherwise unattested feast.

55. Sev. Ant., *Hom. cath.* 56, p. 72.

56. For Arab encampments in the area of Chalcis / Qinnasrin and Beroea / Aleppo, see Shahîd, *BAFOC,* 400–402.

57. Sev. Ant., *Hom. cath.* 57, pp. 83–85.

58. Ibid., pp. 85–93.

59. Ibid., p. 93. The improvised tone of this sermon is echoed in the later *Hom. cath.* 110, delivered in May 517 at the town of Aegae and known from James of Edessa's annotations to have been ex tempore (see Brière, *Introduction,* 61).

aries, in this case their betrayal of a soldier's duty to the emperor and the gods who bestowed authority on him.[60]

Severus's homily is punctuated with quotations, often in abbreviated form, from some of the same scriptural passages cited in the *Passio,* along with near-verbatim rendering of speeches and events the *Passio* relates, such as Maximianus's charge that Christ had been the illegitimate son of a carpenter crucified by the Jews for stirring up trouble, followed by an anti-Olympian response by Sergius and Bacchus.[61] Severus also calls the responsible emperor "Maximianus." Finally, since the feast at Chalcis was in honor of S. Sergius alone, Severus had to reconcile this singular dedication with his own text-bound knowledge of the joint martyrdom of Sergius and Bacchus. He does this by underlining, as he begins to tell the story, that Sergius was martyred *with Bacchus* and that those whom the martyr's crown has joined together should not be separated in the recollection of their shared martyrdom.[62] Severus remarks on their similar appearance and youthfulness—details absent from the *Passio,* but inserted here by the Pisidian-born patriarch in an attempt to flesh out his purely bookish knowledge of the martyrdom for a crowd that in all likelihood knew much better than him.

Severus's homily on S. Sergius is commonly cited as a sign of the cult's spread. But this rather unremarkable sermon offers more than that. It provides a terminus ante quem for the *Passio*'s composition. Severus's dependence on it means that the Greek *Passio* was in circulation at least by 514. The author of the *Passio* does not for a moment pretend to have been an

---

60. The public punishment, designed to return Sergius and Bacchus to their proper place in society, deliberately inverted the soldiers' normal status through the removal of military symbols worn by men who enjoyed great freedom before the emperor and the substitution of both women's clothing and chains, signs of dependence. Mithraism exhibits a similar attempt to confirm desired social order by its temporary, controlled inversion, found particularly in the grade called *Nymphus.* On the top register of a wall painting in the church of Santa Prisca in Rome, a *Nymphus* wears a veil that covers his face. On the bottom register he holds the veil revealing his face. See van Essen and Vermaseren, *Excavations,* 157 (top register), 169 (bottom register). Cf. the Mithraeum of the Painted Walls at Ostia, where a young man, thought to represent a *Nymphus,* again wears female clothing (*CIMRM* 1: 130–31, no. 268). See also Beck, *Studies in Religion* 9; Gordon, *JMS* 3 (1980): 48–64, esp. 50. Greg. Naz., *Or.* 4.89, explicitly likens the public torture of Bishop Marcus of Arethusa to the humiliations inflicted on the body in Mithraic rituals. (I owe this reference to Garth Fowden.) Naguib, *Numen* 41 (1994), esp. 236–43, discusses the martyr's body as a symbolic vehicle for the expression and transgression of cultural norms in her study of Victor, a Christian soldier-martyr in the early fourth century who was exiled from Antioch to the Egyptian desert.

61. E.g., Psalm 135 at *Pass. gr.* 6 and Sev. Ant., *Hom. cath.* 57, pp. 86–87; for Maximinus's speech and the response of Sergius and Bacchus, cf. *Pass. gr.* 8–9 with *Hom. cath.* 57, p. 89; for Maximinus's rage and the parade of the officers, stripped of rank and dressed in women's clothing, cf. *Pass. gr.* 7 with *Hom. cath.* 57, p. 87.

62. Sev. Ant., *Hom. cath.* 57, pp. 85–86.

eyewitness to the martyrdom. In describing the chasm that opened "then" (τότε) to protect the sacred site of Sergius's martyrdom, he writes that even "until the present day" (μέχρι δὲ τοῦ παρόντος) the chasm was a visible witness for the faithless. The author goes on to describe the attempted relic-robbery, which took place a long time after the martyrdom, and the construction, even later, when Christianity had spread throughout the land, of a martyrium within the city walls by fifteen bishops and their translation of the relics to the new shrine. The last events mentioned in the *Passio* are the translation of the relics within Rusafa's walls and yearly celebrations of the martyr's feast at the new church—events well enough established to give an edge to the author's observation that the site of Sergius's execution still produced more miracles than the new martyrium within the walls.

The verse homily on SS. Sergius and Bacchus by Jacob of Sarug (d. 521) also bears the imprint of the *Passio*'s influence.[63] The date of the homily is not known. The somewhat repetitive *mimra* is composed of 152 couplets and, like Severus's homily, was probably intended for public performance at a feast. Jacob took liberties to elaborate particular themes: Sergius's service to two kings, the waywardness of polytheist religion, the martyr's Christ-like endurance of humiliations. He omits details in the *Passio* that Severus picked up on, such as the parade in women's clothing, but makes much of other events in the story. Two themes in particular were selected: the road that Sergius is forced to walk along with nails affixed inside his shoes, and the burial of the martyr's body at Rusafa.

> The iron thorns did not hurt him, while he was running
> to go to the place of Life where He is and to live with Him. (98)

> For the sake of the nails which he saw fixed in the hands of the Pure One,
> he accepted blades in his own feet without grumbling. (111)[64]

The final twenty couplets turn from the martyr's sufferings to his victory, and in these few lines Jacob develops a theology of relics in the frontier region:

> A region full of danger fell to this energetic soldier,
> and his fame and his name made peace in it and he is its pride.

---

63. This homily has received no scholarly attention as far as I am aware. I wish to thank Andrew Palmer for translating it for me. All quotations are from his unpublished translation.

64. Jacob of Sarug, *Mimra on the Victorious Sergius and Bacchus*, AMS 6: 650–61; cf. 10, 83, 96–110. Pitra, *Analecta sacra*, 289–92 with n. 1, published a Greek hymn to SS. Sergius and Bacchus, written by Elias, patriarch of Jerusalem. There are two possible candidates for this Elias, one of whom flourished in the early sixth and the other in the mid eighth century. On which Elias was the author, Pitra's comment was "dictu arduum est." In contrast with Jacob's, this undistinguished hymn reveals no particular familiarity with the *Passio*'s story, or any knowledge of the saints or their cult.

A frightening post full of shuddering was assigned to him,
because he was fit and alert and tough and warriorlike.

The hoard of his bones, like that legion of champions,
guards the country from harms by the power of God.

Joseph's people acquired a wall in his bones;
Jerusalem, too, used to be preserved by the bones of David. (137–40)

The martyr's protective powers became highly prized in the course of the
fifth and sixth centuries. Jacob's homily is but a foreshadowing of Sergius's
role as guardian of the frontier zone.

ALEXANDER OF HIERAPOLIS
AND THE EARLY CULT OF S. SERGIUS

In a brief note, Baumstark asserted that the *Passio* of Sergius and Bacchus
must belong to the fifth century; he arrived at this conclusion only by
grouping the *Passio* with other dated martyr accounts, but without indi-
cating what characteristics the *Passio* of Sergius and Bacchus shares with
them.[65] Considered together with both the external literary evidence and
the epigraphical and archeological evidence now available, the *Passio* does
indeed seem to date from the fifth century, but after the 440s. To reach this
more precise date, we must turn to the activities of Alexander of Hierapolis, who flourished in the first decades of the fifth century.

As we have seen, the *Passio* must have been composed in Greek by 514
when Severus relied on it for his homily at Chalcis; and the *Passio*'s account
mentions the dedication of a martyrium within Rusafa's walls by fifteen
bishops. It is also known that, not long before 431, Bishop Alexander of
Hierapolis invested three hundred pounds of gold in a church at Rusafa
in commemoration of the martyr Sergius.[66] In 431, Alexander was part of
the cohort of bishops who arrived at the Council of Ephesus under the
leadership of John, patriarch of Antioch. Their journey had been delayed,
causing them to arrive only after Nestorius's condemnation, which had
been carefully engineered by Cyril of Alexandria. Alexander remained adamant in his anti-Cyrillian stance even after 433, when John and Cyril accepted the Formula of Reunion. After the reconciliation, John and his supporters made repeated attempts to moderate the stance of Alexander and
the other bishops who held out against Cyril, including many from the

---

65. Baumstark, *Geschichte*, 95 and n. 2. Brock in Lapridge, *Archbishop Theodore*, 41, groups
the *Passio* of SS. Sergius and Bacchus with other Greek *passiones* translated to Syriac in the
fifth–seventh centuries. The earliest manuscript of the *Passio* is sixth-century.

66. *ACOec.* 1.4, p. 185; cf. 1.4, pp. 162–63.

province of Euphratesia.[67] In a letter to Theodoret, bishop of Cyrrhus, Alexander asserted that he could not bear to join in communion with John, even if the latter were to grant Alexander the entire kingdom of heaven (over which, Alexander added, John did not rule), or even Rusafa and the other cities (*civitates*) in the desert (*solitudo*).[68] John resorted to diminishing the influence of the rebellious bishops—the bishop of Doliche was replaced, and in about 434, without consulting Alexander, John traveled to the walled settlement that housed S. Sergius's shrine and consecrated a bishop of Rusafa, which until then had fallen under the direct control of the metropolitan of Hierapolis.[69]

Alexander's activities at Rusafa and John's separation of the town from Alexander's direct patronage are clear signs that Rusafa's stature as a pilgrimage site had grown sufficiently to make it a prized possession. The *Passio* also claims that the miracles of Sergius at Rusafa drew many pilgrims.[70] There is evidence that the cult of S. Sergius had already begun to spread from Rusafa by the early fifth century: Edessa / Urfa and a village now called Söğütlü, northeast of Edessa, had churches dedicated to Rusafa's martyr from around the time when Alexander showed an active interest in Rusafa in the 430s.[71] John took the radical step of wresting a potential seat of influence from a defiant bishop's control. Alexander vainly protested that the Antiochene robbers were after his gold.[72] No fifteen bishops are mentioned in Alexander's letter of protest, where he includes among his losses his investment in the church at Rusafa. We can be confident that Alexander would have rallied as many bishops as he could, including even his friend Theodoret of Cyrrhus, for the consecration of the miracle-working Syrian martyr's shrine.[73] But we should not expect the metropolitan to have distracted the reader from his loss with such details. Alexander took the controversy very personally, and this no doubt only compounded John's wariness of Alexander's direct control over Rusafa. On 15 April 435, deaf to pleas for moderation by fellow bishops, including Theodoret, Alexander was exiled to the Egyptian mines. Rusafa's fame only continued to increase.

67. Frend, *Monophysite Movement,* 23; Devreesse, *Patriarcat,* 51–53.

68. *ACOec.* 1.4, p. 171.

69. Ibid., pp. 162–63, 185.

70. *Pass. gr.* 30; *Pass. syr.,* p. 322. Ulbert in *Actes,* 445, suggests a link between the translation and the growth of the cult's popularity.

71. See chapter 4.

72. *ACOec.* 1.4, pp. 184–85.

73. Cf., e.g., the invitation of neighboring bishops, abbots, and priests by Bishop Perpetuus of Tours to the feast of S. Martin in the 450s, at which Perpetuus consecrated the miracle-working saint's magnificent new church (Greg. Tur., *De virtutibus S. Martini* 1.6).

Discovery of a pivotal inscription originally located in the structure called basilica B by the archeologists, together with excavations beneath this building, have helped identify Alexander's church. The inscription states that the stone-built structure was begun in 518.[74] It also relates that the new building replaced an older shrine built of mud brick; and indeed a brick building, finds from which date it no later than 425, has been discovered beneath the stone basilica.[75] The new evidence allows Konrad, the excavator of the levels beneath basilica B, to confirm that the early fifth-century building is the church known to have been built at Rusafa by Alexander, and the same one consecrated by fifteen bishops, as the *Passio* relates.[76] Allowing a short period of time to justify the observation by the *Passio*'s author that the original site outside the walls worked more miracles than the new shrine, the composition of the *Passio* can be placed safely in the mid fifth century.

The insistence of the *Passio*'s author that the original shrine was still in his day, that is, in the mid fifth century, the site of miracle-working deserves our attention. One way in which the memory of the traditional place of martyrdom could have been kept alive would have been if the feast of the saint included a procession linking the site of martyrdom with the new shrine within the walls that held the relics. One can imagine how, commencing from the shrine within the walls, a procession might have passed from the new shrine to the original tomb outside the walls. The relics would have been carried in the procession, escorted by the region's ecclesiastical and secular leadership, perhaps even a military guard. At the site of the martyrdom, the *Passio* would have been read, litanies performed and hymns sung in honor of the saint.[77]

There is no doubt that by the mid fifth century, Rusafa contained within its walls the shrine of S. Sergius. But no evidence, not even the *Passio*, suggests that S. Bacchus too was buried there. In fact, the *Passio* spends little time on Bacchus. No mention is made, for instance, of his veneration after his body was saved by the Euphratine monks. Bacchus does nonetheless play a part, if only a cameo role, in the story related by the *Passio*, and the consequence of this was that as S. Sergius evolved into one of eastern Christianity's greatest defenders, he would sometimes appear alone, and at other

---

74. Ulbert and Gatier, *DaM* 5 (1991): 169–82. For discussion of the inscription and its place in the cult's development at Rusafa, see below, pp. 80–91.

75. Konrad, *DaM* 6 (1992): 343–44.

76. Ibid., 349 and n. 181; Kollwitz, *Neue Deutsche Ausgrabungen*, 46; Ulbert in *Actes*, 447. Kollwitz was tempted as early as 1959 to identify the church of the fifteen bishops with Alexander of Hierapolis's church (*Neue Deutsche Ausgrabungen*, 46).

77. For processions, vigils, *miracula* readings, and banquets accompanying saints' feasts, see Maraval, *Lieux saints*, 213–21. For the probable location of the tomb outside the walls, see below, pp. 149–73, esp. pp. 157–59.

times with S. Bacchus by his side. From Severus's homily, it appears that, at least in 514, the feast at Chalcis was held in honor of Sergius alone—Severus had to lobby for Bacchus's inclusion. Severus later wrote three hymns in honor of Sergius, but only one featured Bacchus.[78] Severus may have insisted that what God had joined in martyrdom should not be separated in pious remembrance. But those who came to know the powerful martyr Sergius on his own at Rusafa and at local feasts, may have thought it unnecessary to include Bacchus. Others welcomed him. The result was not terribly uniform. In Syria and Mesopotamia, the predominance of Sergius was a given, the appearance of his less-spectacular fellow martyr only occasional.

IMAGES OF S. SERGIUS

Naturally, with the spread of the cult and the *Passio* there arose also a demand for images of S. Sergius, both with and without S. Bacchus. Two types appeared. The first closely reflects the martyr we encounter in the *Passio*, the standing soldier-saint with a gem-studded *maniakion* prominently displayed around his neck. The second is a rider saint with a flowing cape and a martyr's staff. Only the first of these types has been discussed in the scholarly literature, and that briefly. None of the known images can be dated earlier than the mid sixth century.

A good example of a representation of both Sergius and Bacchus together as standing soldier-saints is to be found on an offering dedicated at the church of S. Sergius at "Kaper Koraon," a village somewhere in the limestone hills of northwest Syria (fig. 1).[79] A silver flask, possibly meant for oil, portrays four independent nimbed images in the following sequence: Christ, a soldier-saint, Mary, a soldier-saint. The saints, in the pose of an orans, wear chlamys and chiton fastened at the shoulder by a fibula with prominent *maniakia* around their necks. The flask is thought to date to the mid to later sixth century. Marlia Mundell Mango has proposed that the soldiers represent SS. Sergius and Bacchus, basing her identification on the flask's inclusion in a hoard of objects, many of which are inscribed with dedications to S. Sergius, as well as by comparison with other images.

One of these is the encaustic icon from Sinai, although probably produced in Constantinople, which shows the busts of two very young soldiers, each crowned by a nimbus and dressed in a gold chiton with a carmine

78. James of Edessa, *Hymns of Severus of Antioch* 143–45, pp. 189–91.
79. Mundell Mango, *Silver*, no. 15.

Figure 1. SS. Sergius and Bacchus. Silver flask from the Kaper Koraon treasure, Syria. The Walters Art Gallery, Baltimore, no. 57.639.

Figure 2. SS. Sergius and Bacchus. Encaustic icon from the Monastery of S. Catherine, Sinai. City Museum of Eastern and Western Art, Kiev, no. 111.

clavus and a white chlamys held in place by a gold clasp (fig. 2).[80] Each of the pale figures holds a gold martyr's cross and stares directly ahead with wide, watery eyes. They give the impression of order and total obedience, with their hair and clothes carefully arranged. A tiny bust of Christ floats between them. Later, the soldiers were clearly labeled with inscriptions, Sergius to the left, Bacchus to the right. But their identity would have been immediately apparent from their *maniakia,* here of gold, decorated with two rectangular gems or medallions on either side of one central oblong cabochon gem.[81] The icon is believed to date from the early seventh century.

80. Weitzmann, *Icons,* 1: 39, 28–30, pls. 12, 52, 53. Weitzmann notes that the *maniakia* distinguish the martyrs from other military saints, but inaccurately claims that they are "always depicted as a pair," even though he compares the hieratic rendering of Sergius and Bacchus in the Sinai icon to that of the S. Demetrius figures in the mosaics of the S. Demetrius church of Thessalonica, where S. Sergius appears alone. As a general but not absolute rule, the *maniakion* is distinctive of S. Sergius and S. Bacchus. But other military martyrs do occasionally appear with the gold torque. For exceptions, see, e.g., the Coptic rendering of S. Menas and S. Theodore illustrated by Nicolle in *War and Society,* figs. 61, 62c.

81. Speidel, *Antiquité tardive* 4 (1996): 237–39, sketches the court culture in which bejeweled gold torques were worn by the military elite. He draws attention to a description of such torques in Const. Porph., *De cer.* 2.52, p. 708, which closely coincides with the depictions

What is especially striking about this icon is the extremely youthful rendering of the martyrs.

A hardier portrait of S. Sergius, although unlabeled, appears on the tondo of an elegant silver bowl, dated by silver stamps to the reign of Constans II (641–68), and discovered in Cyprus (fig. 3). Here, a single military saint holds a martyr's cross and wears the chiton and chlamys, the nimbus and the *maniakion*.[82] With a much bulkier body and less orderly rows of curls than the Sinai Sergius, this figure presents a more convincing image of a *primicerius scholae gentilium*. The *maniakion* he wears is studded with a large, round medallion or gem surrounded by four smaller medallions. The configuration is nearly identical to that depicted on the Kaper Koraon flask. The prominence of the saints' neckgear in these objects recalls the *Passio*, where the first stigma is the removal of the officers' *maniakia*. This emphasis on the *maniakia* in the *Passio*, which is repeated in the portraiture, helps verify the identification of the two unlabeled images—on the Cyprus bowl and the Kaper Koraon flask—as representations of S. Sergius.

Another example of the same type is the late seventh-century full-length mosaic icon of S. Sergius that takes a position of honor to the right of the apse in the church of S. Demetrius, another soldier-saint, at Thessalonica (fig. 4).[83] Sergius is depicted as an orans, wide-eyed, staring directly ahead. He wears an elaborately decorated chlamys with a tablion and a chiton, attached at the shoulder by a fibula. Around his neck is the characteristic *maniakion*, very similar in design to that worn by the soldier-martyr on the Cyprus bowl and the Kaper Koraon flask: that is, attached to the gold neckband are four small medallions or gems, which encircle a large central medallion. As in the Sinai icon, here too Sergius's face appears young, austere, and, to the modern eye, effeminate. What appear today as feminine features were often used to evoke youthfulness in portraiture of

in the images of Sergius discussed above. It should be noted that in the *Passio*, the torques are described simply as golden, so we may assume that the addition of jewels reflects the early seventh-century milieu to which the portraits belong. One may hazard the suggestion that the appearance of a gold torque embellished with precious stones in a later Armenian synaxarion was inspired by the visual representation of the soldier saint in this guise (*Armenian Synaxarion of Ter Israel*, 378).

82. Ševčenko in *Age of Spirituality*, ed. Weitzmann, 548–49, no. 493.

83. For color photographs of the seventh-century mosaics, see Bakirtzis, ed., Ἁγίου Δημητρίου, ills. 7–16. Soteriou, Ἡ βασιλικὴ τοῦ Ἁγίου Δημητρίου, 193–94 with pl. 65a. The church of S. Sergius at Gaza, erected during the early years of Justinian's reign, probably before 536, was described in a *laudatio* by Choricius of Gaza. In the mosaic decoration of the church, S. Sergius is portrayed as a mediator between the building's benefactor and the Mother of God and her Son (Chor., *Laud. Marciani* 1.31). Details of the saint's attire are not provided, although perhaps the Sergius mosaic at the church of S. Demetrius in Thessalonica may offer some suggestion of how he was portrayed at Gaza.

Figure 3. S. Sergius (?). Silver bowl from Cyprus. The British Museum, M. and L.A. 99, 4–25, 2.

the period. Perhaps the most evocative attempt to describe this tendency in divine portraiture of the East was penned by Michael Rostovtzeff:

> Most of the Palmyrene gods and some of the goddesses are noble youthful fig-ures with rich curled hair, resplendent in their boyish beauty; and this is true also of many of the heroized men, women, boys, and girls represented in relief or in the round on the funerary monuments. Their features are always some-what effeminate, with peculiar languid eyes—traits which are both highly typical of the later Oriental art of the Near East. . . . Despite their military dress, the military gods of Palmyra are refined, elegant ephebes of the Orien-tal type. This effeminacy is not, however, only sensuous. The graceful figures of the boyish gods and of their curly-haired attendants, the slim proportions

Figure 4. S. Sergius. Mosaic, basilica of S. Demetrius, Thessalonica. Ephoria of
Byzantine Antiquities, Thessalonica.

of their bodies, the romantic eyes, their almost airy appearance enable us to grasp at once, even without the help of the halos and radiate crowns which surround the heads of the gods, their solar, ethereal, and celestial nature.[84]

The last image to fall within this portrait type of S. Sergius is perhaps the most striking, although it is not found in the few brief accounts of the saint's iconography that exist. It appears on a reused cameo dating from the late fourth century onto which the names "Saint Sergius" and "Saint Bacchus" have been etched. The cameo is believed to have been carved as a portrait of the emperor Honorius with his bride Maria, the daughter of Stilicho, on his left (fig. 5).[85] The reuse seems less bizarre when the hair style and general effeminacy of the young soldiers in other representations is taken into consideration. To make interpretation even more complicated for modern viewers, one recent discussion of the cameo proposes that Maria's (later Bacchus's) hair style resembles that of the men rather than the women of the House of Theodosius.[86]

The second type of Sergius image represents the saint with nimbus on horseback. The rider wears military attire, with a flowing cape and a long martyr's staff. The horse does not gallop, prance, or rear up on its hind legs, but rather holds a noble pose with its left forefoot raised. A bronze attachment said to have come from Palestine is decorated with an intaglio image

84. Rostovtzeff, *YCS* 5 (1935): 237. Cf. also Walter, *REB* 53 (1995): 320. At the beginning of the twentieth century, icon painters on Mount Athos used photographs of women or of beardless boys or ancient statues as models for martyrs. To his astonishment, one visitor observed a portrait of Kyra-Basiliki, the concubine of Ali Pasha, standing in as a model for the Protomartyr Stephen (Moyses, Ἁγιορείτικες διηγήσεις τοῦ Γέροντος Ἰωακείμ 35; I owe this reference to Garth Fowden).

85. Delbrueck, *Consulardiptychen,* 260–61, proposed that the reused Sergius and Bacchus cameo served as an icon in the church dedicated to the saints in Constantinople, but this suggestion must remain conjectural. Even Boswell, *Same-Sex Unions,* does not suggest that Bacchus dressed up as a bride. Cf. a bust of Antinous recarved in the third century to represent a middle-aged woman with a Severan hair style (Blanck, *Wiederverwendung alter Statuen,* 45 and pls. 14–15). Another example is the gold reliquary representing the female saint Fides, which in its original form, before the gem- and cameo-encrusted statue was made to do duty as Fides, depicted a Roman emperor—either Marcus Aurelius or Julian (MacMullen, *Christianity,* 128, with n. 87, and 129, fig. 3). I would like to thank Christopher Walter for drawing my attention to another cameo relabeled in secondary use as Sergius and Bacchus. This onyx gem depicts two soldiers en face wearing the cuirass and holding lances. They have been identified as Caius and Lucius, adopted sons of Augustus: *DACL* 6.1.857, no. 5143.

86. Meischner, *AA* 1993: 613–19, with photograph, although the later inscriptions appear only faintly. See also Kiilerich, *Late Fourth Century Classicism,* 92–94, with fig. 46, according to whom Maria's hairstyle most closely resembles that of Constantine's mother, Helen, with echoes back to Livia. Neither study alludes to the subsequent rebaptism as Sergius and Bacchus.

Figure 5. The imperial couple Honorius and Maria, later inscribed as SS. Sergius and Bacchus. Rothschild cameo. Private collection, Paris.

of the saint in this guise, while around the image an inscription proclaims the allegiance of a camel-driver to S. Sergius: "camelarius of Saint Sergius" (fig. 6a).[87] One could imagine that its owner belonged to a company of cameleers working under the banner of Sergius and assuming responsibility for caravan trade from their base at Rusafa—as the Palmyrene companies once had. Or the camelarius could have belonged to a monastery of

87. Καμηλάρης τοῦ ἁγίου Σεργίου: *Muse* 7 (1973): 11. The camelarius would have been under the absolute authority of the caravan leader, the συνοδιαρχηγός. For a vivid account of the practicalities of a caravan, see Grant, *Syrian Desert,* 189–92.

Figure 6. a: S. Sergius. Bronze attachment. Courtesy Museum of Art and Archaeology, University of Missouri–Columbia, no. 72.73.

b: S. Sergius. Bronze bracelet. On Beirut antiquities market in 1960. Published by Mondésert, *Syria* 37 (1960), fig. 4.

c: S. Sergius (?). Lead seal. Courtesy of Mrs. Janet Zacos, Athens.

d: "Holy rider." Silver armband. Royal Ontario Museum, Toronto no. 986.181.93.

S. Sergius at Rusafa, on the model of the Pachomian camelarii.[88] In the late 1950s, a bronze bracelet appeared on the antiquities market in Beirut and was photographed by Henri Seyrig and published by Claude Mondésert, but it has not surfaced in scholarly discussion since that time (fig. 6b).[89] Thirty-five mm in diameter, the bracelet's medallion shows a nimbed saint on horseback, wearing a flowing pallium and carrying a cross staff. An inscription follows the edge of the medallion: "camelarius of Saint Sergius of the Barbarian [Plain]."[90]

---

88. Pall., *Hist. Laus.* 32.9.

89. Mondésert, *Syria* 37 (1960): 123–25.

90. Καμηλᾶϱς τοῦ ἁγίου Σεϱγί[ου τ]οῦ Βαϱβαϱικοῦ. See now the comments of Shahîd, *BASIC,* 507–8. On the "Barbarian Plain," see pp. 1–2 above and pp. 65–66 below, with notes.

The image of a saint on horseback, a speedy guardian of cameleers but also of pilgrims, would have had immediate appeal in the potentially hostile environment of the steppe. In addition to a flask of blessed oil or water, pilgrims to the martyrium would have taken away from Rusafa clay or metal medallions commemorating their visit to the martyr. Such tokens have survived from the busy shrine of Symeon the Younger, the subject of a study by Gary Vikan.[91] The tokens bearing the image of Symeon were ceramic in the sixth and seventh centuries and made of lead during the revival of pilgrimage to the shrine in the tenth century. They were often inscribed with words such as "blessing" (εὐλογία) and "health" (ὑγεία), which crystallized the nature of the bearer's rapport with the saint, particularly in the case of Symeon, who was famous for the miraculous cures worked by his prayers.[92] Such tokens received at the saint's shrine were mementos in a powerful sense—they were made to do more than simply commemorate a visit, like an empty souvenir. The token placed the bearer in continuing contact with the image, the prayer and the healing power of the saint. In the 1920s, the Aleppo collector Guillaume Poche was shown a stone mold on which the inscription "the blessing of Saint Sergius" (εὐλο[γ]ία τοῦ ἁγίου Σεργίου) was carved around an image of Sergius on horseback, with a cross resting on his shoulder.[93] What is more, the mold was said to have been found at Rusafa, a believable claim. Most likely, the object surfaced during clandestine digging and found its way onto the antiquities market. Unfortunately, no illustration accompanies Poche's description as reported by Mouterde and Poidebard. But the description is enough to relate the mold to the image of the rider saint on the two bronze medallions owned by cameleers. To these three nearly identical portraits of Sergius on horseback should be added a lead seal dated 550–650 by Zacos and Veglery (fig. 6c).[94] The authors describe the seal's obverse as follows: "saint riding horse to right, wears nimbus, chiton and himation; holds in right hand cruciform spear with which

91. Vikan, *DOP* 38 (1984): 65–86, esp. 73, on the pilgrim token as both "distillation of and catalyst for" late antique belief in miraculous healing through saints. A seventh-century fragment of parchment shows S. Sergius as a Roman official, nimbed and, uncharacteristically, holding an orb in his left hand, while he blesses with his right. The saint is clearly labeled in Greek Ἅγιος [Σ]έργιος. A cord, part of which is still intact, was attached to the parchment image, so that it could be worn as an amulet (Horak in *Syrien,* 194–95).

92. Vikan, *DOP* 38 (1984): 67–69.

93. Poidebard and Mouterde, *AB* 67 (1949): 115, quote Poche's description from a letter dated 6 October 1924. Vikan, *DOP* 38 (1984): 74, with n. 47, describes molds used to make both lead and clay tokens. Poche, in that portion of his letter quoted by Poidebard and Mouterde, did not include such specifications.

94. Zacos and Veglery, *Byzantine Lead Seals,* no. 2975, with photograph in plate vol. 1, pl. 202, no. 2975.

he attacks a prostrate enemy (not visible)." In the light of the three other images of Sergius on horseback, it seems probable that the prostrate foe is invisible because he does not exist. Zacos and Veglery were induced to imagine the prostrate figure by assimilating this image either to the commonly portrayed figure of the "holy rider," sometimes named as Solomon, other times anonymous, or to later icons of S. George or S. Demetrius.[95]

The inscription on the seal's reverse supports the suggestion that the rider represented is S. Sergius. Abbreviated Latin characters proclaim the seal's owner: *Sergii illustris et commerciarii*.[96] It is relatively rare for a rider saint to appear on a lead seal, and when a saint is depicted, the image is not always identified by an inscription. Often, as seems to be the case with the seal of Sergius the *commerciarius,* the reverse will simply bear the name and title of the seal's owner. The saint shown may be the owner's patron saint, his homonym, although this seems not to be the case automatically. For example, one seal with a rider saint on its obverse is marked on the reverse with what must be the owner's name, Stephen, an unlikely rider saint.[97] But because of the close resemblance between the image used by Sergius the *commerciarius* and that on the mold and the two bronze medallions, there can be little doubt that the lead seal portrays the *commerciarius*'s patron saint, Sergius.

The similarity between the four portraits of Sergius as a rider saint suggests that they represent an image disseminated from the pilgrimage shrine at Rusafa—particularly since the mold, devised for the purpose of reproducing an image, shows Sergius on horseback. The relationship between these four objects, not hitherto discussed, restores to the thoroughly robbed shrine a cult image popular with pilgrims. It also teaches caution. Nowhere in the *Passio* is Sergius associated explicitly with a horse. The *schola gentilium* was, of course, a horse guard, but this fact failed to ignite the imagination of the author of the *Passio,* who not once mentions his hero in connection with a horse. However, the popularity of the rider image is confirmed by a Greek inscription from the Hawran that refers to S. Sergius as a rider.[98] There is also a vivid illustration of personal contact with Sergius the rider

95. Walter in *DCAE* 15 (1989–90): 33–42, focuses on the armed rider who spears a prostrate figure, often a woman or a monster. He traces the development of this widely disseminated image, both pre-Christian and Christian, through several transformations.

96. This is the only lead seal of a *commerciarius* in Zacos and Veglery, *Byzantine Lead Seals* that uses Latin characters. The *commerciarius,* first attested under Anastasius, levied taxes on imports, exports, and commercial transactions (Hendy, *Studies,* 174 and 654 n. 436; Stein, *Histoire,* 2: 214, with n. 1, and 750, n. 1).

97. Zacos and Veglery, *Byzantine Lead Seals,* no. 1311, with photograph in plate vol. 1, pl. 103, no. 1311, dated by the authors to the second half of the sixth century.

98. See below, pp. 110–11.

saint in the Syriac life of Mar Qardagh, datable most likely to the late sixth or early seventh century.[99] In his first night vision of the martyr who was to become a role model for this Iranian aristocrat, Qardagh sees a young man armed and mounted on his horse. The cavalier stands before Qardagh, strikes him on the side with his spear, calls out his name, "Qardagh," and foretells his future martyrdom. When asked who he is, the mounted messenger replies, "I am Sergius, the servant of Christ."[100] The vision reveals not only the power of the rider iconography, but also how well it travels, in this case to late sixth-century Adiabene, due east of Rusafa beyond the Tigris. The story also underscores the influence of established iconography in mortal imaginings of divine figures.[101]

The mounted image of Sergius was inspired by the martyr's role as guide and divine protector in the semi-desert landscape.[102] Armed immortals had long been appealed to in Syria. Rider gods were particularly at home in the Syrian steppe, and their divinity was further charged by the strength and speed of the much-valued horse. Foes mortal or immortal often appeared on horseback: just as the speed of the mounted Arab allies was a tangible asset remarked upon by the historian Evagrius, so too S. Symeon, in his ascetic seclusion, waged war with a spiritual enemy who assumed the outward form of cavalry.[103] A group of stone relief carvings depicting an Arab rider god, sometimes identified as ʿAziz, show the divinity with a flowing cape, lance in the right hand, shield in the other (fig. 7). The stately mount is represented in profile with one foreleg raised, while the rider turns to face the viewer.[104] The resemblance to the image of S. Sergius on horseback is striking. All of the reliefs have been found in the area between the Hawran and Aleppo, that is to say, in the area where the Sergius cult put down its earliest roots. Ernst Lucius, who first drew attention to the similarities between ʿAziz

---

99. See below, p. 120.

100. *Acta Mar Kardagh,* 7. In the mid eighth century, SS. Sergius and Bacchus rode up on horseback to the last Umayyad caliph, Marwan II, as he was torturing the patriarch of Alexandria (*History of the Patriarchs* 1.18, p. 428).

101. Cf. *Mir. Theclae* 12, with Dagron, *Vie et miracles,* 98; and *Mir. Demetr.* 10.

102. In nineteenth-century Cappadocia, Greek Orthodox children were still taught to call on a rider saint—usually George or Theodore—when in need of immediate rescue. See, e.g., Païssios Hagioreitis, Ὁ Ἅγιος Ἀρσένιος ὁ Καππαδόκης, 33.

103. Evagr., *HE* 5.20; Syriac *Vita S. Simeon. Stylit.* 93.

104. Ronzevalle, *CRAI* 1904: 8–12, discusses a relief discovered south of Damascus; Mouterde, *MUSJ* 11 (1926): 307–22, compares two reliefs from south/southeast of Aleppo; Rostovtzeff, *JRS* 22 (1932): 109–10, comments on the iconography of a relief of ʿArsu and ʿAzizu from Palmyra; Seyrig, *Syria* 47 (1970): 77–100, collects evidence of armed Arab deities, often in pairs, that has been found especially in the regions north and south of Palmyra. See also Rostovtzeff in *Excavations at Dura-Europos,* ed. Baur and Rostovtzeff, 199–200, pl. XXIV. 1, 2, 3, for a discussion of three comparable terracottas.

Figure 7. Rider god. Stone relief found south of Damascus. Published by Ronzevalle, *CRAI* 1904, fig. 1.

and S. Sergius, was not familiar with the relief images, but had been impressed by the early appearance of dedications to S. Sergius in Edessa and the Hawran, where the cult of ʿAziz had also left pronounced traces.[105] Lucius's observations have occasionally been cited in passing and without comment.[106] But the close iconographic relationship between the Arab military god and the soldier-saint speaks volumes for the critical role played by the landscape—and the distinctive ways of life it gives rise to—in the formation of religious conception and expression. While attempts to trace the origins of rider iconography have quickly led to tenuous and almost

---

105. Lucius, *Anfänge des Heiligenkults*, 240.
106. See, e.g., Honigmann in *RE*, 4A: 1707.

meaningless associations, the case of S. Sergius and the Arab rider god is bolstered by the geographical framework in which both images circulated.[107] It requires no great leap of the imagination to Christianize the second-century inscription that accompanies an elegant Palmyrene relief showing the camel-riding god ʿArsu, followed by ʿAziz on horseback:

> To ʿArsu and ʿAzizu, the good gods who reward, Baʾlai has made [this], son of Jarhibole, priest of ʿAzizu the good and merciful benevolent god, for his safety and that of his brothers.[108]

At issue here is not some crypto-paganism but rather the instinctive response to particular environmental circumstances unchanged, to a great extent, for millennia.[109]

Another image closely akin to the first four depictions of Sergius as cavalier may confirm the link of the rider Sergius with pilgrimage. In his study of "implements for supernatural healing," Gary Vikan published a photograph of a silver amuletic armband with four medallions, one of a dozen such objects known to scholars.[110] The armbands typically show scenes from holy sites or from the life of Christ, and often include intercessions for the owner's well-being. A figure Vikan calls the "holy rider," associated with healing and the subjection of evil forces, also appears on many of the bracelets, whose iconography, as Vikan argues, originated in pilgrim tokens (fig. 7d).[111] The Christian "holy rider" is a nimbed figure on horseback who wears a flowing pallium and holds a long spear, sometimes topped with a cross, which he aims at the prostrate figure shown below his rearing horse's feet.[112] The silver armband in question is typical, among this category of objects, in its inclusion on its four medallions of the women at the tomb of Christ, the Theotokos and child, and the "holy rider." The Trisagion appears on the fourth medallion, while Psalm 90.1, an apotropaic verse that frequently appears on amulets, is inscribed around the band that links the medallions. "Health" is carved beneath the so-called holy rider, and around the image of the Theotokos and child is written: "Theotokos help Anna Charis." What is unusual about this excellently preserved arm-

---

107. On this problem, see Walter, *ByzF* 14 (1989): 1.657–73 with 2. plates 249–55.

108. Rostovtzeff, *JRS* 22 (1932): 109.

109. Weber, *DaM* 8 (1995): 203–11, draws parallels between iconographic representations of paired Arab caravan gods, the twins Castor and Pollux, and the Christian saints Cosmas and Damian, but with no reference to Sergius and Bacchus.

110. Vikan, *DOP* 38 (1984), fig. 10.

111. Ibid., 75.

112. Bonner, *Studies in Magical Amulets,* 211–12, discusses the pre-Christian antecedents of this image. A recent study of amulets portraying the "holy rider" confirms that the prostrate figure was part of the image in both pre-Christian and Christian tradition: see Spier, *JWI* 56 (1993): 33–38.

band is the rendering of the so-called holy rider. Vikan remarks that this figure "differs from the more common sort . . . insofar as he does not impale an evil prostrate figure or beast." Vikan derives this more "stately version" from adventus iconography, particularly from depictions of Christ's entry into Jerusalem.[113] But in the images discussed by Vikan that portray Christ's triumphal entry into the Holy City, the mount is clearly a long-eared donkey. We do not have to turn to Christ the holy rider to find a good parallel to this unusual representation. The horse's stance in particular, with the left front leg raised in a position of controlled movement, but not of rearing attack, recalls the image of Sergius on the three objects depicted in fig. 6a, b, and c. If the rider saint Sergius is depicted here, then the addition of "health" beneath Sergius's image fuses the portrait of the mounted protector with the martyr Sergius, whose healing powers were demonstrated especially at the pilgrimage site of Rusafa and acclaimed in both the *Passio* and Severus's homily.

It is impossible to divine from the handful of Sergius images that have survived when the two representations first appeared. The class of images in which Sergius is the standing soldier wearing a *maniakion,* sometimes accompanied by Bacchus, was inspired by the verbal *Passio* portrait and closely related to the story's circulation. It may, at least in the early stages of iconographical development, have appealed more to those remote from the Barbarian Plain, and perhaps to a more urban following. The rider image must have arisen locally from the context of the frontier zone, criss-crossed by a wide range of people, including Arab pastoralists. The known rider images seem to be more closely linked with Rusafa and its environs than the standing soldier portraits found at Sinai, Thessalonica, Cyprus, and Kaper Koraon. It is surely significant that, especially in the case of the Sinai and Kaper Koraon images, Constantinople is thought to have been their place of origin.[114] Although much depends on the accidents of survival, the high-quality seventh-century images from Sinai, Cyprus, and Thessalonica may represent a surge of interest in the soldier-martyr as Christian Rome's patron at a time when Arabs, Avars, and Slavs were harassing the empire's frontiers. Perhaps it was his reputation as a celebrated military defender in the East that inspired the Thessalonicans to honor Sergius so prominently in their church of S. Demetrius.

---

113. Vikan, *DOP* 38 (1984): 75 n. 57. See also Vikan's more recent discussion of the "holy rider" image in Θυμίαμα, 341–46, with pls. 197–98.

114. Grabar, *Martyrium,* 2: 26, conjectured the existence of a single prototype at the Sergius shrine at Rusafa, on which five known images of Sergius dating from the sixth to the eleventh centuries were based, namely, the mosaic in Thessalonica; the fresco at S. Maria Antiqua in Rome; the Sinai icon; the Cyprus bowl; and the Sergius mosaic at Daphni near Athens.

The composition of the Passio of Sergius and Bacchus in the mid fifth century gave impetus to, but was probably also itself encouraged by, the spread of the cult of S. Sergius. Until that time, the story of Sergius, and of Bacchus, had been preserved at the martyr's shrine and put into circulation by pilgrims. With the cult's expansion, a written account as well as sacred images were needed to make the martyr more widely available to the many believers who would never visit Rusafa but wished to place their faith in Sergius's miraculous powers.[115] Dissemination of the cult owed much to the mobility of the pastoralists, merchants, and soldiers who traversed the Barbarian Plain. But it must also be seen in the context of the heating up of Roman, Iranian, and Arab relations in the shrine's vicinity, and of the role that was developing for martyr cult more generally in the frontier zone. In the early fifth century, Marutha, the bishop of Mayperqat and a diplomat who traveled back and forth between the Roman and Iranian courts, was busy planting another martyr cult in the frontier zone. The next chapter examines the martyr cult that was deliberately established at Mayperqat in northernmost Syria-Mesopotamia on the frontier between Rome and Iran, just before Alexander's construction within Rusafa's walls of the martyrium to the soldier-martyr Sergius. The example of Mayperqat not only helps to contextualize the Sergius cult at Rusafa, but suggests ways in which martyrs' bones could play a dynamic role in the region's geopolitical developments.

---

115. Cf. Greg. Tur., *Glor. mart.* 63.81, commenting, with reference to the cult of S. Patroclus of Troyes, that "the men of that place had paid little reverence to this martyr, because the story of his sufferings was not available. It is the custom of the man in the street to give more attentive veneration to those saints of God whose combats are read aloud" (tr. Van Dam).

TWO

Martyr Cult on the Frontier

The Case of Mayperqat

RELICS AND DEFENSE

Among eastern Christians, martyr cult had been linked from the start not only to holy objects, the bones and blood of martyrs, but also to holy sites. The bones of martyrs were often enshrined at the reputed site of their martyrdom. But if that spot was inconvenient for practical reasons, as we have seen in S. Sergius's *Passio,* the relics could be translated to a more appropriate place. The establishment of new shrines or embellishment of old became the concern of local groups, who disputed rights of possession and, in doing so, might attract the interest of greater powers—bishops, shaykhs, and kings. Sacred sites in the open spaces of the Syro-Mesopotamian landscape worked on multiple levels and were intimately linked with the maintenance of order among the region's diverse communities.

Relics could be moved around to deal with particular problems. The translation to Constantinople of relics of the Apostles Andrew and Timothy, either at the end of Constantine's reign or in his successor's, was praised by Paulinus of Nola in 405:

Indeed, when Constantine was founding the city named after himself and was the first of the Roman kings to bear the Christian name, the godsent idea came to him that since he was embarking on the splendid enterprise of building a city that would rival Rome, he should also emulate Romulus's city with a further endowment, by gladly defending his walls with the bodies of the apostles. He then removed Andrew from the Achaeans and Timothy from Asia. And so Constantinople now stands with twin towers, vying with the eminence of great Rome, or rather resembling the defenses of Rome in that God has counterbalanced Peter and Paul with a protection as great, since Constantinople has gained the disciple of Paul and the brother of Peter.[1]

Old Rome fell to Alaric in 410 because, according to opponents of the empire's new religion, the traditional divine allies had not been evoked to defend the Eternal City.[2] When the Goths reached Athens in 396, belief in the old gods had still been robust enough to rally Athena and Achilles to the walls and save the city.[3] But in the fifth and sixth centuries, Christian martyrs and saints, usually represented by a relic, were staking their claim as protectors of cities across the empire. In direct criticism of the old gods, Theodoret of Cyrrhus explained the omnipotence of Christian relics:

> The noble souls of the victorious traverse the heavens and join in the dance of the immaterial beings. Their bodies are not hidden away each in its single grave, but the cities and villages that have divided them among themselves call them saviors of souls and bodies and doctors and honor them as protectors of cities and guardians [πολιούχους τιμῶσι καὶ φύλακας] and treat them as ambassadors before the master of the universe and through them receive divine gifts. And even though the body has been divided, the grace has remained undivided, and that minute relic possesses the same power as the martyr, just as if he had never in any way been divided.[4]

The martyrs became champions (πρόμαχοι) and allies (ἐπίκουροι).[5] Severus of Antioch, in a hymn on the martyrs, proclaimed that "the festival of the holy martyrs is the joy and pleasure of all churches, a strong wall for all the inhabited earth, and the victory of kings, and the glory of priests."[6]

When in the early sixth century King Theuderic was besieging the city of Clermont, he lost heart when his general attributed the magnitude of the city's defenses to "the saints whose churches surround the city walls."[7] That saints and fortifications were not associated only in the minds of hagiographers is clear from an inscription found at the southeastern corner of the

---

1. Paul. Nol., *Carm.* 19.329–42; tr. Mango, after Walsh, *BZ* 83 (1990): 53. On the possibility that it was Constantine in 336 and not, as usually believed, Constantius in 357, who translated the relics, see Mango's addendum, *BZ* 83 (1990): 434.

2. Zos., *Hist. nov.* 5.41.

3. Ibid. 6. Cf. Olympiodorus, fr. 27 (Blockley) = fr. 1.27 (Müller-Dindorf), where it is reported that during the reign of Constantius III, three solid silver statues were excavated in Thrace where they had been consecrated and buried to ward off barbarian invasions. Shortly after the statues' removal, the region was inundated with Goths, Huns, and Sarmatians.

4. Theod., *Graec. aff. cur.* 8.10–11.

5. Ibid. 39. Cf. S. Thecla, who dislodged Pallas Athena from Mount Kokysion in Cilicia (*Mir. Theclae*, 2), and later appeared on the walls of Seleucia, letting out a war cry to fend off bandits from the city (ibid., 5).

6. James of Edessa, *Hymns of Severus of Antioch* 216, *PO* 7.5.676.

7. Greg. Tur., *V. Patr.* 4.2.

walls of Calama, modern Guelma in Algeria, commemorating their erection
by Solomon:

> Twelve and one towers altogether rose up in a row;
> It seems a work of wonder, constructed so swiftly.
> The postern gate behind the baths is fastened with iron.
> No enemy could raise a hand against it.
> No one could take by storm the work of the Patricius Solomon.
> The protection of martyrs secures this postern gate.
> The martyrs Clement and Vincentius guard this entrance.[8]

The Solomon of the inscription is Belisarius's commander, known from
Procopius as an energetic fortifier of North African cities against the desert
tribes.[9] Solomon was a native of the region of Dara, a village just west of
Nisibis that had been fortified by the emperor Anastasius with walls and with
relics of S. Bartholomew, described as the guardian of the city.[10]

A relic was the perfect symbol to represent the unity of the world's material and spiritual dimensions. By participating in both, a relic held out to
those who possessed the holy object a hope of divine intervention in the
wavering sphere of material existence. Walls would become impenetrable,
soldiers invincible. The appeal of such a device for rulers grew in strength,
particularly from the reign of Theodosius II. In 421, under the influence of
his sister Pulcheria and as part of Rome's preparation for war with Iran,
Theodosius II sent a gold, gem-studded cross to the bishop of Jerusalem
with instructions to install it on Golgotha.[11] The gift suggested the emperor's desired fusion of Christ's victory with Rome's triumph over its traditional enemy, also a persecutor of Christianity. In return the emperor
received relics of S. Stephen's right arm—both the martyr's name, which recalled a victory crown, and his faithful right arm were ideally suited to the
occasion. When, on their journey from the Holy City to the empire's capi-

---

8. "Una et bis senas turres crescebant in ordine totas; / Mirabilem operam cito constructa
videtur. Posticius / sub termas balteo concluditur ferro. Nu[ll]us malorum poterit erigere
man(um). / Patrici Solomon(is) insti[tu]tion(em) nemo / expugnare valevit. Defensio mar-
tir(um) tuet[u]r posticius ipse. / Clemens et Vincentius, martir(es), custod(iunt) in[t]roitum
ipsu(m)" (*CIL* 8.5352). Cf. Durliat, *Dédicaces*, 11–14. On the fortification at Calama, see
Pringle, *Defence of Byzantine Africa*, 188–91.

9. Proc., *Bel.* 4.19.3, refering to activity in 539–40; *PLRE*, 3: 1167–77 (Solomon 1).

10. ὡς αὐτὸς τὴν φυλακὴν ἐπετράπη τῆς πόλεως: Joh. Diakrin. fr. 2.558, p. 157; see also
pp. 64–65 below. The association of saints or martyrs with walls was widespread. Ephrem
viewed holy men as the wall and shield of Nisibis and her countryside: see, e.g., Ephr. Syr.,
Carm. Nisib. 13.21 on Jacob; ibid. 17.4 on Abraham. Evagr., *HE* 1.13, identifies S. Symeon as
Antioch's rampart and fortress.

11. Theoph., *Chron.*, A.M. 5920, pp. 86–87. See Holum, *Theodosian Empresses*, 102–4;
Holum, *GRBS* 18 (1977): 162–67.

tal the relics arrived at Chalcedon, S. Stephen came to Pulcheria in a dream to announce his imminent arrival. The protomartyr was received in an adventus ceremony and installed in a martyr chapel at the imperial palace: Pulcheria seems to have orchestrated the whole process of the translation. Between 434 and 446, with the aid of an old monk and a vision, she also uncovered the bones of the forty martyrs of Sebaste, soldiers executed in the reign of Licinius and destined to join the ranks of Rome's military martyrs. Theodosius's empress Eudocia also had her part to play in the cultivation of martyrs. At Constantinople she built a church in honor of the previously little known soldier-martyr Polyeuctus. After her fall from favor, Eudocia turned her attention to Holy Land benefaction and became one of the most celebrated patrons of churches, hospices, and poor houses. She also refortified the Holy City, an act that she commemorated in an inscription in which she grounded her endowment in the prophecy of none less than King David.[12]

During the course of the fifth century, martyr cult and the shrines of martyrs came to play an important role in the frontier arena. The construction of a martyrium within Rusafa's walls not long before 425, and the subsequent recording of the *Passio,* were signs of Sergius's rising popularity. But Rusafa was not the only place between the Roman and Iranian empires where martyr cult was blossoming in the fifth century. The accounts of the emerging cult at Mayperqat reveal an instructive variety of motives, and of angles from which Syria and Mesopotamia might be viewed. The cult of the Iranian martyrs at Mayperqat and the collection of their *passiones* may also have provided special stimulus for the development of the Sergius cult only a decade later. Our knowledge of the situation at Mayperqat depends primarily on the *Vitae* of the fifth-century bishop Marutha, the founder of Martyropolis on the site of Mayperqat. Marutha had also served as Theodosius II's ambassador to the Sasanian emperor Yazdgard I. His career crystallizes both the importance of geography in Syro-Mesopotamian martyr cult, and the relationship between political maneuvering and martyr cult that would be expressed also at Rusafa.

AT THE WORLD'S CENTER

As the chief city of Sophanene, Mayperqat served as market and ecclesiastical center for a large and dispersed assemblage of villages whose inhabitants made a living from agriculture and animal husbandry.[13] Situated on undulating ground south of the Hazro range of hills, Mayperqat overlooks

12. Mal., *Chron.* 357–58.
13. See Fiey, *AB* 94 (1976): 57, on Mayperqat before Marutha's appearance; see also Honigmann, *Ostgrenze,* 7 n. 5.

the Tigris basin, which begins to decline some distance to the south of the settlement. Mayperqat (modern Silvan) is watered by the Farkin Su, which in turn flows into the broad but shallow Nymphios (modern Batman Su) 20 kilometers to the south. After draining part of the Taurus mountains, the Nymphios finds a course through the Hazro range and then debouches into the Tigris basin some 40 kilometers south of Mayperqat. The settlement lay at the intersection of many routes, especially those leading southward to the Tigris. Mayperqat was a halt on a route between Bitlis and Amida (modern Diyarbakır), connecting the Black Sea and adjacent Iranian territory with the Syro-Mesopotamian plain and the Mediterranean coast.[14] Situated in the mountainous northeastern limit of Roman control, the city of Mayperqat, "un lieu d'osmose" as Fiey aptly called it,[15] lay at the convergence of the Roman empire to the west, the Iranian empire to the east, Armenia to the north, and Arab lands to the south.[16] Throughout its history, the region has often been caught up in power struggles, not only because of its frontier position, but because its rugged terrain makes it especially difficult to dominate and thus a haven of resilient tradition.[17]

"There is a country district called Sophanene, located in the East between Armenia and Persia, which used to be a wasteland and had not received the faith of Christ," the older of two *Lives* of Marutha preserved in Greek begins.[18] In the fifth century, Sophanene lay within the Roman empire, but was often a bone of contention in Roman-Iranian conflicts.[19] It was a region peripheral to Constantinople's calculations, and in times of persecution, it became, like the desert fringes of Syria-Mesopotamia further south, a refuge for anti-Chalcedonian monks. The *Vitae sanctorum ori-*

14. Sinclair, *Eastern Turkey*, 3: 295; Nogaret, *REArm* 18 (1984): 415–16; Minorsky in *EI*[2], 6: 920; Lewis in *EI*[2], 1: 1242. The topography of Mayperqat has been much discussed because of the city's identification by some scholars with Tigranocerta, a view that now seems untenable. On the difficulty of interpreting ancient accounts of the region, see Syme in *Armies and Frontiers*, 61–71, and now Syme, *Anatolica*, 58–65. For a discussion that argues persuasively in favor of identifying Arzan as Tigranocerta, see Sinclair, *REArm* 25 (1994–95): 183–253.

15. Fiey, *Muséon* 89 (1976): 38.

16. See Sinclair, *Eastern Turkey*, 3: 161–62, 376–77; Minorsky, *EI*[2], 6: 920. On the diversity of cultural, especially artistic, influences, see Nogaret, *REArm* 18 (1984): 421–24.

17. The advantages of this liminal position were clearly perceived. For instance, the monastery of Bar ʿIgra, located hard against the mountains north / northeast of Mayperqat, chose to have its bishops consecrated by the Armenians in order to retain its independence from Antioch: see Fiey, *Muséon* 89 (1976): 31–32.

18. *Vita Maruthae* (*BHG* 2265). When describing the idolatrous state of Marutha's native Sophanene, the Armenian *Vita*, which is a translation from Syriac, assumes the reader's familiarity with the Mesopotamian districts and so does not define Sophanene's geographical position.

19. See Mango, *T&MByz* 9 (1985): 91–93; Minorsky in *EI*[2], 6: 920–21; Fiey, *Muséon* 89 (1976): 5–10; and Dillemann, *Haute Mésopotamie*, 216–17, on the changing political boundaries around Mayperqat.

entalium by John of Ephesus is packed with accounts of trying sojourns in and around Amida and Mayperqat. An episode recorded from the city of Mayperqat involved the holy man Habib, who attracted the faithful from east as well as west of the nearby political frontier.[20] While from Constantinople Mayperqat appeared to lie at the eastern periphery of the empire, one could also see it as the center of the known world, holding a delicate balance between the two great empires and the considerable powers of Armenia and the Arabs to the north and south. Some of our sources for Marutha's activities saw with the eye of the outsider, others with that of the insider. Linguistically the sources, written in Greek, Syriac, Armenian, and Arabic, represent the cultural traditions that surrounded Mayperqat on all sides.[21]

The Greek ecclesiastical historian Socrates wrote around 439, within a generation of Marutha's death ca. 420, and from the vantage point of Constantinople. Socrates briefly records the bishop's two imperial embassies to the Iranian court.[22] Theophanes, drawing on Socrates and Theodore Lector, also attributes two embassies to Marutha.[23] There are also an early, perhaps late fifth-century Greek *Vita* and an eleventh-century *Vita* based on the early Greek account.[24]

Our knowledge of Marutha does not, however, depend exclusively on Greek sources. An Armenian *Vita* exists, which concludes with a prayer to the martyrs of Martyropolis for Gagik and his deacon Grigor, who translated the book from the Syriac, and then continues with a brief account of Kawad I's siege of Mayperqat in 502.[25] This could either be an addendum also translated from the Syriac, or, as is more likely, a later addition to the Armenian translation. There is no explicit indication of the date of composition or translation, but the confusion of Yazdgard II with Yazdgard I in the

---

20. Joh. Eph., *Vita sanct.*, PO 17, pp. 11–12. For the ascetic milieu of the Amida area, see Harvey, *Asceticism*, 57–75.

21. The *Vitae* and other sources will be discussed individually. The many accounts of Marutha's career are surveyed by Tisserant, *Dict. de théologie*, 10: 142–49, and Sauget, *Bib.Sanct.* 8: 1305–9. See also Labourt, *Christianisme*, 87–89, 93; Sako, *Rôle de la hiérarchie syriaque*, 59–61.

22. Soc., *HE* 7.8, mentions two undated embassies. See the discussion in Sako, *Rôle de la hiérarchie syriaque*, 60–61, on the varied ennumeration and dating of Marutha's visits to the Iranian court proffered by the sources.

23. Theoph., *Chron.*, A.M. 5906, p. 82, and A.M. 5916, p. 85.

24. *Vita Maruthae* (*BHG* 2265 and 2266). Both are translated with commentary by Noret, *AB* 91 (1973): 77–103.

25. *Varkʿ ew Vkayabanoutʿiunkʿ Srboç* (*Vitae et passiones sanctorum*) (Venice, 1874), 2.17–32. References below to the Armenian *Vita* (cited as *Vita arm.*) are to the English translation by Marcus, *HThR* 25 (1932): 55–70.

account of Kawad's assault suggests that at least the final section following the translators' names was composed when such details could already have become clouded (after the sixth century?).[26] The lost Syriac original may have been considerably earlier.[27]

The historian Ibn al-Azraq, who wrote a history of his native Mayperqat in ca. 1176–77, and the geographer Yaqut, whose *Kitab mu'jam al-buldan* appeared ca. 1222, derived their accounts of Marutha from a lost Syriac source, very possibly the same one the Armenians translated.[28] In addition, an Arabic Nestorian ecclesiastical history was written by Mari ibn Sulayman in Iran in the twelfth century and revised significantly by 'Amr ibn Matta in the fifteenth. Together with Bar Hebraeus's thirteenth-century *Chronicon ecclesiasticum*, Mari's *Kitab al-mijdal* and 'Amr's later revision relate the main events in Marutha's career, and in greater detail than the Greek historians.[29] The Nestorian accounts belong to the Iranian ecclesiastical world where Marutha earned his reputation as conciliator.

Noret has argued, on the basis of textual comparison, that the early Greek *Vita* is also related to a lost Syriac original.[30] Onomastic evidence supports this claim, but the primary evidence consists of parallels between the Greek and Armenian *Vitae*, and also Yaqut, the latter two certainly dependent on an earlier Syriac source.[31] The Greek *Vita* is very lean, particularly in comparison with the Armenian *Vita*, which shows signs of considerable pious adornment. But the Syriac skeleton is discernible in both accounts— in the narrative order and also in elements such as Marutha's genealogy, the appearance of Jacob of Nisibis, the role of a woman named Mariam in the

---

26. *Vita arm.* 31–32, pp. 68–69 (tr. Marcus). See Marcus's comments, *HThR* 25 (1932): 54.

27. On the lost Syriac account, see Fiey, *AB* 94 (1976): 35 n. 5; Noret, *AB* 91 (1973): 96 n. 5.

28. Ibn al-Azraq, *Ta'rikh Mayyafariqin*, claims to have relied on a manuscript from the Jacobite church at Mayperqat. On the relationship of Ibn al-Azraq to Yaqut and the *Vita arm.*, see Fiey, *AB* 94 (1976): 35–45, on which this study must rely, since no edition of the early part of the history exists. Yaqut, *Mu'jam al-buldan* 5.235–38, draws on Ibn al-Azraq's account. See also Robinson, *JRAS* 6 (1996): 22–27.

29. Mari ibn Sulayman, *Kitab al-mijdal*, fol. 151b–153a; 'Amr ibn Matta, revision of *Kitab al-mijdal*, fol. 151b–153a; Bar Hebraeus, *Chron. eccles.*, 3: 46–52. Marcus translates the relevant passages of Mari ibn Sulayman and 'Amr ibn Matta in *HThR* 25 (1932): 50–54.

30. Noret, *AB* 91 (1973): 96–103, discusses the supporting evidence, although he does not claim that the Greek *Life* is a direct translation from the original Syriac. Fiey, *AB* 94 (1976): 45, accepts Noret's claims and concludes that the *Vita arm.*, Ibn al-Azraq and Yaqut are all translations of an original Syriac that underwent modification over time. The Armenian translation was made, according to Fiey and Noret, at a considerably earlier stage of the Syriac text's elaboration than was the Arabic.

31. Noret, *AB* 91 (1973): 97 n. 4, bases his comparisons with Yaqut on Tisserant's comments in *Dict. de théologie*, 10: 142–49.

Christianization of the region of Mayperqat, and Marutha's successful visits to the Iranian court. The Armenian *Vita* and later Arabic accounts view Marutha's activities from the Syro-Mesopotamian world between Rome and Iran. Variations between these sources—particularly the Armenian ones—and the Greek accounts are explicable in terms of cultural and geographical orientation, and are useful guides in the study of Syro-Mesopotamian martyr cult.

THE ECUMENICAL CITY OF MARTYRS

Marutha's success as imperial ambassador and Christian leader derived from his cultural flexibility, which he owed in large part to the environment that nurtured him. He was the only son of the governor of Sophanene, whose mother, Mariam, had been a Christian woman of noble Armenian blood.[32] Marutha did not follow in his father's footsteps, but instead studied medicine and joined the priesthood. It was the fortunate combination of his medical and theological learning, his native command of the region's languages—he knew at least Greek, Syriac, and Pahlavi[33]—and his increasing involvement with the western Church during a period of nervous calm that made possible his prominence in the shaping of Syro-Mesopotamian political and religious relations. Bishop Marutha's earliest certain participation in Church affairs was in 382, when he took part in the anti-Messalian synod held at Side.[34] His talent as a physician no doubt boosted the success of the Roman embassy to Ctesiphon in 399, when Marutha cured Yazdgard's son of demonic possession or, according to Socrates and 'Amr ibn Matta, re-

32. *Vita arm.* 18–19, pp. 56–57 (tr. Marcus); cf. *BHG* 2265.6 where Mariamne, again an Armenian Christian, is Marutha's mother. See Noret, *AB* 91 (1973): 97–99, for a comparison of the genealogies in the Armenian, Greek, and Arabic accounts.

33. See Baumstark, *Geschichte*, 53, on Marutha's translation into Syriac of the canons of the Council of Nicaea; *Synodicon orientale*, 256, on his translation of the western bishops' letter from Greek to "Persian"; and Sako, *Rôle de la hiérarchie syriaque*, 60. *Chronicle of Seert* 78, p. 198, calls Maruta a philosopher versed in Greek, Syriac, and Hebrew.

34. Photius *Bib.* 52; Soc., *HE* 6.15; Soz., *HE* 8.16; and Mari, *Kitab al-mijdal*, p. 31, fol. 152b (tr. Marcus, 52), record Marutha's attendance at the Council of Constantinople in 381, but Baumstark, *Geschichte*, 53, with n. 6, points to the absence of Marutha's name among the signatories, despite claims that this was Marutha's first appearance at a Church council. Contemporary eastern accounts do not name Marutha's see: e.g., *Syn.or.*, 18–22. 35, 39 (tr. Chabot, 255–62, 274, 280). Only the headings of the acts of the synods, which were probably added later, call him bishop of Mayperqat: e.g., *Syn.or.*, 17 (tr. Chabot, 253). See also Fiey, *Muséon* 89 (1976): 5. In the Greek authors, Marutha's title is bishop of Mesopotamia (Soc., *HE* 6.15 and 7.8). In the fifth century, the bishop of Mesopotamia and of Sophanene were one and the same (Honigmann, *Ostgrenze*, 8).

lieved the king of kings of a chronic headache.[35] But although cures played their part in the Roman visit, the embassy's main concern was Yazdgard's accession in 399 and the Romans' desire to reconfirm peace between the empires and tolerance of Christians under the new shah's rule. All accounts—Greek, Armenian, and Arabic—recognize a good story and linger on the neutral ground of Marutha's successes at court—his miraculous cures of the king and his son and the Christian sage's humiliation of the Zoroastrian priests. Iranian Christians' increased freedom to worship and to build churches during the reign of Yazdgard may have resulted from Marutha's efforts at the bidding of the Roman emperor. But it also owed much to the Iranian monarch's cultivation of minorities as a counterbalance to the Iranian nobility and his wish to avoid conflict with Rome while preoccupied with internal disaffection.[36] Theodosius II sent Marutha in 408 on a second mission, this time in the company of another frontier bishop, Acacius of Amida, most likely in order to proclaim Theodosius's accession to the throne, ensure peaceful relations between the two empires, and refresh the Roman appeal for the welfare of Iranian Christians.[37]

The *Synodicon orientale* records Marutha as "the mediator of peace and concord between East and West."[38] During the Synod of Seleucia-Ctesiphon convened at Epiphany 410, for instance, Marutha revealed the contents of a letter written by the bishops of Roman Syria and Mesopotamia, in which they state their decisions concerning the election and authority of bishops,

35. For Yazdgard's headache, see Soc., *HE* 7.8; ʿAmr ibn Matta, *Kitab al-mijdal*, p. 23 (tr. Marcus, 53). The accounts of Marutha's successes at Yazdgard's court vary in chronology and detail. For instance, Yazdgard's son in Soc., *HE* 7.8; Theoph. *Chron.*, A.M. 5916, p. 85; *Vita arm.* 23 (tr. Marcus, 61); and Mari, *Kitab al-mijdal*, p. 29, fol. 151b (tr. Marcus, 51), is a daughter in *Vita Maruthae BHG* 2265.7 and *BHG* 2266.7. See Sako, *Rôle de la hiérarchie syriaque* 15, 60–61 and 63, esp. nn. 14 and 15, on the diverse accounts of the illnesses and the motivation for Marutha's visit to Yazdgard's court.

36. Yazdgard was criticized by the Iranian nobles for his cultivation of an alliance with the Lakhmids of Hira. On this development, see Bosworth, *CHIran*, 593–612. His non-Christian subjects remembered Yazdgard as "the sinner": Christensen, *Iran*, 269; Labourt, *Christianisme*, 91–92. The reasons for Roman-Iranian conflict in the fifth century are still under debate in modern scholarship. Holum, *GRBS* 18 (1979): 153–72, focuses on the impact of Roman court intrigue on the religious policies of Rome in frontier politics, at the expense of wider political and defense considerations. Rubin in *Defence*, 677–95, and *MHR* 1 (1986): 33–62, discusses the motivation behind Yazdgard's policy toward Rome, but overlooks the role of religious embassies, including Marutha's. Blockley, *East Roman Policy*, 50–51, points to the role of minorities in Yazdgard's macro-politics as a balance to the Iranian nobility and the priestly class of mobads. The question of Iranian cultivation of cultural diversity in Syria and Mesopotamia is discussed further in the context of Khusrau II's involvement at Mayperqat, below, and at Rusafa, pp. 133–41 below.

37. On Acacius of Amida, see Mari, *Kitab al-mijdal*, p. 31, fol. 153a (tr. Marcus, 52).

38. *Syn.or.* 18 (tr. Chabot, 255).

the observance of Church feasts, and the canons of the Council of Nicaea.[39] After brief discussion, the decisions were accepted by the forty eastern bishops who, according to Mari ibn Sulayman, "made known to him (Marutha) that the Westerners were their brethren and comrades," acknowledging the place of Iranian Christians in the Church of Christ that is in the four parts of the world.[40] Grasping at once the power latent in the association of Christians across political borders, Yazdgard is recorded to have responded to the conciliatory efforts of Marutha with the claim that "the East and West shall be one empire under the authority of my rule."[41] In the light of the doctrinal and ecclesiastical interests that the eastern accounts attribute to Marutha on his visits to the Iranian empire, it is significant that the Greek sources focus exclusively on Marutha's mission to convert the king, or at least to dispose him favorably toward Rome and the Christians on Iranian territory. No mention is made of Marutha's efforts to harmonize the western and eastern Churches, a detail that would have diminished Rome's claim to be the sole Christian empire at a period of dynamic missionary activity in Iranian territory.[42]

On his second visit to Yazdgard's court, Marutha made a momentous request of the shah.[43] With the expected worldly detachment of a holy man, Marutha declined all offers of gold and luxuries. His one desire combines the disarming humility of a spiritual leader with the political savvy of an inveterate diplomat: he asked to collect the bones of all Christian martyrs from Iranian territory and take them home to Mayperqat. Without pause, we are told, Yazdgard granted this wish.[44] When the bishop returned with his relics to Roman soil and report of his successes reached the court in Constantinople, Theodosius, deeply impressed, in turn put his resources at the service of Marutha. Not surprisingly, this offer did not fall on stony ground. Like many former diplomats who transform retirement into a second phase of influence, Marutha's next project was to build the village of Mayperqat into a sacred fortress with the emperor's blessing and financial

39. Ibid., 19–36 (tr. Chabot, 257–75). See also *Chronicle of Seert* 66, p. 206; Mari, *Kitab al-mijdal*, pp. 30–31, fol. 152b (tr. Marcus, 51–52); ʿAmr, *Kitab al-mijdal*, pp. 24–25 (tr. Marcus, 54); Bar Hebraeus, *Chron. eccles.*, 3: 49–52; Sako, *Rôle de la hiérarchie syriaque* 68–70; Labourt, *Christianisme*, 92–99.

40. Mari, *Kitab al-mijdal*, pp. 30–31, fol. 152b (tr. Marcus, 52). For the number of eastern bishops in attendance, see *Syn.or.* 19 (tr. Chabot, 257, with n. 1).

41. *Syn.or.* 19 (tr. Chabot, 256).

42. For fifth-century Christian proselytism in eastern Syria-Mesopotamia, see Rubin, *MHR* 1 (1986): 33–36.

43. *Vita gr.* 8; *Vita arm.* 29 (tr. Marcus, 66–67).

44. In the light of the long-standing friction in Iranian-controlled areas caused by Christian burial practices, which Zoroastrians considered an impious contamination of the earth, Yazdgard's permission to take the bones might have been inspired by more than his admiration for the holy man, as Nicholson, *AJA* 89 (1985): 668, has suggested.

support. Between 410 and 420, Mayperqat was fortified with impressive walls and adorned with churches, at whose altars and in whose walls the bones of the martyrs were deposited. The city was christened Martyropolis and elevated to the dignity of an episcopal see.[45]

From the Syro-Mesopotamian perspective, it was not sufficient for Martyropolis, as a fortress at the center of the Christian world, to be protected by the holy relics only of eastern martyrs. According to the Armenian *Vita*, Marutha also received permission from Theodosius to collect "relics from all the saints in his empire."[46] "He went out," the Armenian *Vita* continues, "to Rome and to all the cities and provinces and villages and monasteries and hermitages, and gathered relics." His harvest was impressive — 120,000 from the Roman empire, 20,000 from Asorestan (the Armenian name for Beth 'Arbaya, north-central Syria-Mesopotamia), 80,000 from the Iranian empire, and 60,000 from Armenia, a total of 280,000 relics. Putting aside the hagiographer's enthusiastic hyperbole, what remains is a cult truly centered in Syria-Mesopotamia. Sozomen and Theophanes, Greek sources, are silent about Marutha's collection of relics. The Greek *Vita* mentions only Iranian Christian bones, emphasizing Iranian persecution of Roman reli-

45. One large and two small dark purple marble reliquaries, now in the Diyarbakır museum, were photographed by Gertrude Bell at Silvan (Mayperqat) in 1906: see Mundell Mango's discussion in Bell, *Churches* 129, and Mango, *T&MByz* 9 (1985): 95, who is tempted to believe that they held the bones of Marutha's martyrs. See Fiey, *AB* 94 (1976): 42–43, on pious constructions in the area of Mayperqat according to Ibn al-Azraq in the twelfth century. See also Fiey, *Muséon* 89 (1976): 24–38, esp. 25, on the transfer of the relics from the Melkite church on the city acropolis to another church in 1012/13 by the Marwanid Nasr al-Dawla. Local tradition knew the citadel church as the "fortress," a fitting name in the light its location, but also because of the relics it housed.

46. *Vita arm.* 29 (tr. Marcus, 67–68). Oddly, the Armenian variation has not been remarked on by any commentator. The *Invention of the Relics of Saint Bartholomew* (*BHO* 159) also records that Marutha assembled 270,000 relics from Iran, Syria and Armenia. Van Esbroeck, *REArm* 17 (1983): 190–91, does not date the *Invention,* but conjectures that it had already undergone elaboration by the early eighth century. According to Ibn al-Azraq, Marutha also brought from Constantinople the blood of the Prophet Joshua in a phial, which was kept in a black marble reliquary. Ibn al-Azraq, *Ta'rikh Mayyafariqin,* records that after curing the king's son, Marutha took advantage of his favorable position to negotiate peace between the Iranian king (named Shapur) and Roman emperor (named Constantine). He requested from the shah "the bones of the martyrs and the monks killed by your followers in our country" (summarized by Fiey, *AB* 94 [1976]: 42). Fiey supposes that the reference to "our country" by Marutha, while still in the Iranian empire, implies that the legend recorded by Ibn al-Azraq was written in Iran (*AB* 94 (1976): 42 n. 1). Despite its historical muddle, Ibn al-Azraq's history is closely related to the Armenian *Vita,* except that the native of twelfth-century Mayyafariqin has a habit of telescoping his material. For instance, two generations merge when Marutha becomes both governor and bishop (Fiey, *AB* 94 [1976]: 44). According to the Armenian *Vita,* Marutha placed two requests for martyrs' bones — one to Yazdgard from Iranian territory and one to Theodosius from Roman territory. It may be that Ibn al-Azraq here has fused the two into one request.

gion and subsequent Roman recuperation of their own martyrs' relics to use as protection against Iran.[47] But the accounts closest to home, those preserved in Armenian and Arabic, emphasize the universal Christian intent of Marutha's deeds. Beth 'Arbaya stands distinct in its own right between the empires of Rome and Iran. By assembling the relics at Martyropolis, Marutha not only did his part to ensure that God was constantly worshipped at the martyrs' graves;[48] according to the Syro-Mesopotamian point of view, the effect was also to make present at the core of the Christian world the unity of Christian martyrs and believers across space as well as time.

THE IRANIAN VIEWPOINT

It was in peacetime that Marutha translated the bones of Roman, Syrian, and Iranian Christians to a fortress in the mountains above the Syro-Mesopotamian plain. According to all accounts, the collection of relics was part and parcel of the building scheme for "Martyropolis," undertaken thanks to the patronage of Theodosius II, who would certainly have appreciated the strategic location of Mayperqat and welcomed any additional assistance the martyrs could lend.[49] But, as one would expect, the Armenian *Vita* offers the view from between Rome and Iran, and reveals the constant need for balance. Rome's buildup of this martyr cult at a strategic fortress was bound to elicit an Iranian response. Yazdgard could not afford to be left behind at a critical moment. In the Armenian *Vita*, he too patronizes Martyropolis with an elaborate gift in honor of Marutha—an inscribed gold cup filled with gold to subsidize the building project.[50] This benefaction should be seen as an encouragement of Marutha's efforts to consolidate relations between western and eastern Christians. The usefulness of Christianity for Yazdgard's domestic and foreign policy was obvious, and the Sasanian king could not risk alienating the crucial heartland between the two empires.

47. In the early sixth century, Severus wrote hymns commemorating the Iranian martyrs and other hymns that stress the martyrs' role in the fight against the idolatrous Iranian empire (in James of Edessa, *Hymns of Severus of Antioch* 152, 265, 266, pp. 198–99, 301–2). Not long after Marutha's death in 420, Theodoret, *HR* 24.2, attests the inclusion of Iranian martyrs among the yearly feasts. His language suggests this was a recent development—"Now there are also martyrs under the same roof who suffered at the hands of the Persians and who are honored by us in annual feasts" (ἔχει δὲ νῦν καὶ μάρτυρας ὁμορόφους, παρὰ Πέρσαις μὲν ἠγωνισμένους, ἐτησίοις δὲ πανηγύρεσι παρ'ἡμῖν τιμωμένους).

48. *Vita arm.* 26 (tr. Marcus, 63–64).

49. On the gradual buildup of Mayperqat as a fortified frontier post, see Sinclair, *Eastern Turkey*, 3: 374–75, 381, and 428–29, on Aqbas, an Iranian fort built-up in the sixth century across the river Nymphios.

50. *Vita arm.* 30 (tr. Marcus, 67).

The Iranian martyrs' stories traveled with, or at least close behind, their bones. Accounts of Iranian martyrs were written at different times and places by different authors. Many were composed by eyewitnesses from the Great Persecution under Shapur II and helped to increase the Iranian martyrs' fame outside Iranian territory. A fourteenth-century Nestorian, ʿAbdisho of Nisibis, attributed a collection of Iranian martyr accounts to Marutha himself—not a surprising claim, but one that today seems doubtful.[51] However, even if Marutha played no part in the collection of the martyr acts, it would have been surprising if, when he returned to Mayperqat with the relics, he did not also bring their stories—at least in his memory. Marutha's project to install the relics must have been accompanied by a *translatio* ceremony where the most spectacular martyr accounts would have been narrated, even if they had not yet been recorded in writing. Certainly, Iranian martyr acts were in circulation in the fifth century in the original Syriac, as well as in Greek and Armenian translations.[52] From his see in northern Syria-Mesopotamia, Marutha caught the attention of political and religious observers on all sides: sowing peace between Rome and Iran, fortifying his frontier city with walls and relics, probably also involving himself in the verbal dissemination of the martyrs' stories. This milieu where martyrs were—not so paradoxically—linked with détente and, at the same time, defense, also witnessed the composition of Sergius's *Passio* and the construction of a magnificent church and other buildings within Rusafa's walls.[53]

In 502, Kawad I (488–531) besieged the city of Mayperqat and eventually took it. The capture of such a strategically located fortress was a great boon for his westward campaign. As a last-ditch effort, the city's inhabitants filled with gold and offered as their ransom the gold cup given to Marutha by Yazdgard I, Kawad's grandfather. According to the Armenian *Vita*, which alone records this story, Kawad, in honor of his forefather's esteem for Marutha, withdrew and left the region in peace. Other sources relate that

---

51. Wiessner, *Zur Märtyrerüberlieferung*, 11–39. Labourt, *Christianisme*, 52–53, argued strongly against Assemani's attribution to Marutha of the collection Assemani translated in *Acta martyrum orientalium*. Nevertheless, Labourt conceded that Marutha's role in the collection of *acta* cannot be rejected only on the grounds of the late date of ʿAbdisho. Chabot, *Littérature syriaque*, 40–43, and Baumstark, *Geschichte*, 53–57, did not dismiss Marutha's authorship. Even Peeters could not reject the possibility of Marutha's involvement absolutely (*AB* 56 [1938]: 21, esp. n. 3 and 122).

52. Soz., *HE* 2.14.5; *Martyrum Persarum acta*. Names of Iranian martyrs appear as early as 411 in the Syriac *Calendar of Edessa*. The manuscript (British Library MS. Add. 12150) is the "earliest dated Christian literary manuscript in any language" (Brock, in *Cambridge Ancient History*, 13: 718, with n. 22).

53. *ACOec.* 1.4, p. 163, mentions not only a basilica at Rusafa, but also "illi altissimi muri et alia intra eandem munitionem aedificia."

the city indeed soon reverted to Roman possession after its capture in 502. Later, as part of Justinian's building program, Martyropolis was refortified and named Justinianopolis.[54]

Again at the end of the sixth century, in 589, Mayperqat fell into Iranian hands, only to be returned by Khusrau II in 591 out of gratitude for the emperor Maurice's support of his claim to the Iranian throne against the usurper Bahram.[55] From his position of weakness, Khusrau attempted to maintain a presence at the frontier settlement by recording in a Greek inscription on the city wall Mayperqat's shared Roman and Iranian history and his voluntary cession of it to Roman control.[56] Khusrau returned the city to Roman control, but by emphasizing his generosity at that particular frontier, famous to Christians as the resting place of Iranian martyrs, Khusrau kept his hand in the intricate game of frontier politics. His return of Mayperqat should be seen as a foreshadowing of his gestures at Rusafa, discussed in chapter 5.

Khusrau's maneuvering was immediately countered. When, in 591, Mayperqat was returned to Rome, the bishop of Melitene, Domitianus, inaugurated a feast to celebrate the city's salvation and honor the martyrs.[57] Theophylact relates that at the martyrs' feast Domitianus sang a triumphal hymn composed for the occasion, in which he praised the Iranian martyrs as champions against Iran: "This, martyrs, is your offering from the Babylonian tyrant and foreigner, the fugitive from his own kingdom who is now obedient to the Romans rather than hostile: for such great deeds have you executed against your enemies."[58] Book 4 of Theophylact's *Historia Universalis* closes with this episode about the Iranian martyrs of Martyropolis. At the opening of book 5 we encounter Khusrau before his victory over Bahram, supplicating Sergius, another martyr positioned on the frontier.[59]

The various accounts of Marutha's project illustrate the possibilities of martyr cult in the Syro-Mesopotamian frontier zone. We glimpse in Marutha's career, especially as it is preserved in the Syriac, Armenian, and Arabic traditions, how that zone became a center from which the martyrs' power

54. Proc., *Aed.* 3.2.4–14; Malalas, *Chron.* 18, p. 427. See also van Esbroeck, *REArm* 17 (1983): 183.

55. Theoph. Sim., *Hist.* 3.4.1–5, 3.5.11–6.5, 4.12.6–15.13; Evag., *HE* 6.14–19; Mich. Syr., *Chron.* 2, pp. 360–61; Agap., *Kitab al-'unwan*, pp. 440–47; Sebeos, *Hist.* 9 (tr. Gugerotti, 59).

56. Although the inscription, now lost, was transcribed in fragmentary condition, blocks 6 and 7 preserve enough to reveal Khusrau's vaunting rhetoric. Mango, *T&MByz* 9 (1985): 99–100, republishes the text.

57. Theoph. Sim., *Hist.* 4.15.18–16.28. Garsoïan, *REArm* 10 (1973–74), esp. 120–22, discusses the role played by eastern bishops in the face of siege or attack. Cf. Theophyl., *Hist.* 3.5.8–16; Evag., *HE* 6.14–19.

58. Theop. Sim., *Hist.* 4.16.13 (tr. Whitby and Whitby).

59. Ibid. 5.1.7.

radiated, linking Christians whether Roman, Iranian, or from somewhere in between. It was, after all, during Marutha's lifetime that Symeon ascended his column and became a "great wonder of the oikoumene," attracting visitors from all directions—"Ishmaelites, Persians, Armenians, Iberians, Himyarites, Spaniards, Britons, Gauls, and Italians."[60] The absence from the Greek sources of Marutha's relic-collecting activities west of Iranian territory makes it clear that Rome's leaders aspired to mold martyr cult as a bulwark against Iran. Yazdgard and Khusrau II, on the other hand, through their involvement with Christian communities in Iranian territory and in the frontier zone at Mayperqat, played up the potential unity of Syrian and Mesopotamian martyr cult in their attempts to weaken a dangerous Roman monopoly. In the sixth century, leaders on both sides of the frontier did their best to court the favor of martyr-patrons. It was in this tug-of-war between the martyr cult's natural impetus toward cross-border expansion, and even cohesiveness, and the two empires' impetus toward cultural monopoly that the cult of the martyr Sergius was forged.

60. Theod., *HR* 26.11.

THREE

Rusafa

THE FRONTIER ZONE

In about the year 570, the Piacenza Pilgrim traveled from Antioch across northern Syria and Mesopotamia to Chalcis, Harran, and Barbalissus, where he visited the tomb of Bacchus. At Sura, his final stop, he was told that the neighboring region, wherein lay the shrine of Sergius, was "Saracen country."[1] Judging by his report that Sergius's tomb was to be found at Tetrapyrgium, the pilgrim seems to have made do with Sergius's fellow martyr at Barbalissus.[2] Arab raids posed a threat to travelers, merchants, and settlements in the area of Rusafa long before the late sixth century. Most raids would have been small-scale and aimed at the increase of flocks at the expense of other pastoralists. The vast majority of these would have passed unrecorded.[3] Their impact on individuals could nonetheless be dramatic—

1. Piacenza Pilgrim, *Itin.* 47, p. 191, "inter Saracenos" (tr. Wilkinson, *Jerusalem Pilgrims*, 89).

2. The Piacenza Pilgrim reported that both Sergius and Bacchus had been martyred at Sura, and that Bacchus was then buried at Barbalissus and Sergius, whom he calls Bacchus's brother, at Tetrapyrgium, located "in the desert." Wilkinson, *Jerusalem Pilgrims*, 89 n. 58, 174 (in the good company of Dussaud, *Topographie,* 254) takes the Pilgrim's report at face value and erroneously identifies Tetrapyrgium with Rusafa.

3. Macdonald, *Syria* 70 (1993): 313–14, 328, cautions against confusing brigands and nomads. Accounts of nomad Arab raids on the settled population must be weighed against imperial interest in propagandizing against the Arabs, who were increasingly unavoidable participants in frontier politics: see Macdonald, *Syria* 70 (1993): 326–27, with nn. 154, 155; Sartre in *Désert,* 143–48, 160. That is not to deny that the threat of Arab raids existed: see, e.g., *CIL* 3.128, a Severan building inscription at Khan al-Qusayr on the road between Damascus and Emesa, constructed "for the sake of public security and against the terror of Scenitae Arabs"; with Rey-Coquais, *JRS* 68 (1978): 70 and n. 356. Proc., *Aed.* 2.9, claims that a mud-brick wall provided sufficient deterrence against Arab raids, which also suggests small-scale

as in the case of a camel-herder discovered in the mountains southeast of Sinjar by the Nestorian bishop of Haditha. The bishop approached the figure, whom he heard reciting a Nestorian hymn of resurrection in Syriac. At first the camel-herder responded only in Arabic. But when the bishop bound him with oaths, the man reluctantly explained that in his former occupation as a priest he had been taken hostage forty years earlier in an Arab raid, while praying for rain with his congregation outside Damascus.[4]

In 498, Arabs invaded Syria under the leadership of Iran's ally, the Lakhmid al-Nuʿman. They were defeated at Bithrapsa, "the first district of Syria," by Eugenius, the *strategos* of Syria and Euphratesia.[5] The identification of this site eluded even Alois Musil and Ernst Honigmann. However, Irfan Shahîd seems to have solved the enigma: the Greek Βίθραψα, Bithrapsa, is a corruption of what Shahîd calls "the Semitic form . . . Beth Resapha."[6] The shrine of Sergius at Rusafa had become a desirable object of plunder. But there is reason to suspect that the presence of al-Nuʿman's force near Rusafa was part of a broader trend. The renowned fortified camp, or *hirta*, of al-Nuʿman was located southwest of Rusafa at Hira, be-

---

assaults. Cf. also Teixidor in *Frontières*, 95–103; Whittaker, *Frontiers*, 136–39, 245–46, with n. 4; Sartre, *Trois études*, 121–203, esp. 153–203; Retsö in *Aspects of Late Antiquity*, 31–41; and Graf in *L'Arabie préislamique*, esp. 352, on traditional interpretations of nomads as brigands. For the modern period, see Lancaster and Lancaster in *PSAS* 18 (1988): 55–56.

4. Thomas of Marga, *Book of Governors* 2.41, with n. 3, p. 275. Fiey, *Assyrie chrétienne*, 1: 108, identifies, with some hesitance, Maran Zha in Thomas of Marga with Mar Zaha, who was bishop of Haditha after 740. See also Magoulias, Ἐπετηρὶς τῆς Ἑταιρείας Βυζαντινῶν Σπουδῶν 48 (1990–93): 300–310, for Arab raids on monasteries.

5. Theoph., *Chron.*, A. M. 5990, p. 141. See *PLRE*, 2: 417 and Shahîd, *BAFIC*, 122, for the identification of Eugenius's jurisdiction. Three encounters between Rome and the Arabs are recorded for the year 498. Only the defeat at Rusafa is of direct relevance to the discussion here. For the others, see Shahîd, *BAFIC*, 121–31; Sartre, *Trois études*, 159–60.

6. "[T]he second part of the compound . . . has undergone metathesis, which is common in the (Greek) transliteration of Arabic and other Semitic names" (Shahîd, *BAFIC*, 123). "Beth" has been added to signify the area around Rusafa. Additional evidence in support of Shahîd's suggestion can be found in the Syriac *Hist. Ahud.* 4, p. 29, which refers to Rusafa as Bet Rsapha. Shahîd notes the local parallel of Bizonovias for "Beth Zenobia" on the middle Euphrates (Musil, *Palmyrena*, 268). To this we can add Betproclis for "Beth Forklos" southeast of Emesa (Grimme, *Palmyrae*, 21 n. 8). In the thirteenth century, Yaqut, *Muʿjam al-buldan* 4.255 (tr. Le Strange, *Palestine*, 441) observed the foreign character of the name Betproclis (modern Furqlus). A village on the middle Euphrates refered to in Greek as "Beth Phrouraia" is frequently mentioned in the third-century papyri that appeared on the antiquities market not long before January 1988 and were published by Feissel and Gascou, *CRAI* 1989, esp. 540–45. For further examples from the region, see Morony, *Iraq* 117, with n. 48. Contrary to what Herzfeld suggests in Sarre and Herzfeld, *Archäologische Reise*, 1: 136, with n. 3, in Assyrian cuneiform records of the second half of the ninth century B.C., Rasappa refers not to Syrian Rusafa but to the region between the Khabur river in the west, the Wadi Tartar in the east, the Jabal Sinjar in the north, and the Euphrates in the south (Bernbeck, *Steppe als Kulturlandschaft*, 119).

tween the fertile riverine zone and the desert's fringe. Shapur I and Shapur II developed Hira as a buffer to control Arab incursions eastward, while
Yazdgard I had cultivated the Sasanian alliance with the Arabs of Hira as
a counterbalance to internal political threats.[7] The sixth century saw the
apogee of Hira's prosperity. Its famously salubrious climate and convenient
position for trade from the Arabian peninsula attracted a culturally diverse
population.[8] Hira was an agglomeration of walled enclosures, towers, gardens, and permanent structures, including churches, surrounded by camps.
It is best understood as a permanent camp at the steppe's edge; and the in-
terconnection between the settlement and the steppe is well illustrated by
an incident in the early fifth century. After the *dux* Timostratus routed Iran-
allied Arabs near Callinicum, Arabs allied with Rome launched a successful
raid on a caravan traveling to Hira. The raiders made off with the camels,
but did not linger at Hira, since the inhabitants had taken refuge in the
"inner desert."[9] Local knowledge of the landscape played a critical role in
martial conflict in the region, and was understood by both Roman and
Sasanian leaders as a military advantage.

Traditionally, Iran had launched attacks on Rome up the Tigris or Euphrates, then westward across the Syro-Mesopotamian plain south of the
Taurus Mountains, with the goal of taking Antioch.[10] This pattern had led
to Roman fortification of the major settlements just south of the Taurus
foothills. In 498, al-Nuʿman followed the Euphrates northward, but instead
of continuing as far as the fortified cities below the Taurus, he kept the river
on his right and the steppe on his left, and then cut northwestward in a
direct attempt on Antioch. The first district of Syria he entered on this tra-
jectory was that of Rusafa, where he came up against a Roman commander
with a stronger force. It was not the first, nor would it be the last time that
the steppe approach was taken. The Lakhmid al-Mundhir III, who ruled
505–54, recommended the route to the Sasanian king Kawad as an alternative to the heavily defended northern route, and it continued to be used
throughout the sixth century.[11] According to Procopius, al-Mundhir closed
his remarks to Kawad with the following advice: "As for lack of water or any
kind of provision, let no such thought worry you, for I shall lead the army

7. Brunner in *CHIran,* 3: 757, on Shapur I; Eilers in *CHIran,* 3: 485, 487, on Shapur II and
Bahram V.

8. On the diversity of Hira, see Morony, *Iraq,* 218, 221; Bosworth in *CHIran,* 3: 597–602;
Donner, *Conquests,* 167–73; Musil, *Middle Euphrates,* 102–4, n. 57; Rothstein, *Dynastie,* 12–33.

9. *Chron. Edessa of 506* 283, p. 208; cf. 291–92, p. 215, for another encounter near
Callinicum.

10. For the northern Syro-Mesopotamian route, see Mouterde and Poidebard, *Limes,* 20.

11. Proc., *BP* 1.17.29–39.

wherever it seems most suitable."[12] Procopius also describes the Iranian invasion led by Azarethes, which avoided the fortified northern route and, on the Lakhmid al-Mundhir's advice, cut across Syria-Mesopotamia further south, thereby catching the Roman forces by surprise. Belisarius was stationed in Mesopotamia, and before he was informed of their presence in Roman territory, the Iranians with their Arabs allies were camped at Gaboulon, east of Chalcis.[13] Again, in 540, Khusrau I invaded Syria, traveling from Circesium to Zenobia / Halabiya and Sura, and thence to Rusafa.[14] Later, Procopius describes how Khusrau I took the same route in 542, keeping the Euphrates on his right, and then immediately relates the story of Khusrau's siege of Rusafa.[15] Procopius is not the only source for this use of the steppe routes. John of Epiphania records that in 573 the Iranian general Adarmaanes crossed through the desert from Ambar, south of Circesium, with Iranian and nomad Arab forces.[16] And Theophylact records that Adarmaanes made a surprise invasion through the steppe northwestward from Circesium as far as Antioch, taking Apamea on his way home.[17] This approach expanded the arena of conflict between the Romans, the Iranians, and their Arab allies to include the steppe zone between Ctesiphon and Antioch, the region in which Rusafa lay.

In addition to the route, the timing of Arab attacks at the end of the fifth century is also significant—an incursion into Phoenicia in 491 coincided with the accession of a new Roman emperor, Anastasius; while in 498, the confrontation near Rusafa may have marked the Iranian king Kawad's reestablishment on the throne after a period of internal disruption. One of the major sticking points in Roman-Iranian relations in late antiquity was the guarding of the Caspian Gates undertaken by Iran with Roman subsidy.[18] Kawad made an issue of delinquent Roman payment. But he had failed in 491 to extract payment from Anastasius.[19] It would have been in keeping with traditional Iranian policy to approach the Roman emperor once more when Kawad regained the throne in 498, after a two-year exile. In 491 and 498, the Iran-allied Lakhmids may have offered Kawad a means

12. Ibid. 17.39 (tr. Dewing).

13. Ibid. 18.1–15.

14. Ibid. 2.5.1–33; cf. Proc., *Aed.* 2.6.1–11, on Circesium; 2.8.9–25, on Zenobia; 2.9.1–10, on Sura and Rusafa.

15. Proc., *BP* 2.20.1–16.

16. Joh. Epiph., *Hist.* 1.4 in Müller, *FHG* 4, p. 275.

17. Theoph. Sim., *Hist.* 3.10.6–10.

18. See Rubin in *Defence*, 683–88, on the role of the Caspian Gates in Roman-Iranian relations in the fifth through sixth centuries.

19. *Chron. Edessa of 506* 248, pp. 183–84, where Kawad's gift of an elephant failed to induce payment. See also Blockley, *East Roman Policy*, 88–90; Shahîd, *BAFIC*, 122–25.

of expressing his hostility toward the uncooperative Anastasius without overtly violating the treaty of 442. The two Arab incursions took place after Kawad's diplomatic failures and were designed to remind Rome of the vulnerability of her eastern frontier. Kawad formally broke the treaty when he led a force against Amïda four years later, in 502. Procopius explicitly describes this attack as a response to Anastasius's refusal to pay the Caspian Gates subsidy.[20]

Anastasius was not slow to react to modifications in frontier politics. He began to adjust Roman fortification of the frontier zone, and, in 502, concluded a treaty with Arabs who had been raiding Roman territory between 497 and 502. The verdict is still out on the identity of Ἀρέθας ὁ τῆς Θαλαβάνης, whom Theophanes gives as Anastasius's partner in the treaty.[21] It seems that this Arethas should be identified either with al-Harith the Thaʿlabid, possibly related to the Jafnid dynasty of the Ghassanid tribe, or al-Harith of the Hujrid dynasty, commonly referred to as Kinda.[22]

Major armed conflict at the turn of the fifth century was still drawn to northern Syria and Mesopotamia.[23] Anastasius's answer to Jovian's disastrous cession of Nisibis a century and a half earlier was to fortify the village of Dara in defiance of the treaty of 442 and Iranian protests.[24] During con-

20. Proc., *BP* 1.7.1–3. Cf. *Chron. Edessa of 506* 276, pp. 203, where, having received the out-of-date news of Kawad's preparation for an attack on Roman territory, Anastasius sends Rufinus (*PLRE*, 2: 954–57) to deter Kawad by payment in gold. Rufinus leaves the gold at Caesarea when he learns of Kawad's progress into Roman territory.

21. Theoph., *Chron.*, A.M. 5990, p. 141; cf. A.M. 5995, p. 144. The view espoused by Shahîd, *BASIC*, 1: 3–12, that Anastasius adopted a formal relationship with the Ghassanids as early as 502 (as opposed to Justinian in 529, the date universally accepted), remains controversial. The most recent discussion of this knotty problem is by Robin, *CRAI* 1996: 665–702, esp. 697–99, who brings South Arabian epigraphy into the discussion. For the situation in South Arabia during the reign of Anastasius, see also Rubin in *Eastern Frontier,* esp. 399–403.

22. Various Arab groups, including both longtime rivals and newcomers like the Jafnid dynasty of the Banu Ghassan, were at this time jockeying for position in Syria, Mesopotamia, Palestine, and Arabia, creating a somewhat blurred impression in the sources and no doubt on the ground. It is likely that in 498 when the Lakhmid al-Nuʿman made his foray into Syria, his timing was influenced by the preoccupation of rival Arab groups elsewhere. See, e.g., Malalas's report that the Lakhmid al-Mundhir learned of the quarrel between the Hujrid phylarch al-Harith and the Roman *dux* of Palestine, Diomedes. When al-Harith fled to the southeast into the desert, al-Mundhir met and killed him, seizing the opportunity to resolve an inherited enmity toward the Hujrid dynasty (Mal., *Chron.* 18.16). On Tanukh and Lakhmid migration into south central Syria-Mesopotamia, see Bowersock, *Roman Arabia,* 132–33, esp. n. 42, on Tabari's association of the Tanukh with the frontier zone. For futher discussion of the Banu Ghassan, see chapter 5.

23. See Whitby in *Defence,* 717–26.

24. *Chron. Edessa of 506* 300–301, p. 228. According to Proc., *BP* 1.2.11, the treaty required that neither party construct new fortifications near the boundary between the two empires. See Blockley, *East Roman Policy,* 92 n. 46, for the sources; also Whitby in *Defence,* 737–83; Croke and Crow, *JRS* 73 (1983): 143–59.

struction, S. Bartholomew came to the emperor in a dream, offering to protect the city, and in due course the saint's relics were translated to one of Dara's new churches.[25]

The emergent popularity of the arid steppe approach exerted some pressure further south, where the route left the Euphrates in the neighborhood of Circesium and cut into the eastern extreme of Roman territory. In response, Anastasius turned his attention to Rusafa and to another saint. As we shall see, it is difficult to determine from the sources whether Anastasius played a role in the construction of the impressive gypsum walls that protected the shrine. But certainly Anastasius's elevation of Rusafa's ecclesiastical rank to metropolitan status in the 510s and his translation of Sergius's thumb to Constantinople asserted Roman interest in the well-placed fortress in the frontier zone between the two empires.

By the early sixth century, Rusafa was more than a stronghold in a frontier region. It was a wealthy shrine and pilgrimage center "in the so-called Barbarian Plain." As the name suggests, the region was in the hands of Arabs, commonly known in Greek and Syriac literature as barbarians—βάρβαροι in Greek, barbaroye in Syriac.[26] Procopius describes Rusafa as "in the Barbarian Plain."[27] Theophylact Simocatta uses the short-hand "Barbarikon," as do the authors of the Georgian and later Greek recensions of the original Syriac *Vita* of the Iranian martyr Gulanducht, who visited the shrine from northern Mesopotamia in the sixth century.[28] The name suggests a Roman understanding that Rusafa was set in a region distinct from

25. Joh. Diakrin., fr. 2.558, p. 157, with the editor's note on l. 9. Anastasius's younger contemporary John Lydus, *De mag. pop. rom.* 47, also emphasizes the role of divine intervention with reference to Dara's place in frontier defense: "[U]nless God by the former's [Anastasius's] hand had heavily fortified it at the throats of the Persians, long ago the Persians would have seized the domains of the Romans inasmuch as these are adjacent to them" (tr. Bandy).

26. Kugener, *OC* 7 (1907): 408–12, judiciously corrects Duval's emendation of the Syriac in Severus's homily on S. Sergius, *Hom. cath.* 57, p. 93. Duval prefers to read "men," "population" (*bnaynosha*), instead of "barbarians" (*barbaroye*). Kugener leaves the text as it stands, reading "barbarians." Late antique Syriac and Greek texts that refer to the Arabs of this region as "barbarians" include *Tab. Peut.* 11 ("fines exercitus syriaticae et commertium barbarorum"); *Hist. Ahud.* esp. 3, pp. 24–25; Evag., *HE*, 5.6 (ὑπὸ Σκηνητῶν βαρβάρων); and cf. 3.2, 5.9, 5.20. Steph. Byz., *Ethnica* s.v. βάρβαρος, p. 158, also attests the use of *barbaros* to refer to Arabs. For further comment on the use of "barbarian" in Syriac with reference to Arabs, see Shahîd, *Martyrs of Najrân*, 98–99.

27. Proc., *BP* 2.5.29: ἐν τῷ Βαρβαρικῷ καλουμένῳ Πεδίῳ; cf. Leont. Jerus., *Contra monophys.*, *PG* 86.1900A: ἐν ταῖς κατὰ τὸ Βαρβαρικὸν λεγόμενον λιμιτὸν ἐρήμοις.

28. Theoph. Sim., *Hist.* 5.13.3, reports that the votive gifts of Khusrau II to S. Sergius at Rusafa were taken to the "so-called Barbarikon" (ἐς τὸ λεγόμενον Βαρβαρικόν), meaning, no doubt, the site of Rusafa in the "Barbarian Plain," *pace* de Boor's edition of Theophylact, index 321, where it is suggested that the reference is to a part of the shrine. Whitby and Whitby, *History of Theophylact*, 150 n. 66, follow de Boer; while Schreiner, *Theophylact*, 316 n. 755, goes so far as to suggest that the "barbarikon" was a building where the gifts dedicated to the martyr by

more hellenized territory further west. The first part of the name establishes a distinction between Greek and barbarian and qualifies the second part—the plain. This second part raises important questions about the frontier context of Rusafa. Rusafa does indeed dominate a plain, a wide expanse of stony, monotonous steppeland that continues to the Euphrates and beyond into Iranian territory. But a plain is a poor frontier. A plain is exposed, indefensible, subject to uncontrollable influences. This in part explains why Rome and Iran were constantly fighting over the area—the Syro-Mesopotamian plain, what we might call the greater Barbarian Plain, was not a natural frontier. Situated as it was in this plain, the river Euphrates could not act as a serious frontier. But the plain was, in practice, a frontier zone, and it was given what cohesion it had by the Arab pastoralists who inhabited both Roman and Iranian territory in the region.

The name Barbarian Plain implies recognition that the population of the area was significantly Arab in composition, a fact well illustrated by three incidents spanning over a century. In 504, a Roman officer named Constantine, who two years earlier had joined Kawad's forces as a general, returned to Roman Syria taking with him two wives and a small retinue. They traveled through the desert night and day for a fortnight without meeting a soul, until finally they encountered some Arabs allied with Rome, who took them to the nearby *castrum* at Sura.[29] When not shepherding wayward generals, Rome's allied Arab tribes in the region might occupy themselves with the more mundane business of nomadism. This is clear from the so-called Strata dispute between the Ghassanids and Lakhmids, which probably took place in 539, and nearly drew their imperial allies into armed confrontation.[30] Several particularly dry seasons had forced Lakhmid Arabs beyond their traditional grazing territory into an area controlled by the Ghassanids. The name Strata, by which the disputed region was commonly known, eventually helped to resolve the conflict. The name derived from the Roman road that traversed the grazing lands and linked Damascus, via Palmyra and Rusafa, to the Euphrates. That the entire region through which the Roman road passed could absorb the road's Latin name is strong testimony, not only to the usefulness of artificial markers in the barren steppe, but also to the power of such foreign intrusions over the imagination of the indigenous population. The tenacity of the name Strata is particularly striking in the light of the Arabic origin of much of the region's toponymy, which is attested already from the fourth century.[31] The Roman

the Arab tribes were stored. *Vita Gulanducht* 20.21–22: τὸν σηκὸν τοῦ ἁγίου μάρτυρος Σεργίου καὶ Βάκχου ἐν τῷ βαρβαρικῷ; and cf. the Georgian recension, XV.5.1.

29. *Chron. Edessa of 506* 297–98, p. 219. See *PLRE*, 2: 313–14.
30. Proc., *BP* 2.1–15. For a recent account of the sources, see Shahîd, *BASIC*, 1: 209–18.
31. Bauzou, *Syria* 70 (1993): 48.

word *strata*, meaning clearly marked route, was eventually transformed into the Qur'anic word *sirat*, meaning the way, more specifically, the straight way, the right way.[32] Early Arabic poetry acknowledges this suggestiveness of man-made presences in the desert, as, for example, in the comparison of a favorite camel with a fine Roman bridge, or of the outlines of abandoned camps with the mysterious shapes of Arabic letters.[33]

An incident that occurred about the year 630 again confirms Arab control of the Rusafa region. At that time a monk was traveling from Jerusalem to Dastagird in search of his master's bones. The monk had come from the monastery near Jerusalem that had been the spiritual home of the Iranian refugee goldsmith Magoundat, who became a monk and was renamed Anastasius. Once he had stealthily acquired the relics of Anastasius, the monk was guided across the desert as far as Palmyra by an unnamed Arab phylarch.[34] It was at very much the same time and with regard to the same region that Theophylact commented on the enthusiasm of the Arab nomad tribes for Rusafa's martyr.[35]

A PLACE OF CONVERGENCE

The shrine at Rusafa had the potential to provide Christian emperors with a means of manifesting the Roman presence in a culturally mixed frontier zone—a safety device that had been wanting from Rome's relationship with Palmyra in the third century. At Rusafa, diverse interests converged: it was a watering point for long-range transhumants, regional pastoralists, and caravans.[36] It also lay in the southeastern extension of an area of marginal agricultural land that in the fifth and sixth centuries enjoyed tremendous economic prosperity.[37] And a dense network of well-worn routes and tracks linked the steppe's watering points.[38] The confluence at Rusafa of these various factors helps to explain why it had been the site of a Roman *castrum* since the tetrarchic period.

In the sixth century, the Arabs' role in Roman-Iranian frontier relations

---

32. Ibid., 36.

33. On the bridge, see Tarafa, *Mu'allaqa*, p. 84 (tr. Arberry), and Caussin de Perceval, *Essai sur l'histoire des Arabes*, 2: 354. For the letters, a common image in classical Arabic poetry, see al-Isfahani, *Kitab al-aghani* 2.95 l. 5; and Montgomery, *JSS* 40 (1995): 283–316.

34. *Translat. reliq. Anast.* 5.

35. Theoph. Sim., *Hist.* 5.1.7.

36. Herzfeld compares Rusafa with Hatra: Sarre and Herzfeld, *Archäologische Reise*, 1: 136; see also Pigulewskaya, *Byzance*, 193; Charles, *Christianisme*, 33.

37. See Tate, *Campagnes*, 343–50.

38. Bauzou in *Archéologie*, 205, 213, 216. As we should expect in a context where beasts of burden provided the most suitable form of transportation, most routes were roughly paved or unpaved.

was intricately meshed with their place in pastoralism, agriculture, and trade in the region. In the treaty of 561, the third clause reasserts the exclusive rights over Roman-Iranian trade of the established customs posts: from north to south, at Artaxata, Nisibis, and Callinicum.[39] Clause 5 also treats customs posts, but the specific purpose of this clause is to control Arab merchants in northern Syria and Mesopotamia, namely, at Nisibis and Dara.[40] From Callinicum, trade in central Syria and Mesopotamia was directed westward through Rusafa via the steppe caravan routes. Excavation of rows of shops along a major street at Rusafa has helped to fill in our picture of this important trade center in the Syro-Mesopotamian steppe.[41] Rusafa's commercial prosperity also played its part in the formation of the famous Nestorian holy man Rabban bar 'Idta (d. 611). The son of wealthy Christian merchants in Rusafa, the young Rabban bar 'Idta came under the care of his half-sister after his parents died and left the children an enviable inheritance, making them obvious targets for Rusafa's opportunists.

> Certain men among her kinsfolk were looking to take the chaste woman
>   to wife,
> One for the sake of her great beauty, and another for her riches;
> But when she learned this she left her country altogether.
> Having sold everything which their parents had left them,
> She distributed [the money] among the poor, and the widows, and the
>   monasteries, and the churches.[42]

The two orphans later settled in Nisibis. The report of the physician Ibn Butlan, who visited the city in the mid eleventh century, confirms the tenacity of Rusafa's cultural and mercantile dynamism, which continued into the mid thirteenth century: "[T]he inhabitants of this fortress are steppe folk [*badiya*], most of them Christians, who earn their living by guarding the caravans and bringing in goods and merchandise. There are also vagabonds, as well as thieves."[43]

The few surviving images of the rider saint are potent reminders that, while Sergius's miracles and healing powers made him a desirable patron,

---

39. *Codex Justinianus* 4.63.4. (A.D. 408 or 409); Men. Prot., fr. 6.1(Blockley), fr. 11 (Müller).

40. Blockley, *History of Menander*, 71 n. 51; 73 n. 54.

41. Kollwitz in *Neue Deutsche Ausgrabungen*, 51–53. In the Islamic period, at least, shops encroached on the street.

42. John the Persian, *History of Rabban bar 'Idta* 1.115, pp. 167–69 (tr. Budge).

43. Yaqut, *Mu'jam al-buldan* 3.48 (tr. Conrad in Jabbur, *Bedouins*, 466. I translate *badiya* as "steppe folk," instead of Conrad's "desert folk"). For sources on Rusafa after the Islamic conquest, see Kellner-Heinkele in Sack, *Resafa*, 4: 133–54.

his great influence in the sixth century owed much to his shrine's location at a watered crossroads in central Syria-Mesopotamia.[44] With the control of Rusafa came, at least in theory, the possibility of monitoring movement across central Syria and Mesopotamia—the movement of armies, raiding parties, caravans, pastoralists, and pilgrims. Nearly a millennium before Sergius was executed outside Rusafa's walls, according to tradition, the settlement had held a pivotal position on the political and economic map of Syria-Mesopotamia.[45] The topography of the middle Euphrates region funneled caravan traffic past the site of Rusafa. At Barbalissus, the Euphrates quits its meandering north–south course and turns to flow more consistently southeastward to the Persian Gulf.[46] From near Barbalissus as far south as Dayr al-Zawr, the steppe meets the river in high cliffs.[47] The Euphrates is forced into a narrow gorge by Jabal Bishri, and the river continues past steep banks on the west, which make progress difficult. The Roman and Iranian riverine routes served armies whose supplies traveled by river; but caravan traffic kept a distance from the Euphrates,[48] parallel, but to the west, along the steppe's watering points—both for convenience, since the river banks would be frequently soft on account of rain and flooding between November and June, and to avoid the charges with which the settled population often taxed caravans, significantly diminishing their profits.[49]

44. See Whittaker, *Frontiers*, 136, and Matthews, *JRS* 74 (1984): 163, who observes, with regard to the region east of Palmyra in the third century, that "in this sector the whole concept of territory and its definition and control should be formulated rather differently. It consisted in command of water-points and their associated settlements in an area in which no permanent control or occupation was envisaged."

45. Honigmann in *RE*, 2A: 1684; Musil, *Palmyrena*, 262; Musil, *Middle Euphrates*, 210.

46. The importance of Barbalissus / Balis continued and is underlined in the mid to late tenth century by the merchant-geographers Istakhri and Ibn Hawqal, who describe the prosperity enjoyed in the region before the East Roman raids in the early tenth century. Istakhri (*Kitab al-masalik* 62, tr. Le Strange, *Palestine*, 417) writes: "[Balis] is the first Syrian town you come to from Iraq and the road to it is much frequented and from Balis go many highways. It is, as it were, a port to the Syrians on the Euphrates. However, since the days of Sayf al-Dawla, its buildings have gone to ruin and caravans and merchants go there much less than of old. The city has strong walls and gardens in the lands lying about it and the Euphrates. Its chief crops are wheat and barley."

47. Musil, *Palmyrena*, 260–61. Maps 3 and 4 in Chesney, *Expedition*, well illustrate the relationship between the cliffs and the Euphrates.

48. See Gawlikowski, *Iraq* 56 (1994): 30–31, on the use of the Euphrates for trade as well as for transportation of military supplies; Bauzou in *Archéologie*, 205, on vestiges of the Roman riverine route; Mouterde and Poidebard, *Limes*, 12, on the Roman routes, and 127–36, on the traces of the Iranian Royal Road along the Euphrates; Poidebard, *Trace de Rome*, 89, and Musil, *Middle Euphrates*, 227, on the Iranian Royal Road.

49. See Musil, *Palmyrena*, 261, on caravans' avoidance of the riverine route; Grant, *Syrian Desert*, 42–43, 199, also 148–56, with map opposite 258. And see Mouterde and Poidebard,

The caravan route from Babylonia followed the edge of the steppe on either side of the Euphrates, and then one branch found its passage at the level of Circesium through the well-watered saddle between the western spur of Jabal Bishri and the Anti-Lebanon's furthest outlier, Abu Rujmayn.[50] North of the pass and 30 kilometers south of the Euphrates lay Rusafa, at the intersection of the following routes: (1) the steppe caravan route, which cut inland at Circesium, near where the Khabur meets the Euphrates, or further north at Callinicum, near the intersection of the Balikh and the Euphrates; (2) the major route between the Black Sea and the Gulf of ʿAqaba, running along the Euphrates as far as Sura, where it linked up with the Strata Diocletiana via Rusafa to Damascus, and then carried on through the Hawran plain to Bostra to join what we call the Via Nova Traiana to ʿAqaba;[51] (3) the route to Damascus that runs northwest of the Jabal Rawaq, parallel to the Strata Diocletiana;[52] (4) the Euphrates-Emesa route that passes north of the Jabal Bilʿas hills;[53] and (5) the arid steppe route, or more likely routes, between Ctesiphon and Antioch, which cut into Roman territory around Circesium and thereafter would have been variable according to season.[54]

Despite the topographical features that contributed to Rusafa's importance, it must be emphasized that Rusafa is not, and never was, an oasis.[55] It stands apart from the natural, spring-fed oases—al-Kawm, Tayyiba, Sukhna, Arak, Palmyra, Qaryatayn—that cluster around the mountain chain running northeast from the Anti-Lebanon to the Euphrates north of Dayr al-Zawr. In this sense, Rusafa is exceptional among the settlements in the

---

Limes, 127–32, on the caravan route that diverges from the riverine route north of Barbalissus and passes through Rusafa. Cf. Brunner in *CHIran,* 3: 759, on the arid route west of the Tigris controlled by Arabs, which branched off from Takrit as far as Sinjar, offering an alternative to the populated riverine route. On the dangers of caravan trade, including the imposition of tariffs, see Lukonin in *CHIran,* 3: 740–41.

50. On recent late antique finds at Tayyiba, the well-watered settlement in the saddle between Jabal Bishri and Abu Rujmayn, see Taha, *Cahiers de l'Euphrate* 5–6 (1991): 61, 65.

51. Mouterde and Poidebard, *Limes,* 127, 132, 213; *Tabula Peutingeriana* 10 and 11, and Miller, *Itineraria romana,* 815. See also Bauzou, *Syria* (1993): 27–36; Bauzou in *Archéologie,* 212–13; Dussaud, *Topographie,* 251–55; Poidebard, *Trace de Rome,* 73–84. Archeological finds at Tal Ramad, near Qatara, indicate the existence of trade links between Armenia and Cappadocia and Palestine by way of Mesopotamia and the Rusafa-Sukhna route as early as the sixth millennium B.C. (Contenson, *AAS* 19 [1969]: 29–30).

52. Bauzou in *Archéologie,* 212; Musil, *Palmyrena,* 249–50.

53. Dussaud, *Pénétration,* 82–85; Mouterde and Poidebard, *Limes,* 137, 143–46; Herzfeld in Sarre and Herzfeld, *Archäologische Reise,* 1: 137.

54. Dussaud, *Pénétration,* 86–87, and map on 82. In the context of the development of the semi-desert route during the sixth century, note that Justinian established a *dux* at Circesium (Proc., *Aed.* 2.6.9).

55. *Pace* Gregory, *Roman Military Architecture,* 2: 174.

Syrian steppe.[56] Only the establishment and growth of the cult of S. Sergius at Rusafa can explain the size and sophistication of the settlement, which would otherwise have continued as a modest watering point.

The site of Rusafa dominates the expansive plain west of the middle Euphrates at the point where the land that rises gently from the river valley begins to undulate.[57] In both Syriac (Rsapha) and Arabic (Rusafa), the settlement's name suggests compactness, often meaning "pavement," presumably referring to the site's geological configuration, which makes it a natural gathering place for waters.[58] Although it possesses neither spring nor well, the site lies at the convergence of wadis, most notably the Wadi al-Sila, and is watered by seasonal pools, which gather in depressions to the west after particularly heavy rains.[59] Rainwater can be stored for long periods in dolines, cavelike hollows in the ground that lie northeast, east, and south of the settlement and also run beneath it. Numerous cisterns within Rusafa's walls also preserved rainwater.[60] Small bottle-shaped cisterns sufficed from the fourth and fifth centuries until the city's cavernous cisterns were built in the sixth century.

56. Wirth, *Syrien*, 442.

57. Approached from the west, Rusafa in its ruined state is visible from two hours away by camel (Musil, *Palmyrena*, 154–55). This assumes a clear field of vision. In the morning of 26 December 1992, after a driving snowstorm the previous day, mist obscured the view on my approach from the pass between Jabal Bishri and Abu Rujmayn, almost until I arrived at Rusafa.

58. On the meaning of "Rusafa" in Arabic, see Haase in *EI*[2], 8: 629b, and Stetkeyvych, *Zephyrs of Najd*, 109: "On the one hand it [the word 'al-Rusafa'] implies the compactness and firmness of stone; but that stone is necessarily associated with water, mā' al-raṣaf being 'rock-water.' Furthermore, it brings to mind the idea of the building of a pier or embankment. As such it carries imagist sensibility to the very edge of that which is its semantic opposite. From there, too, it implies the anticipation and the longing for the other bank of the river. Al-Ruṣāfah, in brief, was to the poet a name and a word that implied semantic tension and yearning for its opposite." I would like to thank Sebastian Brock for commenting on the range of meanings in Syriac.

59. Musil, *Palmyrena*, 69. Ulbert in Ruprechtsberger, *Syrien*, 113, ill. 2; Grant, *Syrian Desert*, 160: the top photograph shows a caravan at a water hole between Sukhna and Rusafa.

60. On the cisterns and water supply, see Brinker, *DaM* 5 (1991): 119–46. For pools and dolines, see Musil, *Palmyrena*, 69, 169, 172, 260. Musil recounts how on his second visit to Rusafa, in late March and early April 1912, his party was forced to leave the site for the Euphrates after only two days owing to the inadequate water supply, even for camels (ibid., 65, 167). Heavy snows pose a serious threat to flocks and shepherds, while the ensuing spring flash floods that swell the region's wadis could easily overwhelm shepherds driven to seek shelter there from the harsh northern winds. After the winter of 1912, when snow had covered the region from Rusafa to Jabal Bishri, Musil found the mountain landscape littered in early April with the rotting sheep of shepherds who had failed to cross to the Euphrates before the snows in early January (ibid., 176, and cf. 153, where a heavy snowfall on the route west of Rusafa froze another flock of sheep in late February). On the perils of flooding, see ibid., 176.

Aerial photographs of Rusafa show traces of gardens with enclosures, especially to the south of the site, and built basins and barrages to the west.[61] South of Rusafa the plain continues as far as the limestone Jabal Bishri, whose ravines and gullies also provide pasture for camels and sheep after rain.[62] Arabic writers frequently describe the surroundings of Rusafa as *badiya*, often mistranslated as "desert."[63] The Arabic term describes, not the aridity of a desert, but rather the wide open expansiveness characteristic of the Syrian steppe. The presence of vegetation, as in all steppe and even desert landscapes, depends upon seasonal rainfall, as the following passage referring to the Umayyad Caliph Hisham, most likely outside Rusafa, vividly illustrates: "[Hisham] had gone out with his family, his retinue, his servants, and his companions. And he camped on a barren, stony plain that was elevated and extensive, in a year when the rain had fallen early and abundantly and the land had taken its adornment from the variety of the colors of its vegetation of pretty spring blooms, which were beautiful to behold, and luxuriant, and well watered on a plateau whose soil seemed like pieces of camphor."[64]

With the help of collected rainwater, the area around the walled settlement of Rusafa could conceivably have supported orchards, olive and fig trees, and even grain, but no evidence survives to bear witness to such industry.[65] Seasonal migrations intersected at Rusafa, where the underground reservoirs attracted the region's pastoral Arabs.[66] Fields further to the west can be cultivated only at high risk. For example, those around the al-Abjaz range north of Palmyra flourish or parch depending on the rainfall of March and April.[67] Good pastureland continues from the plain of Rusafa

61. Tchalenko, *Églises syriennes*, 203; Poidebard and Mouterde, *AB* (1949): 110. In 1912, Musil found "old deserted gardens" and a dam southeast of Rusafa (*Palmyrena*, 169). See now Ulbert, *DaM* 7 (1993): 226, with fig. 1.

62. See Musil, *Palmyrena*, 67, 69, and 173–4 on Jabal Bishri; Mouterde and Poidebard, *Limes*, 134, on Jabal Bishri's pasture.

63. For the Arabic sources on the region around Rusafa, see Musil, *Palmyrena*, 270–72. Conrad in *Quest for Understanding*, 275–77, comments on the variety of meanings available for words such as *badiya*, *bariya*, and *sahra*. Groom, *Dictionary of Arabic Topography*, is a fascinating witness to the subtle descriptiveness of the Arabic language of landscape. See also Grant, *Syrian Desert*, 11, on the *badiya*.

64. al-Isfahani, *Kitab al-aghani* 2.129.

65. Musil, *Palmyrena*, 260.

66. The Taghlib tribe, which remained Christian longer than other Arab tribes, was attacked in 692 while camping at the watering place al-Rahub, 36 km southeast of Rusafa (al-Isfahani, *Kitab al-aghani* 12.236). In the thirteenth century, Yaqut records that Taghlib territory included the ridge of Jabal Bishri from the village of Tayyiba (controlling the pass between Abu Rujmayn and Jabal Bishri) as far as the Euphrates (*Mu'jam al-buldan* 1.426). Early in this century, the Jijar tribe spent the winter at Rusafa and the summer north of Aleppo (von Oppenheim, *Beduinen*, 1: 303).

67. Musil, *Palmyrena*, 147.

west along the northern foothills of the Abu Rujmayn and al-Abjaz ranges as far as the fields east of Emesa. This zone is punctuated by wells, many of them perennial.[68] The moisture level in this zone of pasture between Emesa and Rusafa normally remains sufficient to sustain grasses into the autumn.[69] The belt of pasture that the shepherds exploited between these foothills and the stony plain of al-Matyaha to the north is the same followed by the Euphrates-Emesa road.[70] Emesa lay at the juncture of the route from the Euphrates and the major road that followed the Orontes from Antioch to Damascus, the Hawran plain, Bostra, and on south to ʿAqaba. Especially along the Euphrates-Emesa route, and the wide band of pasture along its course, traders and breeders, merchants, soldiers, farmers, and part- and full-time pastoralists would have met at the watering places and settlements that articulate the route.[71]

This east-west route in turn links up with the north–south axis of agricultural villages that flourished in late antiquity on the steppe's fringe northeast of Emesa and stretches from Salaminias / Salamiya toward Apamea and as far north as Chalcis.[72] Several larger villages, such as Seriane / Isriya, Salaminias, and, further north, Anasartha / Khunasira would have served as local markets[73] in this L-shaped zone, which extended in a broad swathe westward to Emesa and northward to Chalcis. The conflux of peoples in this region combined with direct access to the Euphrates-Emesa road to make it a natural choice for the location of several Roman military installations positioned to monitor the region. The *Notitia dignitatum* places the Equites Saraceni Indigenae at Betproclis / Furqlus, 40 kilometers southeast of Emesa; the Equites Promoti Illyriciani at Occariba / ʿUzayribat, east of Emesa, where

68. One such watering place was reported at al-Zarqaʾ between Anasartha / Khunasira, on the steppe's fringe, and Seriane / Isriya (Yaqut, *Muʿjam al-buldan* 3.137, cited by Musil, *Palmyrena*, 212 n. 62); Le Strange, *Palestine*, 555. In the Roman period, before the third-century decline of Palmyra, hamlets existed in the hills northwest of the caravan city thanks to the collection of rainwater in cisterns (Schlumberger, *Palmyrène*, 131–32).

69. Musil, *Palmyrena*, 149, 154. Musil was told that the region's grasses also draw gazelle from the inner desert in the summer.

70. Musil transcribes the toponym as al-Mutayi: see his map in *Northern Arabia*.

71. Along this road in late March 1912, Musil met sheep traders leading large flocks of sheep from the middle Euphrates, where they were raised, to the markets in Aleppo and Hama (*Palmyrena*, 152–53). Dussaud, *Topographie*, 262, describes this band of pasture. On the interdependence of pastoralists and farmers, see Marx in *Nomadic Alternative*, 41–74, esp. 68–71.

72. In late March 1912, Musil met the Hadidiyin tribe, which cultivated land in the environs of the villages northeast of Hama, pasturing their flocks at the foot of Jabal Abu Rujmayn near the western limit of the plain of Rusafa (*Palmyrena*, 151).

73. On the geographical setting and water supply of Seriane, see Gogräfe, *DaM* 7 (1993): 46–48, and Dussaud, *Pénétration*, 84; on the road between Salaminias and Seriane, see Mouterde and Poidebard, *Limes*, 140–43; Honigmann in *RE* 4A: 1723–24; Musil, *Palmyrena*, 58. On Anasartha, see Musil, *Palmyrena*, 204, with n. 58. Ibn Shaddad, *al-Aʿlaq* 22 (tr. Eddé-Terrasse), describes Khunasira's position as on the edge of the *bariya*.

the Bil'as outliers meet the plain; the Equites Scutarii Illyriciani at Seriane at the northern extremity of Abu Rujmayn, approximately halfway between Emesa and Rusafa; and the Equites Promoti Indigenae at Rusafa.[74]

The regions along the routes linking the triangle of Rusafa, Emesa, and Damascus were at the focus of Roman military interest in late antique central Syria. It is significant that the arms of this triangle span the mountainous limits of the Palmyrene plain. After Queen Zenobia's fall, Palmyra continued to function as a town, although its place as a center for trade was vastly diminished.[75] In the late fifth century, Alexander Acoemetes and his band of monks were refused entry into Palmyra, on the grounds that such a ravenous hoard would lead to the town's inhabitants to starvation.[76] Allowing for dramatic exaggeration, the story reflects the vulnerability of resources in cities set in the arid steppe when they are not fed by a booming caravan trade. Thomas Bauzou has convincingly argued that Palmyra and the surrounding plain were abandoned at some point in the early Islamic period, since none of the modern toponyms, with two exceptions, bear any relation to the ancient names.[77] This disjunction between ancient and modern toponyms in the Palmyra region contrasts with the situation in the Hawran, south of Damascus, where a considerable number of ancient toponyms are recognizable in modern place-names.[78] Bauzou ascribes responsibility for the tenacity of Hawranian toponyms to the region's Christian population, which has dwelt in the area continuously since late antiquity.

---

74. *Not. dig. or.* 32, for Betproclis / Furqlus, under the jurisdiction of the *dux Phoenicis,* see above; *Not. dig. or.* 33, for Occariba / 'Uzayribat (cf. Ἀχοράβα, Ptolemy, *Geography* 5.14.13; Occaraba, *Tabula Peutingeriana* 10; Orarabon at Raven. Geogr., *Cosmogr.* 2.15); and for Seriane / Isriya, see Musil, *Palmyrena,* 253. On these routes in the Arabic sources, see Musil, *Palmyrena,* 249–51, 276; Musil, *Middle Euphrates,* 318. On the difficulty of interpreting the terminology that may refer to Arab members of Roman forces, see Shahîd, *BAFIC,* 124, 462–64, 466–67.

75. For evidence of the continuation of urban life after Zenobia's fall, see building inscriptions dated to 279 and 280 in As'ad and Gawlikowski, *AAS* 36–37 (1986–87): 168.

76. *Vita Alex.* 35. Not much in the generalized description (32–35) of Alexander's wanderings in the Syro-Mesopotamian steppe deserves to be taken at face value. It does offer an interesting collection of impressions and stereotypes formed in the mind of a disoriented alien in the steppe. *Castra,* their inhabitants, their defenders, and their gates stand out in sharp relief against the otherwise shapeless landscape. The predictable appearance of a caravan with its cameleers who keep Alexander and his monks from starving outside Palmyra's walls may be invention. But not necessarily.

77. Bauzou, *Syria* 70 (1993): 48–50. This interpretation is supported by the abandonment in the Middle Ages of the Damascus-Palmyra segment of the Strata Diocletiana (Musil, *Palmyrena,* 249).

78. For definitions of the Hawran, see Macdonald, *Syria* 70 (1993): 309 n. 39. I have used the broader definition, which includes not only ancient Auranitis but also Ituraea, Gaulanitis, Batanea, and Trachonitis, that is, from south of Damascus to the Yarmuk, from Hermon and the river Jordan to the the basalt desert, the *harra,* east of Jabal Hawran.

Although Bauzou does not rally evidence from north of the Palmyra region to support his interpretation of Palmyra's history, evidence from the area between Salaminias and Chalcis complements that from the Hawran. In this region too, many ancient toponyms have survived the wear of time. And like the Hawran, the area was home to many Christians until recent years. Both the Hawran and the area between Salaminias and Chalcis were areas of convergence for agriculturalists, semi-pastoralists, pastoralists, and traders, and in both the Sergius cult flourished, as will be illustrated later.[79]

Traces of the Hawranian road system, complemented by a mosaic from the southwestern Hawran, illustrate the mixed agricultural and pastoral nature of the region and help to reknit the less-documented and less-studied area between Salaminias and Chalcis. The primary crops of the Hawran were cereals, olives, and the vine. Villages and larger towns were connected by a dense network of built roads and dirt tracks.[80] Damascus was linked to Bostra by two important paved Roman roads running to the east of the Laja, which would allow for swift movement of troops and supplies. Although much of the course of a third route to the west of the Laja cannot be followed today, it is almost certain that in late antiquity a Roman road followed that route too, which is now the main passage between Damascus and Darʿa. Another Roman road with two bridges is partially preserved between Darʿa and Bostra and then carries on to Mushannaf on the eastern flank of the Jabal Hawran. The visible sections of pavement, even those within the boundaries of Bostra and Maximianopolis / Shaqqa, show no signs of grooves from wheeled transport. In general, there is no evidence that wheeled vehicles were a common feature of Hawranian transportation, particularly in the case of village to village communication, which would have been along dirt tracks. Animals would have been used to transport goods, and a mosaic now in the Bostra museum shows a bearded man clad in a short, sleeveless tunic and sandals leading three camels whose saddles are loaded with storage jars, most likely for wine and oil.[81] The mosaic, dated to 722, decorated the floor of a church dedicated to S. George at Dayr al-ʿAdas, on the main route southwestward from Bostra. The extant panels il-

79. See Peters, *JNES* 37 (1978): 315, who identifies the Chalcis and Beroea region and the Hawran as scenes of intense encounter between pastoralists and agricultural settlements. On the linguistic variety of the Hawran, see Contini, *Felix Ravenna* 4 (1987), esp. 51–66.

80. Bauzou in *Hauran*, 1: 139–58.

81. Donceel-Voûte, *Pavements* 45–54. See Bulliet, *The Camel and the Wheel*, esp. 19–27, for the advantages of camel transport in Syria. Reinvestigation of Roman roads in northwestern Syria has confirmed Bulliet's suggestion that the camel replaced the wheel as preferred means of transport from the sixth century (French, *IstMit* 43 [1993]: 451). See also Graf, *Electrum* 1 (1997): 43–49, who argues that camels and ox-drawn wheeled transport served different purposes: the former were best fit for long hauls, while the latter excelled locally with large and heavy loads.

lustrate a range of activities common to much of the Mediterranean world, but specifically applicable in this instance to the landscape of late antique Hawran: the harvesting of grapes, for example, the capture of birds, and the hunting of hares. The panel shows camels, each with a bell around its neck, kept in single file by a rope attached to their simple harnesses as they pass through a field of flowering plants. The saddles, loaded with two jars on each side of the hump, rest on a tasseled blanket and are secured by ropes around the neck and tail. The cameleer is unarmed and carries only a walking stick—clearly, this is a local scene and not a depiction of a long-distance caravan with armed escorts and greater numbers of beasts. An inscription names the cameleer as Mouchasos, a Semitic name well attested in the Hawran. It is likely that Mouchasos was a pastoralist, full- or part-time, who hired out his services as cameleer to local farmers. The products depicted could well have been his own if he cultivated the rich soil of the Hawran in addition to herding beasts. Certainly during the hot, dry season, when the nomadic segment of the population migrated with their flocks back to the well-watered Hawran and stayed from April until October, the region would have seen the entire spectrum from settled to fully nomadic Arabs.

The Roman buildup of Rusafa can be seen as a response to the vacuum created in the region by the demise of the caravan city and oasis of Palmyra in the late third century. The objects inscribed with "camelarius of S. Sergius" or "camelarius of the Barbarikon" only hint at Rusafa's place in caravan trade.[82] Rusafa, situated in a plain near the Euphrates, was highly accessible to a Roman force, and had a long record of service as a crossroads and watering point. To exploit these advantages was part of Diocletian's larger fortification project in central Syria-Mesopotamia. The new network of roads and fortresses, manned by nine legions, would facilitate rapid concentration of forces in the region, but served primarily for the maintenance of local order,[83] as is depicted in the *Passio* of SS. Sergius and Bacchus when a party from Sura attempted to steal the martyr's relics.[84] While interest in Rusafa as a monitoring station was established by the time of the tetrarchy, the growth of a martyr cult at Rusafa set the fort apart as an unusually useful site. In the eyes of political leaders, an alliance with a powerful divine defender could offer advantages on many levels. The convergence at Rusafa of trade, pastoralism, and pilgrimage, presented an opportunity to monitor the fluidity of movement both within and through the frontier zone. And as the influence of Rusafa's martyr increased, control of the cult and its shrine could offer a step toward control of the mobile populations who passed by

---

82. See above, pp. 35–43.

83. Gawlikowski, *JRS* 84 (1994): 246; Whittaker, *Frontiers,* 135.

84. The debatable nature of the early sections of the fifth-century *Passio* make it rather weak evidence for the monitoring duty of soldiers based in frontier zone *castra.*

the holy site. No doubt with the lesson of Palmyra in mind, Roman emperors from Anastasius to Maurice attempted at Rusafa to exert their authority in the steppe through fortified, non-native urban architecture, and most of all through patronage of the local martyr Sergius.

THE FORTRESS-SHRINE

Like many Syro-Mesopotamian settlements, Rusafa was plagued by the disruptive effects of earthquakes and shifting ground. A complex system of dolines runs beneath the city itself, and this was probably the cause of much of the structural damage from which Rusafa's buildings have suffered. Excavators have unearthed from the fortress-shrine signs of significant late antique rebuilding of older, damaged structures that were dispossessed of their original function and turned into urban quarries, as in the case of basilica B. Excavation is still in progress, and new finds reveal what one would expect—a complicated architectural history. As it is uncovered, material evidence joins the literary to portray a major frontier pilgrimage center, which reached its peak of activity and influence in the late fifth, sixth, and the early seventh centuries. During this period the relics of S. Sergius were moved to a new shrine, the second within the walls. The date of the translation is still uncertain, but both the old shrine outside the walls and the new shrine within provide clues to the nature of the Sergius cult at Rusafa.

Much of the walled settlement today lies hidden beneath up to 4 m of rubble, and soil blown in from the surrounding steppe over the centuries. The visual result was famously captured on film by the scholar-aviator Fr. Antoine Poidebard in 1925–32 (title page).[85] The pocked landscape is punctuated by the ruins of imposing structures—churches primarily—the object of comment by travelers and scholars since the late seventeenth century.[86] The massive gypsum walls that enclose the settlement rise to a height of 14 m and form an uneven quadrangle measuring 536 m on the north, 350 m on the east, 549 m on the south and 411 m on the west. The area within the walls measures 210,000 m^2.[87] Fifteen towers, round or pentagonal, reinforce the walls, which are pierced by four main tripartite

---

85. Poidebard, *Trace de Rome*, pl. 75.

86. Clandestine digging is responsible for the lunar appearance of the area within the walls. Musil, *Palmyrena*, 140–42, provides a good example of how an entire cemetery can be destroyed by treasure hunters in a very short span of time. Trade in antiquities is a long-established business along the Palmyra–Arak–Sukhna–Tayyiba–al-Kawm–Rusafa route (Wirth, *Syrien*, 443). It was well known that the inhabitants of Sukhna conducted profitable freelance excavations at Rusafa (Boucheman, *Petite Cité caravanière*, 82–84).

87. Karnapp, *Stadtmauer*, 8–9.

gates and two minor entrances. The northern gate, facing the Euphrates, is elaborately carved in a style that has especially close parallels in northern Syria and Mesopotamia, most notably at Edessa and Dayr al-Zafaran near Mardin.[88] Although the street plan has been only partially explored by excavation, it is clear that the east–west axis linking the east and west gates intersected two major streets—one leading from the north gate, whose juncture with the east–west axis took the form of an open square, and another further to the east and proceeding from the southern gate, which ran alongside the western courtyard of the city's largest church, basilica A.[89] A visitor entering the city in the mid sixth century through the northern gate passed along a street lined with columns, archways, courtyards, and shops, which sprawled out onto the sidewalks.[90] Three churches in particular would also have caught the eye: basilica A in the southeast quarter, basilica B south of the city center, and a tetraconch basilica surrounded on all sides by a courtyard, which opened onto the northern artery through two tetrapyla (fig. 8).[91]

As was stated in chapter 1, the brick building located below the later construction now called basilica B and dated by finds to no later than 425 has been identified with the martyrium built by Bishop Alexander of Hierapolis.[92] Evidence dating from the Flavian period has also come to light, although not necessarily military in nature. This date corresponds with Vespasianic work on the road between Palmyra and the Euphrates, which passed through Arak and Rusafa. The finds under basilica B also reveal a gap

---

88. Kollwitz in *Neue Deutsche Ausgrabungen,* 50. For discussion of the style of the architectural ornament, see Brands in *Akten,* 590–91, with pls. 73 and 74, and id. in *Spätantike und byzantinische Bauskulptur,* passim, esp. 72.

89. See Ulbert, *DaM* 6 (1992): 403–6, on the south gate street and church courtyard; also the reports in *AA* 1991: 67, on the plaza; *AA* 1990: 613, on a house excavated at the intersection; Ulbert, *Resafa,* 2: 147–48, on the street leading from the south gate; Kollwitz, *AA* 1963: 350–55, on the street in front of the tetraconch church; Kollwitz in *Neue Deutsche Ausgrabungen,* 50–52, for a general overview of Rusafa's street plan, and 51 on the north gate street, first excavated in 1956; Kollwitz, *AA* 1957: 102–9, on the street leading from the north gate and on the khan; and Karnapp, *AA* 1978: 136–50.

90. Sauvaget, *Byzantion* 14 (1939): 126–27, observes the high proportion of space within the walls taken up by nonresidential constructions. In the spring of 1989, a domestic complex near the southern end of the north-south street was excavated. Precise dating was not possible, but it is clear that occupation spanned from late antiquity to the thirteenth century (Wemhoff, *DaM* 8 [1995]: 247–68; and see also Logar, *DaM* 8 [1995]: 269–92, for the ceramic evidence).

91. Also excavated is the small basilica C, located northeast of the basilica A complex, to be published by Thilo Ulbert. On the tetraconch courtyard, see Karnapp in *Studien,* 125–32.

92. See the fuller discussion of the evidence above, pp. 26–28.

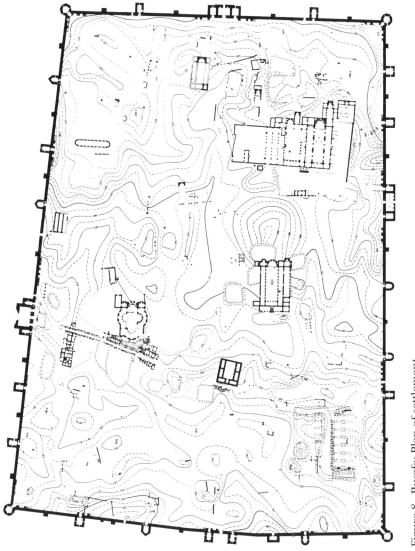

Figure 8. Rusafa: Plan of settlement.

in evidence between the Flavian period and the beginning of the late Roman phase.[93] The finds help to locate for the first time at least one part of the area that lay within the tetrarchic *castrum,* since the early fifth-century martyrium (the forerunner of basilica B) is said in the *Passio* and in the correspondence of Alexander of Hierapolis to have been built within Rusafa's walls.[94] The location of the original martyrium outside the walls remains a mystery, although the cemetery north of the walls may offer a clue.[95]

Basilicas A and B

Basilica A, Rusafa's largest church, lay in the city's southwest corner and the monumental three-aisled basilica was identified by many early travelers as the martyrium of S. Sergius (fig. 9).[96] The basilica is the focal point of a complex assemblage of buildings that underwent considerable elaboration at later stages. On the north, it opens onto a spacious peristyle courtyard, while various annexes, some still not securely identified, grew up to the south.[97] Part of the area to the east has not yet been excavated. From at least the eighth century, permanent shops and workshops lined the perimeter wall of the courtyard west of the basilica.[98] The shops have been interpreted as part of the mosque complex that incorporated one-third of the north peristyle courtyard, but one must wonder whether they replaced more ephemeral installations from earlier periods. The interior of the monumental three-aisled basilica is divided by half piers and wide arches, lend-

---

93. Konrad, *DaM* 6 (1992): 348. Mackensen, *Germania* 61 (1983): 565–78, esp. 578, discusses a mid third-century fibula discovered at Rusafa.

94. Konrad, *DaM* 6 (1992): 350.

95. See Kollwitz in *Neue Deutsche Ausgrabungen,* 48, on the cemetery north and northeast of the walls; and see also pp. 149–73 below.

96. For the history of scholarship on basilica A, see Ulbert, *Resafa,* 2: 1–5.

97. Ulbert, *Resafa,* 2: 118–27, 144–45. Kollwitz in *Neue Deutsche Ausgrabungen,* 64, and *AA* 1959: 88–101, and before him Musil, *Palmyrena,* 157, 268, had hypothetically located a monastery in this complex. Without argument, Ulbert, *AA* 1977: 569, n. 23, disregarded this view, but the possibility of monastic quarters in the basilica A complex, at least at a later stage, has begun to reemerge (*AA* 1993: 730; Ulbert, *Resafa,* 3: 3). Literary evidence of a sixth-century monastery at Rusafa consists of the following: "The humble sinner Joseph, bishop of the holy monastery of Rasiphta" appears in a colophon of a manuscript containing works of S. Ephrem that belonged to a certain Zooras, son of Paul of Tagrit, who gave it to the Syrian monastery in Scetis. The final sentence of the Syriac colophon asks the reader to pray for Bishop Joseph (Assemani, *Bibliotheca orientalis,* 1: 117). Assemani suggests that Zooras might be identified with the non-Chalcedonian stylite who baptized Empress Theodora in 535 and in whose honor a non-Chalcedonian church was dedicated at Amida in 650. On Zooras, see Frend, *Monophysite Movement,* 269–72. If the Zooras in the colophon is to be thus identified, Joseph would have headed Rusafa's monastery in the late sixth century at the earliest and may well have been associated with non-Chalcedonian circles in the region. The existence of such a monastery at that time would not be at all surprising.

98. Ulbert, *DaM* 7 (1993): 115–16.

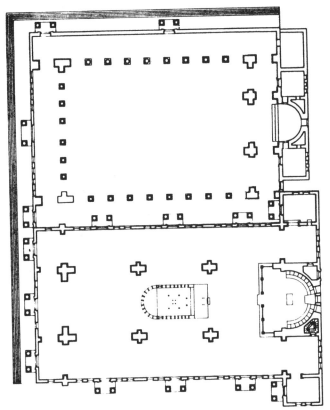

Figure 9. Rusafa: Plan of basilica A.

ing the space an airy grandeur. An upper order was in turn supported on the half piers. In a later phase, and no doubt for structural reasons, the wide span of the arches was filled in and given further support by columns and carved capitals reused from basilica B.[99] At the western end is a nar-thex divided later into three rooms. A large bema in the North Syrian style

99. The date of reuse cannot be determined precisely, but it took place certainly before the eighth century (see below).

crowns the central aisle, and the eastern end is divided into five interconnecting rooms.[100]

The task of dating and identifying the dedications and functions of Rusafa's churches has been an arduous one. And it is by no means complete. Thilo Ulbert's welcome publication of basilica A in 1986 was the first systematic presentation of a building since the professional spade first struck the soil of Rusafa.[101] Recent investigation by the architectural historian Gunnar Brands has radically revised our understanding of the relationship between basilica A on the one hand, and three related projects, the tetraconch, basilica B, and the north gate, on the other.[102] The details will be discussed as necessary, but the crux of the problem is a reused inscription in basilica A that refers to the dedication of an unnamed benefaction to the Holy Cross by Bishop Abraamios in 559. Ulbert understood this inscription to be the key to the building's chronology, dating basilica A to 559. In 1986, after the publication of basilica A as the Holy Cross basilica, the discovery of another inscription, which belonged originally to basilica B, led Ulbert to suspect the need to revise the chronology he had previously established for basilica A.[103] Subsequently, Brands's study of the architectural style of basilica A has stimulated him to date the first phase of the structure to the last quarter of the fifth century. With minor reservations, Ulbert is in agreement with Brands's conclusions and no longer considers basilica A to be the Holy Cross basilica as argued in *Resafa*, vol. 2, *Die Basilika des Heiligen Kreuzes in Resafa-Sergiupolis*.[104] One of the many important implications of Brands's conclusions is that instead of being the last church to be built at Rusafa, basilica A becomes the earliest of those still standing. This qualification is important and will be discussed in turn. The present account accepts Brands's chronology and will attempt to serve as a guide through the somewhat tortuous obstacle course of research at the site.[105]

The inscription on a marble plaque that led Ulbert to identify basilica A

---

100. On the variety of uses made in Syria of the side chambers at a basilica's eastern end, see Descoeudres, *Pastophorien*. Tchalenko, *Églises syriennes*, 206–12, reconstructs the developmental phases of the bema based on his investigation conducted for the Service des Antiquités in 1942. His posthumously published discussion of Rusafa's contribution to the history of bemata ignores the findings of the German excavations. See Ulbert, *Resafa*, 2: 4, 25, 136–37, on the damage subsequently suffered by the bema, which was left exposed to weather and vandals by Tchalenko; also the review by Mango, *JThS* 43 (1992): 263–66.

101. Ulbert, *Resafa*, vol. 2. In 1976 the walls were published by Karnapp, *Stadtmauer*.

102. Brands, *Resafa*, vol. 6 (forthcoming).

103. Ulbert in Gatier and Ulbert, *DaM* 5 (1991): 169–79, esp. 176.

104. Ulbert, letter to the author, 18 October 1996.

105. I would like at this point to express my gratitude to Thilo Ulbert and Gunnar Brands. Both have responded generously to my questions about the architecture of the site and have commented on an earlier draft of this chapter. I am particularly indebted to Gunnar Brands for sharing his work, often in unpublished form.

as a church dedicated to the Holy Cross was discovered over twenty years ago. It was found in the floor of the sanctuary of basilica A, behind the central opening of the templon, but this was not necessarily its original location. It had clearly been at least twice removed during restoration of the floors, broken at some point, and reset for the last time by someone ignorant of Greek. Groups of letters are turned in improbable directions, like a forced jigsaw puzzle. The inscription is, however, complete and gives both a date and the name of a benefactor. Clearly it must have been positioned so that the benefaction itself was obvious, since it is not mentioned in the dedicatory inscription. The inscription reads:

> Abraham by God's mercy bishop of Sergiopolis built in honor of the Holy Cross in order to be made worthy of God's mercy. It was accomplished in the month of Artemisios in the seventh year of the indiction, in the year 870.[106]

The date corresponds to April 559. Abraham was a signatory at the fifth ecumenical council held at Constantinople in 553, and he later opposed Justin's edict espousing Aphthartodocetism.[107] Since the architectural decoration of basilica A places its first phase of construction in the last quarter of the fifth century, the object in honor of the Holy Cross cannot have been the entire church. Instead, the dedication inscription may have referred to the templon, as Brands suggests, or perhaps to the side chapel whose apse is decorated with a large painted cross, admittedly not an unusual decoration.[108]

At this stage, on the basis of architectural style, we know that basilica A was constructed in the last quarter of the fifth century and that, according to the first inscription, in 559 Bishop Abraham adorned the existing building with some further element, possibly a templon. In order to assess the function of basilica A and its relationship to basilica B in particular, we now need to consider the other inscription already mentioned.

106. Ἀβρααμιος ἐλέει Θ(εο)ῦ ἐπίσκο(πος) Σεργιουπό | (λέως) ᾠκοδόμησεν | πρὸς τιμὴν τοῦ Ἁγίου Σταυροῦ ἵνα ἀξιωθῇ | ἐλέους Θεοῦ. Γέγονεν δὲ μη(νί) Ἀρτεμ(ισίῳ) | ἰνδ(ικτιῶνος) ζʹ τοῦ οωʹ ἔτους. Ulbert, *AA* 1977: 563–69; Gatier in Ulbert, *Resafa*, 2: 161. In line two, ἀξιώθη, as in Ulbert, *AA* 1977: 563–69, and Gatier in id. and Ulbert *DaM* 5 (1991): 181, is here corrected to read ἀξιωθῇ. For other inscriptions in basilica A, see Gatier in Ulbert, *Resafa*, 2: 165–69.

107. Devreesse, *Patriarcat* 289.

108. Brands in *Spätantike und byzantinische Bauskulptur*, 67–68, suggests that Abraham's dedication was the templon. For a parallel dedication to a saint of an architectural element within a church, see *IGLS*, no. 1970, in this case a door. Also found at basilica A is an inscription on a large marble plaque decorated with a cross, which was part of the *templon* and records the dedication in August 559, but without mention of a donor (see Gatier in Ulbert, *Resafa*, 2: 166, no. 5). In the remarks following Ulbert in *Actes*, 457, Falla Castelfranchi raises the possibility of a connection between the painted cross in the side chapel and the Abraamios dedication.

This inscription dates the inception of work on basilica B to the spring of 518 under Bishop Sergius. It was discovered in the Umayyad mosque north of basilica A and first published in 1991.[109] Although it was found reused in the mosque, its original home was in basilica B, as the comparison of door profiles has confirmed. Basilica B was constructed on the oldest site at Rusafa to have been used for Christian cult, but the three-aisled structure visible today belongs to the building activity dated to 518.[110] The inscription reads:

> This holy church, once . . . and made of brick, held the holy relics of Sergius the victorious martyr until the other venerable shrine which at present holds the holy sarcophagus was constructed. It was transformed and rebuilt from its foundations with great generosity by the most God-loving bishop Sergius II, the kinsman of Maronius the chorepiscopus. He began the project in the month of Dystros, the eleventh year of the indiction, in the year 829 and completed it in the month of . . .[111]

Three churches are mentioned in this inscription: an old brick church (the former home of Sergius's relics), the new church on the same spot, and "the other venerable shrine" whither the relics had been removed. The *Passio* claims that a church was built within the city, and that Sergius's relics were translated there from outside the walls. The inscription supports the *Passio*, revealing that the church begun by Bishop Sergius in 518 replaced an earlier brick-built church that had formerly held the bones of S. Sergius. Most importantly, it now becomes clear that the "other venerable shrine" is the late fifth-century basilica A, which housed the relics of S. Sergius after they were removed from the first brick church within the walls. This is further confirmed by the plan of basilica A, discussed in detail below.

The east end of basilica A was especially designed to accommodate martyr cult. The room to the south of the apse would have served as a pastopho-

---

109. Gatier and Ulbert, *DaM* 5 (1991): 169–82.

110. Kollwitz in *Neue Deutsche Ausgrabungen*, 53–60; and id., *AAS* 8–9 (1958–59): 24; Donceel-Voûte, *Pavements*, 281–82.

111. † Ἡ ἁγία αὕτη ἐκκλη(σία) πάλαι μὲν [- 4-5 -] κ(αὶ) ἀπὸ π[λ]ίνθων οὖσα τὰ ἅγια ἔσχεν | λίψανα Σεργίου τοῦ πολυάθλου μάρτυρος μέχρ' ο [ὕ] κατασκευῆς τοῦ ἄλλου | σεβασμίου ναοῦ τοῦ νῦν τὴν ἁγίαν ἔχοντος [λ]άρνακα, μετεσχηματίσθη δὲ | κ(αὶ) ἐκ θεμελίων οὕτω φιλοτίμως οἰκοδομή[θ]η ὑπὸ Σεργίου τοῦ θεοφιλ(εστάτου) | β' ἐπισκ(όπου) τοῦ συνγενοῦς Μαρωνίου τοῦ χωρεπισκ(όπου), ἀρξαμένου μὲν τοῦ ἔργου | μη(νὶ) Δύστρῳ ἰνδ(ικτιῶνος) ια' τοῦ θκω' ἔτους, πληρώσαντος δὲ μη(νὶ) *vacat*. Gatier, *DaM* 5 (1991): 179; *SEG* 41 (1991), no. 1537. I would offer a slightly different reading in l. 2. The photograph and drawing show μέχρ[.]κατασκευῆς. The break in the stone allows for only one letter, which I suggest should be an iota, producing μέχρι. Gatier inserts two letters—οὗ—and only brackets the upsilon. But the photograph and drawing indicate no omicron.

rion, while the plan and decoration of the room immediately to the north marks it as the shrine for relics. This room was increasingly elaborated over the course of its four phases of renovation, and the floor, in particular, underwent several stages of embellishment, first with simple gypsum paving stones, followed by limestone and finally by precious marble in green, white, and pink.[112] Other architectural features once distinguished the shrine as a place of heightened importance, such as the towerlike structure that covered the space, a vaulted roof with mosaics, and wall revetments.[113] On a table fitted into the platform, at the focus of the room's splendor, would have rested the silver oblong reliquary sarcophagus of S. Sergius.[114]

Access to the shrine north of the apse was possible from both the north aisle of basilica A and from a chamber that communicated with the shrine from the north. A split-leaf capital inscribed with the name "Sergis," written from right to left in Greek, was reused at the eastern end of the row of columns that divide the central nave from the northern aisle.[115] Of all the capitals reused from basilica B, this one alone bears the saint's name and was no doubt positioned closest to the shrine in order to further emphasize the holiness of the space. The chamber to the north of the shrine opened, in turn, onto the monumental peristyle courtyard on its north side.[116] In this way, pilgrims would have had easy access to the shrine from the northern courtyard. This architectural arrangement could also accommodate the ceremonial display of the relics to a large crowd.[117] The walls of the chamber that communicates with the shrine from the north were carved with pilgrims' graffiti—names, prayers to Sergius and the Trisagion. Fragments of flasks and the recess in the sarcophagus base found in the northern chamber suggest that oil, or water, was poured over the bones, collected, and then distributed among the pilgrims who were drawn to Rusafa by S. Sergius's reputation for healing.[118] The Coptic recension of the *Arab Jacobite Synaxa-*

112. Ulbert, *Resafa*, 2: 43–62, with reference to figs. 28, 30, 31, and 34.

113. A marble plaque with a damaged Greek inscription was found in situ in the final phase of the pavement (Gatier in Ulbert, *Resafa*, 2: 165–66, no. 4).

114. See Evagr., *HE* 4.28, on the silver sarcophagus.

115. For other Syrian inscriptions in Greek writtten backwards, perhaps under the influence of Semitic writing, see Prentice, *Greek and Latin Inscriptions*, 82, 210.

116. Ulbert, *Resafa*, 2: 143.

117. Ibid., 171–77. The courtyard of the healing shrine of S. Thecla at Seleucia was a central gathering place that played an important role in the process of pilgrimage and healing (*Mir. Theclae* 12.24–25, 24.22; Dagron, *Vie et miracles*, 69–70).

118. Ulbert, *Resafa*, 2: 142. We cannot know whether contact with the sarcophagus was permitted, although it seems very likely (Kollwitz in *Neue Deutsche Ausgrabungen*, 57). Sergius's reputation as a healing martyr had reached Gaul by at least the late sixth century (Greg. Tur., *Glor. mart.* 96). On the role in martyr cult of oil blessed by contact with martyrs' bones, see

rion mentions the existence at the shrine at Rusafa of a marble basin into which poured perfumed oil infused with healing powers.[119]

The shrine, like all buildings so far excavated at Rusafa, has been thoroughly robbed of its valuable objects. Here were found only fragments of pilgrims' flasks, small change and hundreds of trinkets—mostly earrings and bracelets of cheap metal or bone. These were the votive offerings of ordinary pilgrims.[120] The greatest number of such objects was found beneath the floor of the second phase of the martyrium in basilica A. A plausible explanation is that the valuable votive offerings had been removed at the time of renovation, while some of those of no monetary value were left behind.[121] These votives can only hint at the irretrievable variety of the offerings to the miracle-working martyr. The objects found in the shrine of basilica A are precisely what we would expect as offerings of the region's pastoral Arab population, among whom the cult of Sergius was especially popular.[122] The only articles of monetary value that have been recovered by archeological investigation are part of a five-piece liturgical assemblage dated to the twelfth century, which allows us a glimpse of the opulence that would once have characterized the saint's treasury.[123] We also have a story told by Gregory of Tours that is set at Rusafa. He relates how a poor woman gave the martyr a few chickens as part of a vow, and when two unscrupulous men stole one of her offerings, Sergius retaliated by petrifying the dedicated bird still in the cooking pot, leaving the thieves to disinvite their hun-

---

Lassus, *Sanctuaires,* 163–67; Delehaye, *AB* 53 (1935): 225. Pieces of cloth rubbed against the holy relics might also have offered the pilgrims contact with the martyr (see, e.g., Greg. Tur., *Glor. mart.* 27).

119. This detail in the undated Coptic recension of the *Arab Jacobite Synaxarion,* 7 October, has not been noticed by students of the Sergius cult or of Rusafa. The recension gives a boiled-down version of the Greek *Passio,* but concludes with this information, added most likely by someone who had visited the shrine, or had heard about it at second hand. Cf. *Mir. Theclae* 7, where oil from the lamp that burned on the holy bema was taken away by pilgrims for its curative powers; also Sophr., *Mir. Cyr. et Io.* 7.3.

120. Ulbert, *Resafa,* 2: 50–52, 59–60, 140, with n. 281. On the coins, see the study of Mackensen in Ulbert, *Resafa,* 2: 181–225. For a photograph of an incense burner, probably seventh-century, discovered in the 1974 excavations (find-spot unspecified), see the catalogue in Ruprechtsberger, ed., *Syrien,* 443, fig. 87.

121. The Piacenza Pilgrim saw armlets, bracelets, rings, tiaras, and emperors' crowns among the votives which adorned the tomb of Christ (*Itin.* 18). Before the redating of basilica A to the last quarter of the fifth century by Brands in *Spätantike und byzantinische Bauskulptur,* 59–74, Ulbert had suggested that the votives found in the church's second phase might have been brought there from the trichoros of basilica B, considered at that time to have been the martyrion of S. Sergius (Ulbert, *Resafa,* 2: 140).

122. On Arab devotion to S. Sergius, see the discussion of the *History of Ahudemmeh* below, pp. 121–28.

123. Ulbert, *Resafa,* vol. 3. See also below, pp. 185–87.

gry guests.[124] Pilgrims left birds as ex-votos in the atrium of S. Thecla's healing shrine near Seleucia. This consecrated petting zoo housed doves, swans,
geese, pheasants and perhaps ibises, and provided innocent distraction for
the pilgrims' children, as well as for the pilgrims themselves, who fed the
birds with grain, no doubt sold on the spot by enterprising locals.[125]

The inscription from basilica B advances our understanding of basilica
A significantly. Less apparent from Bishop Sergius's epigraphy is what purpose his new church served once the relics, formerly in the old brick church
at that site, had been moved to basilica A. The inscription was carved on a
tabula ansata on a door lintel that originally belonged over the main southern entrance of basilica B.[126] Bishop Sergius attached his name to the new
structure's inception and left a blank space at the end of the lintel inscription, presumably for the date of its completion. However, the space was
never filled in. We last hear of Sergius's activities in 524, when he was sent by
the emperor Justin to the conference at Ramla.[127] Under normal circumstances, one would expect the construction of such a church to require an
average of ten years. But perhaps by the time the new church was finished,
a bishop other than Sergius occupied Rusafa's episcopal throne. Bishop
Sergius had also marked his role in the church's progress with another inscription, which was found reused in the apse floor of basilica A:

> By God's mercy, Bishop Sergius II, kinsman of Maronius chorepiscopus, built
> the most holy church and roofed it and supplied doors and various marbles[?].
> Work was begun in the month of Dystros in the indiction . . .[128]

Basilica B was adorned with architectural detail and ornament to glorify
God and awe its visitors. Although smaller than basilica A, its size, 48.50 m
in length and 25.70 m in width, still places it among Syria's largest churches.
The plan reflects the familiar North Syrian basilical style with the typical

---

124. Greg. Tur., *Glor. mart.* 96. Cf. the description of festal picnicking on the feast of
S. Thecla in her shrine at Seleucia (*Mir. Theclae* 26, pp. 356–57).

125. *Mir. Theclae* 24.23–32.

126. Ulbert, *DaM* 5 (1991): 172–73, suggests the southern rather than the western
entrance.

127. Justin's choice of the bishop of Rusafa as Abraham's companion on his diplomatic
mission to the Lakhmid al-Mundhir is another example of Rusafa's ideally suited situation for
mediation between Rome, Iran, and the Arabs. For the Ramla conference, see Shahîd, *Byzantium and the Semitic Orient* VI, 115–31, esp. 122 n. 29.

128. [Ὁ] ἐλέει Θ(εο)ῦ βʹ ἐπ[ίσκοπος Σέργιος ὁ συγγε]ν(ὴς) Μαρωνίου χωρεπισ[κ(όπου)],
| [τὴ]ν ἁγιωτ(άτην) ἐκλ(ησίαν) [ca. 13 ᾠκοδόμησεν] κ(αὶ) ἐστέγ(ασεν), (καὶ) θυρώμ(ατα)
| κ(αὶ) [μαρμα?] | ῥ(ώσεις) διαφόρ(ας) [ca. 12 τοῦ ἔργου ἀρξ]αμ(ένου) μὲν μηνὶ Δύστρῳ
[ἰνδ(ικτιῶνος)]. Gatier, *DaM* 5 (1991): 181 is a revised reading (in the light of the lintel inscription) of the inscription published earlier in Ulbert, *Resafa*, 2: 162–64.

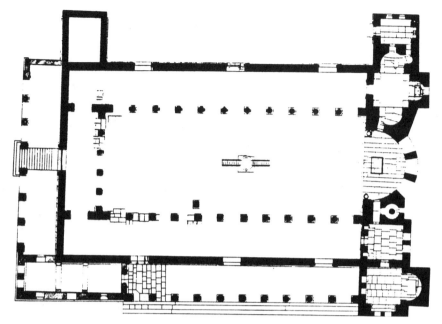

Figure 10. Rusafa: Plan of basilica B.

porch running along the southern face (fig. 10).[129] While the basilica's nave was simple and adorned only by a Constantinopolitan-style ambo, the plan of the eastern end was intricate, although it too followed a pattern common in many Syro-Mesopotamian basilicas. On the south, a square pastophorion communicated with the apse. The pastophorion, in turn, opened on its south side onto an apsidal chamber that may have functioned as a funerary chapel.[130] North of the apse a door led into a triconch room, known as the *trichoros,* whose architecture and ornament drew attention to the importance of the space. The pavement was elaborate *opus sectile,* the conches were covered in gold tesserae, and the profuse architectural decoration was painted. In the eastern niche of the *trichoros* was discovered a rectangular platform with four depressions to hold supports, probably for a table, and

129. Kollwitz in *Neue Deutsche Ausgrabungen,* 54. See also Krautheimer with Ćurčić, *Early Christian and Byzantine Architecture,* 151.

130. In the floor of the apsidal chamber a recess was discovered, which in a parallel installation at Androna held a sarcophagus. On these grounds, Kollwitz, *AAS* 8–9 (1958–59): 31–32, interprets the chamber as a funerary chapel, possibly for the church's founder. Donceel-Voûte, *Pavements,* 180 n. 1 and 284 n. 20, argues that the southeastern apsidal room was, instead, the site of martyr cult, since no sarcophagus has been discovered in the chamber.

a recess in the center connected to a channel that led toward the back of the niche. Most likely the table would have held a reliquary—perhaps of the sarcophagus type found, for example, at Apamea—through which oil or water would be poured and distributed among the pilgrims as an "eulogia."[131] A well in the northeastern corner of the trichoros may also have played a part in the cult, perhaps by providing water to be blessed by contact with the saint's relics.[132] Small finds from basilica B have been negligible.[133]

It has been claimed that the delicate nature of an *opus sectile* floor in the triconch shrine in basilica B excludes the idea that crowds of visitors were allowed to troop through it.[134] This suggestion cannot be ruled out. It overlooks, though, the possibility that the floor was covered with carpets, and is further weakened by the presence of two narrow doorways into the triconch room that would have been accessible to the laity, one from the north aisle and one from the northeast room.[135] Rather than being evidence against accessibility, the narrowness of the entrances can be seen as heightening the drama of encounter with holy relics.[136] Whether or not direct access was

---

131. Donceel-Voûte, *Pavements*, 283 n. 15, draws attention to the similar installation for a table at the center of a side chamber in Huwirta's north basilica. For a discussion of the sarcophagus-type reliquary and the theology of blessed oil, see Gessel, *OC* 72 (1988): 183–202. Writing in the mid tenth century, Mas'udi, *Muruj al-dhahab* 120, claims to have visited a church in which he saw stone coffins containing human bones into which a thick oil was poured so that the Christians could receive a blessing from it.

132. Kollwitz in *Neue Deutsche Ausgrabungen*, 56; id., *AA* 1954: 122–28; and id., *AAS* 4–5 (1954–55): 80–82, for reconstruction of the use made of the triconch shrine and description of the well installed in the northeastern room, which communicated with the triconch shrine. Wells were common features of martyr-cult installations, found also, e.g., at the shrines of S. Demetrius at Thessalonica and S. Thecla at Seleucia. See also Donceel-Voûte in *Akten*, 190–91. Lassus, *Sanctuaires*, 173, discusses parallel martyr-cult installations in Syria. In comparison with the other examples Lassus cites, the ornament of the triconch room of basilica B distinguishes it as the shrine of a particularly revered martyr.

133. In the triconch of basilica B, the only object noted was a marble fragment with a letter A from an inscription (Kollwitz, *AA* 1954: 127).

134. Donceel-Voûte, *Pavements*, 282.

135. On the use of carpets in late antique churches, see Mango in *Byzantium*, 52. Perhaps too obvious to have attracted comment is the long-established practice in the Middle East of removing one's footwear in holy places—a habit maintained, for instance, in the shrine of the Burning Bush at the monastery of St. Catherine, Sinai, where flokata carpets cover the floor. If public access was forbidden, Huwirta offers a possible parallel to the martyrium at Rusafa. There the western entrance to the martyrium north of the apse seems to have been furnished with a low screen with an opening in the middle (Canivet, *Syria* 55 [1978]: 153–62, esp. 155). For general comments on decoration of and circulation around martyr shrines, see Donceel-Voûte, *Byzantion* 63 (1993): 437–38; see also Lassus, *Sanctuaires*, 162–83, esp. 177–81, on arrangement of and activity at martyria.

136. At the holiest of Christian sites, the tomb of Christ, access has always been through a very narrow and low entrance (Wilkinson, *Jerusalem Pilgrims*, 175–76). Donceel-Voûte, *Pavements*, 282, suggests that the narrow entrances into the triconch martyrium would have

allowed, a reliquary sarcophagus, if that is what occupied the space, would certainly have been visible from the two doorways.

On a wide ledge along the eastern wall of the adjoining northeastern annex was discovered another installation for a reliquary sarcophagus, this time with the sarcophagus in situ.[137] In the front of this sarcophagus was a hole from which exuded oil, which was then collected in a recess below. Whose sarcophagus this was is not known. South of the apse, near the passageway between the pastophorion and the so-called funerary chapel, were found two graffiti mentioning the martyr Leontius, a popular soldier-martyr from Tripolis. Kollwitz, who assumed that the triconch housed the relics of S. Sergius, offered the suggestion that it was Bacchus's sarcophagus, since the three soldier-saints shared a dedication at Bostra's cathedral.[138] The evidence that Bacchus's body, or parts of it, was to be found at Rusafa is inconclusive. The Georgian recension of the lost Syriac *Vita Gulanducht* refers only to the reliquary of S. Sergius at Rusafa, while the later Greek recension mentions relics of both saints at Rusafa.[139] The Piacenza Pilgrim and Michael the Syrian report that Bacchus's tomb was at Barbalissus.[140] It would

---

prohibited public access. She does not offer parallels to a popular shrine forbidding direct access to its holy relics, which at Rusafa were protected by a sarcophagus. See, e.g., Joh. Chrys., *Hom. in martyres*, PG 50.664, where he urges his flock to embrace martyrs' sarcophagi. The *Miracula Cyri et Ioannis*, set at their pilgrimage shrine at Menuthis near Alexandria, depicts numerous instances of the pilgrim's close contact with a sarcophagus: see, e.g., Sophr., *Mir. Cyr. et Io.* 1.5, p. 244, where a sick boy's father is pictured drenching (καταβρέχων) the sarcophagus with tears. Elsewhere, it is clearly stated that a grating enclosed the sarcophagus and was opened at set hours: Marcos, *"Thaumata,"* 46. For a vivid description of Western practices, see Brown, *Cult of the Saints*, 87–88.

137. Kollwitz in *Neue Deutsche Ausgrabungen*, 56–57; Kollwitz, *AA* 1957: 70–76, esp. 74, for a photograph of the sarcophagus installation in the northeastern annex.

138. In *Spätantike und byzantinische Bauskulptur*, 64, Brands also suggests that basilica B may have housed the relics of S. Bacchus and S. Leontius. Some later accounts of the martyrdom of SS. Sergius and Bacchus, such as the mid ninth-century martyrologium of S. Adon of Vienna, include a mysterious martyr named Julia, who is said to have been buried with Sergius and Bacchus (cf. *Acta. sanct. Oct* 3.883–85). Cf. also the account in the Coptic recension of the *Arab Jacobite Synaxarion* 114, wherein, on their way to Rusafa, Sergius and his persecutors meet an unnamed young woman who gives them a drink and then follows the party to Rusafa, where she collects the martyr's blood. No further mention is made of the girl, whose appearance in the *Passio* of SS. Sergius and Bacchus may be attributed to the convoluted hagiographical developments shared by accounts of the martyrdom of Victor and Corona (see above, pp. 17–18n. 37 for bibliography). A philological investigation of these sources might be rewarding.

139. *Vita Gulanducht* 15.1 (Georgian recension); 20 (Greek recension of Eustathios).

140. Bacchus is mentioned at Barbalissus in the 570s by the Piacenza Pilgrim (*Itin.* 47, p. 191); and by Mich. Syr., *Chron.* 9.26 (tr. 2: 220), who reports that in 543 the Iranians stole the bones of S. Bacchus and the gold covering from the sarcophagus of S. Sergius from Barbalissus.

not be surprising if a small relic or personal possession once associated with Bacchus, such as his chlamys, was revered at Rusafa. It may also have been the case that a relic or possession of Sergius was housed in the *trichoros*.

Ulbert implies that basilica B, begun in 518, suffered destruction by an earthquake at an early phase of its existence. But the precise date when basilica B, irreparably damaged, became a quarry for other building projects is not known. Ulbert has noted that the use of different architectural fragments from basilica B in basilica A and in the Umayyad mosque suggests that repairs to basilica A, employing reused capitals and columns, were undertaken before the mosque construction in the first half of the eighth century, which exploited much of what materials remained from basilica B, primarily large building blocks from the basilica walls.[141] Still undetermined is who or what was the focus of devotion at basilica B until it was destroyed and its components transferred to basilica A. Unfortunately, the present state of the evidence, both material and literary, helps little with these puzzles.

The Tetraconch

Construction of the tetraconch, dated by finds and style to the early sixth century, belonged to this buoyant atmosphere in which basilica B, erected over the site of Alexander's shrine, also shared.[142] But the function of this building, once thought because of its shape to be the martyrium of Sergius, is still somewhat unclear.[143] The difficulties are linked with the presence in the tetraconch of a synthronon with space for the bishop's throne, a small baptistry communicating with the apse, and episcopal tombs, most notably the tomb found north of the apse, which still bears the name of Abraham.[144] Of course, Abraham was the name of the mid sixth-century bishop who is known also from the inscription found in basilica A. These features might suggest that the tetraconch served as the cathedral, and it has been interpreted by some scholars as such. However, the earlier basilica A seems now a more likely candidate for identification as the cathedral, and it

---

141. Cf. Ulbert, *Resafa,* 2: 151. Private houses were built within the ruins of basilica B by at least the early ninth century (Kollwitz, *AAS* 4–5 [1954–55]: 79, and id., *AA* 1954: 121–22).

142. Brands in *Akten,* 590–97.

143. For the most recent discussion of the tetraconch in the context of Rusafa's architectural development, especially in relation to the north gate and basilica B, see Brands in *Akten,* 590–97, with pls. 73 and 74. For earlier views, see Kollwitz, *AA* 1963: 349–52; Donceel-Voûte, *Pavements,* 268–70; Ulbert in *Actes,* 450; and Kleinbauer, *DOP* 27 (1973): 95–98, who maintains that it was the cathedral. Musil, *Palmyrena,* 156–57, interprets the tetraconch as the martyrium. Kollwitz in *Neue Deutsche Ausgrabungen,* 69, emphasizes the absence of evidence for martyr cult in the tetraconch.

144. See also Kollwitz, *AAS* 8–9 (1958–59): 32; Donceel-Voûte, *Pavements,* 271–72.

too boasts tombs, although unidentified, and a lavishly decorated cross-in-square building in the southeast, which seems to have served as its baptistry.[145] The simultaneous existence of more than one church with a baptistry is attested in other settlements too, such as Zenobia on the Euphrates southeast of Rusafa. One explanation that has been offered in the case of Zenobia is that the two churches served two different rites.[146] A suggestive passage that may go some way toward explaining the opaque situation at Rusafa survives from the synod of Beth Batin near Mesopotamian Harran in 794.[147] It seems that Chalcedonian clergy had been collecting vows to S. Sergius from non-Chalcedonians. The complaint voiced at the synod was that the Chalcedonians had not given any of the collected vows to the non-Chalcedonian church at Rusafa, which is mentioned specifically. At the synod it was decided that in the future, non-Chalcedonians were to give their vows only to their own bishop, whose jurisdiction covered Rusafa. Although it does not make clear whether either Chalcedonians or non-Chalcedonians had a bishop resident at Rusafa, the decision implies that both a non-Chalcedonian and a Chalcedonian church existed at Rusafa, at least in the late eighth century.

PILGRIMAGE TO RUSAFA

At the beginning of the sixth century, several events occurred that might be linked with the construction of the tetraconch, basilica B, and the north gate. In the 510s, the emperor Anastasius had Sergius's thumb translated to Constantinople, a clear sign of the increasing prestige of the saint, whose sacred story was by then circulating in the form of the *Passio* known to us.[148] Also at this time, Anastasius elevated Rusafa to the rank of a metropolitan see,[149] and Rusafa came to be known briefly as Anastasiopolis. More lastingly, Rusafa was also called Sergiopolis—perhaps again the new name should be understood in connection with the earliest imperial interest in the shrine and its relics.[150] In the mid sixth century, Procopius provided

145. Ulbert, *Actes*, 445–56. The second storey on the south side of basilica A has been interpreted as episcopal quarters by Ulbert (*Resafa*, 2: 146).

146. Lauffray, *Halabiyya-Zenobia*, 105–6; Tchalenko too had noted this as a possible solution to the presence in basilica A of a North Syrian style bema, and in basilica B of a Constantinopolitan-style ambo (*Églises syriennes*, 211–12).

147. The decision is discussed by Degen in Ulbert, *Resafa*, 3: 71–72.

148. Joh. Diakrin., fr. 2.554, p. 156.

149. Ibid.; Honigmann, *Evêques*, 102–3; Devreesse, *Patriarcat*, 122.

150. George of Cyprus, *Descriptio orbis romani*, ll. 882–83, pp. 151–52: "Sergioupolis, or Anastasioupolis, the present day Rattapha" (ninth century). Never displaced by the name Sergioupolis, variants of Rusafa are used in the mid fifth-century *Passio;* in 514, by Severus,

a sketch of Rusafa's history, which emphasizes the shrine's acquisition of wealth and influence:

There is a certain church in Euphratesia, dedicated to Sergius, a famous saint, whom men of former times used to worship and revere, so that they named the place Sergiopolis, and they had surrounded it with a very humble wall (τειχίσματι βραχυτάτῳ), just sufficient to prevent the Saracens of the region from capturing it by storm. For the Saracens are naturally incapable of storming a wall and the weakest kind of barricade, put together with perhaps nothing but mud, is sufficient to check their assault. At a later time, however, this church, through its acquisition of treasures, came to be powerful and celebrated. And the Emperor Justinian, upon considering this situation, at once gave it careful attention. He surrounded the church with a most remarkable wall, and he stored up a great quantity of water and thus provided the inhabitants with a bountiful supply. Furthermore, he added to the place houses and stoas and the other buildings which are wont to be the adornments of a city. Besides this he established there a garrison of soldiers who, in case of need, defended the circuit wall.[151]

We have accumulated sufficient evidence for Sergius of Rusafa's gradual rise to fame—from the Surans' attempted theft of his bones to Anastasius's successful, if only partial, translation—to treat with some suspicion Procopius's focus on Justinian as the city's unique provider. The struggle for Rusafa between Alexander of Hierapolis and John of Antioch is clear illustration of the site's attractiveness some fifty years before Justinian's birth.[152] But this does not necessarily convict Procopius of deceit: Alexander's *altissimi muri* may well have seemed a τείχισμα βραχύτατον to Procopius a century later.[153] And whatever their state, there is no doubt that the old walls were replaced by the time of Procopius's composition. Basilica A and the complex surrounding it spread out in the southeast quarter.[154] As for who built the walls: there is a trend toward attributing to Anastasius sites described as Justinianic by Procopius.[155] Early on in the *De aedificiis*,

---

who relies heavily on the *Passio* in his *Hom. cath.* 57; and by John Moschus, *Prat. spir.* 180 (*PG* 87.3052b), in the late sixth century, who calls the pilgrimage shrine "Safas."

151. Proc., *Aed.* 2.9.3–9 (tr. Dewing).

152. See chapter 1.

153. *ACOec.* 1.4, p. 163 (Schwartz): "magnum id ipsum templum fabricatum est et illi altissimi muri et alia intra eandem munitionem aedificia." Kollwitz, *AA* 1954: 120, mistakenly interprets *muri* to indicate a temenos wall around Alexander's church, rather than the *castrum* wall.

154. Ulbert, *Resafa*, 2: 147.

155. For the history of scholarship on Rusafa's walls in the context of Procopius's attributions, see Karnapp, *Stadtmauer*, 51–53; Karnapp, *AA* 1968: 308–11. See Karnapp, *AA* 1970: 99–102, on the north gate. Dussaud, *Topographie*, 254, ascribes Rusafa's walls to Anastasius.

Procopius makes it clear that he includes among Justinian's achievements projects undertaken while Justin was still nominal ruler.[156] The architect Walter Karnapp, in his thorough study of the walls at Rusafa, published in 1976, accepts that Justinian may have been responsible for work at Rusafa already during the reign of his uncle. Karnapp does not, however, conclude that the walls are Anastasian: rather he tends to uphold Procopius's attribution and does not pretend to have reached firmer conclusions, thus leaving the issue open to further investigation.[157] Subsequently, Ulbert and Brinker in the course of excavation have accepted the Justinianic date with only slight reservation.[158] More recently, however, Gunnar Brands in a thorough study of the architectural decoration has built up a strong case for the contemporaneity of the walls and gates, the tetraconch, and basilica B, all of which belong by his calculation to the first decades of the sixth century, which coincided with the final years of Anastasius's rule.[159] Brands does not exclude the possibility that they were finished by Justinian, but notes that no archeological evidence exists to confirm the dating either way.[160] And it should be noted that even Procopius does not claim that Justinian built a church at Rusafa. The "certain church" known to Procopius would have been the Sergius martyrium, that is, basilica A.

In addition to walls, Procopius attests the existence in the mid sixth century of cisterns, stoas, houses, and other buildings characteristic of late Roman urban life. Urban amenities both impressed visitors and provided for them, and while the inhabitants of Rusafa reaped financial profit from the assured influx of visitors, they also bore the responsibility of furnishing the pilgrims with food, water, and beds. Although Procopius mentions only houses and "other structures," inns must have existed, and, in this case, common sense is supported by epigraphy.[161] Kollwitz in his excavation of the sixth-century level of basilica B discovered what seems to be an *enkolpion* referring to an ecclesiastical hostel of S. Sergius.[162] In addition, a two-storey

Croke and Crow, *JRS* 73 (1983): 143–59, reattribute Dara to Anastasius, although they are less successful in redating Rusafa's walls to the earlier emperor. But see also Whitby in *Defence*, 719, on the general difficulties of precise dating, and 724, with n. 8, on the problems of dating the walls and gates at Rusafa in particular.

156. Proc., *Aed.* 1.3.3.

157. See Harrison's review of Karnapp, *CR* 34 (1984): 106.

158. Brinker, *DaM* 5 (1991): 144; Ulbert, *Resafa*, 2: 147–48; Kollwitz in *Neue Deutsche Ausgrabungen*, 46.

159. Brands in *Spätantike und byzantinische Bauskulptur*, passim, esp. 72–74.

160. Brands, letter to the author, 7 December 1996.

161. Proc., *Aed.* 2.9.7.

162. Kollwitz, *AA* 1963: 357–78, fig. 20; Harrauer, *Tyche* 7 (1992): 43; Feissel and Gatier, *BE* 106 (1993): 558, no. 617. Cf. Zacos and Veglery, *Byzantine Lead Seals*, no. 1090A: ξενὼν ἁγίου Θεοδώρου and no. 1318a and b: ξενῶνος τοῦ ἁγίου Θεοδώρου.

khan whose earliest phase belongs to the sixth century, followed by a series of later additions and reconstructions, has been excavated on the main street leading from the north gate.[163] Naturally, in a steppe settlement, the most fundamental necessity for both pilgrims and residents was water. The brackish water drawn from wells provided for general water requirements, while the flask-shaped cisterns collected the rains that served the drinking-water needs of Rusafa from at least the Diocletianic phase. Flask-shaped cisterns have been found beneath basilica B and in the north courtyard of basilica A, and would have been used in private houses too.[164] In the mid sixth century, a water supply system was constructed, consisting of a dam west of the city walls, a main canal leading into the city between two towers and feeding the largest cistern in the southwestern quarter, and another cistern in the northwest. At the beginning of the seventh century, two more cisterns were added to the system, placed parallel to the great cistern in the southwest.[165] Clearly, great effort and expense went into these constructions. Besides the churches, it was the wells and cisterns of Rusafa that fascinated later Arab writers.[166] They were exceptional features at a steppe settlement too far from the Euphrates to exploit that source in any but the most exceptional circumstances.

The pilgrims who came to pray before Sergius's relics spread the martyr's fame and increased Rusafa's prosperity. Theodoret of Cyrrhus, a close friend of Alexander of Hierapolis, noted the rise of the Sergius cult at Rusafa in the context of more general remarks about the shift away from the gods of polytheism toward the cult of Christian saints. In the first half of the fifth century, Theodoret proclaimed that the old festivals, the Pandia,

163. Karnapp, *AA* 1978: 136–50.

164. Brinker, *DaM* 5 (1991): 123–25, 135–36.

165. Ibid., 124–46, esp. 135–43, on the canals and water collection. See also Kollwitz, *AA* 1965: 359. According to Brinker, *DaM* 5 (1991): 144–45, the total volume capacity of the cisterns would have been about 21,000 m^3, and this sixth-century system must have been in operation by 542, when Rusafa's inhabitants successfully withstood a siege by Khusrau I. The same argument has been used for the existence of the sixth-century walls by 542 (see Karnapp, *AA* 1970: 121). According to Proc., *BP* 2.20.14–15, Khusrau withdrew after a short siege because of lack of water for his troops, while according to Evagr., *HE* 4.28, S. Sergius miraculously saved the city. Neither outcome necessarily depended on a new water supply system within the walls. See Gatier, *DaM* 10 (1998): 237–40, for a dedicatory inscription of a δεξαμενή.

166. See Hamza al-Isfahani in Yaqut, *Mu'jam al-buldan* 3.47, where Hamza attributes the repair of Rusafa's cisterns to al-Nu'man ibn al-Harith. On the identity of this figure, see Kellner-Heinkele in Sack, *Resafa*, 4: 146 n. 114. Ibn Butlan in Yaqut, *Mu'jam al-buldan* 3.48, describes the cavernous underground cistern with its vaults and marble columns, like the church above ground; and al-Asma'i in Yaqut, *Mu'jam al-buldan* 3.47, notes that when, as sometimes happened in the summer, the cisterns ran dry, the wealthy inhabitants sent slaves with donkeys overnight to the Euphrates to fetch water.

Diasia, Dionysia, had been superseded by feasts in honor of Peter, Paul, and a company of Syrian martyrs, Thomas of Edessa, Sergius of Rusafa, Marcellinus, Antoninus, Mauricius of Apamea, Leontius of Tripoli.[167] At the beginning of the sixth century, Severus of Antioch in his homily on Sergius remarked how the Arabs from the region around Rusafa were drawn to Sergius's tomb to "take on the yoke of God," in other words, to be baptized.[168] Images of Sergius and his martyrdom, along with their exegesis, must have played a crucial role in conversion, but also in the maintenance of the cult.[169] This would have been the case particularly at Rusafa, where a wide variety of visitors converged, some of whom were surely drawn to enter the shrine out of curiosity. Unfortunately, no images have survived at Rusafa.[170] Gregory of Nyssa's portrait of the martyrium of another popular Eastern saint, Theodore of Euchaita, suggests what we should expect at Rusafa: the ornate decoration is described as "psychagogic," the mosaic floor deserves high praise, and the walls are painted with the martyr's *passiones*.[171] The *Acta* of Anastasius the Persian is one of many late antique accounts that link conversion with images. Anastasius's story is especially illuminating in the context of Rusafa's inevitable linguistic diversity. A defector from the Iranian army in the early seventh century, Anastasius settled in Hierapolis, where he, unfamiliar with Greek, apprenticed himself to a fellow Iranian goldsmith. This man was a Christian and introduced Anastasius to the martyrs of his religion through the wall paintings of his parish church.[172]

Although Sergius received visitors year-round, his annual feast must have provided the opportunity not just for a communal celebration, but for a market of notable size and diversity, which would have assembled around the fortified settlement located at a major crossroads. In the mid sixth century, Choricius of Gaza described the vibrant feast of S. Sergius celebrated at Gaza in terms that might also characterize the scene at Rusafa on Octo-

167. Theod., *Graec. aff. cur.* 8, p. 335.

168. Sev. Ant., *Hom. cath.* 57, p. 93; Kugener, *OC* 7 (1907): 408–12. For the use of yoke imagery for baptism, as well as the less probable use to indicate tonsure or marriage, see Lampe, *Lexicon*, s.v. ζυγός.

169. On the images of S. Sergius, see chapter 1.

170. Tesserae from the destroyed dome mosaic and traces of wall painting are discernible in the shrine north of the apse. Cf. also Ulbert in *Pietas*, 1562–63, where he discusses the sigma-shaped mensa plate of verde antico found in the last phase of the shrine. On the traces of mosaic decoration found in the basilica B trichoros, see Mundell in *Iconoclasm*, 67–69, who suggests on the basis of the colors of the fallen tesserae that the pattern was more probably floral than figural.

171. Greg. Nys., *De Sancto Theod.* 62–63.

172. *Acta Anast.* 8, with Flusin, *Saint Anastase*, 1: 50 n. 27 and 2: 228 n. 45, on the role of martyrdom depictions in conversions.

ber 7, noting that it took place "[d]uring the best time of the year, when the bodies are neither oppressed by cold nor enervated by heat, and when day and night have just made their truce with one another and agreed to have an equal share; when the weather is especially pleasant for everyone and gathers for us many people from everywhere, when there are no winter showers or the burning rage of the sun which ravage travellers."[173]

Already in the mid fourth century, bishops and others had attempted to exploit the overlapping of spiritual, social, commercial, and political interests at Christian feasts. Basil of Caesarea, for example, took the opportunity to extract favors for his clergy from government officials who were drawn to *panegyreis* along with the sick, the hopeful, and the ecclesiastical hierarchy.[174] He also warned against the excesses that came in the wake of the week-long festivities—bawdy mimes, dancing, and overindulgence of all varieties. That religious festivals inspire a wide range of activities—from divine visitations to daylight robbery—has always been the case. Some saw in the Arab conquest God's wrath against the Christians of Syria who instead of celebrating the martyrs' feasts with fasts, vigils, and psalms, indulged in drunkenness, dances, and other forms of debauchery.[175] From the many examples of late antique *panegyreis,* two in particular stand as close parallels for Rusafa's early autumn feast. Still in Sozomen's day, the Oak of Mamre near Hebron was the scene of annual summer festivities celebrated together by Christians, Jews, and polytheists: "the panegyris draws . . . locals and others from further afield, Palestinians, Phoenicians, and Arabs; many others, both buyers and sellers, gather there on account of the fair."[176] Similarly, Ammianus reported that merchants flocked to Batnae just west of the Euphrates for the yearly festival (*annua solemnitas*) held there in early September.[177] The celebration and accompanying market would spread out before and after the

173. Chor. Gazae, *Laud. Marc.* 1.14 (tr. Litsas). Litsas, *JÖB* 32 (1982): 430–31, searches through obscure Sergii and unusual festal dates for Sergius and Bacchus in order to find a date in late May for the Gaza feast of S. Sergius. Although the setting depicted could easily be in springtime, there is, in fact, no need to look beyond 7 October for a date that fits Choricius's description of the weather conditions.

174. Basil, *Ep.* 142, 2.64–65; *Hom. in divites* 80–81 (*PG* 31.281c; 31.1020b–d), on the mercantile dimension of martyrs' *panegyreis,* a characteristic feature also of pre-Christian festivals. See also Mitchell, *Anatolia,* 2: 69–70.

175. Mich. Syr., *Chron.* 11.7 (2.422, tr. Chabot).

176. Soz., *HE* 2.4.1–3. On the tree's environment, see Hepper and Gibson, *PEQ* 126 (1994): 94–105.

177. "[A] great crowd of every condition gathers for the fair, to traffic in the wares sent from India and China, and in other articles that are regularly brought there in great abundance by land and sea." (Amm. Marc. 14.3.3, tr. Rolfe). See also Amm. Marc. 18.9.13, on the annual fair in Amida's suburbs, which drew the region's peasants as well as foreign merchants. For another festival held in honor of the saints at Arsamosata, see *Chron. Edessa of 506* 261–62, p. 193.

religious climax, and one can easily imagine the merchants traveling with great profit from feast to feast, as they still do, for example, in modern Greece.[178]

The martyrium of S. Sergius at Rusafa had by the sixth century become one of the major eastern shrines included on late antique pilgrimage itineraries. On a grand tour of eastern martyrs, for example, the monk John, who made his home in a cave in the Judaean wilderness, visited S. John at Ephesus, S. Theodore at Euchaita, S. Thecla at Seleucia, and S. Sergius at Rusafa.[179] There is no doubt that Rusafa was a major shrine. But Rusafa's setting in the steppe necessarily influenced its everyday clientele, made up primarily of the mobile population of Syria and Mesopotamia, merchants, pastoralists, even migrant workers whose path brought them to the shrine.[180] The majority of late antique pilgrims' accounts of eastern holy places were written by Westerners, which helps to explain their occasional confusion in the face of so many exotic places and their stories. Rather than itineraries and narrative descriptions, the student of eastern Christian pilgrimage is often obliged to piece together more scattered evidence—references in saints' lives, homilies on martyrs and saints, and inscriptions left at holy sites. The heterogeneity of this evidence should cause us to reflect on the variety of pilgrims and their ways of encountering the shrine at Rusafa. To begin with, many eastern pilgrims to Rusafa did not share the western pilgrims' habit of recording their observations in writing. Many of the eastern pilgrims were pastoral Arabs.[181] Pilgrimage for easterners was often an accompaniment of journeys taken for other reasons, such as trade or seasonal migration with flocks of sheep, goats and camels.

As has been noted already, Rusafa lay on the natural route for migration dictated by the existence of a major pass through the steep-sided Jabal Bishri and Jabal Abu Rujmayn. The concluding section of the *Passio* states that at the time of the feast on 7 October, wild animals were wont to gather at Rusafa. It was at precisely this time that the seasonal rains were expected to begin and that wild animals, especially gazelle, as well as pastoralists, would be migrating southward from summer pastures north of the mountains to winter pastures in the Syro-Arabian desert.[182] The addition of this

178. Tardieu, *Paysages*, 13–14, notes that the major Syrian *panegyreis*, including one at Salaminias, occurred during the summer season, which extends into late September.

179. Joh. Mosch., *Prat. spirit.* 180 (*PG* 87.3.3052b).

180. A wealthy man from Sheba learned from merchants of the healing powers of S. Symeon on his pillar (Syriac *Vita Sim.* 79). Bowersock in *Archéologie*, 68, draws attention to a fleeting reference to harvesters working southeast of Palmyra; for the Palmyrene inscription, see Teixidor, *Syria* 40 (1963): 33–37, esp. 34–35.

181. Theophyl., *Hist.* 5.1.7: Sergius "whom the nomad tribes are also wont to revere."

182. For discussion of these migration routes, see G. Fowden in *Roman and Byzantine Near East*, 2: 121–27.

detail by the *Passio*'s author lends credibility to his local knowledge, at least at the time of composition in the fifth century. Rusafa's place in this landscape at the convergence of wadis north of the main pass, suggests that it may also have served as a sanctuary for animals, who would have been protected here by the saint from slaughter during their seasonal migrations.[183]

These physical conditions of Rusafa's setting combined to make it a natural site for a *haram*—a hallowed space carefully demarcated and maintained, usually by a particular tribe for whom the privilege was hereditary.[184] A *haram* might be considered sacred by association with a holy tree or spring, but most often it was centered on the tomb of a holy man, a saint. Usually it occupied a strategic position, most commonly at a source of water near a crossroads.[185] It was a natural magnet for the region and usually the site of a market. The *haram* was also understood to be neutral ground where conflicting parties could meet and seek resolution of their disagreement. And it was often an asylum for animals. The tomb might be open-air or covered with a simple building. The authority of the saint was the backdrop for all activity that transpired at the site: judgments, business deals, social agreements. The *haram* was not simply a saint's tomb; it was a sacrosanct site, distinguished by the saint's presence, where worldly leaders exercised their authority under the saint's protection.

It is clear that the pilgrims who congregated at Rusafa to stand in the saint's presence cannot easily be typecast. The faint traces that they have left behind convey at least an outline of the people who sought the martyr's help—but also of the saintly company Sergius kept. Among the graffiti that anticipant pilgrims carved on the walls of the northern annex, while waiting just outside Sergius's martyrium, Syriac and Arabic messages seem to have been mixed in with Greek. Unfortunately, the non-Greek graffiti are illegible today, with the exception of two late Arabic inscriptions.[186] The

183. In *RE*, 2A: 1684–85, Honigmann notes the emphasis given in the *Passio* to Sergius's power over animals, an attribute the Christian saint shared with the Arab god ʿAziz. For other similarities between these two, see above, pp. 40–42. It would not have been unusual if animals were also brought to the saint for healing, as at the shrine of S. Thecla (*Mir. Theclae* 36). Cf. also Evagr., *HE* 1.14, where it is reported that pilgrims would circumambulate the column of S. Symeon with their beasts of burden. In the medieval Greek epic *Digenis Akritis* (Grottaferrata 3.141), Mecca is evoked as a sanctuary for animals, as well as pilgrims.

184. Donner, *Early Islamic Conquests*, 34–37; Serjeant, *Studies in Arabian History* III. It is a matter of ongoing debate just how far back the *haram* tradition reaches, although few would doubt the existence of such a pattern in the pre-Islamic steppe and desert.

185. In the modern period, beduin gathered in the steppe year after year at the same site. A well or cistern, caves or ancient buildings usually marked the frequented spot, which would be used while they waited for the next seasonal signs for migration: see, e.g., Lewis, *Nomads and Settlers*, 127–29.

186. Khoury in *Resafa*, 2: 179–81, publishes the Arabic inscriptions. Syriac graffiti noted in *AAS* 33.2 (1983): 70, were not published in *Resafa*, vol. 2. On the important differ-

name Sergius is recorded as Sergios and Sergis.[187] Some of the names carved in Greek on the wall are clearly of Semitic origin: Abbibas, Salmis, Marousa.[188] The frequency of the name Symeon may reflect the popularity of the famous Syrian saint, who, according to the accounts of his life, was especially beloved by Arab pastoralists.[189] Not all of the names belonged to the pilgrims themselves. Some seem to evoke saints—such as John and Thecla, whose shrines, along with Sergius's, had been numbered by John Moschus among the East's greatest. The martyr Sergius was anything but isolated in his Barbarian Plain, where Arab raiders threatened caravan trade and faint-hearted pilgrims. His shrine had grown over the course of two and a half centuries into a stable center within a complex network of routes, which joined often dissimilar regions both within and without Syria and Mesopotamia.

---

ences in the uses to which various scripts found in Syria were put, see the excellent article by Macdonald, *Syria* 70 (1993): 303–88, esp. 382–88.

187. Römer in *Resafa,* 2: 173, no. 17; 175, no. 41. On Arabic and Syriac forms of Greek Sergios, see Gero in *Syrie,* 51 n. 24.

188. Römer in *Resafa,* 2: 171–77. See Gatier, *Inscriptions,* 2: 69, 97; Sartre, *Bostra,* 215, 236; Wuthnow, *Semitischen Menschennamen,* 7, 103; with Macdonald's cautionary discussion of the difficulties involved in distinguishing different Semitic names from a consonantal skeleton and identifying that skeleton with a Greek version (*Syria* 70 [1993]: 378–79).

189. Römer in *Resafa,* 2: 172; *Vita Sim. Styl.* (Syriac) 67, 77; Theod., *HR* 13,16,18, with Canivet's comments.

FOUR

The Spread of the Sergius Cult in Syria and Mesopotamia

Abba Sergius, a sixth-century anchorite in Sinai, was traveling with a party of mules and muleteers when they came face to face with a lion. Before the lion had an opportunity to seize its prey, Abba Sergius stepped forward, held out a piece of bread, an *eulogion,* and ordered the beast to move off the track. Sated by this substitute, the lion allowed the party to carry on its way.[1] Lions, raids, heat, and cold were the obstacles that travelers encountered along waterless tracks, not only in the Sinai wilderness, but across Syria and Mesopotamia too.[2] Shelters from these threats, such as the monastery of Saint Catherine in Sinai, were bolstered by saints' relics. At shrines, travelers would pray for the saints' guidance and protection. Many Christian travelers carried with them from their baptism the name of a saint: "and to their children they take care to give the names of these [martyrs], engineering for them in this way security and protection."[3] The dramatic rise of Sergius's popularity, apparent in personal names and church dedications, reflects the sixth-century growth of belief in Sergius's power as protector.

From the early sixth century, the name Sergius was commonly borne by men of religious vocation. A deacon Sergius from Amida oversaw Anastasius's fortification of Dara.[4] A presbyter named Sergius co-built a church dedicated to S. George at ʿAmra, west of Maximianopolis / Shaqqa in the

---

1. Joh. Mosch., *Prat. spir.* 125.

2. On the threat of raids in the Sinai peninsula, see Gatier in *L'Arabie préislamique,* 499–523. Lions still posed a threat to inhabitants of and travelers in the middle Euphrates region in the last century. Blunt, *Bedouins of the Euphrates,* 1: 89–93, describes an attack in 1878.

3. Theod., *Graec. aff. cur.* 8.334.

4. *Chronicle of Amida of 569* 7.6.

Hawran.[5] East of Emesa, the area of Salaminias was served by a periodeute and also by a chorepiscopus, both named Sergius.[6] Further east and a century later, Rabban Sargis, "destroyer of the mighty," recorded the history of the Nestorian holy men of Beth Garmai, the central Mesopotamian region north and east of Takrit.[7] Sergii also rose to sit on patriarchal thrones: in Antioch from 557 to 560 and in Constantinople under Heraclius (Sergius I, 610–38); while Sergius of Rome, who reigned between 687 and 701, was one of five Syrians who took their place on Peter's throne between 686 and 730. It was this Pope Sergius who introduced to Rome the cult of the Holy Cross.[8]

By the early sixth century, bearers of the name Sergius had risen to high positions outside ecclesiastical circles too. The *Prosopography of the Later Roman Empire* reveals a dramatic increase in the name's attestation among higher-ranking officials between the late fifth and the early seventh centuries: from two Sergii between 260 and 395 to nine between 395 and 527, and to fifty-five attested between 527 and 641. Since the name Sergius was already attached to a famous Roman family in the Republican period, not every Sergius necessarily owed his appellation to the saint. This seems to be the case with the earliest attestations in the *Prosopography*.[9] But the great popularity of the name in the East, attained over a short period of time, strongly associates the increase with the growth of the Sergius cult. A debt to the Syro-Mesopotamian saint is certain in some cases, such as Sergius, son of Bacchus, who from his birthplace near Dara became a governor of Tripolitania and by 559 had been made *patricius*.[10] The family of another prominent Sergius came from Rusafa—the father of this Sergius had probably become a *vir illustris* at Edessa, where in 590 he vied with Edessa's elite in banqueting the fugitive Khusrau II. The son Sergius was later taken hostage by the same Iranian despot, but spent his time among Khusrau's inner circle until he returned to Edessa, most likely after the truce with Heraclius in 628–29.[11] In the early to mid sixth century, Sergius of Rhesaina, also in northern Syria-Mesopotamia, rose to fame as a medical doctor and theologian.[12] Another Sergius, probably also a Syrian, was prized by Khusrau I as

5. Waddington, *Inscriptions*, no. 2092. Sartre, *IGLS* 13.197 n. 3, mistakenly includes this church in a list of dedications to Sergius in the Hawran.

6. *IGLS*, no. 2517, for the periodeute; Lucas, in von Oppenheim and Lucas, *BZ* 14 (1905): 29, for the chorepiscopus, whose inscription is dated to 564.

7. Thomas of Marga, *Book of Governors* 1.33.

8. Bishop, *Liturgica historica*, 144–46.

9. E.g., *PLRE*, 1: 826. Like any prosopography, the *Prosopography of the Later Roman Empire* must be used with discretion: see Barnish, *JRS* 84 (1994): 171–77, esp. 175.

10. *PLRE*, 3: 1124–28.

11. Ibid., 681, for the father, Ioannes 102, and 1133, for Sergius 38.

12. Ibid., 1123–34, Sergius 1.

an interpreter and relied on by Agathias as a translator of Iranian royal archives.[13] Less glamorous jobs were held by other Syrian Sergii—one was a baker at Constantia / Viranşehir east of Edessa; another was a stone cutter at Maximianopolis / Shaqqa in the Hawran.[14] On a church floor at Dionysias / Suwayda, south of Maximianopolis, a full-length mosaic portrait commemorates a Sergius, probably an important local donor.[15] In various oriental Christian versions of the Bahira legend, the name Sergius, or Sergius-Bahira, is given to the famous monk who discerns in the young Muhammad his as yet unrevealed identity as the Prophet.[16] Sergius, or rather, Sarjis, was a popular name among Arab Christians: "I was a Christian called Sarjis, the surest and best guide in the sandy desert," explains an early follower of Muhammad in Ibn Ishaq's *Life of the Prophet.* "During the pagan period [*jahiliya*] I used to bury water which I had put in ostrich shells in various places in the desert and then raid men's camels. When I had got them into the sand, I was safely in possession of them and none dared follow me thither. Then I would go to the places where I had concealed the water and drink it."[17]

A saint's name could be grafted onto a family tree and reappear generation after generation, as once purely secular names had. The name's original association might become dissipated through force of habit. But name-giving in late antique Syria and Mesopotamia must be seen in the context of the saints' annual festivals. No evidence could prove that each Sergius thought of the martyr Sergius as his personal patron simply because his parents had chosen to give him the name. Nonetheless, the calendar of religious feasts that punctuated late antique conceptions of time forced on the bearers of such an important saint's name a consciousness of their name's history. Names, especially saints' names, carried powerful associations, and popular names in particular should be read as indicators of cultural trends. It was not coincidence that joined the widespread adoption of the name Sergius from the late fifth through the early seventh centuries with other

13. Ibid., 1129, Sergius 9. Cameron, *DOP* 23–24 (1969–70): 162, discusses the Syrian origin of Sergius; see Agathias, *Hist.* 4.30.284–300; also *PLRE,* 3: 1124, Sergius 3, an Edessene envoy to Iran in 543, 544–45.

14. Lucas, in von Oppenheim and Lucas, *BZ* 14 (1905): 61, no. 96, for the ἀρτοκόπος; Waddington, *Inscriptions,* no. 2162, for the stone carver.

15. The figure has been variously interpreted: see Donceel-Voûte, *Pavements,* 310–13, with fig. 305. This selection attempts to represent the variety, but by no means the quantity, of Syrians and Mesopotamians named Sergius in late antiquity. Clerics named Sergius appear frequently in the *Synodicon orientale.* See also the examples cited by Poidebard and Mouterde, *AB* 67 (1949): 113–14. The female form Sergia is also recorded. A Sergia wrote *De translatione Sanctae Olympiadis,* and another is mentioned in a dedication in the so-called Riha treasure (Mundell Mango, *Silver,* no. 35).

16. For the oriental sources, see Gero in *Syrie,* 47–58.

17. Ibn Ishaq, *Sirat* 985, p. 668 (tr. Guillaume).

signs of the growth of the martyr Sergius's reputation, such as building projects at Rusafa and the spread of sanctuary dedications beyond the cult center. That a name could reflect a political and religious climate is clearly illustrated by the frequent adoption of names such as Mu'awiya, Yazid, and Walid in Umayyad Syria. The choice of these names expressed engagement with the current political and religious situation. The Umayyad caliphate offered a new set of names that stood in deliberate contrast to names such as 'Ali, Hasan, or Husayn, which were seldom given in Syria, but common in Egypt.[18]

Sergius's name, whether simply chosen at baptism, or carried on the lips of pilgrims, was the most mobile accessory in the martyr's cult. Its use in dedications must serve as tracing dye in any attempt to recapture the cult's spread. A bird's-eye view of Syro-Mesopotamian dedications to Sergius at the time of the erection of basilica B at Rusafa in 518 describes a great arc, from the Hawran southwest of Rusafa through the villages east of the Anti-Lebanon and continuing along the southern foothills of the Taurus mountains. At that time, starting in the southwest and traveling clockwise among dated inscriptions only,[19] Umm al-Surab had a church of Sergius and Bacchus from 489, while Bostra's cathedral honored Sergius, Bacchus, and Leontius in 512/13. In northeastern Hawran, a well-preserved inscription records a martyrium of Sergius in 517 at Raham,[20] and at the same date, on the southern edge of the rocky basalt Laja, a temple to Sergius is recorded at Busr al-Hariri. Moving further northward, Severus of Antioch preached at the Sergius church of Chalcis in 514, while Zabad in the basalt country southeast of Chalcis honored Sergius with a martyrium in 512. West of Edessa, near modern Nizip, a Sergius church was consecrated in the village of Söğütlü as early as 431. No evidence of dedications east of Edessa before 518 has been discovered, but the eastern arm of this arc of dedications would begin to take form by the middle of the century.

What follows is an attempt to evoke from a selection of dedications in late antique Syria and Mesopotamia a picture of where the cult of Sergius was spread, by whom, and for what reasons. A striking characteristic of the Sergius cult that will emerge from this overview is the cult's adaptability to the distinctive Syro-Mesopotamian landscape and the various populations inhabiting it. Springing from Rusafa, the cult was woven into pastoral migration and trade patterns, defense organization, and the fabric of monastic and village life. The densest cluster of surviving dedications from the late fifth and early sixth centuries is found in the Hawran and the zone

---

18. Gilliot, *Arabica* 40 (1993): 357–58.

19. Bibliography appears with the discussion of individual sites, with the exception of Raham, which is only mentioned here.

20. On Raham, see Dunand in *Mélanges syriens,* 571, no. 290.

from Salaminias to Chalcis. In these areas, as we saw in chapter 3, agricultural and pastoral societies overlapped, and both regions were touched by much-traveled trade routes.[21] One of the great nodes along the routes in Syria was the city of Damascus. On the *decumanus,* the famous "Street called Straight," a shrine (ναός) dedicated to Rusafa's martyr had already been established before the fifth- or sixth-century widening of the road that absorbed part of the shrine.[22]

THE HAWRAN

South of Damascus and its oasis, the Ghuta, the Hawran plain provided an environment suitable for both pastoralism and agriculture.[23] At the village of Eitha / Hit, northwest of Maximianopolis, the deacon and oikonomos Sabinianos built a church dedicated to Sergius and dated it by reference to a trio of local clergymen: an archimandrite who was also a priest, another priest, and a deacon.[24] The presence of an archimandrite suggests that the church belonged to a monastery.[25] What is most intriguing about the inscription is its date, which, according to Waddington, reads ἔτους σμθ' μ[η]ν(ὶ) Μαρτί(ῳ) (March 249). Waddington assumed that the date is to be reckoned according to the calendar of Provincia Arabia and arrived at a date of 22–31 March 354 or 1–21 March 355 of the Christian era, making the Sergius sanctuary at Eitha one of the earliest-known examples of a building dedicated to the memory of any saint at a site other than that of his or her martyrdom. In this case, it would have been only four decades after Sergius's death under the tetrarchy, according to the *Passio* tradition. The date 354 has been almost universally accepted, usually without any refer-

21. Donner in *Tradition and Innovation,* 73–85, and *Conquests,* 16–20, esp. 16 n. 5, provides a succinct discussion of social, economic and political interrelations of settled, seminomadic, and nomadic populations.

22. The shrine is mentioned in the *Vita* of S. Stephen of the Saba monastery, the eighth-century hymnographer and nephew of S. John of Damascus, *Acta Sanct. Jul.* 3.555 §61. See Sack, *Damaskus,* 16, with a plan of late Roman Damascus in fig. 5. Will, *Syria* 71 (1994): 16 with n. 38, considers the shrine, known as the Maqsallat al-Baris, in the context of the city plan of Damascus.

23. Villeneuve, *Hauran,* 1: 121–25; Bauzou in *Hauran,* 1: 158. For a general account of Hawranian architecture, see Farioli Campanati, *Felix Ravenna* 141–44 (1991–92): 177–232.

24. Waddington, *Inscriptions,* no. 2124. I am indebted to Kalliope Kritikakou for discussing the problems of Syrian calendars with me, with special reference to Eitha/Hit. I would also like to thank Maurice Sartre for his comments on my interpretation of the Eitha inscriptions and for sending his most recent view, which is in agreement with my own.

25. Sartre, *IGLS* 13.197 n. 3, identifies the church as monastic, presumably because of the inclusion of an archimandrite in the inscription. The inscription does not allude to a monastery or the type of sanctuary dedicated, but employs the general term ἱερόν.

ence to its uncertainty.[26] In 1982, Maurice Sartre consulted the stone again and read the date not as CMΘ, as had Waddington, but as CME, with the result that the date, if reckoned according to the era of Provincia Arabia, would be March 350–51, instead of Waddington's 354–55.[27] Still, either of these dates in the 350s would be the second-earliest attestation of the use of Roman months with the chronological system of Provincia Arabia. The earliest was found southeast of Bostra at Imtan, the site of a Roman fort and explicable by that association.[28] No other inscription from Eitha uses the era of Provincia Arabia,[29] and also unusual for the mid fourth century is the accumulation of clerical names. The earliest-known evidence of a bishop at either Maximianopolis or Philippopolis / Shahba is their attendance at the Council of Chalcedon in 451—but lack of earlier evidence does not necessarily mean lack of a bishop. Nevertheless, a date according to the era of Provincia Arabia would place Eitha at the forefront of various trends, not only reception of the Sergius cult, but also the honoring of any martyr with a church, and the use of Roman months and ecclesiastical titles in inscriptions. This accumulation of irregularities certainly seems to demand some explanation.

It is not out of the question that the cult of Rusafa's martyr had begun to spread by the mid fourth century and that the earliest surviving material evidence comes from Eitha, located between the Laja and the Jabal Hawran near the two main roads linking Damascus and Bostra. But as Honigmann pointed out in a review of Robert Devreesse's *Le Patriarcat d'Antioch* in 1947, a calculation of the inscription's date according to the local era of Maximianopolis would place the dedication in the mid sixth century, where it would correspond to the known development of martyr cult in general, and that of the veneration of Sergius in particular.[30] The era of Maximianopolis begins either in 287 or 302, which would mean that the Sergius church at

---

26. To their credit, Poidebard and Mouterde, *AB* 67 (1949): 112 n. 8, note that the date is suspect. Meimaris with Kritikakou and Bougia, *Chronological Systems,* 154, acknowledge the unusual features of the early date, stating that the alternative to the era of Provincia Arabia would be a local era; but they conclude in favor of 354. Before revising his reading of the inscription, Sartre, *Bostra,* 121 n. 184, took the early date as certain : "Pour ne parler que de celles où une inscription permet d'assurer la date, mentionnons l'église Saint-Serge de Hit, vers 354 au plus tard." Trombley, *Hellenic Religion,* 2: 343–44, 373–74, who also accepts 354, is silent about the problems surrounding the date.

27. Sartre, letter to the author, 30 January 1997.

28. Waddington, *Inscriptions,* no. 2037; Meimaris with Kritikakou and Bougia, *Chronological Systems,* 154, 190.

29. Sartre underlines this point, noting that other inscriptions at Hit employ royal or imperial dating systems (ibid.).

30. Honigmann, *Traditio* 5 (1947): 159–60.

Eitha was dedicated in either 536/37 or 551/52, dates coinciding with the period of greatest building activity in honor of Sergius in the Hawran, according to known inscriptions.[31] It was a time when Roman months were commonly in use in inscriptions, as well as the clerical titles that appear in the Eitha dedication. In the light of other inscriptions from Maximianopolis, we might expect an inscription dated by the local era to be marked by ἔτους τῆς πόλεως, which is lacking from the Eitha inscription. But the use of this phrase is by no means systematic.[32] No other inscriptions have been discovered outside the city of Maximianopolis that are dated by that city's era. However, Eitha's proximity to Maximianopolis, only a few kilometers to the southeast, makes the possibility of attraction to that city's era very likely. The historical context is weighted heavily against the early date. The argument for a sixth-century date according to the Maximianopolis calendar would be further strengthened by new evidence, such as whether or not Eitha belonged to the territorium or ecclesiastical jurisdiction of Maximianopolis. Nonetheless, it should be clear that no arguments for the precocious spread of the Sergius cult in the Hawran can be based on the evidence from Eitha.

Situated on the road between Mushannaf and Bostra, the village of Kafr boasted several churches. In 1939, Maurice Dunand published an inscription whose damaged second line begins with space for two or three letters followed by PΓΙΩ, and could allude to the popular martyr George just as well as Sergius. Dunand did not note the possibility of reading George, and his [Σε]ργίῳ has been accepted without comment in subsequent publications.[33] However, already at the time of Dunand's publication another

---

31. Meimaris with Kritikakou and Bougia, *Chronological Systems*, 321–23. Koder and Restle, *JÖB* 42 (1992): 79–81, are unaware of the solid arguments for 287 or 302 for the beginning of the era of Shaqqa put forward by Jones, *Cities*, 465 n. 82, and discussed at length by Robert, *Hellenica* 11–12 (1960): 306–15. The problem has been discussed more recently in Meimaris with Kritikakou and Bougia, *Chronological Systems*. Koder and Restle, who date the beginning of the era of Shaqqa to 286, do not in their brief discussion even raise the vital issue of which calendar was used in the inscriptions dated by the era of Shaqqa. The crux of the problem for the Eitha inscription (if we accept that it employs the era of Shaqqa, as I believe we should), as for all inscriptions dated by the era of Shaqqa, is our ignorance of which calendar was used—either the Graeco-Arabic, which began on 22 March, or the Julian, which began on 1 January. For this reason, the question of whether the era of Shaqqa began in 286 or 287 must still remain open.

32. I thank both Glen Bowersock and Maurice Sartre for insisting on this point. Sartre observes that in neighboring villages, such as ʿAmra and Hayat, the use of the provincial era is made explicit, in order, it seems, to draw attention to the exceptional use of that era. The implication of this practice is that usually a local era would be expected.

33. Dunand in *Mélanges syriens*, 559, no. 245 with drawing; followed by Poidebard and Mouterde, *AB* 67 (1949): 112; Devreesse, *Patriarcat*, 231; Sartre, *IGLS* 13.197 n. 3.

inscription was known that attests the dedication of a church to S. George at Kafr in 652. Unless the village possessed two churches dedicated to S. George, Dunand's interpretation was justified.[34] The inscription published by Dunand attracted the attention of Robert and Aigrain for its unusual use of μάγαρον for the building dedicated to Sergius.[35] Aigrain explains the rare usage as another instance of Christian absorption of a pre-Christian name of a holy place, such as ἱερόν, ναός and μεμώριον—all of which are likewise attested in the Hawran in the context of the Sergius cult.[36] Other names used to mark Sergius dedications in Syria-Mesopotamia are ἐκκλησία, οἶκος, εὐκτήριον and μαρτύριον.

In the foothills of Jabal Hawran, two monasteries were dedicated to Sergius. The first inscription was found in situ over a door in the ruined buildings of Dayr al-Qadi, west of Suwayda.[37] The undated metrical dedication commemorates in archaizing style renovations made to the sanctuary of Sergius: μάρτυρι Σεργίῳ περικαλλέα νηὸν ὀπάσας. East of Salkhad, at Dayr al-Nasrani, another lintel, this one found on the ground near the eastern entrance of the monastery courtyard, preserves in a partially illegible inscription a prayer to the "God of Sergius and Bacchus."[38] Seen in conjunction with the three crosses etched across an inscription that Αβδοβαλος (that is ʿAbd Baʿal, servant of Baal) carved over the door of a tower later incorporated into the monastery, the Christian prayer proclaims forthrightly that the God of Sergius and Bacchus has supplanted the region's older god, Baal.[39]

South of Dayr al-Nasrani, another dedication was made to the pair Sergius and Bacchus. Umm al-Surab, on the road leading from Bostra to Gerasa, twelve kilometers northwest of Umm al-Jimal, preserves the basalt remnants of a prosperous late antique village. The dedicatory inscription, carved on a *tabula ansata* flanked by two damaged crosses, still stands over

34. Brünnow and Domaszewski, *Provincia Arabia*, 3: 360.

35. Robert, *Bull.* (1940): 232, no. 189; Aigrain, *OCP* 13 (1947): 22–24. Both Robert and Aigrain accept Dunand's reading.

36. In general, Christian use of μεμώριον is only rarely attested in the Hawran, although it is common in Syria and Palestine for Christian and Jewish tombs. More common in the Hawran are μνῆμα and μνημεῖον, the latter attested twenty-eight times (Sartre, *Bostra*, 38–39).

37. Waddington, *Inscriptions*, no. 2412.

38. *PAES*, 3A5: 333–34, no. 722, with drawing, where Littmann reads the dedication to the "God of Sergius and Bacchus" in the first line and the first half of the second line. Only the first two letters of the first line were legible to Dussaud and Macler, *Nouvelles archives* 10 (1902), no. 48, with drawing. Littmann's reading also diverges significantly from that of Dussaud and Macler. For one of many examples of this phrase, see Mundell Mango, *Silver*, 256, no. 85: "The God of S. George"; and for a general discussion, see Peterson, *Εἷς θεός*, 210–12.

39. *PAES*, 3A5: 334, no. 723; *PAES*, 2A5: 334–35, on the tower's incorporation and the possibility that the site was formerly a polytheist high place.

the western entrance of Umm al-Surab's largest church.[40] The benefactors were Ameras and Kyros, sons of Ulpianos, although Littmann's restoration of (A)μεϱας is conjectural.[41] Littmann's suggested reading of the date as 489 is accepted in the recent publications of Sartre and King.[42] The ruins at Umm al-Surab include two undated churches in addition to the Sergius and Bacchus church, and many examples of domestic architecture, much of which has been modified over centuries of habitation, which continues today.[43] Howard Crosby Butler described the basalt church of Sergius and Bacchus, which he thought it one of the most interesting in the southern Hawran, as "medium-size."[44] In form, it is a three-aisled basilica with two rows of five columns, which supported a gallery. Three doors in the western façade opened onto the aisles, the façade was sheltered by a portico, and the main entrance was flanked on either side by a *kolymbion*, a basin for blessed water. Above the door was the inscription. The dreary effect of so much basalt was relieved by painting and mosaic, traces of which have been found in the church.[45] To the north and south of the church extend courtyards surrounded by small buildings. Butler is silent about the southern courtyard, but interpreted the northern complex as "the complete domestic establishment of an ecclesiastical community." However, King has recently called into question the architectural and chronological unity of the northern structures and their relation to the church.[46] Both Butler and King agree that the church of Sergius and Bacchus was perhaps already converted into a mosque and fitted with a minaret under the Umayyads.[47]

Moving west of Bostra, a cluster of villages allied themselves with Rusafa's martyr in the last decade of the sixth century. Ghasm, on the road between Bostra and Darʿa, commemorated Sergius and Bacchus together in a

40. *PAES*, 3A2: 57–58, no. 51, with drawing. The building's dedication to SS. Sergius and Bacchus is clear on the inscription, but the beginning of l. 4, where the type of building was named, is damaged and only an initial μ can be read. Littmann restored the word as μ[νημεῖον]. See above for the frequency of this term in the Hawran. For a discussion of the architecture with reconstructions, see *PAES*, 2A2: 94–99.

41. Sartre, *Bostra*, 174–75, endorses Littmann's reading without mentioning that it is a conjecture, and considers it a unique variant of the Semitic name Amerus, especially popular in the Hawran. Trombley, *Hellenic Religion*, 2: 321–22, also generalizes from the inscription without qualification.

42. Sartre, *Bostra*, 197 n. 3; King, *DaM* 1 (1983): 112, 116; King, *DaM* 3 (1988): 47, 50.

43. On the two churches, see King, *DaM* 3 (1988): 40–51. Butler, *PAES*, 2A2: 95, describes Nabataean and early Roman epigraphical and architectural fragments from Umm al-Surab, whose remains are primarily late antique.

44. *PAES*, 2A2: 96.

45. King, *DaM* 1 (1983): 117, 125–26.

46. *PAES*, 2A2: 99; King, *DaM* 1 (1983): 124.

47. King, *DaM* 1 (1983): 133–36.

μεμώριον, where relics of the saints were perhaps revered.[48] The inscription, found reused as part of a manger, dates the original building to 593. Straddling the Wadi al-Zaydi, the village of Jiza has produced two dedicatory inscriptions: one for a church of Theodore, and one for Sergius—the word used in both cases is ναός.[49] The Sergius consecration is dated to 590. At Tayyiba, where a bridge dated to the reign of Marcus Aurelius carried the Bostra-Darʿa road across the Wadi al-Zaydi, a church (ναός) was built in 589 to 590, possibly to Sergius, but damage to the inscription's first line makes that reading conjectural.[50] And a fourth, but undated, dedication was recorded in this small area—this one called a martyrium of Sergius, at the non-Chalcedonian monastery of ʿAllmat.[51]

A remarkable lintel inscription found in Zorava/Azraʿ, at the southern limit of the Laja, was published with commentary by Claude Mondésert in 1960.[52] Discovered in situ, having been missed by earlier scholars, its fourteen lines tell with striking poetic style the story of the dedicant's devotion to Sergius and that martyr's passion and victory:

And now, seeing the power of the savior, master, God,
glorify the holy king, who has destroyed the works of idols.
For this house was once adorned with images of demons
and bound by rough stones, which the logos of Christ
has freed and has reestablished, with finely polished stone,
the house of his servant, the well-mounted Sergius,
through the zeal and efforts of the children of noble Theodore,
who desired to have Sergius himself as their divine defender,
he who spurned worldly authority,
and accepted bitter tortures from head to foot.
Although his feet were pierced with nails, he did not spare his head,
but having given his spirit unto his master and savior, he delivered it up
    to death,
and in exchange for a worldly life, received his portion of celestial life.

The inscription falls into three interrelated parts. The first six lines allude to the erection of a church on the site of a polytheist temple. In this category it joins the better known church of S. George also at Zorava, where Christians still worship today, as well as another church of S. Sergius, also on

---

48. *PAES*, 3A5: 278–79, no. 619.

49. Savignac and Abel, *RB* 2 (1905): 597–98.

50. Dussaud and Macler, *Nouvelles archives* 10 (1902): 693, no. 155, for the possible Sergius inscription, no. 154 for the bridge. The drawing of the church dedication shows CEB, whereas Dussaud and Macler read Σε[ργίου].

51. In the so-called "Letter of the Archimandrites," in *Documenta* 218 (tr. Chabot, 151–52). For other Sergius monasteries mentioned in the letter, as well as general comments on the *Documenta*, see below, pp. 143n.45, 144.

52. Mondésert, *Syria* 37 (1960): 125–30.

the edge of the Laja but to the east, at Busr al-Hariri.[53] The verbal image of Sergius as a horseman is a welcome partner to the visual representation of the rider saint found on the metal medallions, the seal, and the stone mold discussed earlier. This image is immediately followed in lines seven and eight by the church's benefactors—the children of Theodore—who chose the cavalier saint expressly for his power as a divine defender.[54]

What follows in the last six lines is a distilled version of Sergius's martyr-dom along the lines of the *Passio,* punctuated by carefully weighted con-trasts, as elsewhere in the inscription: Sergius renounces earthly power; he undergoes ruthless punishment with nails in his feet; he surrenders his body to be killed, but receives his heavenly reward.[55] This inscription bears witness to the circulation in the Hawran of the story as told in the written *Passio.* Since the *Passio* has been shown in chapter 1 to date from after the 430s, the erection of the otherwise undated church must belong to the late fifth or sixth century, the most intense phase of the cult's dissemination.

Between September 512 and March 513, Archbishop Julian of Bostra consecrated a church (ἅγιος ναός) near the Arabian capital's center—a tetraconch in form with echoes of Mesopotamian architectural style.[56] The church bore a unique dedication—to SS. Sergius, Bacchus, and Leontius. The soldier who joined Sergius and Bacchus was martyred at Phoenician Tripolis (modern Tripoli in Lebanon), possibly in the reign of Trajan.[57] Two churches in the Hawran were dedicated to Leontius: one in 483 at Dur, southeast of Busr al-Hariri, and the other in 565 at Sur in Auranitis.[58] Also, Justinian built a church (οἶκος) dedicated to Leontius in Damascus.[59] Known dedications to Leontius were concentrated in southern Syria and the coastal city of Tripolis. The period of the Bostra church's construction and consecration was fraught with ecclesiastical controversy in this city.

53. For the Azraʿ church of George, see Waddington, *Inscriptions,* no. 2498, where the dedication describes the substitution of choirs of angels for the sacrifices to idols at the old shrine. For Busr al-Hariri, see ibid., no. 2477, where it is persuasively suggested that τὸ πρὶν ἔνθα ἀπόθητον refers to a polytheist shrine.

54. Mondésert, *Syria* 37 (1960): 129, suggests that Theodore may have been a philosopher or rhetor and the children his disciples, although he admits that no external evidence supports this interpretation.

55. See Mondésert's comments on the rhythm and rhetoric of the inscription in ibid., 127–28.

56. *IGLS,* no. 9125. See Sartre, *Bostra,* 124–26, with nn. 215, 216, for studies of the church, which has yet to be published systematically. On its architectural style, see Lassus, *Sanctuaires,* 95–96, and Farioli Campanati, *Felix Ravenna* 141–44 (1991–92), esp. 222–24.

57. After studying law at Beirut, Severus of Antioch received the sacrament of baptism in the church of Leontius at Tripolis and later composed a hymn to the martyr (Evagr., *HE* 3.33; James of Edessa, *Hymns of Severus of Antioch,* 138).

58. For Dur, see Waddington, *Inscriptions,* no. 2412p; for Sur, see *PAES,* 3A7: 426, no. 797[3].

59. Proc., *Aed.* 5.9.26.

Bishop Julian opposed Severus's election as patriarch of Antioch in November 512, which eventually cost him his see.[60] According to John Moschus, who heroizes the opponent of Severus, before Julian's exile in 513, several Bostran "enemies of Christ," that is, non-Chalcedonians, bribed an attendant to poison the archbishop. But, informed by divine revelation that he would remain unharmed, Julian humiliated his would-be assassins by drinking the tainted cup before their eyes.[61] By the early sixth century, Sergius was acquiring a history of mixed associations, with devotees among both Chalcedonians and non-Chalcedonians. Severus of Antioch wrote three hymns in honor of Sergius, one with Bacchus, and in 514, the year after Julian consecrated Bostra's cathedral, Severus preached a sermon on Sergius at Chalcis.[62] In the same climate, Jacob of Sarug (ca. 451–521) composed his metrical homily on Sergius, and the emperor Anastasius openly declared his support for the non-Chalcedonian cause and for the martyr Sergius of Rusafa.

WEST OF THE STEPPE

Leaving the Hawran, we travel northward to Salaminias at the southern base of another basalt landscape. Situated northeast of Emesa, on the main route to the important settlement of Seriane / Isriya, Salaminias is set in the fertile zone of hills and depressions that reaches as far north as Chalcis, but to the east and south is bordered by an arid landscape. The town was integrated into the network of routes that linked the many villages between Emesa and Chalcis, as well as the east-west route in the direction of Rusafa.[63] An inscription found near the city gate commemorates local patronage of Salaminias's fortification wall:

> This is the gate of the Lord, the righteous shall enter through it.
> The noble namesake of the glorious martyr Sergius,
> made it secure by restoring the entire citadel,
> this stronghold that was the salvation of many mortals,
> and has won him eternal memory.[64]

---

60. On Julian's opposition to Severus, see Evagr., *HE* 3.33. See Sartre, *Bostra*, 109–13, for an account of Bostra's ecclesiastical history in the early sixth century.

61. Joh. Mosch., *Prat.spir.* 94.

62. James of Edessa, *Hymns of Severus of Antioch*, 143–45.

63. For a description of Salaminias's setting, see Waddington, *Inscriptions*, in his discussion of no. 2633. On Salaminias's place in this network of communications, especially with regard to Rusafa, see Mouterde and Poidebard, *Limes*, 139–47; for the Emesa-Salaminias-Anasartha-Barbalissus route, see 177–78.

64. *IGLS*, no. 2524. The first line is Psalm 117.20. Trombley's location of Salaminias as "Salamis [*sic*] on the riverine plain of Orontes," needs correction (*BMGS* 21 [1997]: 173).

Unfortunately, this inscription is undated. One of the few dated inscriptions from Salaminias records the consecration of a church to the Theotokos in 604.[65] Despite its regional importance, little evidence remains to help reknit the town's history. Bishop Julian of Salaminias was present at the consecration of Severus as patriarch of Antioch.[66] Traveling from Jerusalem to Emesa, the ailing English pilgrim Willibald spent Lent of 726 at Salaminias.[67] Besides the walls and the church of the Theotokos, Willibald may have visited the church of "the holy and victorious martyr Sergius," in honor of whom an inscription attests the construction of an oratory (εὐκτήριον) "from the foundations."[68] No date accompanies the dedication, although suggestions include an early date of 430–31, which is not impossible, but arrived at, it seems, by the association of the Sergius inscription with a dated, but unrelated, colonnette also discovered at Salaminias.[69] A safer date between 550 and 620, when the cult was especially vigorous, has also been advanced.[70]

Sergius was also honored at Sabbaʿ, a small village between Epiphania / Hama and Qasr ibn Wardan.[71] The damaged inscription, probably from the lintel of a main entrance, mentions the door of Sergius and is dated to 890 or 806 in the Seleucid era, that is, A.D. 578/79 (Prentice), or A.D. 494/95 (Jalabert and Mouterde).[72] To the east at Nawa, one of the largest late antique settlements in this basalt region, the exterior of an impressive church was decorated with excerpts from the Psalms and the Song of Songs, the letters rendered in fine, high relief.[73] A lintel inscription from another church at Nawa is dated to A.D. 468–77.[74] After the date, it reads ἐπὶ Δανι | ήλου φρ | τοῦ μ Σε(ρ)γίου. Prentice supposed φρ to stand for πρ[εσβυτέρου] and supplied μ[άρτυρος], so that a priest named Daniel built a church to the martyr Sergius. But Jalabert and Mouterde propose an interpretation that is preferable in the light of nearby parallels. They read φρ as φρ[ουράρχου] and μ[ητάτου] for μ, so that an unspecified church at Nawa was dedicated by Daniel, captain of the guard of the fortified post of Sergius. Just north of Nawa, at Tal al-Dahab, an inscription dated 489

65. *IGLS*, no. 2512; Prentice, *Greek and Latin Inscriptions*, 237, no. 287, including a photograph.

66. Devreesse, *Patriarcat*, 207; Honigmann, *Evêques*, 31.

67. Hugeburc, *Life of Willibald*, ch. 26, p. 100.2–13.

68. *IGLS*, no. 2530.

69. *IGLS*, no. 2525, with commentary.

70. Hartmann, *ZDPV* 23 (1901): 110.

71. Dussaud, *Topographie*, map 8 at 2C. See also Butler's map of the ʿAla opposite *PAES*, 2B: 1.

72. *IGLS*, no. 1970; *PAES*, 3B1: 9, no. 823, with drawing.

73. *IGLS*, nos. 1945–49; Dussaud, *Topographie*, map 8 at 2D.

74. *IGLS*, no. 1952; *PAES*, 3B1: 14, no. 834.

records some unnamed construction Βεεσωνος φρ, which Prentice this time interpreted as φρουράρχου.[75]

Most towns in the region had towers, although the settlements on the whole were unwalled. Where dated, the towers, like the churches, belong to the sixth century.[76] To the southwest of the basalt plateau, Raphanaea / Rafniya guarded the pass through the Anti-Lebanon that connected Emesa with Tripolis. Along with traders and soldiers, the cult of Sergius took this route and was established at Orthosias, an important caravan stop just north of Tripolis, where Peter the Iberian saw a church dedicated to Sergius and Bacchus.[77] At Raphanaea, an undated inscription on a limestone lintel identifies the μητάτον τοῦ ἁγίου Σεργίου [μ]άρτυρο[ς].[78] In the Nawa and Raphanaea inscriptions, fortified posts are defended by the same divine patron. At Ghur, southeast of Raphanaea, another fortified post (μητάτον) was protected by a trio of military saints: Longinus, Theodore, and George.[79] In the same region, at Burj, the tower that gave the village its present name was marked in 526 as the μητάτον of the archangel Michael and Saint Longinus.[80]

In 540, after Khusrau I had come besieging and plundering along the northern route to Antioch, he took a southward detour on his homeward journey to empty Apamea of its treasures. No doubt smaller settlements along the way were also exposed to Khusrau's raiding army. Among these may have been a village known from Greek inscriptions as Kaper, or Kapro, Koraon.[81] The name was made famous in this century thanks to an impres-

75. *IGLS*, no. 1924; *PAES*, 3B1: 20, no. 850.

76. Butler, in *PAES*, 2B1: 1–5, gives a general account of the 'Ala and its context.

77. *Vita Petri Iberi* 109; on Orthosias, also known as Artousa—the name is preserved in the modern Ard Artousa—see Dussaud, *Topographie*, 78–80 and map 14 at 3A; *Tabula Peutingeriana* 10.3 (Ortosias); Miller, *Itineraria romana*, 823.

78. *IGLS*, no. 1397; Mouterde, *MUSJ* 28 (1949–50): 37–38, with a barely legible photograph, pl. XV.2. Raphanaea appears on the *Tabula Peutingeriana* 10.4 (Raphanis). See Mouterde and Poidebard, *Limes*, 30–31, on Raphanis.

79. *IGLS*, no. 155. Mouterde, *MUSJ* 12 (1927): 274, identified the site of Ghur with Carion, placed twelve Roman miles southeast of Raphanaea on the *Tabula Peutingeriana*. This identification was accepted by Honigmann in *RE*, 4A: 1674, but has more recently been reconsidered by Rey-Coquais, who suggests that a location southwest of Raphanaea is preferable since the site of Carion was on the route between Raphanaea and Orthosias: *Arados*, 85–88. See Dussaud, *Topographie*, map 8, for Rafniyé (3A) and Ghour (3B).

80. *IGLS*, no. 1610; *PAES*, 2B: 103; Dussaud, *Topographie*, map 8 at 3A.

81. Mundell Mango proposes an identification with the modern village of Kurin—suggesting that Kafr (Arabic for village) has fallen away to leave only Kurin. For her hypothetical reconstruction of the history of Kaper Koraon, see Mundell Mango, *Silver*, 33–34; and on the Hama region's political and cultural links in late antiquity, see ibid., passim, but esp. 6–7. More recently, Fiaccadori has argued in favor of an identification of Kaper Koran with Burj Haydar, a village with conspicuous late antique architecture in the central region of the Jabal Sim'an (*PP* 48 [1993] 287–91).

sive hoard of over fifty silver objects discovered in the Hama region and now attributed to the village of "Kaper Koraon"—in particular to its church of S. Sergius. The identification of precisely which village was known in late antiquity as Kaper / Kapro Koraon has not been made for certain, although it seems most likely that it was located in the Hama area. The mainly undated objects have been assigned dates on the basis of stamps and style to between 540 and 640, suggesting pious activity in the wake of Khusrau's visit. Many of the liturgical objects declare that their donors dedicated them to the treasure of S. Sergius, sometimes also adding "of Kaper / Kapro Koraon."[82] A particularly elaborate paten showing Christ celebrating the first Eucharist with his disciples has attracted attention because it was dedicated to Sergius by Megas, an honorary consul, *patricius* and *curator domus divinae* known from the reign of Maurice.[83] Another impressive gift, consisting of two lamp stands, was offered by four brothers to Sergius and Bacchus.[84] They are described by Marlia Mundell Mango as "the finest Byzantine lampstands in silver . . . produced by the most complicated manufacturing methods of any object in the Kaper Koraon treasure."[85] Mundell Mango ascribes the joint attribution to Sergius and Bacchus to coincidence or "simple misunderstanding." What sort of misunderstanding can, in fact, be identified. The words of the dedicatory inscription are identical on both objects, although the word order has been muddled on no. 11 (*IGLS* 2034 II), where the opening εὐξάμενοι has been transposed to the end of the dedication.[86] On both objects, the inscription runs first along the base of the lampstand and is continued on a second line directly above the first:

† εὐξάμενοι τὴν εὐχὴν ἀπέδωκαν τῷ | ἁγίου Σεργίου (καὶ) Βάχχου | † Σέργις (καὶ) Συμεὼν (καὶ) Δανιὴλ (καὶ) Θωμᾶς | υἱοὶ Μαξιμίν(ου) κώμης Καπρο Κοραω.[87]

†Having vowed, they fulfilled their vow to (the church) of S. Sergios and Bacchos †Sergis (and) Symeon (and) Daniel (and) Thomas, sons of Maximinos, of the village of Kapro Korao(n).

---

82. E.g., Mundell Mango, *Silver*, no. 3, a chalice from the early seventh century; no. 4, a paten from the mid sixth century; no. 7, a cross from the sixth to seventh centuries; no. 14, a ewer from the mid sixth century; no. 28, a chalice from the sixth to seventh centuries.

83. Mundell Mango, *Silver*, no. 35, and 8–10 on Megas; also *PLRE*, 3: 870–71, Megas 2; Feissel, *T&MByz* 9 (1985): 465–76. Megas also dedicated two ewers to Sergius at Kaper Koraon.

84. Mundell Mango, *Silver*, nos. 11 and 12.

85. Ibid., 99.

86. Jalabert and Mouterde publish the lampstands as *IGLS*, no. 2034.I (= Mundell Mango no. 12) and no. 2034.II (= Mundell Mango no. 11). They include the text of only no. 2034.I and neglect to mention the different word order in their no. 2034.II.

87. *IGLS*, no. 2034.I.

Another item, a ewer, was dedicated to Sergius alone by five men: Daniel, Sergius, Symeon, Bacchus, and Thomas, but without additional identification as sons of Maximinus.[88] Comparing the names in the dedications of the lampstands and the ewer, it becomes clear that we are dealing with the same names—only Bacchus is a saint in the lampstand dedication and a brother on the ewer inscription. What transpired to produce a dedication to Sergius and Bacchus must have been the following: the craftsman was given a written copy of the dedication he was to inscribe, and after τῷ ἁγίου Σεργίου followed the list of brothers, which happened to begin with the brother named Bacchus. The craftsman, who was not from the area, was familiar with Sergius and Bacchus as a pair, made a natural slip and sanctified the first brother, Bacchus. The result was a unique dedication at Kaper Koraon to Sergius *and Bacchus.*

Two more building dedications to Sergius appear in northwestern Syria. At Dar Qita, the ruins of several churches have been studied, including one consecrated to Sergius in 537, adjoined on the southeast by a baptistry. Although no date is recorded for the baptistry's dedication, it was in need of repair in 566–67, when the door was renovated by five priests named John, Sergius, Danos, Bacchus, and Ramlys.[89] Nineteen years earlier at Babisqa, the next village to the east, a Syriac inscription records the purchase of gardens by Sargon, Theodore, and Bacchus, and most likely the construction of a stoa by John.[90] Given the proximity of place and date of the two inscriptions, it is probable that the same John, Sergius and Bacchus took part in the construction of Babisqa's stoa and Dar Qita's church. Babisqa also had a church, dedicated in 609–10, whose lintel inscription reads: Ἅγιε Σήργι, βοήθεσον. Πρόσδεξε τὴν καρποφορ(ίαν) Σολομονίδα τῶν Ζορυν (or Ζαρυλ). Prentice translates the dedication as "Holy Sergius, help (us)! Receive the offering of Solomonidas, of the (family?, tribe?) of Zoryn (or Zaryl)," without commenting on the ethnic background of the name Zoryn or Zaryl, but assuming, probably rightly, that it refers to a family group, rather than a region or town.[91] This is the last-known dated Greek inscrip-

88. Mundell Mango, *Silver* no. 14 = *IGLS,* no. 2033.

89. Prentice, *Greek and Latin Inscriptions,* 80–81, no. 61 (church); no. 62 (baptistry), with Prentice's commentary. *PAES,* 3B4: 125–26, no. 1086 (church), and no. 1088 (baptistry) with same commentary as in Prentice, *Greek and Latin Inscriptions;* map of Dar Qita opposite *PAES,* 3B: 119. Cf. *IGLS* 545 (church), 546 (baptistry). See also Tchalenko, *Villages antiques,* 2: pl. 134, no. 24; pl. 9, no. 3 (church).

90. See Littman, *PAES* 4.B: 64–65, for the Syriac inscription. For discussion of the Syriac name Babisqa (*BYT BZQ'), in the light of other toponyms in the regions, see Feissel in *Ἑλληνισμός,* 296–97.

91. Prentice, *Greek and Latin Inscriptions,* 88 no. 71 (tribe?); Prentice in *PAES,* 3B4: 132–33 (family?). Although the designation τῶν with a proper name is not commonly found in sixth- or early seventh-century epigraphy, it has parallels in, e.g., a late seventh-century document

tion in northern Syria, and the spelling of the martyr's name offers an additional variant: Σηϱγίς.[92]

NORTHERN SYRIA AND MESOPOTAMIA

At Sujin, southeast of Beroea/Aleppo, a dedication inscription was discovered worn by reuse in an irrigation canal. The highly abbreviated text states simply that a martyrium of Sergius was built in the year 839, that is, A.D. 527/28.[93] Further southeast of Beroea, the famous trilingual inscription of Zabad records in Greek and Syriac the laying of the first stone of a church dedicated to Sergius on 24 September 512, the feast of Thecla, another popular eastern saint. The Greek and Syriac dedicatory inscriptions flank a disk with a chi-rho monogram.[94] The texts differ slightly, reflecting the liberties taken by the two carvers.[95] One Greek and one Arabic inscription consisting mainly of names were added along the lintel's lower edge below the dedications and the central medallion. Adding to Littmann's reading of the Arabic inscription, Kugener has shown that the Arabic names correspond to those in Greek, and represent other, possibly later benefactors of the church, although this point is still unclear. Semitic names appear in all four of the inscriptions and two (perhaps three) of the dedicants recorded in Arabic bear the saint's name. One is called Sergius, son of Imru' al-Qays, a familiar name in the history of Roman-Arab relations in the eastern provinces.[96] Arab enthusiasm for Sergius at Zabad in the early sixth century corresponds to Severus's contemporary witness to the popularity of the shrine at Rusafa among the region's Arab population. Between Zabad

---

from the Nessana papyri, where it clearly refers to a tribal affiliation (Kraemer, *Excavations at Nessana*, 3, no. 92.40–45). Although it is never stated, it is perhaps against this background that Trombley, *BMGS* 21 (1997): 182, 195, has interpreted the dedication to refer to an Arab devotee of S. Sergius. It is unnecessary to create a female name Σολομονίδα, which Trombley Arabizes to Sulaymana, suggesting that she was "probably the wife of a sheikh." The inscription clearly reads Σολομονίδα, the genitive of the masculine name Σολομονίδας.

92. *IGLS*, no. 563; *PAES*, 3B4: 132–33, no. 1100, with a drawing of the inscription on the lintel of the western entrance and a plan of Babisqa opposite 128.

93. *IGLS* 258, with drawing; Robert, *Bull.* (1940): 228, no. 172, accepts the *IGLS* reading; Dussaud, *Topographie* map 10.

94. *IGLS*, no. 310, with drawing. Kugener in *JA* 9 (1907): 509–24; *RSO* 1 (1907): 577–86 offers important interpretations of the inscription and corrections of *IGLS*. Littmann responds to Kugener in *RSO* 4 (1911): 193–98. See also Kugener, *RSO* 1 (1907): 577–79, on the tradition of lintel disks in Syria and Mesopotamia.

95. Kugener, *JA* 9 (1907): 519–20, argues persuasively that two separate hands carved the Syriac and the Greek.

96. The inscription at Zabad is one of the oldest examples of Arabic script. See Shahîd, *BASIC*, 1: 699–702.

and Rusafa lay the monotonous, arid plain of al-Matyaha, literally, the place without landmarks where one loses one's way. But having traversed this exposed plain east of Zabad and descended from the watershed to the Euphrates, one traveled easily to Rusafa along the caravan route that ran west of the river. It was also possible to cross directly to Rusafa through the steppe along the tracks used by pastoralists. Located in a mixed zone of agricultural and pastoral land, at the northern edge of the basalt Jabal Shbayt, the Sergius church with its inscriptions in Greek, Syriac, and Arabic illustrates with particular clarity the power of this cult to draw together the region's diverse cultural strands.

North of Beroea a somewhat unusual inscription was carved onto the lintel of a small building preceded by a vestibule at Kafr Antin.[97] In the lintel's center is a square plate in relief—perhaps it held an image of the saints mentioned in the inscription. Around the square runs a prayer for the builder and a date, August A.D. 523. Left of the blank plate is a separate inscription invoking S. Theodore and S. Sergius, spelled Σέργειος. Farther to the northeast of Beroea, at the modern village of Söğütlü, just west of the Euphrates, an important Sergius dedication was discovered in 1974.[98] The mosaic inscription is part of a geometrically patterned mosaic floor. Column bases and fragments of capitals scattered among the adjacent houses must originally have been part of the same church. The inscription is clear and dated: ἔτους γμψ' ἐκτί[σθη] | τοῦτον μαρτύρ[ιον] τοῦ | ἁγίου Σεργ[ίου]. The Seleucid date of 743 places the martyrium's consecration in A.D. 431, precisely when Alexander, bishop of Hierapolis, was constructing the first martyrium of Sergius within Rusafa's walls. Southwest of Söğütlü, another mosaic inscription at Ikizkuğu also evoked the name Sergius, presumably as the church's dedicatee.[99] East of Söğütlü, on the west bank of the Euphrates just north of ancient Zeugma, the village of Ehnesh (Turkish Gümüşgün) preserves a chapel of Sergius in a grove alongside a stream, known still at the beginning of this century as the Serkis-su.[100] Although the

---

97. *PAES,* 3B6: 203–4, no. 1202, with drawing; Dussaud, *Topographie,* map 8 at 3B.

98. Candemir and Werner in *Studien zur Religion,* 1: 230–31.

99. Ibid., 226–27. Robert, *Bull.* (1979), no. 603, accepts the view of Candemir and Werner that the isolated name Sergis refers to the church's dedication. Robert also repeats the authors' innaccurate comment that attestations of the cult of Sergius (not George, a common confusion made in antiquity and also here by Robert) appear in Syria from the early sixth century, overlooking the mid fifth-century church of Sergius nearby at Edessa.

100. Cumont, *Études syriennes,* 152–53, records the stream's name and the primarily Armenian composition of the village in 1907. Palmer in *Polyphonia byzantina,* 45–84, has thrown much light on Ehnesh's rich, but until now blurred, epigraphical record. See also Palmer, *Seventh Century,* 71–74. Chabot first recorded the inscription (although he could not recall whether it belonged to a church of Sergius or George), without a map or careful commentary in *JA* 9 (1900): 285–88. For sketch maps of the vicinity, see Palmer in *Polyphonia byzantina,* 81, and Cumont, *Études syriennes,* 289, map 7; for a broader geographical context,

church itself is not dated, its antiquity and original association with a non-Chalcedonian community is confirmed by the unusual Syriac inscription carved in estrangela script on the church's exterior.

Continuing around the northern edge of the Syro-Mesopotamian plain, the city of Edessa could boast two churches dedicated to Sergius, one within the walls and another outside the eastern city gate. The church outside the walls was built by Bishop Hiba, the successor to Rabbula, who died in 436.[101] S. Symeon was added to the church's dedication sometime between the Stylite's repose in 459 and 498, when it is first identified as the church of SS. Sergius and Symeon. In May of that year, when Anastasius abolished the chrysargyron tax paid by artisans, a jubilant celebration broke out and spread to the church outside Edessa's walls: "The whole city rejoiced and they all, both small and great, put on white garments, and carried lighted tapers and censers full of burning incense and went forth with psalms and hymns, giving thanks to God and praising the emperor, to the shrine of S. Sergius and S. Symeon, where they celebrated the eucharist."[102]

In 503, Kawad besieged Edessa, against the good advice of a Christian from Hira, who knew of Christ's prophecy that the city would never fall into enemy hands. Before the shah's arrival, the Edessenes gathered the relics into the city from the surrounding countryside, both to save the holy objects from desecration and to bolster the city's defenses. Areobindus, the Roman commander at Edessa, accepted to emerge only a short distance from the city walls, in order to treat with the Sasanian general Bawi at the church of S. Sergius.[103] The church was later burned by the Iranian forces after their failure to take the city. The presence of a church dedicated to SS. Sergius and Symeon just outside Edessa reflects the popularity of both saints among the pastoral and semi-pastoral Arabs, whose control over the region could at times reach as far as the city walls.[104] But its location outside the walls did not inhibit city dwellers from participating in festivities there.

A sanctuary dedicated to Sergius in the sensitive military zone east of Edessa, between Dara and Nisibis, served as funerary chapel for the Iranian

---

although Ehnesh is not marked, see Honigmann, *Ostgrenze,* map 3, between Zeugma / Balqis and the Merziman-çay.

101. *Chron. 1234* 1.180.

102. *Chronicle of Edessa of 506,* 257–58, tr. Chabot, 190. See also Luther's commentary, *Syrische Chronik,* 166.

103. *Chronicle of Edessa of 506,* 284–87, tr. Chabot, 209–11. Although the *Chronicle* refers to the church as that of S. Sergius only, it must be identified with the church (referred to earlier) of SS. Sergius and Symeon.

104. See ibid. 308–9, tr. Chabot, 207, on Iranian and Roman attempts to control Arab raids against the villages of northern Syria-Mesopotamia. Dilleman, *Haute Mésopotamie,* 76–77, describes the threat of raids that characterized this region, especially between Edessa and Nisibis and at times of drought.

martyr Gulanducht, who died there in 591. The ruins of a fortress named Sargahan correspond to the location given in the *Vita*, and the name preserves the dedication to Sergius.[105] The *Vita* also records that Gulanducht, on pilgrimage to the Holy City from Nisibis, visited the shrine of Sergius in the "Barbarian Plain."[106]

THE IRANIAN EMPIRE

The Sergius cult spread beyond the western part of Mesopotamia that was under Roman control into the heavily Christianized eastern region in Iranian territory. Theophylact, writing in the 630s, calls Sergius "the most efficacious saint in Persia."[107] In the *Acta* of Mar Qardagh, S. Sergius makes three encouraging visits to Qardagh, a probably fictional marzban of Arbela during the reign of Shapur II (310–79).[108] The appearance of the military martyr Sergius to another in the making is a vivid illustration of the spread of the Sergius cult eastward.[109] Although the date of the *Acta* is not secure, the wide dissemination of S. Sergius's influence in the sixth century points to the period between 550 and 650 for the *Acta*'s composition.[110] S. Sergius's role in the *Acta* also demonstrates that the military saint had not been monopolized by the Romans. At a critical turning point in the story, Qardagh, the protégé of Rusafa's martyr, successfully engages and routs the "Romans and Arabs" who have been raiding his territory.[111]

The known dedications to Sergius within the Iranian empire are primarily found west of the Zagros, where most of the Christians lived. Qaraqosh, a village near Mawsil, had a church of Sergius and Bacchus, probably dating back to the growth of anti-Chalcedonian influence in the area during the second half of the sixth century.[112] Not far from Hira and ʿAqula, a Nesto-

---

105. *Vita Gulanducht* 24 and 26. The classical or late Roman fort preserved at Sargahan, in the borderland between Roman and Iranian territory, has elicited discussion from, e.g., Peeters, *AB* 62 (1944): 121; de' Maffei in *Seventeenth International Byzantine Congress*, 240–42, with photographs 1–5; Sinclair, *Eastern Turkey*, 3: 341–42, 367.

106. See above, pp. 65–66.

107. Theoph. Sim., *Hist.* 5.14.3.

108. *Acta Mar Kardaghi martyris* 7, 30, 34, 53.

109. See chapter 1 on the image of the saint in Qardagh's visions.

110. In his excellent article in *Festgabe*, ed. Eilers, 150 with n. 40, Wiessner argues persuasively for a sixth-century date. Cf. also Peeters, *AB* 43 (1925): 298–99, who preferred a seventh-century date. For a recent discussion of the date and historical context of the *Acta*, see Walker, "Your heroic deeds," esp. 27–32.

111. *Acta Mar Kardaghi martyris* 41. See the translation by Walker, "Your heroic deeds," 235–36.

112. Fiey, *Assyrie chrétienne*, 2: 458–59. This church preserves traces of an ambo (Fiey, *Mossoul chrétien*, 98–99).

rian monastery dedicated to S. Sergius flourished from before the reign of Khusrau II until at least the tenth century.[113] As a Zoroastrian, the future Mar ʿAbda observed the catechumens gathering at the church of S. Sergius to receive the sacrament of baptism during the night of the Easter service. By God's grace, he saw the angels crown the newly baptized as they emerged from the font, their garments radiant with the true light. The Zoroastrian too was moved to shed his old skin and receive the seal of baptism. After spending time in Hira as a disciple of Mar Babai, ʿAbda later took up residence in a cave, where he once applied healing oil to a hunter who had been savaged by a lion. George of Izla, an Iranian aristocrat who converted to Nestorian Christianity and was martyred in 615, was buried in a monastery dedicated to Sergius at Mabrakta near Seleucia-Ctesiphon.[114] The *Acta* of Anastasius the Persian (d. 628) mention a monastery dedicated to the holy martyr Sergius six miles outside Dastagird, at the village known in Greek as Bethsaloe (Βηθσαλωέ) where the king had a residence.[115]

These scattered signs of the Sergius cult in the Iranian empire do not on their own justify Theophylact's grand claim. Fortunately, two exceptional sources survive to shed further light on the cult's eastern dissemination. They are both *Histories* of non-Chalcedonian bishops who encouraged devotion to the saint as they evangelized the countryside. In 559, Ahudemmeh was consecrated bishop of the non-Chalcedonian diocese of Beth ʿArbaya and metropolitan of the East.[116] He had grown up in Balad near the Tigris, the eastern limit of Beth ʿArbaya. The city of Takrit formed the region's southern extremity, Nisibis marked the north, and the Khabur the west. Through a shrewdly articulated mission, Ahudemmeh promoted non-Chalcedonian Christianity in Mesopotamia, particularly among the "barbaric" tent-dwellers of the Jazira, until his martyrdom in 575.[117] Christ's exhortation "feed my lambs" rang with immediate clarity for the newly consecrated bishop.[118] His missionary strategy was founded on the establishment of a clerical hierarchy, cultivation of pious habits, and construction of

---

113. *Chronicle of Seert*, pp. 549–50. See Fiey, *AB* 79 (1961): 110.

114. *Syn. or.* 625. See also Fiey, *AB* 79 (1961): 110.

115. *Acta Anast. Pers.* 32, 39, 43. On the Christian community of Bethsaloe, see Flusin, *Saint Anastase*, 243–46. The village Bethsaloe and its Sergius monastery, located one mile outside the village, is otherwise unknown. Hoffmann, *Auszüge*, 120, located Bethsaloe on the Diyala river (*Acta Anast. Pers.* 38), which flows six miles to the north of Dastagird.

116. According to Bar Hebraeus, *Chron. eccl.* 2.100–102, Christophorus, catholicus of the Armenians, consecrated Ahudemmeh as bishop, while the tireless non-Chalcedonian missionary Jacob Baradaeus made him metropolitan. Nau convincingly argues, in his edition of the *History of Mar Ahudemmeh*, 20 n. 3, that Jacob Baradaeus was the hierarch who, according to the *Hist. Ahud.* 20, consecrated Ahudemmeh to both dignities at the same time.

117. See also Bar Hebraeus, *Chron. eccl.* 2.99–100.

118. *Hist. Ahud.* 4, p. 21.

sacred buildings among the tribes in order to focus Arab devotion within the Church's control.

Of course, conversion was the prerequisite, but both the language and manner of the nomads presented daunting obstacles.[119] Traveling from campsite to campsite, Ahudemmeh worked a spell of conversion over the tribes by a twofold plan of negation and revelation. Old forms of worship were shattered: the Arabs saw their holy places destroyed and stone idols broken by the power of his prayer.[120] Like flies, demons were chased from their accustomed seats of worship, the sick cured, lepers purified.[121] With a flood of miracles and signs, Ahudemmeh affirmed the true religion. Yet as he followed the tribes' movements, some encampments still met him with a hail of stones.[122] Only after the dramatic exorcism of a shaykh's daughter were Ahudemmeh and his God finally embraced by one camp. Others were to follow. After breaking through the first barrier, he traveled among the encampments, sharing the hardships of extreme cold, heat, difficult tracks, and scarce supplies of water, while at the same time teaching, baptizing, and consecrating a priest and a deacon for each community. He also made certain to name churches after the heads of each clan, in order to encourage their leadership in ecclesiastical affairs.[123]

Ahudemmeh was credited with the conversion to non-Chalcedonian Christianity of Arab pastoralists in the region of Beth 'Arbaya between Nisibis, Jabal Sinjar, and Balad, but also in the area of Takrit, as far south as Hira.[124] Christianity had to adapt to the demands of the landscape and the way of life it imposed. Impromptu or portable altars served the needs of Arab Christians, who would seize the opportunity, whenever it presented itself, to participate in the divine mysteries.[125] Stories about Arab conversion

119. Ibid., p. 22.

120. Ibid., p. 23.

121. Ibid., pp. 23–24.

122. Ibid., p. 24.

123. Ibid., p. 26 for baptism and p. 27 for clergy and the naming of churches. Cf. Sozomen's description of Arab Christians: "[Some of the Saracens] began to convert to Christianity not long before the present reign [Theodosius II]. They became familiar with faith in Christ through their encounters with the priests and monks who lived close to them, virtuous men and wonder-workers, who were living a contemplative life in the neighboring desert" (Soz., *HE* 6.38.14).

124. Morony, *Iraq*, 374. On Beth 'Arbaya, see Dillemann, *Haute Mésopotamie*, 75–78; and see also Donner, *Early Islamic Conquests*, 157–73.

125. E.g., Leontius of Jerusalem, *Contra monophysitas*, PG 86.1900–1901 (I thank Garth Fowden for this reference). Use of portable altars by the Christian Taghlib tribe is attested as late as the eleventh century in the *Murshid* of Abu Nasr al-din Yahya ibn Jarir, cited by Fiey, *L'Orient Syrien* 8 (1963): 320–21. In this account, a bishop attired in ecclesiastical dress traveled with the tribes and celebrated the liturgy in Arabic. When presbyters and deacons journeyed in a desert land, taking with them a chalice and paten, but lacking an altar, it was per-

often include renunciation of camel meat, a feature of desert life particularly repugnant to many settled people and no doubt woven into conversion stories for that reason.[126] An eleventh-century account of the conversion of a Turkish king illustrates the creative flexibility demanded of the spiritual shepherds of pastoral communities. The unnamed ruler had converted to Christianity, thanks to a rescue mission by S. Sergius, who saved him when he lost his way on a hunting expedition. His subjects were nomadic peoples, and in order to nourish their newly adopted Christianity, "the king set up a pavilion to take the place of an altar, in which was a cross and a Gospel, and named it after Mar Sergius, and he tethered a mare there, and he took her milk and laid it on the Gospel and the cross and recited over it the prayers which he had learned, and made the sign of the Cross over it, and he and his people after him took a draught from it."[127] In the case of the Lenten fast, the Nestorian patriarch allowed that, since their diet consisted of only milk and meat, the nomad Christians should abstain from meat and consume only sour milk, a sacrifice, since they usually took it sweet.

The tactics Ahudemmeh employed to encourage the Arabs' affection for the Christian religion were not designed to disrupt the established rhythms of nomadism. For example, the *History* nowhere hints that the bishop encouraged sedentarization among the Arab groups. Instead, he stressed care for the indigent, for strangers, and especially for the monasteries of central Syria-Mesopotamia—in both Roman and Iranian territory.[128] Care for these communities in practical terms meant subsidy, and this was possible only if the Arab pastoralists maintained the traditional migrations with their flocks, their primary source of income. The tribes "made generous gifts that would sell at high prices" to sustain the monks' bodily needs.[129]

---

mitted that the deacon hold the two sacred implements and himself become the altar (see *West Syrian Synodicon* 237, ed. and tr. Vööbus). Portable plaques carved with crosses have been discovered in the ruins of a Christian monastery from the early Islamic period at Ain Sha'ia in the southwestern Iraqi desert (Okada, *al-Rāfidān* 11 [1990] 103–12). The excavators interpret the plaques as personal icons. I would like to thank Yasuyoshi Okada for providing me with offprints from *al-Rāfidān*.

126. E.g., Theod., *HR* 26.13. Some established forms of behavior were especially resistant to change. John Moschus relates an incident involving a group of Ghassanid-allied Arabs whose booty from a successful raid included an adolescent boy. After some argument in Greek, a priest who happened to witness the event managed to rescue the boy from becoming a first-fruits offering, made in honor of the priest back in the Arabs' camp (Joh. Mosch., *Prat. spir.* 155). The identification of the Arabs as allied with the Ghassanids, well-known non-Chalcedonians, should be taken with caution in the light of Moschus's commitment to Chalcedon.

127. The account is from the Nestorian patriarch Mari, *Kitab al-mijdal,* cited in Mingana, *BRL* 9 (1925): 310–11. (I owe this reference to Peter Brown.)

128. *Hist. Ahud.* 4, pp. 27–28.

129. Ibid., p. 28.

Once Christian customs had been planted among the tribes, Ahudemmeh initiated the next stage of mission, the construction of a shrine to Sergius.

He built a great and beautiful house of dressed stone in the middle of Beth 'Arbaya in a place called 'Aynqnayya. He placed in it an altar and some holy relics and called the house by the name of Mar Sergis, the famous martyr, because these Arab peoples bore great devotion to his name and had recourse to him more than to all other men. The saint (Ahudemmeh) attempted by means of this house, which he had built in the name of Mar Sergis, to keep them (the Arabs) away from the shrine of Mar Sergis of Beth Rsapha, since it was far distant from them. He made it, as far as he was able, resemble the other, so that its beauty might hold them back from going to the other. Near this shrine he had built, he further constructed the great and famous monastery of 'Aynqnayya.[130]

The project was, in other words, a deliberate attempt to interrupt the flow of local Arab pilgrims across the Euphrates to the Sergius shrine at Rusafa. Ahudemmeh carefully channeled their enthusiasm for local benefit. Not only its name, but the very plan of the new shrine imitated its rival at Rusafa.

In 1956, J. M. Fiey identified Ahudemmeh's complex as the ruins of Qasr Sarij, east of Jabal Sinjar near Balad, and he was followed by David Oates, who studied the complex and dated it to 565.[131] The church, like that described by Ahudemmeh's biographer, is of dressed limestone. Its plan is unique in Iraq, but immediately identifiable as the fifth- and sixth-century North Syrian model also adopted at Rusafa. The central nave with semi-circular apse at the eastern end was flanked by two aisles. The northern aisle terminated in a diaconicon, which communicated with the apse. To the south of the apse was a martyrium,[132] which opened onto the southern aisle, not through a small door, as in the case of the diaconicon, but through a wide arch nearly spanning the aisle's full width. Access was not allowed from the apse to the north, as considerations of symmetry might have dictated. Instead, a door led into the martyrium from the porch on the south side. In this way, the martyrium south of the apse was accessible from the south porch, as the martyrium in basilica A was from its north courtyard. This porch, a feature especially suited to the region's heat,[133] seems to have ex-

---

130. Ibid., p. 29. Cf. Symeon of Beth Arsham's activities at Hira also in the mid sixth century. After converting Arabs of the Lakhmid tribe, Symeon induced the leaders to build a church (Joh. Eph., *Vita sanct.* 140).

131. Fiey, *Sumer* 14 (1958): 125–27, with figs. 1–5; Oates, *Ancient Iraq*, 106–17. See Okada, *al-Rāfidān* 12 (1991): 71–83, where he notes that of all late antique churches in Iraq, only the two in the north, Qasr Sarij and the basilica at Tal Musayfna, are built of dressed stone and have semi-circular apses.

132. See *Hist. Ahud.* 4, p. 29, for the installation of relics.

133. Amm. Marc. 20.6.9 describes the area surrounding Sinjar as especially desiccated.

tended around the southern, western, and northern sides of the church, and on the west, it evidently acted as a narthex, since there are no traces of an internal narthex.[134]

Near the shrine, Ahudemmeh constructed a monastery, now largely destroyed, where he brought together a substantial community.[135] Poor and stranger received hospitality in this "garden filled with goods for the entire country where it was situated."[136] Nearly half a century later, Maruta, the non-Chalcedonian metropolitan of Takrit (629–49), erected a monastery dedicated to Sergius beside a spring called ʿAyngagga in the middle of the desert between Takrit and Hit on the Euphrates.[137] Situated on the main route to ʿAqula, the new Sergius monastery became, like Ahudemmeh's foundation, a harbor in the wilderness carefully chosen for its well-watered location. The arid region south of Takrit between the two great rivers was controlled by Arabs who monitored the steppe route passing between the rivers and provided an alternative to the riverine routes, where merchants paid heavy tolls. Maruta's monastery attracted the Arabs of the region as well as merchants and travelers. Not only the physical setting, but also the splendor and holiness of the establishment drew visitors. The *History of Maruta* describes the elaborate decoration and equipment that embellished the monastery: elegant architecture, costly fabrics, and precious sacred vessels. The monks who moved into the foundation and served as missionaries for the neighboring region were described as vigorous ascetics.

> By them [the monks] and by this monastery all Mesopotamia was pacified because [the monastery] was situated at the center of it. God, by the hands of our father [Maruta], made of it a refuge, a harbor [λιμήν], and a place of repose for all who travel and dwell in this desert, and at the same time a joy, a refuge, a protection against danger, against hunger and thirst, for all who pass the place. Those who cross the desert to reach ʿAqula find rest there, it is their harbor. Those who travel from the Euphrates to the Tigris or the Tigris to the Euphrates stop there. One must see the [multitudes who] camp there and pass on, and others who dwell there; feeding their hunger they are sated, drinking, they are refreshed. The indigent, the afflicted, the sick, and the feeble are brought there, above all by the people who live in Mesopotamia, and are cured and leave strengthened, in good health and succored as much in body as in spirit. [This monastery] saved many men, it protected them and guarded them from lions, from chill, from heat, and from other dangers and rescued them. The monks who live there led many souls that were far from God and

---

134. Oates, *Ancient Iraq,* 107 n. 4.

135. *Hist. Ahud.* 4, p. 30. Traces of the monastery remain, but the structures were built, not of dressed limestone like the church, but of rubble and mortar, making reconstruction of the plan impossible (Oates, *Ancient Iraq,* 106).

136. *Hist. Ahud.* 4, p. 30.

137. Denha, *Hist. Marut.* 6, pp. 85–86; see also Morony, *Iraq,* 375–78.

from knowledge of Him to the orthodox faith, and they were a cause of good to them. This was the case not only for travelers in the desert, but also for those who dwell in the fortresses of the Euphrates.[138]

This flow of visitors across Syria and Mesopotamia was essential to the function of the holy sites created by Ahudemmeh and Maruta. Their services were carefully tied to the terrain—shelter for travelers, food, drink, and security for their financial resources.[139] The cool and green of a monastery could easily conjure up images of paradise among desert-dwellers. Monastic settings, including those within the urban surroundings of Rusafa and Hira, were known to offer refuge in times of plague, but on a more regular basis played a vital role in social life.[140] When Hind, the eleven-year-old daughter of the Lakhmid king al-Nuʿman of Hira went to church on Great Thursday to communicate, she was espied for her beauty by ʿAdi ibn Zayd, the Christian poet and diplomat. Her maids noticed and indulged his attentions, while their mistress remained for some time unaware that she was being watched. Once she realized her maids' complicity with the man's illicit gazes, Hind fell into a rage, even striking one of the girls. A year after the incident in Hira, one of Hind's maids described to her mistress the splendid church at Tuma, also in Hira, lingering on the monks, the beautiful lamps and building, and the girls who visited it. Intrigued by the description, Hind received permission from her mother to visit the church herself. The maid then tipped off ʿAdi, who arrived at the church adorned in his richest Iranian finery, surrounded by a great entourage of young men. Hind's maid drew her mistress's attention to ʿAdi, praising his beauty as even greater than that of the lamps and all the other decorations in the church.[141]

After the coming of Islam, the Umayyads in particular were impressed by these built oases, by their soothing atmosphere and architecture.[142] Especially during great feasts, when wine and song filled the sheltered spaces, monasteries could also provide an inviting backdrop for courtly love. The ʿAbbasid poet ʿAbdallah ibn al-ʿAbbas sang the praises of the garden around a church dedicated to S. Sergius, where he met with his beloved at the

---

138. Denha, *Hist. Marut.* 6, p. 86 (tr. adapted from Nau); cf. pp. 88–89.

139. Theod., *Graec. aff. cur.* 8.63, describes how travelers prayed for guidance and protection at martyrs' shrines before setting off on a journey and, when possible, returned to give thanks.

140. Caliph Hisham retired to Rusafa in order to escape the plague and to be near the monastery (Yaqut, *Muʿjam al-buldan* 2.510, 3.47, tr. Le Strange, *Palestine,* 432, 522). On the commonplace of retiring to the desert in time of plague, see Conrad in *Quest for Understanding,* ed. Seikaly et al., 269–71.

141. al-Isfahani, *Kitab al-aghani* 2.122–23.

142. See, e.g., Hamilton, *Walid and His Friends,* 86.

saint's feast.[143] A similar scene is described in the *Miracula* of S. Thecla. At her shrine near Seleucia, a group of pilgrims gathered for a meal after the saint's feast, and entertained themselves by describing, each in turn, what they had found most delightful: the brilliance and the splendor of the church, the magnitude of the crowd, the noble assembly of bishops, the inspired teaching, the melodious chanting and the well-ordered vigils, prayers, and ceremonies. One man confessed that he was so transfixed by the dazzling beauty of a young woman also attending the service, and so consumed by his desire for her, that he could not tear himself away to pray to the martyr. After a visitation from the indignant Thecla, the lecherous man died three days later.[144]

Clearly, monasteries, especially when set near roads, could exercise extraordinary magnetism over a region's settled and mobile population. Ahudemmeh's justification for his new Sergius shrine, namely, the great distance that separated Beth ʿArbaya from Rusafa, was in fact an attempt to conceal his effort to control the pastoral Arabs, whose migration patterns stretched across the Syro-Mesopotamian steppe.[145] The monasteries established by the leaders of non-Chalcedonian Christianity served to anchor mobile groups into a program of Christian behavior focused on monastic communities. And the monasteries depended in turn on a reciprocal relationship with visitors. Our accounts of the activities of Ahudemmeh and Maruta reveal the centrality of economic factors to religious and political life in Syria-Mesopotamia. Here Procopius too is useful. In his description of Rusafa he explains how "this church, through its acquisition of treasures, came to be powerful and celebrated."[146] The *History of Ahudemmeh* relates how even before the construction of the shrine of Sergius and the adjacent monastery at Qasr Sarij, the Arabs supported monasteries by rich donations that the monks could in turn sell to provide their daily bread. Sanctuaries and monasteries became repositories of material as well as of spiritual wealth; a pious donation might augment the dedicant's local prestige and power, since investment at these holy places took the form of display before peers. But the sphere of influence within which the holy places operated

143. al-Isfahani, *Kitab al-aghani* 19.251. The tenth-century poet Abu'l-Nasr al-Basri records his fascination with a statue in a convent of Sergius (cited by Farès, *Vision chrétienne,* 7). The Sergius church is not identified more specifically in either poem. The poet Abu Nuwas similarly evokes the pleasures of pilgrimage to a Sergius monastery, possibly that near ʿAna, attested in the mid tenth century, even comparing it to the great Meccan hajj (cited in Wagner, *Abū Nuwās* 111, 197–99).

144. *Mir. Theclae* 33; cf. 34.

145. Until the imposition of the modern borders, the Jazira tribes traveled regularly between the Upper Tigris and the Middle Euphrates (Oates, *Ancient Iraq,* 116).

146. Proc., *Aed.,* 2.9.5–6 (tr. Dewing).

was not limited to their immediate locality. Maruta's Sergius monastery was said to attract visitors from as far afield as the "fortresses of the Euphrates," which must refer to Circesium, Zenobia, Callinicum, Sura, and even Rusafa.

For the political leaders of Rome and Iran, the consolidation of Arab religious allegiance at shrines and monasteries was not important only for political and economic reasons. Through permanent holy places, settled powers could attempt to exercise political control over transhumant as well as settled tribes. Roman and Iranian negotiators in the peace treaty of 561 took pains to monitor Arab involvement in cross-border trade and in tribal conflicts across the political frontier.[147] Arab disputes over pasture had been known to escalate into Roman-Iranian confrontation.[148] Competition for control inspired not only bishops in the Iranian empire, but also the king of kings. When Nestorians burned Ahudemmeh's complex, it was Khusrau I who immediately had it reconstructed, sparing nothing on its ornament. Later, in 575, near the end of Khusrau's long reign (531–79), Ahudemmeh died in the prison to which the Iranian king had committed him after the bishop converted an Iranian prince and aided his flight to Roman territory. Despite the beneficial effects of Ahudemmeh's activities among the Arab tribes, Khusrau did not forget that tolerance of Christianity was a policy in the service of political expediency. Khusrau's ostentatious rebuilding of the Sergius monastery at 'Aynqnayya was just one response to the increasing involvement of Roman emperors from Anastasius to Maurice at the popular frontier shrine of Rusafa.

In late antique Syria and Mesopotamia, the name Sergius became a byword for power and success. Ahudemmeh claimed in the mid sixth century that love for the name of Sergius would keep the Arabs bound to his new shrine at Sinjar. Jacob of Sarug saw the world through the same lens when he wrote "beautiful name Sergius, which is beloved to all ears" and "a region full of danger fell to this energetic soldier, and his fame and his name made peace in it and he is its pride."[149] In his ex-voto dedication to the saint, Khusrau II ascribed his wife's conception of their child to Sergius's "most holy name."[150] Adopting the martyr's name and evoking the name Sergius were considered tantamount to making the martyr present instantly. The name was believed to possess the power to break through the deceptive constructions of time and space that were thought to separate the living from

147. Men. Prot., fr. 6.1, ll. 314–407; see also Shahîd, *Byzantium and the Semitic Orient* VII, 181–213.

148. For the dispute near Nisibis in 484 caused by a two-year drought, see Nau, *Arabes chrétiens*, 13–15. See the discussion of the political dimension of the grazing disputes of 536 and 539 (the "Strata dispute") above, pp. 66–67.

149. Jacob of Sarug, "Mimra on the Victorious Sergius," tr. Palmer, 118 (see epigram) and 137 (see pp. 25–26 above).

150. Theoph. Sim., *Hist.* 5.14.8.

the dead. In a story set in the reign of Leo I, a Jew who was burning at the stake called out, "God of Sergius, help me. Saint Sergius, you know!" and immediately was rescued by the saint on horseback, accompanied by Bacchus. When the Jew was later baptized, he adopted the name Sergius as a constant protection.[151] That the story may be a literary invention is of little interest. It is the vivid link between name and presence that we must retain.

The power and influence of the name Sergius were expressed, not only in the spiritual life of the individual, but also in the political arena. One example of this, discussed in chapter 5, is the reinstallation of Khusrau II on the Sasanian throne. By the late sixth century, Sergius's fame had reached the shores of the Atlantic, where a Syrian merchant had installed the martyr's index finger in a house-chapel in Bordeaux. Bishop Bertramn of Bordeaux had heard rumor of an eastern king who charged victoriously into battle with S. Sergius's thumb attached to his own. Craving such miraculous triumphs, the bishop attempted to wrest the relic from the Syrian. But in the struggle that ensued, Sergius's finger was splintered into tiny fragments.[152] Considering the potential for garbling reports between Mesopotamia and Bordeaux, it is not improbable that the eastern king of the rumor was originally Khusrau II.[153] Sergius had become a preeminent patron of victory, and of military victory especially. But the distant king in the East could easily have been Anastasius, Justinian, Khusrau, or the Ghassanid phylarch al-Mundhir, all of whom showed their faith in the saint's power.

151. The story, whose source is unknown, is told in the fourteenth-century ecclesiastical history of Xanthopoulus, *Eccles. hist.* 25.24.

152. Greg. Tur., *HF* 7.31.

153. Tillemont, *Memoires*, 5: 496, makes this suggestion.

FIVE

Frontier Shrine and Frontier Saint

JUSTINIAN, THEODORA, AND S. SERGIUS

At the heart of Constantinople rose the most elegant church ever erected in honor of Rusafa's martyr. Its plan is an octagon set in a square. The eastern wall of the square has an apse and the western wall is pierced by five doorways linking the narthex with the main body of the church. Through the narthex, the church was connected on the south to the now destroyed basilical church of SS. Peter and Paul, with which it shared a propylaeum and courtyard.[1] Between the central octagon and the outer square is a sheltered ambulatory on the ground floor, with a gallery on the second storey. Eight piers are joined by exedrae, either rectangular or deep semi-circles, arranged in an alternating order to create a dynamic, undulating movement around the central space. Two columns of colored marble with elegant folded or Ionic capitals punctuate the space within each exedra. Finely wrought columns support the architrave on the ground floor, while on the gallery level arches spring from the piers to crown each niche. From these eight piers and arches ascends a pumpkin dome divided into sixteen segments with alternately straight and curved surfaces. According to Procopius, the walls were richly adorned with marble revetment and gold mosaic.

The monogram carved on the ground floor capitals and the dedicatory inscription running along the entablature leave no doubt that the church was dedicated by Justinian and Theodora to the holy martyr Sergius:

> Other sovereigns have honored dead men whose labor was unprofitable, but our sceptered Justinian, fostering piety, honors with a splendid abode Sergius

---

1. Proc., *Aed.* 1.4.1–9. Janin, *Géographie ecclésiastique,* pt. 1, 3: 470, notes another, later church dedicated to Sergius and Bacchus in Constantinople, known only from synaxaria.

the Servant of Christ, Begetter of all things; whom not the burning breath of fire, nor the sword, nor any other constraint of torments disturbed; but who endured to be slain for the sake of Christ God, gaining by his blood heaven as his home. May he in all things guard the rule of the sleepless sovereign and increase the power of the God-crowned Theodora whose mind is adorned with piety, whose constant toil lies in unsparing efforts to nourish the destitute.[2]

The epigram praises the martyr's spiritual and physical endurance in a generic manner, without specific reference to the tortures described in the *Passio*. Likewise, Sergius's fellow martyr Bacchus, although present in the *Passio,* is absent from the epigram. Justinian beseeches the soldier-martyr Sergius to guard his rule. Theodora seeks the martyr's aid in the accomplishment of good works, an interest of the empress admired by Procopius and often shared by the emperor.[3] Despite the original dedication to S. Sergius alone, which was maintained by some later writers, others, as early as 536, included S. Bacchus.[4]

The church has attracted attention mainly from scholars interested in the debate over centrally planned palace churches, and little has been said about the church's broader significance for the cult of S. Sergius.[5] This

2. *CIG* 4.8639. See von Hammer[-Purgstall], *Constantinopolis und der Bosporos,* 1: xii–xiii; van Millingen, *Byzantine Churches,* 74; Ebersolt and Thiers, *Églises,* 24; Mercati, *Rendiconti* 3 (1924–25): 197–205, for the history of the publication of the inscription and the text. Tr. Mango, *JÖB* 21 (1972): 190, with slight alteration.

3. For example, after the fire started by the Nika Riot in 532 had destroyed a hospice that nestled between the old churches of Hagia Eirene and Hagia Sophia, Justinian and Theodora rebuilt and expanded the hospice, absorbing two other hospices nearby in the process (Proc., *Aed.* 1.2.14–18). An embroidered cloth adorning the altar in the church of the Holy Wisdom depicted the couple's ministry to the sick at hospices and their visits to churches; another portrayed them with hands entwined with those of the Mother of God and Christ (Paul. Silent., *Descriptio Sanctae Sophiae* 796–805).

4. The dedication to S. Sergius alone is maintained in *ACOec.* 3.174; Joh. Mal., *Chron.* 18.485; the ninth-century Georgian *Life of John, Abbot of S. Sergius* by John the Sceuophylax, 159, 163, but at 165 the dedication is to both; Const. Porph., *De cer.* 1.11; *Anth. gr.* 1.8. On the other hand, a dedication to S. Sergius and S. Bacchus appears in Proc., *Aed.* 1.4.3; in the tenth-century *Patria Konstantinoupoleos,* in *Script. orig. Const.* 2.231–32; and in the twelfth-century historian Cedrenus, *Hist.* 1.642 (Bekker). Pierre Gilles, who visited the church in 1544, discerned in the pilaster carvings of vines intermixed with clustered grapes hints at the church's association with Bacchus (*De topographia Constantinopoleos* 95–97). Three hundred years later, Joseph von Hammer [-Purgstall] arrived at the same conclusion after viewing the elaborate carving of the entablature (*Constantinopolis und der Bosporos,* 1: 376–77); van Millingen, *Byzantine Churches,* 72, corrects this misperception, noting that "though the flower points upward it has been mistaken for clusters of grapes," and adding that if the carving did portray grapes, the symbol would refer to the vine in the Gospel of John, and not to the god Bacchus.

5. Mango, *JÖB* 21 (1972): 189–92; Krautheimer, *JÖB* 23 (1974): 251–53; Mathews, *Revue de l'art* 24 (1974): 22–29; Mango, *BZ* 68 (1975): 385–92. I would like to thank Irfan Shahîd for sending the abstract of a paper in which he touches on some issues of general importance to the subject of Justinian and Sergius.

brief discussion does not aspire to join in the architectural controversy, but rather to shed some light on the importance of this Constantinopolitan church in the context of frontier religion during Justinian's reign.

To begin with, it is worth recalling that Procopius describes the church as an adornment for the entire city. Regardless of whether or not public access was allowed originally, as it certainly was by the twelfth century, the monumental church of S. Sergius could not have escaped the notice of the city's inhabitants and visitors. As Mango has underlined, it was built at a smart address. The decision made by Justinian and Theodora to dedicate the church to S. Sergius deserves to be seen within the broader context of the benefactors' activities, and not just Theodora's charities, which were sometimes enjoyed by non-Chalcedonian monks. Justinian's interest in the Syro-Mesopotamian martyr has been given short shrift. Mango justifiably disregards the dramatic early seventeenth-century account in which Sergius and Bacchus appear to the emperor Anastasius to warn him against executing the pair of officers, Justin and Justinian, who stood accused of treason.[6] In gratitude for the martyrs' intervention, the legend continues, Justinian erected a church in their honor in Illyricum, where the story was set. But this late fantasy is hardly Justinian's only association with Rusafa's martyr. Justinian followed the lead of Anastasius, whose defense of Rome's eastern frontier zone employed frontier martyrs as well as fortifications. Procopius mentions a well or cistern built by Justinian at a monastery of S. Sergius on Mount Cisseron in Palestine (possibly Galilean Kisra), and a chapel (οἶκος) of S. Sergius in Phoenician Ptolemais.[7] It is not out of the question that the church at Constantinople would have housed the thumb of Sergius translated to Constantinople by Anastasius and never heard of again. Anastasius may have planned a church for the martyr but simply run out of time, since the translation took place at the end of his life, between 514 and 518. Justinian, in turn, took an interest in Rusafa and at some point between 527 and 540 sent to the shrine a gold, gem-encrusted cross dedicated to S. Sergius by both himself and Theodora.[8] Perhaps also, on the model of the cross sent to Jerusalem by Theodosius and Pulcheria, the royal pair had expected to receive a relic of the martyr Sergius in return for their gift. Through building projects and this impressive joint gift, Justinian and

---

6. The legend and the "Life of Justinian" in which it is found are discussed by Bryce, *EHR* 2 (1887): 657–86, a good piece of detective work. Cf. also Mango, *JÖB* 21 (1972): 191, with n. 7. One goal of this "Life of Justinian" is to provide an etiology for the dedication to SS. Sergius and Bacchus of the monastery that stood on the banks of the river Bojana, near Shkodra in northern Albania. The adjacent fortress, which commands the surrounding plain, is known as Rozafat: on the toponomy, see Jireček, *Sitzungsberichte der kaiserlichen Akademie der Wissenschaften* 136 (1897): 49–54; Norris, *Islam in the Balkans*, 61–62, with n. 38.

7. Proc., *Aed.* 5.9.20 and 25.

8. Evagr., *HE* 4.28, reports that the gift was joint; *HE* 6.21, that it was from Theodora alone.

Theodora allied themselves with Rusafa's popular saint: they imposed their presence at Sergius's shrine in the frontier zone where defense, the fidelity of Arab allies and opposition to Chalcedon were live issues. The alliance was advertised at the capital too. While reinforcing their authority at the martyr's frontier shrine, they at the same time claimed the soldier-saint as their own by establishing S. Sergius in a position of honor in Constantinople.

The gift was a potent gesture at Rusafa, particularly if seen in the light of Sergius's reputation among the Arabs of Syria, whose political and religious allegiance to Constantinople was often suspect. In 542 or 543, Justinian bestowed on the Ghassanid leader al-Harith the title of *patricius*.[9] But as head of the Ghassanid confederation from 529 to 569, al-Harith zealously supported the non-Chalcedonian cause. At more or less the same time as Justinian was conferring honors on him, al-Harith turned to Theodora to approve the consecration of two non-Chalcedonian bishops, Jacob Baradaeus and Theodore.[10] Seen in the context of two of Justinian's most considerable preoccupations during his reign—reconciliation between Chalcedonians and their opponents, and maintenance of the eastern frontier—it was a wise decision to ally himself and his empress with the most influential martyr in the frontier zone, a military saint who enjoyed great popularity among the region's Arab and mainly, but not exclusively, non-Chalcedonian inhabitants.

IRANIAN INTEREST IN S. SERGIUS

Making his way up the Euphrates with his army in the spring of 540, Khusrau I bypassed the naturally fortified site of Circesium and made a halfhearted attempt to force Zenobia's surrender before moving on to Sura.[11] The soldiers at Sura put up a valiant resistance until their commander was killed. On the following day, the Surans, in despair, sent their bishop to Khusrau's camp to negotiate a surrender. But once the city gates were opened, Sura was taken by trickery, its houses looted, and many inhabitants slain. The survivors were taken hostage and their fate was put in the hands of Bishop Candidus of Rusafa by Khusrau, who presented the bishop with the opportunity to ransom 12,000 captives for two hundred pounds of gold. Candidus reluctantly promised to raise the money and the hostages were set free. Two years later when Khusrau returned to collect his due, Candidus emerged from Rusafa empty-handed to plead with the king.[12] Under tor-

9. Shahîd, *BZ* 52 (1959): 321–43, with additions in id., *Byzantium and the Semitic Orient* XI.

10. Joh. Eph., *Vita sanct.* 499–504; Bar. Hebr., *Chron. eccles.* 1.46; Mich. Syr., *Chron.* 9.29 (tr. Chabot, 2: 245–46).

11. Proc., *BP* 2.5.1–33.

12. Ibid., 20.1–16.

ture, Candidus bade Khusrau take the sacred vessels from Rusafa's shrine, and in due course an armed escort accompanied some of Candidus's men into Rusafa, where they emptied the treasury, save the martyr's silver reliquary. In particular, they took with them the gem-encrusted gold cross dedicated to the saint by Justinian and Theodora.[13] But these holy goods were not enough for Khusrau, who had been informed that the rest had been hidden by the inhabitants. Six thousand men were sent to besiege the city, but the plan to take it by stealth was foiled by an informant, an Arab Christian named Ambrus who was fighting in Khusrau's army. Only two hundred Roman soldiers were present to defend Rusafa, and the population was on the verge of surrender. At this point, Ambrus detached himself again from the Iranian camp to inform the inhabitants that the Iranian army had enough water for only two days longer, and would then be forced to retreat. According to this version, told by Procopius, faith in S. Sergius among the region's Arab population saved Rusafa. In Evagrius's account, the martyr's intervention was more direct—although the Iranians had heard that only women, children, and invalids remained within the walls, an immense army miraculously appeared on the battlements to defend the fortress-shrine.[14] According to both reports, Khusrau's army retreated the next day.

Half a century later, Khusrau II inherited a complicated history of invasion and détente between his empire and Rome's. Both the conflict and its resolution revolved not around differences but around shared interests, making trade, Arab allies, and Christians central issues in the empires' confrontations. The virtually self-governing community of Christians in the Iranian empire provided Khusrau II with a bridge into Roman Syria and Mesopotamia. Association, not simply with the Christian faith, but with the cult of S. Sergius in particular became a means of making his influence felt in the sensitive frontier zone between the two empires. During his long reign from 590 to 628, Khusrau II learned from his grandfather's political shrewdness in dealing with Christians. The later king's involvement with Christianity was, however, more subtle and more complex.[15] Evagrius and Theophylact provide evidence for Khusrau's involvement with S. Sergius within Roman territory, while for his patronage of the cult in the Iranian empire material must be drawn from more scattered and often later sources. The difference in sources does not necessarily impede a broad view of Khusrau's interest in Rusafa's saint. That interest makes most sense when understood, not according to territorial divisions, but in the context of frontier politics.

Rusafa played a pivotal role in Khusrau's relationship with Maurice. It

13. See Theoph., *Chron.* 5.13.1–2.

14. Evagr., *HE* 4.28.

15. Flusin, *Saint Anastase,* 2: 95–127, traces the fluctuations in Khusrau's policies toward Christians.

was the Roman military commander at Rusafa whom Khusrau chose as the mediator who would convey to the emperor his plea for protection.[16] In the west Syrian *Chronicon ad annum Christi 1234,* that commander is identified as "the Arab general who dwelt at Rusafa as a subject of the Romans, a zealous Christian man named Abu Jafna Nuʿman b. al-Mundhir."[17] This Jafna may, as his name suggests, have been the son of the Ghassanid phylarch al-Mundhir. Maurice embraced Khusrau's cause with enthusiasm and established him at Edessa with John of Rusafa, in whose household the exiled king could easily have heard stories of the miracles performed by Rusafa's saint.[18]

Khusrau's flight from his empire and eventual restoration had been prophesied by the Iranian apostate Gulanducht, who was born into a Zoroastrian family in Seleucia-Ctesiphon and married to a well-placed husband, but spent her Christian life in the frontier zone. Inspired by a vision, she was baptized and subsequently imprisoned in the Castle of Oblivion. After countless tortures, culminating in decapitation (from which she recovered, with the help of an angel, who reunited her head and body), Gulanducht journeyed into Roman territory, and on her way to Jerusalem as a pilgrim, she visited Rusafa. Later, she returned to live in Hierapolis, where she dreamt about Khusrau's future struggles. Her association with the frontier saint Sergius extended beyond her repose in 591, since she was buried at a chapel dedicated to Sergius between Nisibis and Dara, in order to intercede on behalf of all the region.[19] Evagrius gives a highly condensed account of Gulanducht's life in which he mentions the tortures she underwent at the hands of the Zoroastrians and the miracles she wrought, and then refers the reader to the *Vita* written by Bishop Stephen of Hierapolis.

Evagrius uses the story of Gulanducht to make a transition from the events following Bahram's usurpation to the thank offerings dedicated to S. Sergius at Rusafa by Khusrau after his restoration. Evagrius describes the gifts and includes their dedications, which are nearly identical to Theophylact's transcriptions, all of which will be discussed in due course. But first it is worth noting the last three items that follow Evagrius's extended account of Khusrau's gifts to S. Sergius and close his *Historia ecclesiastica.* In

---

16. Mich. Syr., *Chron.* 10.23 (tr. Chabot, 2: 371–72).

17. *Chron. 1234* 90 (Lat. tr. Chabot, 1: 169; Eng. tr. Palmer, 115). On this chronicle, which preserves parts of the secular history of Dionysius of Tall-Mahre (d. 845), see Palmer, *Seventh Century,* 85–104.

18. For John of Rusafa, see above, p. 102.

19. *Vita Gulanducht* (Georgian redaction) 20.2. The Georgian *Vita* is considered to be a faithful redaction of the original *Vita* (probably Syriac), composed by Bishop Stephen of Hierapolis, who knew Gulanducht and recorded her life story between the saint's death in 591 and Evagrius's mention of the work in 593–94 (Garitte, *AB* 74 [1956]: 419–25). For an abbreviated Greek account written by the priest Eustratius before 602, see Peeters, *AB* 62 (1944): 74–125.

these items, the Antiochene historian focuses on important participants in the political life of the frontier zone: Arab allies, Christian leaders, both Chalcedonian and oppositional, and miracle-working saints. The Lakhmid leader al-Nuʿman, who had formerly delighted in human sacrifice, is converted to Christianity and commits to the flames his gold statue of Aphrodite; Gregory, the patriarch of Antioch, after solemnly depositing Khusrau's gifts at S. Sergius's shrine, makes a whirlwind tour of the frontier zone, where, Evagrius reports, he reclaims from the Severan heresy many fortresses, villages, monasteries, and entire tribes; and Symeon the Younger, who, like the elder stylite, had by his miracles attracted both Romans and "barbarians," finishes his earthly days.[20]

The order and substance of what Theophylact chose to relate about Khusrau's reinstallation on the throne also conveys a clear sense of the primary political and religious influences in the frontier zone. As was noted in chapter 2, the account of Khusrau's gifts to Sergius at Rusafa opens Theophylact's fifth chapter, directly following Bishop Domitianus's triumphalist hymn in honor of the Iranian martyrs of Mayperqat at the end of book 4. Theophylact gives a fuller account of Gulanducht's life story than Evagrius, but both authors clearly assume the reader's familiarity with the famous saint's deeds. The history of John of Epiphania, Evagrius's contemporary, provided the organizational framework within which both Theophylact and Evagrius wrote. Differences arose from their diverging interests—Theophylact's in Khusrau's relationship to Rome and Evagrius's in church history.[21]

The chronology of Khusrau's fall and rise can be briefly outlined as follows:

15 February 590	Khusrau II is crowned
9 March 590	Bahram II is crowned
spring/summer 590	Khusrau appeals to Maurice
7 January 591	Khusrau prays to S. Sergius
9 February 591	the head of Zatspharam, one of Bahram's main commanders, is brought to Khusrau
late summer 591	Bahram is defeated and Khusrau is restored
autumn 591–winter 592	Khusrau sends his first offering to S. Sergius
592	Khusrau marries Shirin, an Aramaean Christian
April–August 593	Khusrau sends his second offering to S. Sergius[22]

20. Evagr., *HE* 6.22–23.

21. Khusrau's dedications to Sergius at Rusafa are described by Evagr., *HE* 6.21, and Theoph. Sim., *Hist.* 5.13.1–14.12. See also Higgins, *BZ* 48 (1955): 98–102.

22. For a political narrative, see Whitby, *Emperor Maurice,* 234–36.

We should not underestimate the influence of the widespread faith in S. Sergius's supernatural power on Khusrau's decision to turn for assistance to the Christian rider saint. Neither should we overlook that the choice also allowed the Sasanian king to establish a presence in the Barbarian Plain and create a rapport with the audience of S. Sergius's major shrine at Rusafa. Khusrau's first offering to S. Sergius was a gold cross, accompanied by the gem-studded gold cross dedicated by Justinian and Theodora to the saint and plundered from the treasury by Khusrau I. Khusrau II sent to Antioch a request for the manufacture of a cross, along with funds and a letter stating his motivation for the offering. After slight editing, the letter (or, for practical reasons, more likely an abbreviated version) was inscribed on the cross made for Khusrau and then sent to Rusafa.[23] The inscription reads:

> This cross I, Chosroes [Khusrau], King of Kings, son of Chosroes [dedicate]. When we departed for Romania on account of the devilish operations and villainy of the most ill-starred Baram son of Bargusnas and of his associate cavaliers, and because the ill-starred Zadesprates left the army and made for Nisibis in order to seduce the cavaliers of the district of Nisibis into rebellion and complicity in revolution, we also sent cavaliers with an officer to Charcha and, through the fortune of the most holy and renowned saint Sergius, when we heard that he was the granter of petitions, in the first year of our reign, on the seventh of January, we petitioned that if our cavaliers should kill or defeat Zadesprates, we would send a bejeweled gold cross to his shrine for the sake of his most holy name. And on the ninth of February they brought before us the head of Zadesprates. So, since we were successful in our petition, because each part was unambiguous, we have sent to the shrine of the most holy Sergius the cross made by us in honor of his most holy name, together with the cross sent to his shrine by Justinian, king of the Romans, which was brought here in time of estrangement between the two states by Chosroes our father, King of Kings, son of Koades, and which was discovered in our treasuries.[24]

Once reinstalled on his throne, Khusrau took a Christian named Shirin as a wife. Ten days after Khusrau prayed to S. Sergius that Shirin conceive, the saint visited him in a dream.[25] In thanksgiving for Sergius's intervention, in the spring or summer of 593, Khusrau sent to Rusafa a golden paten and chalice, along with a gold cross and a silk curtain embroidered in gold to be

---

23. For Higgins's reconstruction, see *BZ* 48 (1955): 92–98. The main difference between Evagrius and Theophylact here is that the former understands the text as an inscription on the gift, while the latter takes it to be an accompanying letter. The same is true of the second offering.

24. Theoph. Sim., *Hist.* 5.13.4–6 (tr. Whitby and Whitby, with alterations).

25. Evagr., *HE* 6.21; cf. Theoph. Sim., *Hist.* 5.13.1–14.12. For Khusrau's involvement with Christians in Iran, see Nau, *Arabes chrétiens*, 46–49, and Morony, *Iraq*, 332–83.

deposited at Sergius's shrine.[26] The gold paten's inscription elaborately denies possible misconstructions of Khusrau's gift:

> To the great martyr Sergius, Chosroes, King of Kings. I, Chosroes, King of Kings, son of Chosroes, have dispatched the gifts accompanying the paten not for the sight of men, nor so that the greatness of your most holy name be known from my words, but so that the truth about the events be recognized as well as the many favors and benefactions which I had from you: for it is my good fortune that my name should be carried on your holy vessels. During the time when I was in Berthamaïs, I petitioned of you, holy one, to come to my aid and that Seirem (Shirin) conceive in her womb. And since Seirem is a Christian and I a Hellene, our law does not grant us freedom to have a Christian wife. So on account of my gratitude to you, for this reason I disregarded the law, and I held and hold from day to day this one among my wives as legitimate, and thus I resolved now to beseech your goodness that she conceive in her womb. And I petitioned and ordained that if Seirem should conceive in her womb, I would send to your most holy shrine the cross that she wears. And with regard to this both I and Seirem have this purpose, that we should have possession of this cross in remembrance of your name, holy one. And we have resolved that for its value, although this does not extend beyond four thousand three hundred standard *miliaresia,* five thousand standard coins should be dispatched in its place. And from the time when I had this petition in my mind and made these calculations, until the time we came to Rhesonchosron, ten more days did not elapse and you, holy one, not because I am worthy but because of your goodness, appeared to me in a dream at night and thrice declared to me that Seirem had conceived in her womb. And in the dream itself, I thrice answered you in return and said, "Wonderful, wonderful." And because of your holiness and charity, and because of your most holy name, and because you are the granter of petitions, from that day Seirem did not know what is customary for women. I was in no doubt of this, but trusted in your words, even because you are holy and a true granter of petitions. After she did not experience womanly ways, from this I recognized the power of the vision and the truth of what you had spoken. So straight away I sent the cross and its value to your most holy shrine, giving orders that from its value one paten and one chalice should be made for the sake of the divine mysteries, but also that a cross, which is owed, be fixed on the honored altar, and a solid gold censer and a Hunnic curtain adorned with gold; and that the remaining *miliaresia* are for your holy shrine, so that through your fortune, holy one, in all things, but especially in this petition, you may come to the assistance of myself and Seirem. And what has come to us through your intercession by the mercy of your goodness, may it also advance to completion at the

---

26. Evagrius describes the fabrics as Hunnish; on this term, see Kislinger and Diethart, *Tyche* 2 (1987): 8. According to the Piacenza Pilgrim, who visited the Holy Land in the 570s, the entrance to the tomb of Christ was shrouded with gold-embroidered hangings (*Itin.* 25.7).

wish of myself and Seirem, so that both I and Seirem and everyone in the world may have hope in your power and still trust in you.[27]

According to Evagrius, who was primarily interested in ecclesiastical affairs, Khusrau did not send the first offerings directly to the shrine, but to Gregory, the Chalcedonian patriarch of Antioch, who personally, after receiving Maurice's blessing, dedicated them to the saint at Rusafa. The passage in Evagrius makes clear that this process guaranteed that the Iranian king's gifts would be delivered to the saint by Chalcedonian hands. By sending his offering first to Antioch, as diplomacy must have dictated, Khusrau acknowledged Roman control of the shrine, for the crosses were more than private ex-votos: they were symbols of the Iranian king's alliance with the widely invoked frontier saint. Khusrau's offerings joined those of countless other devotees, many of whom were responsible for the maintenance of Roman control of the region. Sergius's reputation among the Arab tribes who inhabited the territory joining the two empires had helped to create a Syro-Mesopotamian world that on one level ignored political allegiances. But the same Arab tribes that were joined through the cult of Sergius were often drawn into the political conflicts between the two empires.

Khusrau's dedications to S. Sergius need also to be seen in the context of political tensions in Iran, where Iranian Christianity was evolving an important political as well as cultural identity. Reverence for the rider saint Sergius was particularly fervid in Iran, where dissemination of the cult was aided by the way in which Sergius fitted so comfortably into the traditional heroic ideal that permeated Iranian culture.[28] Through his elaborate donations, Khusrau was not only associating himself with the Arab and Iranian devotees of Sergius. In their thank offering of a gold cross for Shirin's conception of a son, Khusrau and his wife also stepped deliberately into the place of Justinian and Theodora, whose gold cross Khusrau had returned with his first dedication.[29] The parallelism between the royal couples extended also to building projects, since after his return to power Khusrau constructed three churches in his empire: one for the Apostles, one for the Theotokos, and one for the martyr Sergius.[30] Although no source states

27. Theoph. Sim., *Hist.* 5.14.2–11 (tr. Whitby and Whitby, with alterations); cf. Evagr., *HE* 6.21. The intrusion of the Greek editor is especially evident when Khusrau refers to himself as a "Hellene," i.e., a non-Christian.

28. See Wiessner in *Festgabe*, 141–55, esp. 150–55.

29. In the context of the interest that Khusrau and Shirin showed in S. Sergius and the Holy Cross, it should be recalled that in 559, Bishop Abraamios made a dedication to the Holy Cross, probably in the basilica A complex (see chapter 3).

30. Flusin, *Saint Anastase*, 2: 101–6. Accounts of the churches vary. Mich. Syr., *Chron.* 10.23 (tr. Chabot, 2: 372), lists the Mother of God, the Apostles, and the martyr Sergius; Agapius,

explicitly for which of his two Christian wives, Maria or Shirin, the Sergius church was built, in the context of the miraculous bond linking Khusrau and Shirin to S. Sergius, and manifested in their votive offerings to S. Sergius at Rusafa, it was most probably for Shirin.[31] The Nestorian *Chronicle of Seert* is somewhat more specific, agreeing that Khusrau built three churches, but adding that two were for Maria and one large one (together with a palace) in the region of Beth Lashpar for Shirin the Aramaean.[32] The palace can be identified with the extensive ruins of Khusrau's summer palace, which give their name to the modern Kasr-i Shirin, Shirin's palace. Thirty-three kilometers northwest of the ancient city and important Christian center of Hulwan, the palace was sited beside the river Hulwanrud and on the important caravan route between Ctesiphon and the Zagros plateau.[33] Babai the Great's *History* of the early seventh-century martyr Giwargis mentions a famous monastery dedicated to the martyr Sergius, where the queen would celebrate the saint's festival. This monastery was located in the Hulwan region and should no doubt be identified with the church of S. Sergius built for Shirin by Khusrau II.[34]

Like Theodora, Shirin involved herself in court politics and, in particular, in disputes between the non-Chalcedonians, whose patroness she was, and rival Nestorians.[35] Khusrau, however, had his own quarrel with the Nestorian catholicos Ishoyahb of Arzun (582–95), who had made the unfortunate decision to remain in his see rather than follow Khusrau when the deposed king was forced into exile in the Roman empire.[36] In a move demonstrating to Maurice Khusrau's respect for the Chalcedonians, and by extension for the Roman emperor's religious stance—and at the same time putting Khusrau's own treacherous catholicos in his place—Khusrau invited Anastasius, the patriarch of Antioch, to consecrate the new churches between 593 and 595. The choice illustrates beyond a doubt Khusrau's mastery of the intricate relationship between Christianity and political allegiance in Roman and Iranian relations. When Ishoyahb died in 595, he was succeeded at the helm of his Church by the elderly Sabrisho, whose reign was distinguished by good relations with Khusrau, who even took part in

---

Kitab al-'unwan, pp. 186–87, speaks of one at Ctesiphon to S. Mary and the other to S. Sergius the martyr; while the *Chron. 1234* 171, mentions S. Sergius and the Mother of God, both for his wife.

31. Flusin, *Saint Anastase*, 2: 102–4, with n. 42, also arrives at this conclusion.

32. *Chronicle of Seert* 58, pp. 146–47 (Scher).

33. Streck and Lassner in *EI²*, 4: 730–31.

34. Babai the Great, *History of Mar Giwargis* 518 (tr. Braun, 258). See Hoffmann, *Auszüge,* 120, for the identification.

35. For a discussion of Shirin's role in Iranian religious politics, see Flusin, *Saint Anastase,* 2: 106–18.

36. Labourt, *Christianisme,* 201–7.

Sabrisho's consecration. The choice also pleased the emperor Maurice, who sent an artist to Ctesiphon to paint the pontiff's portrait. Maurice kept the portrait in his treasury, along with holy relics and a hat belonging to Sabrisho. As a sign of great favor, the emperor sent the catholicos a piece of the True Cross contained in a reliquary covered in jewels. In a foreshadowing of his later translation of the True Cross to his capital from Jerusalem, Khusrau intercepted the first piece of the Cross that had been sent to Sabrisho, making a gift of it to Shirin.[37]

After the fall of Maurice in November 602, Khusrau again exploited his familiarity with tensions among Christian groups, this time outside Iranian territory. When he invaded and occupied all Syria and Mesopotamia, he decided, in order to undermine the region's links with Constantinople, to refrain from requiring apostasy from Christianity. Instead, he offered a choice between allegiance to the non-Chalcedonian or the Nestorian Church, since the decision of Chalcedon had come by the early seventh century to stand for Orthodox Roman Christianity.[38] Non-Chalcedonian Christianity was widespread throughout Syria and Mesopotamia, in the villages, cities, monasteries, and among the tribes—that is, the same places Patriarch Gregory had visited on his eastern tour. A large part of the region's pastoral Arab population, in particular those allied with the Banu Ghassan, was non-Chalcedonian. Khusrau's aim in cultivating Rusafa's saint and non-Chalcedonian Christianity was to shift the political balance of Syria and Mesopotamia in the Iranian empire's favor. Almost two centuries earlier, Yazdgard had attempted to associate himself with Marutha and the cult of martyrs at the strategic site of Mayperqat. Khusrau I had supported Ahudemmeh's cultivation of devotion to Sergius as a means of monitoring Arab pastoralists who crossed the frontier zone. The Arab tribes who inhabited and defended the frontier zone were crucial for the maintenance of both empires' territorial claims. They were allied with either Rome or Iran, but had been known in the past to change sides, so by making his presence felt at an important center such as Rusafa, Khusrau II was also courting their favor, just as Justinian had tried to do in the 530s and 540s.

THE GHASSANID CONFEDERATION

Any investigation of Ghassanid involvement with the Sergius cult in Syria, and at Rusafa in particular, runs up against serious difficulties with the

---

37. *Chronicle of Seert* 67, pp. 172–77. On the Cross in Ctesiphon, see Flusin, *Saint Anastase*, 2: 170–72.

38. Agapius, *Kitab al-ʿunwan*, pp. 198–200, referring to the terms offered at Edessa. For the broader historical context of the association of the Chalcedonian position with the Roman Empire, see Fowden, *Empire to Commonwealth*, 123.

sources. Irfan Shahîd has labored to fill in the gaps of evidence and recon-
stitute a living picture of Ghassanid control in Syria, Palestine, and Arabia.[39]
Because of his particular interest—which he shares with the sources of
the period—in the political and religious relations between Rome and its
Ghassanid allies, Shahîd has focused his attention on the Ghassanid, specifically Jafnid, ruling elite. As Shahîd has often emphasized, the leaders
of the Ghassanid confederation, those whom Nöldeke called the Princes of
the House of Jafna, were settled Arabs interested in the horse and the hunt,
occupations closely linked to their role also as a mobile fighting force.
There is no reason to claim, in contradiction to Shahîd, that the Jafnid elite
followed their own flocks in the manner of Arab pastoralists. But on the
other hand, it cannot be overlooked that they were leaders of a confederation that spanned a region including rich agricultural land, villages on the
fringe of the steppe, and arid steppeland, swathes of which were never cultivable. The present study of Ghassanid interest in the Sergius cult will en-
deavor to bring into the picture the pastoral dimension of the Ghassanid
confederation, which our literary sources, on the whole, leave to one side.

Shahîd has underscored the sophistication with which the Ghassanid
elite conducted their relations with other political and religious leaders.[40]
What is commonly called the Ghassanid confederation—properly speaking, the body of Arab allies united under the leadership of the Jafnid dynasty of the Banu Ghassan, originally from South Arabia[41]—performed a
twofold service for the Roman empire. On the one hand, it guarded the
frontier zone against external penetration, in particular by Iran's Lakhmid
allies. At least equally important—but much less well documented—was
the Ghassanid federation's role in the internal policing of Roman territory,
in particular of nomadic groups in relation to each other and to the settled
populations. Unfortunately, little is known in detail about the political and
military organization of this confederation, although it seems that members
of the Jafnid dynasty may have been responsible for particular regions and
the tribes based there.[42]

In addition to the culturally diverse political world in which the Ghassanid leaders exercised their admirable diplomatic skill, it is also necessary
to see them in the Arab context, which embraced Arab pastoralists as well
as farmers, merchants and the ruling elite. Ghassanid power in the eyes of

39. Shahîd, *BAFIC* and *BASIC*, 1. For a rich but utterly neglected account of the Ghassanids, see Musil et al., *Kuṣejr ʿAmra*, 130–51.

40. For Ghassanid involvement with the anti-Chalcedonian cause in Syria, see, with discretion, Shahîd, *BASIC*, 1: 691–995; on the Sergius cult in particular, see 949–62.

41. Robin, *CRAI* 1996: 698 n. 118, stresses that it is by no means certain that the entire
tribe of Ghassan migrated north to Palestine and Syria.

42. Donner, *Early Islamic Conquests*, 43–44; Shahîd, *Byzantium and the Semitic Orient* I,
63–65.

Rome was founded both on the speed of their cavalry and on their knowledge of the land. Such intimate knowledge is rooted in the world of steppe pastoralism. It is to the further credit of al-Harith's diplomacy that he understood when to play on Roman cultural stereotypes of Arab life, which were certainly familiar to him. Perhaps the best example of this is an incident preserved by Michael the Syrian, which probably took place in 536/37 at a meeting between al-Harith and the notoriously zealous Chalcedonian patriarch of Antioch, Ephrem.[43] The latter was pressing al-Harith to enter into communion with the Chalcedonian Church, an invitation the Ghassanid patron of the non-Chalcedonian cause repeatedly refused. Finally, in order to drive his point home, al-Harith invited the patriarch to a banquet at which camel meat was the only fare offered. When, as expected, Ephrem was repelled, al-Harith seized the opportunity to compare the hierarch's disgust with his own at the thought of taking communion from Chalcedonian hands. al-Harith's coup worked because it tapped into deep-running prejudices against the nomadic Arab way of life, in which the consumption of camel meat was a mainstay.[44] Even though there is no evidence to suggest that al-Harith was himself a pastoralist, to assume that he was somehow remote from this nomadic way of life is to sever an important bond that linked the Ghassanid elite to the varied constituency the confederation embraced. Because of the biases of the written sources, it is only with great difficulty that a picture of the diversity of the Syro-Mesopotamian and, specifically, the Ghassanid sphere can be recaptured. But that diversity contributed to the important role played by Rusafa as a fixed center in the steppe, and every attempt must be made to reach a fuller understanding of the ways in which settled and nomadic groups interacted in this region.

Literary evidence records a number of Ghassanid-associated churches south of Damascus that were dedicated to S. Sergius. In the sixth century, there was a non-Chalcedonian monastery dedicated to S. Sergius at BWŞʿ near Jilliq, some 20 kilometers south of Damascus and the site of a Ghassanid residence.[45] At the same time, another non-Chalcedonian monastery dedicated to S. Sergius flourished at Jabiya (Gabbitha in Syriac) in the Jaw-

---

43. Mich. Syr., *Chron.* 9.29 (tr. Chabot, 2: 246–48). See Shahîd, *BASIC*, 1: 746–55, for a discussion of the passage.

44. Cf. Theoph., *Chron.*, A.M. 6122, p. 333: Jewish converts to Islam realized that Muhammad was not the Messiah when they saw him eating camel meat. On the unflattering and common identification of Arabs as camel eaters in Greek literature, see Cook, *al-Qanṭara* 13 (1992): 10, with n. 55. For the provision of meat—mutton, goat, and camel—to the settled population by Arab pastoralists in the modern period, see Jabbur, *Bedouins of the Desert*, 35.

45. "Letter of the Archimandrites," in *Documenta* 221 (tr. Chabot, 154). The precise vocalization of the site BWŞʿ is not known. Lamy published an earlier edition and translation in *Actes du onzième congrès international des orientalistes* (1898): 117–37. See also Nöldeke, *ZDMG* 29 (1875): 427. For discussion of the *Documenta*, a redaction of non-Chalcedonian documents

lan, the celebrated *hirta* and principle residence of the Jafnids.[46] This monastery was perhaps built by al-Harith.[47] In 587, the phylarch Jafna offered this church of S. Sergius as the site for a meeting between the quarreling non-Chalcedonian patriarch Damian of Alexander and the dethroned patriarch of Antioch, Peter of Callinicum.[48] Jabiya, which spread out over several hills, was the most famous of many sites associated with the Ghassanids in the Hawran. The area was renowned for its mild climate, plentiful grasses, and perennial waters, as the name suggests: *jabiya* in Arabic indicates the shallow, man-made depressions from which animals would drink water supplied from wells or springs.[49] The situation of the Ghassanid-allied Arabs of the Hawran bears close resemblance to that created by Ahudemmeh and Maruta of Takrit, in which pastoral Arabs were linked through their migratory patterns to the life of monastic communities.[50] The pastoral as well as settled Arabs would have provided gifts and protection to the monasteries, which, in turn, served as permanent centers of spiritual sustenance and venues where the Arabs could exhibit their influence but also as bases in the Hawranian agricultural zone where many pastoralists would spend the summer months. Active Ghassanid patronage of non-Chalcedonian monasteries in the Hawran is explicitly attested in the "Letter of the Archimandrites," signed in 570 by 137 non-Chalcedonian abbots, priests, and deacons (fifteen of whom were named Sergius) in condemnation of the "pseudopastors" of the tritheist heresy. This document provided the raw material for Nöldeke's groundbreaking study of Hawranian topography in 1875, in which he mapped the monasteries and sites with known Ghassanid associations. The past century of scholarship has fine-tuned Nöldeke's work, and Irfan Shahîd's recent study of the document has further clarified our picture of how the association between the Ghassanid confederation and the non-Chalcedonian monasteries worked, a potentially important parallel for Rusafa.[51]

We can glimpse this overlapping of settled and pastoral life in the Hawran

---

dating between 535 and 580, with the majority between ca. 560 and 568, see van Roey and Allen, *Monophysite Texts,* 267–303, esp. 290 on the so-called Letter of the Archimandrites.

46. "Letter of the Archimandrites," in *Documenta* 215 (tr. Chabot, 149); Mich. Syr., *Chron.* 10.22 (tr. Chabot, 2: 367); Nöldeke, *ZDMG* 29 (1875): 430; Aigrain in *DHGE,* 3: 1218–19.

47. Shahîd, *BASIC,* 1: 958.

48. Mich. Syr., *Chron.* 10.22 (tr. Chabot, 2: 364–70). See also Shahîd, *BASIC,* 1: 932, and id., *ARAM* 5 (1995): 491–503.

49. Conrad, *BMGS* 18 (1994): 46 n. 131; *EI²,* 2: 360.

50. See chapter 4.

51. See Shahîd, *BASIC,* 1: 824–43, esp. n. 118, on the problems of transliteration. See also Sartre in *Trois études,* 177–88, a study of the Ghassanids and non-Chalcedonian monasteries primarily from a topographical point of view.

in poetry composed by Hassan ibn Thabit (ca. 570–ca. 659), who spent time in the company of the Ghassanid princes of the house of Jafna before offering his talent to sing the Prophet's praises shortly after 622.[52] "Its banners descended on Busra, and in Rumah like whirlwinds it left the smoke of its blazing passage": the image of this opening verse of the shorter of two poems composed by Hassan between 590 and 610 on the theme of the plague, comes straight from the open steppe, conjuring up the dust devils that have struck the imagination of countless travelers. Hassan animates the plague—it is the jinn, the demons who overturn both daily routine and annual celebration, bringing calamity upon laborer and prince alike. His lament takes on the texture of the landscape with its variety of inhabitants: he follows after the bereaved, naming their villages, recalling their tents nearby, their herds of horses, thereby tracing the epidemic's path, but also the Ghassanid presence in the Hawran:

> To whom belongs the abode rendered desolate in Maʿan,
>> From the heights of al-Yarmuk unto al-Khamman,
> Then al-Qurayyat down from Balas, then Darayya,
>> Then Sakkaʾ, then the compounds [*qusur*] close by,
> Then the hinterland of Jasim, then the wadis
>> Of al-Suffar, where herds of horses and fine white thoroughbreds feed?
> That was the abode of him whose tent is raised on lofty poles,
>> The one dear unto me beyond the measure of his friendship and favour.
> Their mother was bereaved, and was bereaved of them
>> On the day they stopped to camp at Harith al-Jawlan.
> Easter approached, so the young girls
>> Sat to arrange garlands of coral,
> Gathering saffron in finely perforated cloths,
>> Wearing saffron-dyed gowns of linen,
> And not busying themselves with resin, nor with gum,
>> Nor with the seeds of the colocynth.
> That was a home of the al-Jafna when calamity struck,
>> As the vicissitudes of the ages claimed their due.
> I did indeed consider that there I behaved as a resolute man should,
>> When the place where I sat and stayed was in the presence of the wearer
>> of the crown.[53]

All the toponyms are identifiable and all represent known haunts of the Ghassanids. They form a triangle that closely follows the major, paved Roman roads from Damascus in the north to Dayr al-Kahf southeast of Bostra,

---

52. Conrad, *BMGS* 18 (1994): 12–58.
53. Hassan ibn Thabit, *Diwan* 1.255, no. 123 (tr. Conrad, *BMGS* 18 [1994]: 30).

continuing along the Bostra-Dar'a road as far west as Gadara / Umm Qays, moving northward again through the Jawlan past Jabiya and Jasim, and back up to the Ghuta plain of Damascus.[54] The sites that Hassan and an anonymous reviser of his poem mention share certain important characteristics besides an association with the Ghassanids and a position on main routes. Most command a defensive advantage, are near water and fertile fields and include a monastery, thus confirming the association suggested in the "Letter of the Archimandrites." Sufferers include those living in tents and in *qusur,* which Conrad translates here as "compounds" rather than the more traditional "castle," "palace," or "fortress." Spreading south from Damascus, the plague devastated the fertile Ghuta, described as a patchwork of villages and *qusur.* While Hassan evokes the "wadis of al-Suffar, where herds of horses and fine white thoroughbreds feed," a contemporary reviser of his poem substitutes the "buildings of Suffar."[55] This alternative is not, however, incompatible with the pastoral image. Encampments included a wide variety of structures, from the heavy basalt houses and churches that have outlived centuries of inhabitants in the Hawran, to more ephemeral structures that usually elude archeologists.[56]

To the number of Ghassanid-associated sites known from the "Letter" and from Hassan ibn Thabit's poems, archeological survey may have recently added another. Only the site's modern name is known, al-Ramthaniya,[57] located on well-watered ground surrounding a volcanic summit in the east-

---

54. See the map in Conrad, *BMGS* 18 (1994): 22.

55. The variant reading is recorded in 'Arafat's edition, 1.257.

56. Rather than associating permanent buildings more or less exclusively with the sedentarization of pastoral nomads, it is helpful to look at the use made by beduin in the modern period of permanent structures. For example, a shaykh of the Banu Sakhr in the 1920s built what was called a *qasr* in the Syrian steppe. This residential compound is described as follows in Lewis, *Nomads and Settlers,* 231 n. 30: "[P]art storehouse, part family and tribal headquarters, they [the *qusur*] were used by the shaykhs particularly to entertain guests and as the venue of tribal gatherings." See also 139. Usually, the skaykh lived with his family in a tent pitched nearby.

57. Note the older transcription al-Rumsaniyya in Schumacher, *Jaulan,* 231–35, 292; Oliphant, *PEQ* (1886): 81. I would like to thank Claudine Dauphin for providing me with offprints. A full appreciation of the interesting work of Dauphin and her team is frustrated by the absence of a detailed plan of the ecclesiastical complex on the summit. Only a schematic plan of the entire settlement and field systems, as well as photographs of limited use, are available in print. For a general plan, see Dauphin in *Early Christianity,* ed. Manns and Alliata, 70, fig. 2, and id. in *Akten,* 668, fig. 1, with pl. 83a, a photograph of the summit showing the monastery and martyrium from afar. See also Dauphin, *Archéologia* 297 (1994): 52–64; 294 (1993): 50–57; Gibson and Dauphin, *BA-IAS* 12 (1992–93): 7–31; Dauphin and Gibson, *IEJ* 41 (1991): 179; Gibson and Dauphin in *Archéologie et espaces,* 35–45; Dauphin, *IEJ* 36 (1986): 274–75; 34 (1984): 268–69; 33 (1983): 112–13. For publication of the Greek inscriptions, see Gregg in Dauphin et al., *POChr* 46 (1996): 324–28.

ern Jawlan, approximately twenty kilometers due west of Jasim.[58] A spring rises in the northwest sector of the settlement, and at the eastern foot of the volcanic summit is a built pool. The dense assortment of secular and ecclesiastical buildings at the site includes facilities for storing water and corralling animals. Enclosures have been discovered on the northwest, north, and northeast of the settlement, and traces of fields marked out by boulders stretch out toward the west and southwest.[59]

At the highest point of the settlement is a large rectangular structure with ancient foundations, but rebuilt at various periods, in part with re-used cut stones, some decorated in relief with vines, palm trees, crosses, and geometrical designs. A Greek inscription carved on the far upper right-hand corner of a basalt lintel gives a date in the Seleucid era of 685, that is, A.D. 373–74.[60] This date would seem to mark the erection of the building, while another Greek inscription from the same building identifies the structure as a martyrium of S. John the Baptist and is dated June 377.[61] This longer inscription of eleven lines records that the *illustrius ordinarius* Flavius Nuʿman, who had been responsible for a military division, built the martyrium after completing his military service. The inscription's date, 377, may record the consecration, since it postdates the first inscription by at least three years.[62] The presence of relics of S. John the Baptist at al-Ramthaniya has been plausibly explained in the context of the destruction of the shrine dedicated to the prophet and saint at Sebaste under the emperor Julian. Once the relics were dislodged from their original cult site, it is not difficult to imagine that some of them ended up in the Jawlan. Another inscription, discovered on the ground outside the western entrance by a late nineteenth-century traveler who published a drawing, records the restoration of the martyrium by a *clarissimus* Balbion.[63] The rebuilding included wall carvings in high relief and a mosaic floor. The restoration is undated, but on the basis of the letter forms, the survey team has assigned it to the

58. For al-Ramthaniya's proximity to Jabiya and Jasim, which is not mentioned in any discussion of the site, see Dussaud, *Topographie*, map 1.2D for "Roumsaniyé" and 2.2A for "Djabiya" and "Djasim."

59. Dauphin, *IEJ* 36 (1986): 274.

60. Gregg in Dauphin et al., *POChr* 46 (1996): 326, no. 26, with drawing in VI, fig. 20.

61. Ibid., 325–26, no. 25, with photograph in XV, pl. Va.

62. Dauphin in Dauphin et al., *POChr* 46 (1996): 335–36.

63. Gregg in Dauphin et al., *POChr* 46 (1996): 327, no. 28, with drawing 7, fig. 22 and photograph at XVI, pl. VIa. See also the brief discussion by Dauphin in Dauphin et al., *POChr* 46 (1996): 336–37. Schumacher, who published his work in 1888, discusses the site briefly (*Jaulan*, 231–35); fig. 125 is a drawing of the inscription without translation or commentary; see also fig. 117, for a plan of the building now on the site of the martyrium. Oliphant, *PEQ* (1886): 81, also includes a drawing of the inscription. On use in the eastern provinces of the title *clarissimus*, see Shahîd, *Byzantium and the Semitic Orient* III, 323–22.

sixth century. In addition to the inscriptions that clearly identify the original building and its rebuilding by Balbion as a martyrium, the Christian nature of the building is also indicated by the many stone blocks carved with Christian symbols, some of which are scattered near the site, while others were incorporated in later reconstructions of the building.[64] That the present rectangular construction is a product of the Islamic period is suggested by the pointed internal arches and the plan, which is unlike that of any known Christian martyrium, with no eastern apse, entrances on the east and west sides, and a long, narrow annex attached on the north side.[65] A reused block from the vicinity seems to have been fitted out to hold an icon of the saint, since over an oval recess in the stone the name of John was carved and adorned with a vine trellis.[66]

John the Baptist was commemorated on several occasions throughout the year, the two most popular falling in the summer (his birth on 24 June and his beheading on 29 August), when the Hawran, and related Jawlan, would have been host to nomadic groups pasturing their flocks in the dry season. The remains of al-Ramthaniya suggest that the martyrium of John was part of a cluster of related buildings, perhaps including a funerary chapel to the west, a ring of natural caves to the southeast, and a monastery arranged around a courtyard to the south.[67] This group of ecclesiastical buildings dominated the settlement. It was surrounded by an enclosure wall and linked to the enclosures southwest of the settlement by a processional way, which can still be made out. Evidence of ancient tent enclosures mixed in with a few permanent structures suggests that pastoralists would have pitched camp just beyond the settled area in order to exploit the pasture and water supply around al-Ramthaniya.[68] Additionally, they would have been drawn to the feast of the saint, perhaps also for baptism, as at the shrine of Symeon at Qalʿat Simʿan and of Sergius at Rusafa, where groups of Arabs gathered for that purpose.[69] Discovered in the area northeast of

---

64. Schumacher, *Jaulan*, figs. 118–25.

65. Dauphin, *IEJ* 34 (1984): 268, states that the rectangular building represents the western end of the martyrium. The existence of a late antique martyrium on the site is clear from the inscriptions.

66. Gregg in Dauphin et al., *POChr* 46 (1996): 326–27, no. 27 with VI, fig. 21; XV, pl. Vb. See also Dauphin, *IEJ* 34 (1984): 268. Cf. the similar arrangement at Kafr Antin in northern Syria (see above, p. 118).

67. Dauphin in Dauphin et al., *POChr* 46 (1996): 337; Dauphin, *IEJ* 34 (1984): 268.

68. Dauphin in *Akten* 671–73; Dauphin, *BA-IAS* 8 (1988–89): 83–4; Dauphin, *IEJ* 36 (1986): 274. For a discussion of the archeology of nomadic enclosures, see Rosen, *J. Field Archeology* 20 (1993): 441–51, with useful drawings and a consideration of a camp in the Negev within the wider context of nomadism in the surrounding region.

69. Sev. Ant., *Hom. cath.* 57, p. 93. Dauphin does not draw attention to parallel evidence for nomad baptism at great pilgrimage sites, although she does conjecture that a pool of undisclosed dimensions, located in the area of the enclosures, would have been used for mass bap-

the pool, perhaps at the head of the processional way, is what seems to have been an open-air shrine, with stones set up to mark the perimeter and an apse with an upright stone at the eastern end.[70] The suggestion that the stone served as an altar for the seasonal shrine should be treated with caution, since it would be highly unusual to leave an altar exposed to the elements and potential desecrators. More likely it would have marked the correct orientation for worship.

The seasonal nature of nomadic association with al-Ramthaniya should be underlined more than it has been in the published reports, which assume that nomadic presence at a settlement implies a gradual sedentarization. As we have seen in the case of the Arab interaction with monasteries recorded in the *History of Ahudemmeh* and the *History of Maruta,* the popularity and influence of certain cult sites in Syria and Mesopotamia depended to a significant extent on the mobility of groups in the region, especially the Arab pastoralists. The evidence at al-Ramthaniya, in particular, ought to be seen in the context of the site's close proximity to the important Ghassanid centers at Jabiya and Jasim, in a strategically important zone between the Syro-Mesopotamian steppe and the Mediterranean coastal cities. The patronage of Flavius Nu'man and Balbion may reflect their attempts as leaders in the region to capitalize on the link between cult sites and pastoralist movement. Despite the shortcomings of our present knowledge of al-Ramthaniya's architectural history, the accumulation around the site's water supply of a martyrium, enclosures, fields, and, it seems, a small monastery, points toward its inclusion among sites associated with the Ghassanid confederation. Like Hassan ibn Thabit's poems, the evidence from al-Ramthaniya reveals the wide spectrum of pastoralists and agriculturalists that flourished in the Hawran and Jawlan. But what is more, these examples reinforce the importance in nomadic life of permanent centers, especially cult centers, a relationship political leaders in the region were keen to control.

AL-MUNDHIR

Outside Rusafa's northern gate is a cemetery in which stands a small cross-in-square stone building, measuring 17 m in width and 20 m in length

---

tisms. Without more evidence about the context and construction of the pool, the suggestion cannot be evaluated. Even if the pool is more likely to have been intended for storage of water for animals than for Christian ritual, the suggestion that mass baptisms occurred should be taken seriously, since these could easily have been facilitated by a movable font.

70. Dauphin, *Archéologia* 297 (1994): 64; Dauphin and Gibson, *BA-IAS* 12 (1992–93): 28–29; and Dauphin, *IEJ* 36 (1986): 274, pl. 35c, a photograph of the stone at the eastern end of the temenos.

Figure 11. Rusafa: al-Mundhir building, interior from west.

(fig. 11).[71] The building, positioned 150 m northeast of the gate, stands on an eminence east of the main road leading into the town. Entering through the main door, which is located on the building's west side, one sees four central piers whose capitals are decorated with the split leaf design typical of northern Syria and Mesopotamia. The central space was probably covered by a pyramidal wooden roof, while barrel vaults covered the main axes. Pendentive domes still today cover the small bays in the building's four corners. At the eastern end an apse was flanked on either side by a separate, small rectangular room. The arch that spans the apse is supported on piers to the south and north, and the corner capital of the southern pier was adorned with a bird with outstretched wings, now much damaged.

71. I would like to thank Thilo Ulbert who, over the course of several years, has responded to my queries about the excavations at Rusafa and has read and commented on earlier versions of my discussion of the al-Mundhir building. I am also indebted to Gunnar Brands, who provided extensive comments on the discussion of the al-Mundhir building in my dissertation, "Sergius of Rusafa: Sacred Defense in Late Antique Syria-Mesopotamia" (Princeton, 1995). The argument that I advanced there concerning the building's identification remains unchanged here, but is supported by further evidence. Neither Ulbert nor Brands should be held responsible for my conclusions. For a much needed reconsideration of the building's architecture and decoration, see Brands, *DaM* 10 (1998), 211–35. Also, Fowden, *DaM* 11 (2000).

Crosses carved on some of the capitals were later lopped off.[72] Other crosses were scratched on the interior walls of the building. A cross in relief marked the apex of the apse and it is very likely that another was carved on the now seriously damaged medallion at the center of the molding over the double apse window. The upper band of the molding is decorated with an elaborate and finely carved frieze with marine motifs. The lower band bears a Greek inscription: +Νικᾷ ἡ τύχη Ἀλαμουνδάρου, "the fortune of Alamoundaros triumphs," or, more loosely, "Long live al-Mundhir."[73] The inscription refers to the Ghassanid leader al-Mundhir, called Alamoundaros in Greek, who held the office of phylarch from 570 to 581.

Standing just outside the gypsum walls of Rusafa, the al-Mundhir building occupies a space between the densely built-up pilgrimage center and the open Syrian steppe (see title page). This building is important to the study of the Sergius cult for various reasons. First and foremost, thanks to the inscription, the structure is a concrete link between the Ghassanid phylarch and S. Sergius at the martyr's primary cult site. The building's presence at Rusafa is an indication of the geographical range of Ghassanid involvement in Syria. Secondly, the phylarch's building, I argue, offers another example of S. Sergius's mediating power in this region. This point in particular requires some explanation, which must begin with the task of identifying the structure's purpose.

In 1939, Jean Sauvaget published an interpretation of this building that has been almost universally accepted ever since.[74] The success of Sauvaget's views owes much to the author's familiarity with the landscape and the early Islamic cultural history of Syria. Excavation of the monument began over a decade ago, and a full publication of the building is now being prepared by Thilo Ulbert. While a reexamination of the evidence may, in the circumstances, seem premature, there are still many points that can usefully be

72. Guyer in Sarre and Herzfeld, *Archäologische Reise*, 43; Spanner and Guyer, *Rusafa*, 66.

73. Guyer discussed Rusafa's architecture in Sarre and Herzfeld, *Archäologische Reise*, 2: 39–43; fig. 156 illustrates the inscription; fig. 152 is a plan and fig. 154 a reconstruction of the building with pyramidal roof. Spanner and Guyer, *Rusafa*, also publish a plan, pl. 31, and the inscription, fig. 16. For discussion of the accentuation of the acclamation—which should here be taken as the present indicative—see Cameron, *Porphyrius*, 76–80. See now also the discussion of the inscription by Shahîd, *BASIC*, 1: 501–5, esp. 503 n. 354, with photograph opposite 502. On the basis of the inscription's relationship to the decoration on the molding, Sauvaget, *Mosquée omeyyade*, 159 n. 2, concludes that the inscription is original and excludes the possibility that it could be a later graffito.

74. Sauvaget, *Byzantion* 14 (1939): 115–30. The thorough dissemination of this theory is remarkable. To mention only two recent examples from books with a wide readership, Cameron, *Mediterranean World*, 181, writes that Rusafa was "the main Ghassanid centre," while Isaac, *Limits of Empire*, 256, asserts that "an inscription shows that a modest building north of the town served as *praetorium* for the Ghassanids." As we shall see, the inscription itself "shows" nothing with regard to the building's function as either a praetorium or anything else.

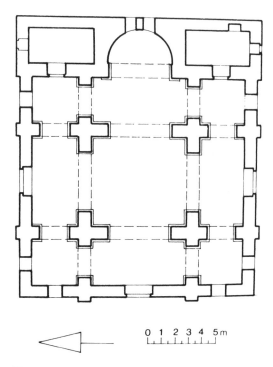

Figure 12. Rusafa: Plan of al-Mundhir building.

discussed, even if new archeological findings, when published, may impose some modifications. My interpretation of the function of al-Mundhir's building outside Rusafa's walls owes much to Sauvaget's emphasis on the site's function as a meeting place for the Ghassanid confederation. However, my understanding of the relationship between the sacred and the profane, as it is made manifest in the structure in question, diverges from his and, consequently, leads to a difference of opinion regarding the building's identification. Attention must be given to the building's details, some of which were overlooked or misrepresented by Sauvaget. These details can contribute to a wider understanding of the place of al-Mundhir's building within the context of steppe architecture, but also in relationship to the history of early Islamic architecture and culture.

Sauvaget's first concern was the building's plan (fig. 12). Architectural historians from Guyer to Lassus understood the structure as a church and drew parallels with several similar cross-in-square buildings in Syria. Sauvaget discounted this identification because of what he saw as three inescapable problems: (1) its plan is an anomaly in the context of Rusafa's other churches; (2) no other Syrian church possesses an identical plan, and the only one that bears comparison, the chapel at Androna, is excluded because its apse is much larger than that in the al-Mundhir building; (3) the inscription in the apse is out of place in a church, funerary or not.[75]

Sauvaget's first objection, as he admits himself, does not carry much weight. No canon stipulates that churches in one place must be stylistically related. But as it happens, excavation at Rusafa has brought to light a very close parallel to the al-Mundhir building: a cross-in-square building erected in the southeast part of the basilica A complex. Like the al-Mundhir building, its orientation is east-west, with the apse at the eastern end. The building was part of the original plan, which is now dated to the last quarter of the fifth century.[76] This structure has been identified by Ulbert as the baptistry of basilica A. As regards Sauvaget's second point, a few years after he published his article, the conclusion that the building was not a church was accepted by Lassus in his important book on the Christian architecture of Syria. However, in his discussion of cross-in-square churches, Lassus included sixth-century churches whose kinship with Rusafa's building is difficult to discount.[77] In particular, the church at al-Tuba, one of the largest ruined towns of the basalt plateau north of Salaminias, is dated to 582 and strikingly similar in plan, even in the apse's proportion to the rest of the building.[78] The al-Mundhir building and the church at al-Tuba were erected within a span of ten years at the end of the sixth century—and both buildings were erected roughly a century after the cross-in-square building southeast of basilica A.

The decoration of the al-Mundhir building likewise falls within the standard repertoire of fifth- and sixth-century church decoration. First, maritime iconography, such as that carved on the molding above the apse windows, commonly adorned churches throughout the late Roman empire,

75. Guyer in Sarre and Herzfeld, *Archäologische Reise,* 42, suggested that the building was intended as the phylarch's mausoleum, a view that at least takes into consideration the building's context. This view was also considered possible by Tchalenko, *Villages antiques,* 1: 262 n. 1.

76. For publication of the "Vierstützenbau I," see Ulbert, *Resafa,* 2: 98–101, 122–23, and fig. 62. For the redating of phase one of basilica A, see above, pp. 80–91.

77. Lassus, *Sanctuaires,* 143–50, fig. 61.

78. On al-Tuba, see Butler, *Early Churches,* 163–64, with n. 299 by Baldwin Smith, who notes the similarity between the plans of al-Tuba, Androna/Andarin, and Rusafa's extra-muros building. Despite Sauvaget's objection, apse size has not excluded Rusafa's building from consideration among cross-in-square churches: see, e.g., Tchalenko, *Villages antiques,* 1: 262 n. 1. Mango, *Byzantine Architecture,* 52, with figs. 74–75, concludes that the size of the apse—"a little too small with regard to the proportions of the building"—is not sufficient to disqualify the building as a church, although for Mango, as for Sauvaget, the inscription makes the identification as a church impossible. For other parallels among Syrian churches, see now Brands, *DaM* 10 (1998), 211–35.

including basilica B and the tetraconch at Rusafa.[79] At the most general level of interpretation, the scenes represent the bounty of creation or allude to Paradise. The bird carved on the southern apse capital is now damaged, but was most likely an eagle, also characteristic decoration in churches of the period.[80] Like the marine scenes, the representation of an eagle, the bird that soars higher, closer to the sun than all others, can be variously interpreted.[81] The eagle may, for instance, symbolize the presence of angels, witnesses to the worship offered there—a particularly apt interpretation since the eagle appears on a capital belonging to the apse. So often a symbol of the sun or the supreme god in pre-Christian art, the eagle in Christian iconography may represent the fusion of celestial and earthly power, the two sources of authority that overlap in a princely church. Two contemporary parallels to the use of the eagle in the al-Mundhir building, one from Lebanon, the other from Syria and both from churches, help to illustrate this point. First, the well-preserved mosaic pavement of a church at al-Ghina, located in the mountains 11 kilometers southeast of Byblos / Jbayl, is decorated with geometric designs in the side aisles, while medallions with fish and animals cover the floor of the central nave. On a raised podium in front of the sanctuary is portrayed a lone eagle, depicted frontally with wings widespread.[82] As at Rusafa, the eagle is given a prominent position at the threshold between the nave and the sanctuary. Presumably, the eagle was chosen because of its own liminal nature between heaven and earth. Again in the second example, the Adam mosaic from the north church at Huwirta (Huarte), the eagle appears near this potent threshold.[83] At Hu-

79. See Kollwitz, *AA* 1963: 346, fig. 13, for a cornice in the tetraconch that shows a scallop shell flanked by dolphins. The marine decoration from basilica B will be published by Brands in *Resafa*, vol. 6 (forthcoming). Brands provides further examples of marine imagery from ecclesiastical contexts in *DaM* 10 (1998), 227–31.

80. A phoenix has also been suggested. Brands, *DaM* 10 (1998), 227, does not rule out this possibility, but prefers the eagle interpretation. On eagles in the context of the al-Mundhir building, see ibid. 225–27.

81. It has been suggested in a recent discussion of the reused material in the al-Aqsa mosque in Jerusalem that the representation of an eagle on a capital identifies the sculpture's original context as a church (Wilkinson in *Bayt al-Maqdis*, 1: 129, 134–35). For a range of interpretations of the eagle in the Christian context, see Schneider, *RAC*, 1: 91–94; Maguire, *Earth and Ocean*, 65–66, with notes. Eagles appear frequently in both non-Christian and Christian art in the Hawran and the Jawlan, familiar territory for the Banu Ghassan. For eagles in the basalt synagogues of the Jawlan, see Hachili in *Roman and Byzantine Near East*, 1: 185–86, 198–201; and see also Grabar, *CArch* 11 (1960): 62, figs. 15 and 19.

82. Donceel-Voûte, *Pavements*, 347–53, with figs. 334–38; for further bibliography on the symbolism of eagles, see 352 n. 11. Also on the eagle at al-Ghina, see Stern, *CArch* 15 (1965): 35, who discusses parallel iconography on both the lintel decoration and floor mosaic of a synagogue at Jaffa.

83. Donceel-Voûte, *Pavements*, 102–16, with figs. 71–79 and pl. 5. Note that a phoenix also appears in the upper southeast corner of the Adam scene.

wirta, the eagle takes up its position of honor at the right hand of Adam, just as the eagle in the al-Mundhir building hovers over the right side of the sanctuary. At Huwirta, too, the mosaic ensemble is located in the central nave, just in front of the sanctuary proper. In the al-Mundhir building, the eagle, straddling both celestial and terrestrial worlds, would have served to represent the phylarch's secular authority, while at the same time alluding to the heavenly authority behind it.[84]

Sauvaget's positive identification of the building outside Rusafa's walls grew out of his discussion of the al-Mundhir acclamation. In his opinion, the victory cry excluded the possibility that this was a sacred building, and parallels therefore had to be sought in secular architecture. Sauvaget's preferred comparison was the second-century so-called praetorium at Mismiya on the northern edge of the Laja, whose apsidal recess bore close resemblance to that at Rusafa.[85] The year before Sauvaget published his article on the building outside Rusafa, Edmund Weigand published what is still regarded as the most exhaustive study of the building at Mismiya.[86] Weigand concluded that it was a temple, and that the nearby temples at Sanamayn and Slim offer the closest parallels to Mismiya.[87] More recent considerations of the building by Stephen Hill and Ze'ev Ma'oz emphasize the similarities between the Mismiya temple and later church architecture. Photographs of the building, which had been destroyed by the beginning of this century, reveal a very grand cross-in-square structure with an intricate tripartite façade. While the second-century edifice may have been an important link in the chain of architectural developments from the second to the sixth centuries, it is difficult to deny that the impression left on a visitor by the modestly adorned building outside Rusafa would have been more akin to that of the humble church at al-Tuba than to that of the building at Mismiya. And there is one further consideration that Sauvaget overlooked. Structural changes to the building at Mismiya indicate that it was converted into a church, probably before 450.[88] In the 570s or 580s, when al-Mundhir had his name inscribed on the Rusafa building, Mismiya was a church, regardless of its original function.

Certain details of Sauvaget's theory also require modification. For in-

---

84. At the church of the Studite monastery in Constantinople, the eagle was associated with imperial and consular rank, again as a reflection of heavenly authority on earth (Kramer, *Skulpturen,* 82–84); see also Brands, *DaM* 10 (1998), 226.

85. Spanner and Guyer, *Rusafa,* 67, had already drawn attention to the similarity between the Mismiya and Rusafa buildings. For a recent reexamination of the monument, see Ma'oz, *DOP* 44 (1990): 41–46, with excellent photographs from the Dumbarton Oaks archive.

86. Weigand in *Würzburger Festgabe,* 71–92.

87. See Freyberger, *DaM* 5 (1991): 1–38, for the type of Roman temple to which the Mismiya temple originally belonged; see also id., *DaM* 4 (1989): 89 n. 15.

88. Hill, *DOP* 29 (1975): 349; de Vogüé and Waddington, *Syrie central,* 45–46.

stance, he assumed that the feast of S. Sergius was celebrated on 15 November.[89] But both the Chalcedonian and non-Chalcedonian Churches celebrated the feast of S. Sergius in October, on the first or the seventh. October first is recorded as the feast date in 514 when Severus of Antioch delivered his homily in honor of S. Sergius at Chalcis. A date in October corresponds more accurately with the date of the seasonal migration than does 15 November, since already in early October, transhumants near the steppe's fringe would be preparing to move to winter pastures.[90] Furthermore, Sauvaget's assertion that the feast would have been celebrated according to the non-Chalcedonian calendar (which in fact did not differ from the Chalcedonian, at least as regards S. Sergius) betrays a dangerous assumption that the church hierarchy at Rusafa was dominated by non-Chalcedonians, simply because the site was associated with the Ghassanids thanks to the al-Mundhir building. As was noted earlier, the only bishop of Rusafa who was certainly non-Chalcedonian was the Sergius who attended the council of Ramla under Justin I. After 536, in Roman Syria and Mesopotamia, monasteries rather than metropolitan sees were the usual power centers for the non-Chalcedonian cause. It is a great misfortune that no clear evidence of everyday interaction between supporters and opponents of Chalcedon exists from Rusafa.[91] But it is reasonable to assume that as a pilgrimage center, Rusafa would have seen visitors of all persuasions. The *Vita* of S. Gulanducht offers a hint that has not been taken: after emerging from an instructive vision in which an angel shows Gulanducht two cups, one (Chalcedonian) resplendent with light and the other (non-Chalcedonian) hidden by shadows, Gulanducht sets off to Jerusalem via Rusafa, where she worships. The passage suggests that Rusafa at the end of the sixth century was a holy place acceptable to supporters of Chalcedon.[92] It is also instructive, in the absence of direct evidence relating to the cohabitation of supporters and opponents of Chalcedon at Rusafa, that John of Ephesus records a situation at Amida where both groups at-

89. In this, Sauvaget followed Charles, *Christianisme,* 33.

90. Macdonald, *JRAS* 2 (1992): 4 and 9; Schlumberger, *Palmyrène,* 131 with n. 2; and Musil, *Manners and Customs of the Rwala,* 7–8.

91. The important study by Mundell (Mango) in *Iconoclasm,* 59–74, recognizes the contemporary interest in S. Sergius at Rusafa of both supporters and opponents of Chalcedon. More recently, Walter too has insisted that both Chalcedonians and non-Chalcedonians would have enjoyed Justinian's patronage at Rusafa: *REB* 53 (1995): 375. Cf. the otherwise admirable *Making of Orthodox Byzantium,* where Whittow, with less care, simply describes the shrine at Rusafa as Sergius's "great Monophysite shrine" (47–48).

92. *Vita Gulanducht* (Georgian redaction) 14.7–15.1; the story exists also in the Greek summary of the *Vita Gulanducht* made by the priest Eustratius before 602: see Peeters, *AB* 62 (1944): 88–89.

tended the same church, but did not receive the Eucharist from the same chalice.[93] Another solution for a mixed congregation at a holy site was found at the shrine of Cyrus and John at Menuthis near Alexandria. There non-Chalcedonians appear to have imbibed oil taken from the lamp that hung over the holy sarcophagus, as a sort of *antidoron*.[94] Throughout the region, S. Sergius was cultivated by Chalcedonians, non-Chalcedonians, Nestorians, and even non-Christians. No evidence indicates that any group managed to monopolize the shrine at Rusafa.

Another important detail in need of further attention concerns the site of the building. Sauvaget explains that it lies outside Rusafa's main north gate, but mentions only in passing that it is surrounded by Christian and Muslim graves.[95] On his first visit in 1908, Musil saw a large, undisturbed Christian cemetery extending east from the building, but when he returned in 1912, he found all the graves opened and looted. Muslim graves northwest of the city walls had already suffered the same fate at the time of his first visit.[96] None of the ruined graves have been published, but the only graves to be found near Rusafa are located to the north of the city, extending east and west.[97] A ruined mausoleum, also unpublished, north of the al-Mundhir building has been informally dated by Ulbert to the fifth century.[98] No parallels to the situation outside Rusafa have been discovered at other Ghassanid-associated sites, in the Hawran, for instance. It must be asked, then, why this building was set among graves.

To find an answer, we must turn to the *Passio* of SS. Sergius and Bacchus and to the overall plan of Rusafa. Sergius, shod in spiked sandals, led a ducal procession along the Strata Diocletiana from Sura and Tetrapyrgium to Rusafa. Approaching Rusafa from the north, the party would have entered the castrum through the north gate. Sergius was brought one last time before the *dux* Antiochus, who condemned him to death by the sword. The young officer was then displayed before the people of Rusafa and taken to the place of execution, where he was allowed a final prayer before his head was cut off. A chasm opened where his blood fell to spare the holy site from

93. Joh. Eph., *Vita. sanct.* 101–2.

94. Marcos, *"Thaumata,"* 46 with n. 19.

95. Spanner and Guyer, *Rusafa*, pl. 1, show the necropolis to the north and northeast of the city walls on their map. See also Brands, *DaM* 10 (1998), 220, on the grave chambers in this region north of the walls.

96. Musil, *Palmyrena*, 165.

97. Although none of these graves have been systematically excavated, many of the coins found in beduin digging in this grave area are said to be late antique.

98. Ulbert, letter to the author, 18 October 1996. Thilo Ulbert and Stephan Westphalen plan to publish the building in the near future. For a plan of the mausoleum, see Musil, *Palmyrena*, 211, fig. 83.

desecration by unbelievers, and the martyr was buried at the site of his execution, where countless miracles occurred, even into the 430s or soon after, when the *Passio* was written.[99] The attempt by a party of Surans to steal the body was averted by the emergence of armed defenders from within Rusafa's walls. Even on the most skeptical reading of the story, it is clear that in the fifth century, Sergius's grave was considered to have been located outside the city walls. We are not told on which side of the settlement.[100]

As stated above, in addition to the presence of Christian graves, the northern cemetery's antiquity is suggested by a mausoleum of late Roman date located north of the al-Mundhir building. Nor is any other cemetery visible today. The author of the *Passio* clearly implies that the holiness of the site of Sergius's martyrdom persisted even after the saint's body was translated within the walls for security reasons and honored by a magnificent shrine. The memory of the original site could easily have been preserved in oral tradition for centuries after the translation. And the grave of a miracle-working saint would naturally have attracted the graves of those who desired to rest near the holy tomb.[101]

A clue to the site of Sergius's original tomb may be provided by the conspicuously large, decorated gate in Rusafa's north wall. Each of its three portals is flanked by two columns, which in turn support five arches upon their exquisitely wrought acanthus capitals. The carving on the arch moldings is of the highest quality and is dense with luxuriant floral and vine motifs. A carved cross marks the keystone of the central arch. Considerable skill and effort clearly went into the adornment of the north gate of this heavily fortified settlement. Rusafa did occupy a strategically important site for the security of the frontier zone, and the entrance was no doubt designed to impress all visitors to the fortress and pilgrims to the popular shrine. The significance of Rusafa as fortress and shrine might be thought sufficient explanation for the grandeur of the settlement's main entrance. But the northward orientation toward the Euphrates (or "the pacified parts of the empire," as Krautheimer saw it)[102] is a weak explanation of why the north gate in particular was chosen for special elaboration. The elaboration of the gate becomes more intelligible, however, if Sergius's original tomb was lo-

99. *Pass. gr.* 28–29. On the date, see chapter 1.

100. The text simply does not support the curious assertion made by Woods, *JECS* 5 (1997): 364–65, that the grave was located midway between Rusafa and Sura, more or less near Tetrapyrgium: see *Pass. gr.* 27, 29; *Pass. syr.*, pp. 317, 320–21.

101. On *ad sanctos* burials, see Duval, *Loca sanctorum Africae,* 501–16. The belief that holiness lingered at places that formerly housed relics is expressed in the inscription from basilica B, which identifies the site of the church that was begun in 518 by its earlier status as the house of Sergius's relics.

102. Krautheimer with Ćurčić, *Early Christian and Byzantine Architecture,* 262.

cated north of the city. Then the impressive entrance would have marked out Rusafa's sacred orientation.

All the gates, including the northern one, were built at the same time as the walls, in the first third of the sixth century.[103] These walls embraced the buildings within the older walls and, in particular, the shrine built for Sergius's relics by Alexander of Hierapolis, which has been located beneath basilica B.[104] Given the antiquity of the graves north and northeast of the north gate, it is certainly possible that this northern graveyard grew up around the traditional site of the tomb of Sergius, and that al-Mundhir's building stood on an eminence among the graves in this area is because it was at or near the site that local memory held sacred as Sergius's original resting place.[105]

With the architectural background and position of the building now placed more firmly in context, the meaning of the inscription can be addressed. Sauvaget's attempt to explain the common Greek acclamation at Rusafa as a translation of an Arabic phrase is unnecessary in the context of al-Mundhir's deliberate adoption in the building of other Roman conventions, such as the plan, which is strikingly similar to the baptistry within Rusafa's greatest architectural complex surrounding basilica A. The acclamation underscores al-Mundhir's skillful adoption of the cultural language of Rome. Alan Cameron's study of acclamations has demonstrated that the phrase in question was entirely standard, even hackneyed, in the eastern provinces and attested epigraphically from the late fifth to the seventh centuries.[106] The name given in the genitive indicated a favored faction, or else an individual—sometimes an emperor—usually in association with a faction. The phylarch's inscription imitated the simplicity of the well-worn acclamation formula, omitting, for example, any titles. Its attractiveness must have lain precisely in its simplicity and familiarity. And, of course, in its association with success.

To reconstruct the cultural context in which these acclamations were used, Alan Cameron refers to a characteristic passage from the *De cere-moniis*—a tenth-century document that here preserves sixth-century prac-

---

103. Karnapp, *Stadtmauer,* 37–49, 52–53.

104. Konrad, *DaM* 6 (1992): 313–402.

105. Alois Musil, whose interpretations always deserve serious consideration, suggested, in passing, that the al-Mundhir building was the church originally built to house Sergius's relics by the Surans and "rebuilt and richly endowed" by the Ghassanid phylarch (*Palmyrena,* 264). This observation has escaped the notice of subsequent students of the building, including myself in my dissertation (see above, n. 71).

106. Cameron, *Porphyrius,* 74–75. Already at the time of the publication of Sauvaget's article, the editor of *Byzantion,* Henri Grégoire, had noted that the acclamation of al-Mundhir "est du type byzantin le plus banal" (Sauvaget, *Byzantion* 14 [1939]: 117, below n. 1).

tice.[107] The following excerpt describes hippodrome ceremonial during which the emperor might have been present, surrounded by the sacred symbols of his power:

> And again the cheerleader cries in a loud voice: "Holy, thrice holy"; and they all shout back: "Victory for the Blues" . . . ; the cheerleader cries: "Lady, Mother of God"; and the people cry: "Victory for the Blues" . . . ; and the cheerleader cries: "The power of the Cross"; and the people respond: "Victory for the Blues." . . .108

Modern students may not feel immediately at home with this antiphonal interplay of sacred and profane that, as Cameron observes, "is so characteristic of the unselfconsciously religious Byzantine." But, I suggest, it is precisely this interplay that informed al-Mundhir's choices as an Arab ally of Rome, with pronounced political and religious interests. Acclamations using sacred language were inscribed in the auditorium of the hippodrome at Alexandria, an example from the field that complements the *De ceremoniis*.[109] Acclamations also played a prominent role in ecclesiastical assemblies, many of which were held in churches and related buildings.[110] The acclamation "The fortune of the Christians triumphs" (Νικᾷ ἡ τύχη τῶν Χριστιανῶν) has been found on a column in the courtyard of a church at Zenobia, east of Rusafa, on the Euphrates. Closer to home, "The faith of the Christians triumphs" (Νικᾷ ἡ πίστις τῶν Χριστιανῶν) is carved on a column inside the north gate of Rusafa itself.[111]

Two questions that naturally arise next are: who was the intended audience, and what was the intended purpose of the inscription? The latter question is closely linked with the more general issue of the building's function and so will be left until later. Obviously, since the text is in Greek, only those who knew that language would be able to read it. Whether it would in fact have been legible is less apparent. Although the apse is the most symbolically potent place in the building, the inscription's location in the innermost recess of the apse is certainly not the most prominent position from which to proclaim the phylarch's success.[112] The acclamation is legible if one stands in front of the apse, but not from much further away.

---

107. Cameron, *Porphyrius*, 69.

108. Const. Porph., *De cer.* 1.69, p. 311.6–14 (Reiske)

109. Borkowski, *Inscriptions*, 75–96; see also 144–46 and the companion sketch of the auditorium, which illustrates the location of the different acclamations.

110. Roueché, *JRS* 74 (1984): 186–89.

111. For Halabiya: Lauffray, *Halabiyya-Zenobia*, 2: 231–37, no. 6; *SEG* 41 (1991), no. 1531d; Rusafa: Seyrig in Tchalenko, *Villages antiques*, 3: 33–34, with drawing in vol. 2, pl. 148, no. 36. Cf. Gatier, *DaM* 10 (1998): 241.

112. The apse measures ca. 4.35 m in width and ca. 3.35 m in depth.

Approximately 1.20 m long, the text follows the curved molding over the double window (fig. 13). Set in the back of the apse, with letters standing only 12 cm high and no sign of color, we cannot take it for granted that many, in fact, would have read it. And what effect would the inscription have had on any of al-Mundhir's Arab visitors who were not literate in Greek? For them, it is likely that the Greek letters would have expressed the phylarch's link with the Roman authority that had invested him with special privileges among the Arab allies. In this respect the carved characters were a cultural marker that operated in a fashion similar to the familiar architectural style of the building itself. Even among those for whom a text is inaccessible either because of its language or location, writing can nonetheless fulfill a nonliterary function by symbolizing authority, especially religious authority.[113] That different visitors would interpret it at different levels is only to be expected and does not necessarily conflict with the intended purpose, or better, purposes, of the building. The phylarch may well have behaved in a different manner according to the audience, but we must leave this issue for later, after considering the structure's possible functions within the Syro-Mesopotamian cultural milieu.

For a fuller picture of the range of religious, social, and political uses to which churches in late antique Syria were put, we must consider some parallel situations in the region. As a framework within which to assemble these examples, it is helpful to think of the tribal church, which was common in predominantly Arab Hira. For example, at Hira the Biʿa (church) Bani Mazin was named after an ancestor of the Banu Zimman, a clan of the large al-Azd tribal group, which included the Banu Mazin and the Banu Ghassan.[114] The tribal church would be a structure where the tribe would gather, both its settled members and those who did not live permanently at Hira. It may be recalled that in the mid sixth century, the missionary Ahudemmeh had made a point of assigning the names of clan chiefs to the new churches he established, explicitly "so that they would assist in every affair and matter of business, as much as they were needed."[115]

The stone martyrium dedicated to the "holy martyr Thomas" outside the city walls of Anasartha provides another useful parallel to the al-Mundhir

---

113. For examples of this nonliterary function in the early Roman Empire, see Beard in *Literacy in the Roman World,* 48, and id., *PBSR* 53 (1985): 139.

114. For Hira, see al-Baladhuri, *Futuh al-buldan,* p. 281 (tr. Hitti and Murgotten, 1: 442); Ibn Hazm, *Jamharat ansab al-ʿArab* 374–75; ʿAbd al-Ghani, *Taʾrikh al-Hira* 44. Likewise at Kufa, after the original establishment at the settlement's center of a mosque, government building, and open space for the market and camels, various tribal groups such as the Banu Makhzum, a clan of the ʿAbs tribe, built separate tribal mosques. See al-Tabari, *Taʾrikh* 2.734.

115. *Hist. Ahud.* 4, p. 27.

Figure 13. Rusafa: al-Mundhir building, apse. Photograph by R. Anderson. Courtesy of Dumbarton Oaks.

building at Rusafa. Its Greek inscription states that in 425 a woman with the unusual Arab name Mavia (Μαουια in the inscription) dedicated the martyrium.[116] Southeast of Chalcis, Anasartha was a major market center for the cultivated fringe of the steppe, where pastoral and agricultural life met, and still do today. It was the region controlled by the Tanukhids in the fourth century. Located east of Anasartha is Zabad, where a famous early sixth-century inscription identified a Sergius church in Greek, Syriac, and Arabic.[117] The Arab dedicant of the Anasartha martyrium used Greek alone. But the Arab association of the martyrium is undisputed thanks to the name Mavia (Arabic Mawiya) in the inscription. This Arab building in honor of a Christian saint was constructed outside the walls of a regional center on the steppe's edge, foreshadowing the role of the al-Mundhir building at Rusafa. Both suggest the importance of permanent buildings as unifying points along the wide spectrum between settled and fully pastoral Arabs.[118]

At Harran in the Laja, a bilingual Greek and Arabic inscription carved on a lintel identifies a martyrium dedicated to S. John by "Sharahil son of Zalim, phylarch," in the Greek. The first line of the Arabic reads "I, Sharahil, son of Zalim, have built this martyrium in the year 463."[119] The year, reckoned here according to the era of Bostra, is A.D. 568. The inscription offers a glimpse into the phylarchal system, although it is not certain whether Sharahil would have been associated with the Ghassanid phylarchate, since this name is otherwise unattested. But the prominent

116. Mouterde and Poidebard, *Limes,* 194–95. The building has now been destroyed. Shahîd, *BAFOC,* 222–38, and *BASIC,* 1: 243, argues that the Mavia in the inscription should be identified as the famous Tanukhid queen.

117. *IGLS,* no. 310, with drawing. See the discussion in chapter 4.

118. Shahîd's insistence, with reference to the Tanukhids, that "they [the *foederati*] were not nomads but were sedentaries who had their own permanent establishments outside the big cities" (*BAFOC,* 227) seems here to sacrifice an opportunity to appreciate how Arab buildings served to mediate between the very diverse population that inhabited this region. The statement that follows is characteristic of Shahîd's thought on Arab building projects throughout his work and deserves a brief commentary: "Far from being a nomadizing and unsettling element, they [again, the *foederati*] were the watchmen of the imperial frontier against the inroads of the nomads from the Arabian Peninsula, and as builders of castles, palaces, churches, and monasteries, they were active participants in the development of settled life in the Byzantine limitrophe." First of all, pairing of "nomadizing" with "unsettling" implies that the nomadic way of life is unsettling. Secondly, the deliberate contrast of "nomadizing" and "unsettling," which represent mobility and impermanence, with the static image of the "watchman" and his permanently built environment sweeps away all the gray area in between, which includes, e.g., ephemeral architecture and semi-nomads.

119. Dussaud with Macler, *Nouvelles archives* 10 (1902): 726–27, for the Arabic; Waddington, *Inscriptions,* no. 2464, for the Greek.

display of the phylarch's association with the church again bears witness to the close, personal links of Arab leaders to particular churches, perhaps especially martyria.

Perhaps the most interesting and persuasive evidence for the existence of tribal churches within the Ghassanid orbit is the church referred to as the "church of the glorious, Christ-loving and patrician Mundhir" that appears in the "Letter of the Archimandrites," dated to ca. 570.[120] Also included in this list is the monastery of 'Isnaya, convincingly identified by Irfan Shahîd as a Syriac form of the Arabic "Ghassaniya."[121] The churches and monasteries affiliated with the Ghassanid confederation, and with specific phylarchs, would have served to affirm their Christian identity, as well as to provide a permanent base for the spread and maintenance of non-Chalcedonian Christianity in the region. In similar fashion the building outside Rusafa, with its ecclesiastical architecture and the prominently placed inscription linking the structure with the Ghassanid phylarch, could have served as a tribal church.

The greatest obstacle to our understanding of the al-Mundhir building and its inscription is the underdeveloped nature of our knowledge of how churches worked—especially tribal churches. What may seem to us an impossibly blasphemous combination, such as a personal acclamation in the apse of a church, may have seemed laudable to some contemporaries, tolerable to others and unforgivable to still others. Response to what we may choose to assume were abrasive actions would depend on the context, and particularly on the balance of power among those involved.

An incident recorded in the *Vita Euthymii* by Cyril of Scythopolis illustrates the confusion over boundaries that animated relationships between secular and clerical authorities in this period. During Euthymius's two-year absence from his monastery in Palestine, the Arab phylarch Terebon had established the habit of standing near the altar, just behind the chancel screen (κάγγελον) during the liturgy.[122] After Euthymius's return, Terebon, in his usual manner, was resting his hands on the chancel screen during the liturgy celebrated by Euthymius. Suddenly, during the anaphora, the phylarch saw a veil of fire descend in front of the altar. In terror, he retreated to the back of the church. This incident first makes clear that

---

120. In *Documenta* 223 (tr. Chabot, 155). The location of this church, named as 'Uqabta, is still uncertain. See the discussion of 'Uqabta by Shahîd, *BASIC*, 1: 830–31, 834–35, and also 862–65. Nöldeke's tentative suggestion that it may be identified with 'Aqabat, south of Damascus, has received cautious acceptance from Shahîd.

121. In *Documenta* 224 (tr. Chabot, 156). See the discussion in Shahîd, *BASIC*, 1:833–38, with an important parallel from a letter of Simeon Beth Arshan.

122. Cyr. Scyth., *Vita Euthym.* 28.

Terebon's adopted place was next to the altar and that in Euthymius's absence this preference had been accepted. Secondly, with the return of Euthymius's authority came the ultimatum that the phylarch's behavior was not acceptable for a secular ruler. It was abruptly terminated, thanks to divine intervention. Terebon's behavior could in this case be curtailed because of the pressure exerted by a more powerful authority than himself— Euthymius and his God.

Other evidence survives from the late sixth and early seventh centuries to illustrate a range of activities that took place in churches of the region. ʿAdi ibn Zayd, a Christian Arab counselor of Khusrau II was reported to have held a banquet in a church in order to mark an alliance with some Arab clients.[123] As we have seen, the histories of the sixth- and early seventh-century missionaries Ahudemmeh and Maruta also refer specifically to the Syro-Mesopotamian Arabs and their social and charitable activities centered on churches and monastic complexes.[124] What we need to explore further is how the region's leaders used the space within a church, whether such use varied according to local geography, climate, and culture, and whether this would have differed from standard use in, for example, a highly urban context. In the misunderstanding between Terebon and Euthymius we see the gaps that could easily open up in practice. The episode may also point to varying practices from region to region, even from church to church.

An incident at Dara a decade after al-Mundhir's fall from grace provides a helpful context for interpreting the phylarch's building outside Rusafa. Theophylact recounts how in early 591 Khusrau was proclaimed king and, surrounded by an armed Roman contingent, advanced with the Roman general Narses to Dara. There, "the barbarian king entered the city and enshrined himself at once within the walls in the city's celebrated shrine, in which the Romans conducted the mysteries of religion."[125] This act of Khusrau galled the city's inhabitants, who protested that even upon taking the city Khusrau I had not committed such an outrage against their religious observances (σέβασμα). Bishop Domitianus's threat to withdraw the Roman alliance quickly chastened Khusrau, who sent his highest-ranking representatives to plead with Domitianus on his behalf. Once he had evicted

---

123. al-Isfahani, *Kitab al-aghani* 2.100.

124. See chapter 4 above.

125. Theoph. Sim., *Hist.* 5.3.4: εἰσήρρησε τοιγαροῦν πρὸς τὸ ἄστυ ὁ βασιλεὺς ὁ βάρβαρος καὶ ἐντεμενίζεται ἅμα τοῖς τειχίοις παρὰ τῷ περιφανεῖ τεμένει τῆς πόλεως . . . Παρά can be interpreted as either "in" or "belonging to." In his translation of Theophylact, Schreiner finds the meaning of the sentence so opaque that he emends τειχίοις, which appears in the MSS, to τευχίοις, from τευχίον, producing an unnecessarily innovative translation: "Der barbarische König trat in die Stadt ein und schritt in Waffenrüstung in die berühmte Kirche der Stadt."

Khusrau from the shrine (ἐξοικίσας τοῦ τεμένους Χοσρόην), Domitianus relented.[126]

The episode is a prime example of crossed cultural signals. Over the course of two years Khusrau had been raised from exile to the throne again, thanks to the assistance of his traditional enemy, Rome. Khusrau's cause had been advanced by Roman bishops and commanders; he had prayed to S. Sergius; Roman forces rallied, and a month later he received the head of Zadesprates; Khusrau grew impressed with the Christian God, encouraged by close contact with Bishop Domitianus of Melitene and Patriarch Gregory of Antioch;[127] the emperor Maurice granted reinforcements and a loan for Khusrau to keep the Iranian forces faithful to him. In this buoyant atmosphere, Khusrau arrived at Dara with a new Roman general and took what to him, a king with a brilliant future, must have seemed the most natural step—to display his personal authority in the city's most prestigious space, the sanctuary of the Great Church. It is even possible that Khusrau intended the gesture as a compliment to Domitianus and Gregory, whose enthusiasm for his interest in Christianity must have been transparent to the exiled king.

By occupying the site most sacred to Christians, Khusrau was allying himself with the powerful Christian God. But Khusrau was not a Christian king. That Khusrau established himself in the sanctuary itself and not, as Michael and Mary Whitby suggest, in "part of the complex of ecclesiastical buildings attached to the Great Church,"[128] is certain from Theophylact's significant repetition of ἐντεμενίζεται and τεμένει. Khusrau did not raise a tempest simply by moving into the bishop's guest rooms without an invitation. The Sasanian king was no fool, and given his dependence on Roman support (emphasized by Theophylact), the fiasco must have taken Khusrau by surprise just as much as it did Domitianus and the Darans. Already while staying at Edessa Khusrau had offended his host, John of Rusafa, by insisting that the hostess serve wine to their foreign guest by her own fair hand—as, he attested, was the Sasanian custom.[129] We can only conclude that Khusrau's self-installation at the church was a ritual gesture of power based on a precedent familiar to the Sasanian king at home in Iran, but which backfired in this particular context.

In Khusrau's time, though, there still persisted a traditional function of

126. Theoph. Sim., *Hist.* 5.3.7.
127. On the role of Domitianus and Gregory during Khusrau's exile, and in particular Domitianus's correspondence with Pope Gregory the Great with regard to what the clerics believed was Khusrau's imminent conversion, see Paret, *REB* 15 (1957): 45–50; Peeters, *AB* 65 (1947): 11–17.
128. Theoph. Sim., *Hist.* 5.3.4 (tr. Whitby and Whitby, 135; see also n. 12 for comment).
129. Mich. Syr., *Chron.* 2.380–81.

the Zoroastrian fire temple that is highly relevant to Khusrau's action at Dara. On the occasion of a Sasanian monarch's coronation, the king of kings lit a fire in what then became his fire temple. The king's reign was reckoned from that moment.[130] And although this is the most powerful testimony to the joining of political rule with divine authority in Khusrau's immediate cultural environment, there are other examples from late antique Syria and Mesopotamia where sacred spaces witnessed the long-term demonstration of political authority.

While the examples of Terebon and Khusrau are helpful in that they illustrate the often uneasy interaction between priests and kings in sacred space, in many ways it is more illuminating to find evidence of the day-to-day established use of holy places for functions other than the explicitly liturgical. It cannot be overstressed that the transaction of judicial matters in churches was a long-established practice in Syria and Mesopotamia. Already in 497/98 Alexander, the governor of Edessa, established a reform by sitting in judgment every Friday in the martyrium of S. John the Baptist and S. Addai the Apostle.[131] This is perhaps the most important key to our understanding of how the secular and the sacred were integrated in the al-Mundhir building outside Rusafa. Sasanian precedent also existed, since judicial proceedings relating to the temple treasury took place inside fire temples.[132] As we have seen, the authority of Sasanian kings was also intimately linked with the fire temple: some early Sasanian coins show the fire altar on the reverse, together with a legend which describes the fire as belonging to the king on whose coin the image appears.[133] The throne-altar appears on several Sasanian and later pseudo-Sasanian silver plates, again as a fusion of the religious and secular power of the king. In his *Chronology of the Ancient Nations,* al-Biruni describes the appearance and function of thrones in fire temples. For example, the emperor Peroz, seeking relief for his country from a severe drought, entered a fire temple, embraced the fire, and then "descended from the altar, left the cupola, and sat down on the (seat) made of gold, similar to a throne, but smaller."[134]

The example set in churches and fire temples may also have had some influence on the similar use made of mosques in early Islamic Syria and Mesopotamia. For instance, not long after the Muslim conquest of Meso-

130. Lukonin, *CHIran,* 3: 695; Chaumont, *JA* 252 (1964): 59–75, esp. 65–75.

131. *Chronicle of Edessa of 506* 29; see also Morony, *Iraq,* 83–85.

132. Lukonin, *CHIran,* 3: 734. On the relationship between fire temples and palaces, see Schippmann, *Iranischen Feuerheiligtümer,* 499–515.

133. Harper, *Iran* 17 (1979): 51–52, 63 with pl. 4b, illustrating a Sasanian throne in front of the royal fire altar.

134. al-Biruni, *Kitab al-athar al-baqiya* 228 (tr. Sachau, 215). On the altar-throne, see Harper, *Iran* 17 (1979): 63.

potamia, mosques became the favored venue where public announcements were made and where *qadi*s would hear lawsuits.[135] Of course, this practice is traced back to the Prophet himself, who prayed, preached, and settled disputes in his house-mosque at Medina. In late antique Syria and Mesopotamia, examples of the use of mosques for political and social purposes are not difficult to find. For example, in early Umayyad Syria, the Caliph Mu'awiya held audiences in both mosque and palace, but at the mosque he cultivated a more informal atmosphere with his public.

> Then he would come out and say: "Boy, bring my chair." He would go into the mosque and humble himself [before God], after which, leaning his back against his stall [*maqsura*], he sat on his chair, attended by his guards. There would approach him the weak, the Arabs of the desert, children and women, and whoever had no [protector], and they would say: "I have been wronged," to which he replied: "Console him." Or: "I have been attacked," and he replied: "Send [men to occupy themselves] with him." Or: "Somebody swindled me," and he gave the order: "Go and look into his affairs."[136]

The cumulative effect of these examples is to suggest that to discuss the al-Mundhir building as if in late antique Syria and Mesopotamia church and audience hall were mutually exclusive categories is simply to miss the point. The eastward orientation, plan, and decoration of al-Mundhir's building belong to the world of ecclesiastical architecture. When considering the structure, we must remember the powerful interplay between sacred and imperial symbolism that enlivened church architecture at this period.[137] One may recall the prominence of the monograms of Justinian and Theodora in their church dedicated to S. Sergius in Constantinople. An instructive parallel comes from Huwirta's Michaelion, also known as the north church, mentioned earlier for its representation of an eagle. The Michaelion is a three-aisled basilica dedicated to the archangel and dated to the end of the fifth century.[138] Unlike the al-Mundhir building, where the complete absence of a pavement creates serious difficulties of interpretation,[139] sections of the mosaic floors of the Huwirta basilica are well preserved. At the east end of the central aisle, just in front of the apse, Adam is depicted in the act of naming the animals. His throne, cushion, and footstool allude to standard Roman imperial images, for God had given Adam royal au-

---

135. According to *hadith*, some *qadi*s sat next to the minbar (Pedersen, *EI*², 6: 670–71, with examples of churches used for litigation in the Islamic period).

136. al-Mas'udi, *Muruj al-dhahab* 1833.

137. Krautheimer with Ćurčić, *Early Christian and Byzantine Architecture*, 262.

138. Canivet and Canivet, *Ḥuārte*, 1: 315–17.

139. Ulbert, *AAS* 33 (1983): 71, reports that no trace of the floor was discovered during excavation. On the rarity of finding clear archeological evidence of altar installations in apses, see Donceel-Voûte, *Pavements*, 112 n. 38.

thority over Creation. But at the same time the image anticipates the throne of Christ the heavenly king—the altar, in other words, that stood within the apse.[140] We might also compare the contemporary Chrysotriclinos built by Justin II (565–78) in the Great Palace at Constantinople, which could even have been seen by al-Mundhir on his official visit to the capital two years after the structure's initial construction. The decoration, executed under Tiberius II (578–82) and restored by Michael III (842–67), depicts Christ enthroned in the vault of the eastern apse, in which the emperor would preside from his throne over a wide range of ceremonies, many of explicitly religious character. In Krautheimer's words, "it served as audience hall for the Emperor's Majesty and palace chapel."[141] One example of a multilayered religious ceremony celebrated in this space took place each Palm Sunday. After receiving high dignitaries in the Chrysotriclinos early in the day, the emperor would return after a series of processions outside the Palace, and take his place on the right-hand side of the Chrysotriclinos. The priests then entered and stood in the center, while a deacon placed the Gospel on the royal throne and recited the litany.[142]

Bearing in mind this cultural context where sacred and secular power were commonly fused, we can also speculate about how the building outside Rusafa's walls would have been used. In addition to attending services there when he was present in the area, we can imagine that the phylarch might also have used the space as the governor Alexander of Edessa had, as a potent venue for settling disputes. Perhaps, like Adam in the Michaelion, the phylarch would have sat before the apse as God's earthly regent, the phylarch over the Arab confederacy who would have held meetings in this tribal church with Arab encampments spread out in the plain around Rusafa (fig. 14).[143] Seasonal rhythms would have dictated the building's use. For the Ghassanids whose primary *hirta*, Jabiya, was in the Hawran, Rusafa was a far-flung northeast extension of their influence. But as we have seen, the settlement was well placed to bring together, once a year, the Ghassanid-allied Arabs whose pastures were far from the Hawran. The building constructed outside the walls served the Arab pastoralists who came to Rusafa en route to winter pastures. It provided a permanent struc-

140. My husband kindly drew my attention to this parallel.

141. Krautheimer with Ćurčić, *Early Christian and Byzantine Architecture*, 78.

142. Const. Porph., *De cer.* 1.32 (Reiske); 1.41 (Vogt), with commentary 1.8–10 (Vogt); see also Lavin, *Art Bull.* 44 (1962): 1–27, for discussion of the interplay of sacred and profane in late Roman architecture, esp. 22–23 on the Chrysotriclinos.

143. Cf. Cyr. Scyth., *V. Euthym.* 15, where the Christianized Arabs under the leadership of Aspebetus-Peter camp in their tents around the church founded for them by Euthymius at some distance from his monastery. Sauvaget, *Byzantion* 14 (1939): 130 n. 1, draws attention to the late antique placement of Tanukh encampments outside the walls of Aleppo. See also Mich. Syr., *Chron.* 12.8 (tr. 3: 31).

Figure 14. The fourteenth-century Armenian monastery of the Apostle Thaddeus between Lake Van, Turkey, and Lake Urmiya, in northwest Iran, surrounded by pilgrims' tents for the patronal festival. Courtesy of Domas Publications.

ture where the phylarch could be present during the festal period of a favorite saint to hear suits and meet with other leaders within the confederation. A gathering of these leaders under the auspices of a single saint would have served to reaffirm and strengthen the no doubt sometimes fragile federate bonds.[144] The importance of fixed, congregational centers in nomadic society is also expressed in early Arabic poetry, as in the *Muʿallaqa* of Labid b. Rabiʿa, a younger contemporary of the Prophet Muhammad and a convert to Islam:

> They have built for us a house whose elevation is high,
> and the old and the young of the tribe have ascended to it.[145]

The association of the al-Mundhir building with Rusafa and S. Sergius would have served to reinforce the authority of the phylarch in the same way that a holy man buttressed the authority of the ruling clan at a *haram*.

144. For comparable federate gatherings at a temple dedicated to a single deity in South Arabia, see, e.g., Doe, *Monuments*, 207.
145. Labid b. Rabiʿa, *Muʿallaqa* 84 (tr. and comm. Jones, *Early Arabic Poetry*, 2: 200).

Especially if, as seems likely, the building was near the place of Sergius's martyrdom, and perhaps even stood upon the very ground sanctified by it, al-Mundhir's own authority would have been further sanctioned by the saint's prior presence. If the collective memory of Rusafa recalled that al-Mundhir's building rested on or near the site where according to tradition Sergius's blood had been spilt, then the various religious and political purposes that merged at the building would also be stamped by the saint's authority. The inscription would have served as another sign of al-Mundhir's intimate association with the saint, this time with the authority of the written word behind it. It was less important that all who entered the building could see or read his name in the inscription than that the words were simply present in the most sacred space of the building.

If we are to understand the al-Mundhir building as a church, it should be seen within the broad spectrum of church functions sketched here. Perhaps the most important precedent is the use of churches, such as that at Edessa, for judicial proceedings. And as we have seen, Edessa was not an isolated example, but part of a long-standing tradition in west Asia. Inevitably conflicts of interest and interpretation arose. In the cases of Terebon and Khusrau II, clerical authorities possessed power enough to override the political leaders' claims within the sacred space of the church. Our written sources for Rusafa do not preserve any clerical response to al-Mundhir's inscription in the apse, or to his actual use of the building. Nor, as we have seen, do the sources provide any clear impression of the nature of either the Chalcedonian or the non-Chalcedonian hierarchy at Rusafa. The record leaves no trace of a dynamic religious leader like Euthymius or Domitianus who would have been in a position to challenge al-Mundhir. Certainly a non-Chalcedonian cleric would have thought twice about opposing his most powerful patron. And Chalcedonians too would have been acutely aware of the critical role played by the Ghassanids in the protection of the frontier zone, despite al-Mundhir's tumultuous relationship with Roman authority. The Roman portrait of al-Mundhir as headstrong and independent-minded is an exaggeration of the qualities that made him an undeniably distinguished commander and a leader capable of buttressing his own authority by close association with S. Sergius.

al-Mundhir and his forces had been highly successful in defending Roman territory, especially north and east of the Hawran, from Iranian and Arab attacks. In 570, they had routed the Arabs of Qabus, Iranian allies who had provoked an encounter with the Ghassanids by invading Roman territory.[146] After 575, al-Mundhir took the initiative in attacking and plundering Hira and was said to have distributed the booty among monasteries,

146. Men. Prot. fr. 17; Joh. Eph., *HE* 3.6.3; Mich. Syr., *Chron.* 10.8. (tr. 2: 308–9).

churches, and the needy.[147] After an official visit to Constantinople in 580, he returned to find the area he protected exposed to the raids of the Iranians and their Arab allies, a situation he soon put straight;[148] and later that year, after an unsuccessful campaign with Maurice, then the emperor Tiberius's *magister utriusque militiae per orientem*, he routed the Iranian and Arab forces that attacked him on his return home.[149]

At least as early as May 570, al-Mundhir held the title of phylarch, but only two years later Tiberius was plotting his death. The emperor sent a letter to Marcianus, the *magister utriusque militiae per orientem*, with instructions how to ensnare the Arab leader; and he sent another letter to al-Mundhir himself. But somehow, each letter was delivered to the other's addressee, and al-Mundhir, alerted in this way to Tiberius's treachery against him, withdrew his protection against raids in the frontier zone for three years. When, in early 575, al-Mundhir agreed to a reconciliation, he and Justinianus, Marcianus's successor, sealed their alliance with oaths at the tomb of S. Sergius at Rusafa.[150] The commanding personality that had caused Romans to distrust al-Mundhir almost from the start of his career as phylarch, was perhaps also what inspired him to link his authority so intimately with that of Rusafa's saint. If the building outside Rusafa's north gate was built during the first part of al-Mundhir's service, between 570 and 575, he may have first met Justinianus there before entering Rusafa together. But if, as is also possible, the inscription +Νικᾷ ἡ τύχη Ἀλαμουνδάρου was carved after 575, the building would have been intended as a trophy of his restoration as protector of the frontier zone and as a symbol of thanksgiving for Sergius's aid in that achievement. The site and function of the building would then have represented the inalienable alliance between the soldier saint Sergius and the phylarch al-Mundhir. Before the reconciliation in early 575, Justinianus was preparing a force made up in part by "barbarian" mercenaries for engagement with Iranian forces, and al-Mundhir must have perceived that his estrangement was by then only working against him. The walled settlement of Rusafa was conveniently near the front and enshrined the region's most revered saint, a powerful guarantor of the two parties' promises.

In 581, Roman imperial plotting against al-Mundhir finally bore fruit, and at the consecration of a friend's church at Huwwarin, al-Mundhir was arrested, "like a lion of the wilderness shut up in a cage."[151] The phylarch was taken to Constantinople, where he and his immediate family were

147. Joh. Eph., *HE* 3.6.4.
148. Ibid., 4.42.
149. Ibid., 6.18.
150. Ibid., 6.4.
151. Ibid., 41. See Shahîd, *BASIC*, 1: 459–61.

placed under house arrest. The phylarch's son al-Nuʿman stayed on to raise havoc in the frontier zone his father had once protected. After the accession of Maurice, who had tarred al-Mundhir as a traitor in the reign of Tiberius, the captive phylarch was exiled to Sicily. Not long afterward, probably in 584, al-Nuʿman too was arrested and exiled to the same island. The leadership vacuum left behind was soon filled by fifteen splinter groups, each controlled by an unnamed prince. Syriac sources refer to an Arab commander allied with Rome again in 587: Abu Jafna ibn al-Mundhir, who was living at Rusafa.[152] To judge from his name he was probably another of al-Mundhir's sons, who remained in Syria during the former phylarch's exile.

S. Sergius embodied qualities, such as military prowess and healing powers, that were required for survival in the environment where his cult flourished. What is so striking about his cult is how tightly enmeshed it was with the place where it thrived. As we have seen, the focal point of the relationship that had developed between the saint and the Arab population during the course of the fifth and sixth centuries was the frontier shrine, where the political, economic, and religious interests of Rome, Iran, and the Arabs converged. But it should never be overlooked, despite the site's impressive architecture and its famous saint, that this shrine lay fully in the steppe. It was by no means inevitable that the Roman fortress would grow into a celebrated city in the sixth century. Without belief in the saint's ability to benefit his wide range of devotees through the powers he embodied, the site would have remained a modest watering point.

---

152. For Nuʿman's revolts, see Joh. Eph., *HE* 3.42–43; for the splinter groups, see Mich. Syr., *Chron.*10.19 (tr. 2: 349–51); *Chron.1234* 74 (tr. 1: 166). For Jafna at Rusafa: *Chron. 1234* 90 (tr. 1: 169), which preserves the secular history of Dionysius of Tell Mahre (d. 845); and also for Jafna, see Agapius, *Kitab al-ʿunwan*, p. 182, which refers to Jafna as a *qadi,* here best translated as leader. Cf. also Yaqut, *Muʿjam* 3.156, for later Ghassanid associations with Rusafa. For one account of the Ghassanid phylarchate after the reign of al-Mundhir, see Shahîd, *BASIC,* 1: 540–63, and id. in *ARAM* 5 (1993): 491–503.

SIX

The Cult of S. Sergius
after the Islamic Conquest

UMAYYAD RUSAFA

ʿAmr ibn Maʿdikarib, the warrior-poet who fought at Yarmuk, wrote of the Ghassanids: "They were lords in the *jahiliya* and stars in Islam."[1] Certainly Ghassanids were among the Arab allies of Rome who fought at the protracted battle of Yarmuk in August 636. After this signal Roman defeat, the victors collected their booty at "Jabiya of the kings," the site of the famed Ghassanid *hirta*.[2] Jabiya was established as the region's main military camp, and in 638, the caliph ʿUmar met there with his principle advisers to hammer out the terms under which the newly conquered lands would be governed. With the Islamic conquests and the collapse of Sasanian and Roman control in Syria and Mesopotamia, the Syrian steppe ceased to be a frontier zone. Some of the Ghassanids moved to Anatolia, while others remained in Syria. Little or nothing is heard of Rusafa during the first decades of Islamic rule.

The Umayyads, Syria's rulers from 661 to 750, left behind a legacy characterized most of all by its synthesis of the region's traditions: political, economic, architectural, and religious.[3] Ghassanid rule was obliterated, but the path carved out by the Ghassanid confederation as Arab allies of the Roman empire was often followed by the new Arab elite. Through their formal alliance with Rome, the Ghassanid elite had been drawn into the political

---

1. Quoted by Shahîd in *Islamic World,* 329; and see generally 323–36 for the fate of the Ghassanids after Yarmuk.

2. For an account of the battle and its background, see Kaegi, *Byzantium and the Early Islamic Conquests,* esp. 112–46.

3. For general discussions of Umayyad rule and its cultural context, see Kennedy, *The Prophet and the Age of the Early Caliphates,* 82–123; Grabar, *Formation,* passim.

establishment with its titles and rituals. Of particular importance in the context of Umayyad Syria was the Ghassanid integration of Graeco-Roman architectural forms into the framework of Arab culture in Syria. As we have seen, this is strikingly manifest at al-Mundhir's building outside the walls of Rusafa. Many of the surviving and identifiably Ghassanid buildings, such as Qasr al-Hayr al-Gharbi, continued to be used in the Umayyad period, some certainly by the Umayyads themselves.[4] Some of the fortified settlements near the Euphrates also continued to be inhabited under the Umayyads, including Tetrapyrgium and Rusafa.[5] Rusafa was chosen by the Umayyad caliph Hisham as the site of a country residence outside the walls, and came to be known by Arabic writers as Rusafat Hisham.[6] During Hisham's sojourn at Rusafa, literary Arabic flourished, and countless poets passed through his court, reciting their poems beside the reflecting pool and awaiting praise or censure.[7] To judge by the number of poems recounted in the setting of Hisham's court in the *Kitab al-aghani*, the potential reward was deemed worth the risk.[8] After the Umayyad conquest of Spain in 711, the first amir of al-Andalus, ʿAbd al-Rahman I, built a palace (*qasr*) and gardens northwest of Cordova and baptized it Rusafa (Arruzafa).[9] ʿAbd al-Rahman was the grandson of Hisham and had spent part of his childhood at Syrian Rusafa. The gardens of Arruzafa boasted plants from Syria, and the palace was ranked among ʿAbd al-Rahman's most remarkable constructions, along with the Grand Mosque and the palace at Cordova. Like his grandfather's residence, Arruzafa became a center for poets and country pleasures such as hunting.[10]

Hisham's contribution to Syrian Rusafa included the mosque built due north of basilica A, which encompassed one-third of the church's monumental courtyard (fig. 15).[11] The worshipper could enter this courtyard

4. Shahîd, *Byzantium and the Arabs in the Sixth Century*, vol. 2 (forthcoming), will discuss the buildings attributed to the Ghassanids by Hamza al-Isfahani. See Gaube, *Ein arabischer Palast*, who argues a Ghassanid origin for Khirbat al-Bayda.

5. Konrad, letter to the author, 14 October 1996. See Konrad's forthcoming *Resafa*, vol. 5: *Der spätrömische Limes in Syrien*.

6. For the Arabic sources on Rusafa, see Honigman in *EI*[1], 6: 1183–86; Haase in *EI*[2], 8: 630–31; and Kellner-Heinkele in Sack, *Resafa*, 4: 133–54.

7. Hisham's palace has not been excavated. It is believed to be located in the ruins that occupy an area of 4 km[2] south of the walls (Sack, *Resafa*, 4: 49–52). Ulbert has excavated what he interprets as an Umayyad pavilion outside the walls of Rusafa to the southeast (Ulbert, *DaM* 7 [1993]: 213–31).

8. See, e.g., al-Isfahani, *Kitab al-aghani* 3.216–17; 4.413–15; 5.191–92.

9. For Spanish Rusafa, see Marin, *EI*[2], 8: 631–33.

10. The suburb that spread between Cordova and the residential complex also became known as al-Rusafa (Marin, *EI*[2], 8: 632).

11. The mosque is dated by numismatic evidence from the foundations to Hisham's reign (Sack, *Resafa*, 4: 47–49).

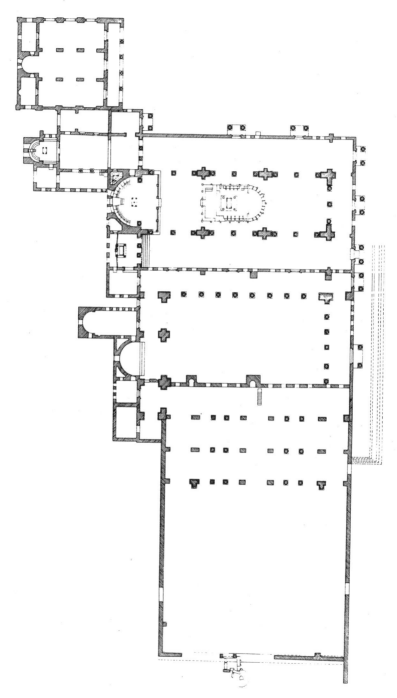

Figure 15. Rusafa: Plan of basilica A and mosque.

directly from the mosque's prayer hall, through a door in the south, *qibla,* wall. The result of this architectural innovation was that the mosque shared the courtyard and its stoa with the city's main church, which housed the martyrium of S. Sergius. Two mihrabs, as well as the stone minbar that later replaced the original wooden one, are still visible on the interior *qibla* wall. North of the prayer hall is another open-air courtyard, with the formal entrance to the whole complex in its north perimeter wall.

In order to understand the relationship between basilica A and the Umayyad mosque at Rusafa, it is helpful to consider briefly the Dome of the Rock and the Church of the Resurrection in Jerusalem, and the shared temenos of S. John at Damascus. The Muslim sanctuary in Jerusalem, ranking third in importance after Mecca and Medina, was built by 'Abd al-Malik.[12] It clearly upstaged the Church of the Resurrection, the holiest monument of Christendom, expressing Muslim sovereignty over the Holy City without direct, physical impingement on the Christian shrine. The location chosen instead for the Dome of the Rock, the Temple Mount, was among the most symbolically potent within the monotheist tradition. What is of interest here, though, is not Muslim use of sacred topography, but more specifically the form that Muslim interaction with Christianity took. In terms of cult, the Church of the Resurrection presented little of interest to adherents of the Muslim faith. There was, naturally enough, no relic of the ascended Jesus there to reverence. What was important in Jerusalem was not so much to absorb current religious practice, but rather to construct a symbol of Muslim hegemony in the ancient holy city of Judaism and Christianity, now adopted by Islam. The message is powerfully conveyed by the monument's position, but also by the lengthy monumental inscription inside the building. This elegant compilation of Qur'anic texts includes a rebuttal of the Christian doctrine of the Trinity. But since Muslims rather than Christians would have frequented the building, the inscription was aimed more at cementing Islamic faith and averting conversion from Islam to Christianity, than at proselytizing among Christians.

Early Muslim leaders were not unaware of the spell cast over the Arabs by Christianity, with its liturgical, charitable, and festal traditions, often based at churches and monasteries. In 706, on the order of al-Walid I, a mosque finally usurped the entire site of Damascus's main church, dedicated to John the Baptist, which had stood there since at least the time of Theodosius I.[13] From 635 until 706, however, Christians and Muslims had

12. On the Dome of the Rock, see Grabar, *Shape of the Holy,* esp. 21–134; id, *Formation,* 47–71; and Raby and Johns, ed., *Bayt al-Maqdis.*

13. For the architectural history of the pre-Christian temenos and the buildings it enshrined, see Sack, *Damaskus,* 16–19; see also Freyberger, *DaM* 4 (1989): 82–84 on the reuse of pre-Christian architectural fragments in the church complex.

worshipped in separate areas within the same temenos. The church housed as its most cherished relic the head of John the Baptist, revered by Christian and Muslim alike as one of the greatest prophets. Even though we can assume that the church would still have been a great attraction in its own right in the early eighth century, it should not be forgotten that it was located in the heart of the political capital of the Umayyad empire. This fact must have militated against the sharing of the city's most important shrine by Christians and Muslims. During the period of symbiosis, the visual balance within the temenos would have been tipped toward the preexisting Christian basilica, renowned for its grandeur. The mosque seems to have taken the form of an open-air arrangement, and occupied the southeast corner of the temenos.[14]

What we see at both Jerusalem and Damascus is the upstaging of a Christian holy place. In the case of Damascus, the price was total absorption of what had once been a shared precinct. The tenth-century historian Muqaddasi records an interchange about Walid's decision to build the Great Mosque that recaptures the late antique cultural climate in which the belief that architecture had the power to hold hearts and minds flourished:

> "O my uncle, verily it was not well of the Caliph al-Walid to expend so much of the wealth of the Muslims on the mosque at Damascus. Had he expended the same on making roads, or for caravanserais, or in the restoration of the frontier fortresses, it would have been more fitting and more excellent of him." But my uncle said to me in answer, "O my little son, thou hast no understanding! Verily al-Walid was right, and he was prompted to a worthy work. For he beheld Syria to be a country that had long been occupied by the Christians, and he noted herein the beautiful churches still belonging to them, so enchantingly fair, and so renowned for their splendor, even as are the al-Qumama[15] and the churches of Lydda and Edessa. So he sought to build for the Muslims a mosque that should prevent their regarding these, and that should be unique and a wonder to the world. And in like manner is it not evident how the Caliph 'Abd al-Malik, noting the greatness of the dome of the al-Qumama and its magnificence, was moved lest it should dazzle the minds of the Muslims, and hence erected above the Rock the Dome which now is seen there?"[16]

The situation at Rusafa offers another possible form of cohabitation, not far from the original arrangement in Damascus. By incorporating the three-aisled mosque into the preexisting north courtyard of basilica A, Hisham's architects linked their building to the shrine of S. Sergius, but without at-

---

14. See Creswell, *Early Muslim Architecture*, 1: 151–96, esp. 180–96.

15. Qumama (which means garbage) is a derogatory name for al-Qiyama, the Church of the Resurrection at Jerusalem.

16. Muqaddasi, *Ahsan al-taqasim* 159 (tr. Le Strange, *Palestine under the Moslems*, 117–18).

tempting to replace the Christian cult and its material apparatus. Judging from the unadorned structure that remains, he did not attempt to rival the dazzling beauty of basilica A. Despite its important role as a pilgrimage center, Rusafa was not a leading political center in Umayyad Syria. Even though it served as a refuge for Hisham, Rusafa never carried Damascus's political weight, so it did not require the same show of Muslim hegemony, which was what imposed the destruction of the Christian basilica of S. John and the erection on its site of a monument to Umayyad rule.

Acknowledgment of the martyr's importance is implied in the mosque's very location. Its proximity to basilica A suggests an effort to benefit from the saint's miracle-working presence and to provide Muslims with a place nearby to worship—even to participate in the cult of Sergius.[17] The close symbiosis of church and mosque might also be interpreted as a Muslim attempt to ease Christians into Islam by not rejecting outright the patterns of Arab involvement in Christian establishments, especially in the steppe, where, as we have seen, churches and monasteries were important fixed points in pastoral Arab life. It would not be surprising if the mosque were known as the masjid of Mar Sarjis, since dedications of mosques to local saints were not uncommon even in the early years of Islam.[18] The Masjid Nabi Allah Jarjis mosque at Tarim in the Wadi Hadramawt of South Arabia is also popularly known still today as the holy place of the prophet Sarjis.[19] The appearance of both Jarjis and Sarjis in variants of the mosque's appellation is not surprising. It represents another instance of the frequent confusion of these two popular military saints, both of whom were also blurred with the Muslim Khidr.

By the time of the Islamic conquest of Syria in 636, in the minds of many Arabs, Sergius had become so closely identified with the Christian religion that he stood as a symbol of the faith itself. This tendency was strong also among those Arabs who adopted the new religion of Islam. The early

17. For modern examples of shared cult between Christians and Muslims, see Curtiss, *Ursemitische Religion,* passim, esp. 103–5 and 283, on the cult of S. Thecla and S. Sergius; Hasluck, *Christianity and Islam,* passim, esp. 63–97; and Bowman, *Man* 28 (1993): 431–60. In Urmiya in northwest Iran, both Christians and Muslims sought healing by incubation and anointment at the church of SS. Sergius and Bacchus (Fiey, *Mossoul chrétienne,* 146–47, n. 2).

18. See, e.g., Palmer, *Monk and Mason,* 23.

19. Serjeant, *Studies in Arabian History* II.574–75, concludes that the dedication was to S. Sergius, popular among the Arabs of Syria—although Serjeant strangely confuses Rusafa with Babisqa. His comments are extremely brief and include no attempt to explain the obvious connection between the Arabic Jarjis and Greek Georgios, or the relationship between S. George and S. Sergius. In July 1997, a banner hung outside the mosque clearly identified it as the Masjid Sarjis. Shahîd in *DOP* 33 (1979): 85–87, favored S. George as the dedicatee, but has more recently considered the identification with S. Sergius more likely—in fact, he simply calls the building the Masjid Sarjis: Shahîd, *BASIC,* 1: 956 n. 35. On the frequent conflation of the two saints, see, e.g., Hasluck, *Christianity and Islam,* 570–71.

Islamic poet Jarir accused one of the remaining Christian tribes in Syria of having been deluded by the Cross and by S. Sergius.[20] This tribe, the Taghlib, was famous for carrying into battle "a cross held high and Mar Sarjis."[21] Most commentators have taken this to refer to either an icon of S. Sergius or a banner bearing the martyr's image. Both suggestions are plausible. Another possibility might be a relic of the warrior saint—recalling the famed eastern king who led his forces with Sergius's thumb attached to his own.[22] This close association of Sergius and the Cross anticipates and helps explain a telegraphic story about Christianity's adoption by a Roman king that was recorded by the historian Ibn Ishaq in the eighth century. This king, upon hearing about the miracles of a man among the Israelites, and his death at the hands of the Jews, summons the holy man's apostles to preach their master's message to him. Embracing the religion of Jesus, the king then "took down Sergius and concealed him."[23] Then he proceeded to preserve and revere the cross on which Sergius was crucified. A key to unraveling this chronologically confused passage is that some Muslim traditions provide a double for Jesus, in order to avoid the (to them) unacceptable view that he was crucified. That Sergius was chosen to stand in for Christ in this instance further highlights the saint's prominence in Muslim understanding of Christianity. Sergius's inclusion as one of the essential features that even a boiled-down version of early Christianity must retain is perfectly consistent with the Taghlib talismans of Sergius and the Cross, and with Jarir's jibe. The known dedications at Rusafa—to S. Sergius and to the Holy Cross—underscore once again the fortress-shrine's prominent position in the cultural and religious developments of the late antique world.

The Cross was widely perceived by Muslim Arabs as a symbol not only of Christianity but of Rome,[24] and Sergius seems to have shared this distinction. Umayyad reaction to the Cross was not uniform, ranging from outright proscription to the adoption of more subtle alterations, as seen in the coins

20. Jarir and Farazdaq, *Naqa'id* 2.904, ll. 85–90. For additional brief references to this Christian Arab weakness for S. Sergius, see Trimingham, *Christianity* 236 n. 60.

21. al-Akhtal, *Diwan* 309 (tr. Lammens, *Syrie,* 73).

22. For banners associated with South Arabian saints, see Serjeant, *Studies in Arabian History* III.53–54. The Christian Arab history of northern Syria is remembered with pride by modern Christian Arabs: both the schools operated by the Syrian Orthodox archdiocese of Aleppo are named after the Banu Taghlib. For the relic-bearing king, see Greg. Tur., *HF* 7.31, and above, p. 129.

23. Ibn Ishaq, preserved in Tabari, *Tar'ikh* 1.739 (tr. Perlmann 4.124, who mistakenly makes "Jesus" rather than "Sergius" the subject of the passive verb *suliba*). Cf. Newby, *Making of the Last Prophet* 210–11, translating this passage from the *Ta'rikh*, and 205–9, discussing and translating other passages from Tabari's *Tafsir* that refer to "Sergius" as Jesus's double.

24. King, *BSOAS* 48 (1985): 269

of 'Abd al-Malik.[25] Treatment of Sergius also varied, and the case of his shrine at Rusafa reveals a sequence of responses over time. What is certain is that Hisham confronted head on this issue of the saint's conspicuous cult establishment at Rusafa. In the choice of the mosque's location, proximity to the shrine clearly overrode more practical factors, such as the fact that the ground under the mosque was riddled with dolines. At the time of the mosque's construction, subsidence had already damaged the nearby basilica A.[26] The three-aisled mosque absorbed one-third of the north courtyard attached to basilica A, so that the courtyard was thereafter shared by those who visited the church and the mosque. The entrance to the courtyard, which led directly through the *qibla* wall, is a highly unusual feature in Umayyad architecture. The arrangement appears, for example, in Damascus and Kufa, but only when connecting a mosque to a palace.[27] At Rusafa, there is no sign that the *qibla* door was reserved for the caliph, imam, or any other authority entering from a palace. On the contrary the juxtaposition of the public courtyard and the prayer hall at Rusafa suggests that the *qibla* door was designed to facilitate public movement between the mosque and the shrine at the southeast corner of the courtyard.

In order to explain the impractical location chosen for the mosque and its architectural links with basilica A, the site's excavator, Dorothée Sack, has suggested that Hisham must have been personally devoted to S. Sergius.[28] In saying this, Sack follows Yaqut, who claims that Hisham built his residence at Rusafa in order to be near its monastery.[29] Certainly, the Umayyads were famous for the catholicity of their religious tastes. But the choice to tie the mosque architecturally to the famous church sprang from more than the personal fancy of Hisham's. The intimate association of the mosque with the shrine should be seen in the context of the wider political arena in which the cult of S. Sergius operated in late antique Syria and Mesopotamia. Although the frontier between Rome and Iran had dissolved in the wake of the Islamic conquests, the new rulers of Syria and Mesopotamia still needed to exert control over the populations who inhabited the region, the mobile Arabs in particular.[30] As a place for worship and arbitration, a space in which the identity of the community was affirmed, the mosque at Rusafa would have been a powerful site for mediation, thanks to the divine au-

---

25. For a recent discussion of the coins, see Blair, in *Bayt al-Maqdis,* 1: 64–68.

26. Sack, *Resafa,* 4: 41–42.

27. Ibid., 53–54, with n. 192, and 69, with n. 239; also, Hamilton, *Khirbat,* 106–7.

28. Sack, *Resafa,* 4: 156.

29. For Yaqut, see below.

30. For the political situation, especially with regard to the Arabs of Iraq, see, e.g., Kennedy, *Prophet,* 82–123.

thority of S. Sergius. At Rusafa, Hisham would have stepped into the shoes of Anastasius, Justinian, Khusrau, and, perhaps in particular, the Ghassanid phylarch al-Mundhir, who had all allied themselves in various ways with the mediating influence of S. Sergius among the region's population. Hisham would have hoped to benefit from the flow of pilgrims to the neighboring shrine of the miracle-working saint, but the Christian cult would simply have been too well established and influential beyond the bounds of Rusafa to have been clothed fully in Muslim garb.

At a much later phase, possibly after the earthquake in the twelfth century, a tomb was built in the courtyard north of the mosque.[31] Sack has suggested that it was a Muslim tomb, or *mashhad,* of S. Sergius.[32] It seems unlikely that the Muslim tomb had replaced the Christian holy site, since Christians were still dedicating offerings at the shrine of S. Sergius at Rusafa in the thirteenth century. If the tomb in the mosque's courtyard was also considered a tomb of S. Sergius, it might signify a separation of Christian and Muslim cult, of which there are otherwise no such definite signs, either literary or archaeological. However, another interpretation can be offered, based on parallel evidence of cultic continuity in northern Syria and on a twelfth-century literary tradition about Rusafa. al-Hawari (d. 1215), an ascetic of Shi'ite leanings who composed a guide to pilgrimage sites, includes in his entry for Rusafa "tombs of the companions and followers" of the Prophet. He adds that he has not seen the names himself, and that God alone knows the truth.[33] Yaqut, in the early thirteenth century, reports that a *mashhad* had been built in the place of an abandoned Christian monastery outside Aleppo, in honor of 'Ali, who had been seen there by several Shi'as.[34] What these two examples may point toward is Rusafa's place in the wider Islamicization of holy sites in twelfth- and thirteenth-century Syria. At Rusafa, Muslim accommodation of S. Sergius represented the first phase that is clearly reflected in the mosque's intimate proximity to the Sergius church. The second phase that we may postulate here moves beyond the shared holy man Sergius / Sarjis to the installation at the holy site of purely Muslim holy men. The degree to which the Prophet's companions would have cohabited comfortably with S. Sergius must have varied over time, in accordance with historical circumstance and religious function.[35]

31. Evidence also exists of a small chapel built to the south of basilica A at an unspecified, but late, date (Ulbert, *Resafa,* 2; 152; id. in *Syrien,* 124).

32. Sack, *Resafa,* 4: 45–46.

33. al-Hawari, *Kitab al-isharat,* p. 61 (tr. Sourdel-Thoumine, p. 136).

34. Yaqut, *Mu'jam al-buldan* 2.691 (tr. Le Strange, *Palestine under the Moslems,* 430–31).

35. Different views of the Prophet Sarjis at the mosque of Nabi Allah Sarjis at Tarim in South Arabia offer an illustration of how understanding of a holy man can be influenced by contemporary political and religious developments. In the early 1950s, Serjeant reported that "the prophet Sarjis is generally reckoned in Tarim to be pre-Islāmic" (Serjeant, *Studies in*

We should be careful to observe the real boundary that did stand between Christianity and Islam, despite what appears to have been a willingness, especially in the early Islamic period, to recognize common ground. Muslims were discouraged—on pain of death—from conversion to Christianity. To underscore the reality of this boundary, Hisham created a new Rusafan martyr in 737, when, outside the city's walls, he executed an Armenian prince named Vahan who had converted to Islam and then reverted to Christianity.[36] The martyr Vahan is remembered by Armenian Christians and not usually by students of Rusafa, but it is our only explicit literary evidence pertaining to Hisham's relations with a Christian at the site. Although Vahan did not reside at Rusafa and was martyred there simply because he was brought to appear before Hisham, his fate would have been a lesson to all potential converts to Christianity.

RUSAFA AFTER HISHAM

First the obliteration of the Syro-Mesopotamian arena of Roman and Iranian confrontation, and then the ʿAbbasid shift of the caliphal capital from Syria to Iraq, meant increasing political irrelevance for Rusafa, and consequently a lack of interest in it by contemporary historians. Rusafa's peripheral location between two empires had boosted the circulation and prestige of its saint on both sides of the frontier. But once it was absorbed into the Islamic commonwealth, Rusafa seems to have been demoted to the status of a minor regional center that still bore signs of its luminous past. From the time of the conquest onward, evidence for the survival of the Sergius cult at Rusafa must be inferred from the continuing prosperity of the fortified town itself. Around 1154, al-Idrisi described the settlement as the goal of travelers and merchants; an attractive place, vibrant with bazaars, merchandise, craftsmen, and its own flourishing inhabitants.[37] Three Arabic inscriptions in Hebrew script discovered in a much-damaged khan at the junction of the town's main east-west artery and the street leading to the north gate suggest that some of the merchants doing business at Rusafa were Jewish. The oldest commemorates the establishment of a room in the southwest corner of the courtyard as cult place in 1105.[38] Ibn Butlan commented half a century later that most of the inhabitants were Christian and most were

---

Arabian History III.574). Some forty-five years later, in a climate of strong Wahhabi influence in Hadramawt, the bearded, middle-aged man standing watch outside the mosque assured me that Sarjis is not in the Qurʾan and should be regarded with suspicion.

36. Peeters, *AB* 57 (1939): 330–33.

37. al-Idrisi, *Nuzha* 649 (tr. Kellner-Heinkele in Sack, *Resafa*, 4: 144–45).

38. Caquot, *Syria* 32 (1955): 70–74. On the khan, see Karnapp, *AA* 1978: 136–50.

occupied with the caravan trade.[39] According to al-Idrisi, Rusafa still occupied its place on the important route between the Euphrates and Homs that skirted the steppe to the north.[40]

Ibn Shaddad, a native of Aleppo who died in Cairo as a refugee after the Mongol invasion of Syria in 1259, records that the Mongols spared Sergius's city. Until 1269, a Mamluk governor was stationed at Rusafa, now on the front line in the confrontation between the Mamluks and the Mongols. Perhaps in connection with this tension, and perhaps also because of related damage to the settlement, which shows signs of fire damage in its last phase, the inhabitants soon abandoned Rusafa for towns further to the west, such as Salamiya and Hama.[41] The city would not be reinhabited, aside from a goat-headed snake that haunted the ruins thereafter and terrified passing beduin.[42] Rusafa's buildings, rebuilt manifold times over the centuries, had suffered from fire, earthquake, and subsidence. Basilica B, damaged most likely by an earthquake or subsidence, was allowed to be quarried as early as the late sixth century for materials used in basilica A and, later, in the Umayyad mosque. Eventually, houses were built within its ruins. The main church, basilica A, was frequently restored and reworked to accommodate changing needs. An inscription set into its western wall records restoration in 1093 by Symeon, metropolitan of Sergiopolis, perhaps after the earthquake of 1068 that devastated Palmyra.[43] Ibn Butlan, in a letter written in 1051, says that inside Rusafa's walls there was "a mighty church, the exterior of which is ornamented with gold mosaics, begun by the order of Constantine, the son of Helena."[44] No traces of such decoration have come to light, but the statement captures the legendary allure that Rusafa's religious architecture still held in the eleventh century. It seems that the southern or southwestern part of the basilica A complex housed monks, although neither archeological nor literary evidence helps pin down the chronology of such a community.[45] Yaqut in 1225 describes "a convent in the city of Rusafa Hisham ibn 'Abd al-Malik on the western bank of the Euphrates and in the desert, a day's march from Raqqa for those who are laden . . . I myself have seen this monastery, and it is one of the wonders of the world as regards its beauty and its structure. I have heard that Hisham built his city to be near

39. Ibn Butlan in Yaqut 2.955 (tr. Le Strange, *Palestine under the Moslems,* 522; cf. tr. Kellner-Heinkele in Sack, *Resafa,* 4: 146–47).

40. al-Idrisi, *Nuzha* 649 (tr. Kellner-Heinkele in Sack, *Resafa,* 4: 145).

41. Ibn Shaddad, *al-A'laq al-Hatira* 394 (tr. Eddé-Terrasse, 21–22; cf. tr. Kellner-Heinkele in Sack, *Resafa,* 4: 151). See also Ulbert, *Resafa,* 2: 151–53; and Sack, *Resafa,* 4: 132.

42. Musil, *Manners and Customs,* 414.

43. Gatier in Ulbert, *Resafa,* 2: 169, no. 19; see also Musil, *Palmyrena,* 271.

44. Ibn Butlan in Yaqut, *Mu'jam al-buldan* 3.48 (tr. Le Strange, *Palestine under the Moslems,* 522; cf. tr. Kellner-Heinkele in Sack, *Resafa,* 4: 146–47).

45. For evidence of a monastery at Rusafa, see p. 80n.97, above.

this monastery, and that it existed before the city. There are monks in it and religious men. It stands in the middle of the town of Rusafa."[46]

BETWEEN EAST AND WEST

Some glimmer of the sanctuary's beauty shines through the five silver objects discovered in 1982 during the excavation of the western end of the northern courtyard. The impressive assemblage includes a hanging lamp, a eucharistic chalice, the foot of another chalice, a paten, and a nonliturgical drinking cup. The objects were buried in a clay jar just before the Mongol onslaught of 1259/60, and represent the only finds in precious metal, other than a few coins, that have been uncovered and recorded as part of systematic investigation at this once famously wealthy site.[47] All five can be dated to the thirteenth century and all attest to the enduring cultural diversity of those who revered Rusafa's martyr. Apart from their exquisite decoration, the objects are particularly fascinating for the phases of use and influence they reveal. The lamp, wrought in silver and adorned with gold and intricate niello friezes, was designed originally as a drinking vessel about 1200 A.D. The style suggests a Syrian origin. Sometime before 1258/59, the cup was fitted out as a hanging lamp and presumably intended for use at Rusafa in honor of S. Sergius. The paten introduces another type of reuse, or rather rededication, most likely by a secondary owner of the object. A central medallion depicts the hand of God. The paten's form and iconography indicate a western origin, either in northern Germany, northern France, or England, where depiction of the hand of God was a common feature of patens dating from the early thirteenth century. After it had been transported from its native land, a man of Edessene descent donated the paten to "the church of Mar Sargis of Rusafa," according to the Syriac inscription.[48] The nonliturgical drinking cup too originated in the west, and in this case the central heraldic figure identifies it with the noble Coucy family of Picardy.[49] Most likely, the vessel would have been part of the baggage of Raoul I, sire de Coucy (d. 1191), who had come to Syria with the Third Crusade. This connection helps more generally to explain the proliferation of western-produced objects in Syria at this time. The elegant silver cup shows signs of numerous repairs and a damaged secondary Arabic in-

---

46. Yaqut, *Mu'jam al-buldan* 2.510 (tr. after Le Strange, *Palestine under the Moslems*, 432; cf. tr. Kellner-Heinkele in Sack, *Resafa*, 4: 146).

47. For their publication, see Ulbert, *Resafa*, 3, esp. 1–64, on the objects; and Degen in ibid., 3: 65–76, on their inscriptions.

48. Degen in Ulbert, *Resafa*, 3: 68–74.

49. See de Pinoteau in Ulbert, *Resafa*, 3: 77–78.

Figure 16. Silver chalice found at Rusafa. National Archaeological Museum, Damascus.

scription explains that it was dedicated at a church, probably at Qalat Ja'bar on the Euphrates. How it reached Rusafa is unknown.[50]

While the single chalice foot seems also to come from France or England, a subtler fusion of East and West is represented by the one intact chalice (fig. 16). The half-round shape of the cup and the large ribbed nodus that links the cup and foot are characteristic of late Romanesque chalices in Germany, France, and England. But the delicate niello ornament and figural representations are clearly native to northern Syria, suggesting that the chalice was made in Syria and its form inspired by a western model.[51]

The estrangela dedicatory inscription of the priest Iwannis (John) is original, in contrast to that inscribed on the western paten. The representation of the Theotokos with Christ child in the tondo, and of Christ the Pantokrator on the external border of the cup, belong to the Byzantine iconographical tradition, and are even accompanied by the typical Greek abbreviations in Greek characters. Although the subject requires further investigation, the combination of standard Byzantine religious iconography and a dedicatory inscription in Syriac by a priest named John suggests that perhaps the chalice was commissioned by a Chalcedonian whose liturgical language was Syriac.

While, as we have seen, no depictions of S. Sergius have been preserved on the walls of Rusafa's churches, frescoes of the saint dating to the twelfth and eighteenth centuries adorn three other Syrian churches. The monastery of Mar Musa al-Habashi, near Nabak, the church of Mar Sarjis at Qara and the church of Mar Sarjis at Sadad are all located west of Rusafa, roughly between Damascus and Homs.[52] As in the case of the thirteenth-century silver paten found at Rusafa, the Latin influence is evident in the twelfth-century paintings and is in fact more pronounced than any Byzantine debt. At both Mar Musa and Qara, Sergius is mounted on a white horse. The rider saint wears typical Crusader dress and turns his torso to face the viewer. He carries in one hand the characteristic Crusader pennant, a red cross on white ground, and in the other he holds a martyr's cross. A third portrait of this type is the famous Crusader icon of S. Sergius at Sinai.[53] Western influence in this medieval portrait of Sergius as a rider saint is undeniable. However, it was not the only source for the rider portrait of Sergius, which, as we have seen, has Syrian roots planted in the early phases of the cult's development.[54]

At Sadad, in the church dedicated to SS. Sergius and Bacchus, the exuberant wall-paintings seem to reflect an idiosyncratic style more than a particular iconographic tradition. The saints' portraits occupy the south wall next to the sanctuary and are the only unlabeled depictions of rider saints in the church's highly animated iconography. Their prominent position and the building's dedication would have made their identity obvious. Sergius is shown crowned, but with a much more elaborate headpiece than he wears at Mar Musa and Qara. And at Sadad, the young martyr has acquired a beard. Also exceptionally for Sergius, but within the wider tradition of soldier-saints, he spears a demon who struggles beneath the forefeet of the martyr's horse. His accomplice's mount also rears above the pros-

52. Cruikshank Dodd, *Arte Medievale* 1 (1992): 61–130; Velmans, *CArch* 42 (1994): 134–38; Johann Georg, Herzog zu Sachsen, *OC* 2 (1927): 233–42.

53. Hunt, *BMGS* 15 (1991): 96–145.

54. See above, pp. 35–44.

trate figure. This smaller rider, no doubt Bacchus, is also crowned. Sergius carries a diminutive passenger seated just behind him on the horse. Given the eccentricity of these late paintings, such deviation from the standard iconography of SS. Sergius and Bacchus is not terribly surprising. The Sadad painter's Sergius is a collage of attributes characteristic of several powerful eastern saints—the riders Sergius and Bacchus; the beloved George, spearing the dragon and carrying a tiny figure behind him; and the other popular Sergius, whose son Martyrius accompanies him on his steed, much in the manner of George's companion. Sergius and Martyrius may be lesser known today, but they were sufficiently esteemed in the eighth century for the poet Jarir to reprove the Christian Taghlib for embracing "Sergius and his son" instead of Muhammad—a barb that suggests that the Sadad painter was not alone in confusing the two powerful Sergii.[55]

In the wall just in front of the head of Sergius's horse a stone reliquary still containing bones was discovered.[56] That the relics came from Rusafa cannot be excluded, since the cult spread earliest precisely in this southwestern direction from Rusafa. It may be recalled in this context that the conclusion of the *Passio* notes that miracle-working relics of S. Sergius could be found elsewhere in addition to Rusafa.[57] But there is also the question of what happened to the relics after Rusafa's abandonment. Some of Rusafa's inhabitants were said to have fled westward and taken refuge in the Hama region and at Salamiya.[58] No explicit mention is made of who was responsible for the relics. Miscellaneous references to the relics of SS. Sergius and

55. Jarir, *Diwan* 474. A few of the Sadad wall paintings (but not SS. Sergius and Bacchus) are illustrated by Johan Georg zu Sachsen, *OC* 2 (1927), pls. 3–4. See Littmann, *OC* 3–4 (1930): 288–91, and Littmann in *PAES* 4.B.56–62, for the Garshuni (Arabic written with Syriac letters) legends on the wall paintings. For the iconography of SS. Sergius and Martyrius, see Mirzoyan, *REArm* 20 (1986–87), 441–55, esp. fig. 1. I would like to thank Mat Immerzeel, who prefers to identify the painting as S. George with Amiras, for his correspondence about this painting.

56. In May 1996, the Syrian Orthodox priest of Sadad showed me a small stone sarcophagus-shaped reliquary and a silver reliquary containing small pieces of bone. He claimed that both had been found in the wall next to the painting of S. Sergius. The hole in the wall is clearly visible. The recently published history of this Christian village does not mention the reliquary, but it describes the paintings in detail (al-'Arab, *Sadad fi al-ta'rikh*, 293–96). On a similar stone reliquary now in the Aleppo Archeological Museum, the name Mar Sargis is scratched lightly on the lid. This Syriac inscription is considered to be secondary; cf. Hunter, *Studia Patristica* 25 (1993): 309–10.

57. *Pass. gr.* 30.

58. Ibn Shaddad, *al-A'laq* 21–22 (tr. Eddé-Terrasse). Jabbur, *Bedouins,* 465–66, quotes Ibn Butlan on the Christian makeup of Rusafa as late as the eleventh century and considers it possible that the Slayb tribe may be descended from Christians of Rusafa and the Euphrates region.

Bacchus are nonetheless to be found: a Georgian translation of the original Greek *Life* of John, abbot of the S. Sergius monastery in Constantinople in the later ninth century, claims, for example, that John discovered the relics of S. Sergius in the S. Sergius church in Constantinople. According to this account, the relics had been hidden for many years in the ground by heedless men.[59] In the eleventh century, a Russian pilgrim to the church of S. Sergius in Constantinople, Stephen of Novgorod, claims to have reverenced the heads of Sergius and Bacchus there; and the martyrs' chlamydes were reportedly housed there also since before the thirteenth century.[60] At the beginning of the fourteenth century, relics of SS. Sergius and Bacchus were kept in the Nestorian monastery at Maragah just west of Lake Urmiya, in northwest Iran.[61] In 1377, Armenian raiders are said to have scattered bones of S. Sergius at the Sergius monastery of Sergisiyah, in the region of Melitine.[62] Today the monasteries of Vatopedi and Simonopetra on Mount Athos both preserve parts of the skull of S. Sergius.[63]

BETWEEN CHRISTIANITY AND ISLAM

Besides Hisham's activities at Rusafa, there is some modern evidence that Muslims too embraced Sergius as their saint. Charles Doughty, the Victorian traveler in Syria and Arabia, observes of Sergius that he "was an old Christian saint at Damascus, 'but he is now of Islam'; you may see his shrine in the sûk by the street fountain, the bars of his windows are all behanged with votive rags." And he relates a story he had heard about S. Sergius in connection with the Muslim massacre of Christians at Damascus in 1860. "Upon a morrow, in the beginning of the rebellion, Sergius his lamps were found full of gore, also his fountain ran blood, prodigies which great learned turbans interpreted to presage 'great destruction of Christian blood!'"[64] Despite his adoption into Muslim cultic life, Sergius still retained—as the shaykhs' interpretations reveal—his Christian heritage. These mixed associations allowed the saint to find a place simultaneously in both traditions.

Today, perhaps the best-known Syrian church dedicated to S. Sergius is located at Ma'lula, not far from Sadad, in the Anti-Lebanon mountains

---

59. See van Esbroeck, *OC* 80 (1996): 163, §15.

60. Majeska, *Russian Travellers,* 38–39; cf. 165–65, for the fourteenth century; see also 264–65, with n. 5, for the chlamydes.

61. *Monks of Kūblāi Khān* 245–46 (tr. Budge).

62. Mich. Syr., *Chron.* 15.1 (tr. Chabot, 3: 162).

63. In contemporary Greece, S. Sergius's healing powers are sought especially for head injuries, inspired, it is said, by the gash in the cranium kept at the monastery of Simonopetra.

64. Doughty, *Travels* 1.522. For the Sergius shrine in Damascus, see p. 105n.22, above.

northwest of Damascus.[65] Maʿlula today is famous for the dialect of Aramaic that is still spoken by its inhabitants, both Christian and Muslim. Two monasteries, one dedicated to S. Sergius and the other to S. Thecla, perch in the mountains above the flat-roofed houses, among which there is also a church dedicated to S. George. The church of the Sergius monastery houses an exquisite icon of SS. Sergius and Bacchus on horseback by Michael of Crete, dated to 1813. Another by the same hand depicts S. Thecla enthroned.[66] The monastery of S. Thecla is built around a cave revered according to local tradition as Thecla's tomb. Maʿlula's trio of martyrs, Sergius, Thecla, and George, are among the select few who were reckoned by John Moschus as the greatest saints of the East, a distinction that they still claim not only among Christians but also among Muslims.[67] Pilgrims of both faiths visit the shrine of Thecla for healing. Maʿlula is today the best-known example in Syria of the overlapping of Christian and Muslim practice.

In the East, both S. George and S. Sergius have often been identified with the Muslim prophet Khidr, thanks to the healing and protective powers associated with both the Christian and the Muslim figures. It has been thought that this identification was encouraged by Muslims in order to induce a gradual assimilation of the two faiths, which would eventually lead to the conversion of Christians to Islam.[68] More likely in most cases, it simply underlines the shared hopes and aspirations for supernatural healing and protection of both groups. S. Sergius is especially identified with Khidr in areas with strong Armenian influence, since Sarkis is one of the most highly revered saints in Armenian Christianity.[69] There can be no doubt that the appeal of S. Sergius to both Christian and Muslim had roots at Rusafa, where the church and mosque stood side by side for six centuries.

The cult of S. Sergius was established in late antiquity around the relics of a martyr whose power as a healer and defender was sought by the Romans, Iranians, and Arabs who shared an interest in Syria and Mesopo-

---

65. The monastery of S. Sergius preserves reused architectural elements that date back as early as the fourth century, although the present church belongs to the Middle Ages (Ulbert in *Pietas,* 559–62).

66. On Michael of Crete and the large number if icons by him at this monastery, see Candea and Agémian, eds., *Icones Melkites,* 196–202, and Hatzidakis and Drakopoulou, Ἕλλη-νες Ζωγράφοι, 2: 301–2, with figs. 202, 204.

67. At Maʿlula, the feasts of SS. Sergius and Thecla are both celebrated on 7 October (Reich, *Études sur les villages araméens,* 146).

68. See Hasluck, *Christianity and Islam,* 145, 335 n. 1; and Canaan, *Mohammedan Saints,* 14–15.

69. On S. Sergius in Armenian culture, see Hasluck, *Christianity and Islam,* 570–71; Peeters, *Recherches,* 1: 25–36; and Thierry, Monuments Arméniens 508. Further research needs to be done on the Armenian life of S. Sergius and his son Martyrius (Peeters, ed., *Bibliotheca hagiographica orientalis,* 231–32) in the context of frontier politics and culture.

tamia. The spread of belief in S. Sergius's power and subsequently of the influence of the saint and his cult center drew much of its distinctive strength from Rusafa's location in the fluid frontier zone, where knowledge traveled widely and among varied groups. By the time of the Islamic conquests, when the Barbarian Plain lost its political significance, the cult was widely disseminated in Syria and Mesopotamia, and even further afield, where Sergius could not anyhow be so closely associated with frontier defense. What started as a frontier religion very much part of a place and a time, had acquired the momentum to cross other boundaries, less mindful of geography, between Christianity and Islam.

BIBLIOGRAPHY

Articles in encyclopaedias, the *Bulletin épigraphique*, and *The Cambridge History of Iran* are not included in the bibliography.

PRIMARY SOURCES

Acta Anastasii Persae. Edited and translated by B. Flusin. In id., *Saint Anastase le Perse et l'histoire de la Palestine au début du VIIe siècle*, 1: 3–91. Paris, 1992.

Acta conciliorum oecumenicorum. Edited by E. Schwartz. Strasbourg, 1914–.

Acta Mar Kardagh martyris. Edited by J. B. Abbeloos. *AB* 9 (1890): 5–106

Acta S. Theclae. Edited by G. Dagron in *Vie et miracles de Sainte Thècle*, 167–283. Brussels, 1978.

Agapius of Manbij. *Kitab al-'unwan*. Edited and translated by A. Vasiliev. *PO* 5.4, 7.4, 8.3, 11.1.

Agathias. *Historiae*. Edited by R. Keydell. Berlin, 1967.

al-Akhtal. *Diwan*. Edited by A. Salhani. Beirut, 1891–1925.

Ammianus Marcellinus. *Res gestae*. Edited by C. U. Clark. Berlin, 1910–15.

'Amr ibn Matta. Revision of Mari ibn Sulayman, *Kitab al-mijdal*. Edited by E. Gismondi. In *Maris Amri et Slibae de patriarchis nestorianorum commentaria*. Rome, 1896–99.

Anthologia graeca. Edited by H. Beckby. Munich, 1957–58.

Arab Jacobite Synaxarion. Coptic recension. Edited and translated by R. Basset. *PO* 1.3, 3.3, 11.5, 16.2, 17.3, 20.5.

Armenian Synaxarion of Ter Israel. Edited and translated by G. Bayan. *PO* 5.3, 6.2, 15.3, 16.1, 18.1, 19.1, 21.1–6.

Babai the Great. *History of Mar Giwargis*. In *Histoire de Mar Jabalaha, de trois autres patriarches et de deux laïques nestoriens*, ed. P. Bedjan, 416–571. Leipzig, 1895. Translated by O. Braun under the title *Ausgewählte Akten persischer Märtyrer mit einem Anhang: Ostsyrisches Mönchsleben* (Kempten, 1915), 221–77.

al-Baladhuri, Ahmad ibn Yahya. *Futuh al-buldan.* Edited by M. J. de Goeje. Leiden, 1866. Translated by P. K. Hitti and F. C. Murgotten under the title *The Origins of the Islamic State* (New York, 1916–24).

Bar Hebraeus. *Chronicon ecclesiasticum.* Edited and translated by J. B. Abbeloos and Th.-J. Lamy. Louvain, 1872–77.

Basil of Caesarea. *Epistolae.* Edited and translated by Y. Courtonne. Paris, 1957–66.

——. *Homiliae. PG* 31.164–617.

al-Biruni, Abu'l-Rayhan Muhammad ibn Ahmad. *Kitab al-athar al-baqiya.* Edited by C. E. Sachau. Leipzig, 1876–78. Translated by C. E. Sachau under the title *The Chronology of the Ancient Nations* (London, 1879).

al-Buhturi. *Diwan.* Edited by R. Sarkis. Beirut, 1911.

Calendar of Edessa of 411. Edited and translated by F. Nau under the title *Un Martyrologue syriaque. PO* 10.1.11–28.

Cedrenus, George. *Compendium historiarum.* Edited by I. Bekker. Bonn, 1838–39.

Choniates, Nicetas. *Historia.* Edited by J. L. van Dieten. Berlin, 1975.

Choricius of Gaza. *Laudatio Marciani* 1. Edited by R. Foerster and C. Richtsteig in *Choricii Gazaei opera,* 1–26. Leipzig, 1929.

Chronicle of Amida of 569 = Historia ecclesiastica Zachariae Rhetori vulgo adscripta 2. Edited by E. W. Brooks. Paris, 1921. Translated by F. J. Hamilton and E. W. Brooks under the title *The Syriac Chronicle Known as That of Zachariah of Mitylene* (London, 1899).

Chronicle of Edessa of 506. In *Chronicle of Zuqnin 775.* Edited by J.-B. Chabot in *Incerti auctoris chronicum anonymum pseudo-Dionysianum vulgo dictum,* 1: 235–317. Paris, 1927. Latin translation by J.-B. Chabot in *Incerti auctoris chronicum anonymum pseudo-Dionysianum vulgo dictum,* 1: 174–233 (Paris, 1949). English translation by W. Wright under the title *The Chronicle of Joshua the Stylite, Composed in Syriac* A.D. 507 (Cambridge, 1882).

Chronicle of Seert. Edited and translated by A. Scher and others. *PO* 4.3, 5.2, 7.2, 13.4.

Chronicle of Zuqnin of 775. In *Incerti auctoris chronicum anonymum pseudo-Dionysianum vulgo dictum,* ed. J.-B. Chabot, vol. 2. Paris 1933. French translation by R. Hespel in *Incerti auctoris chronicum anonymum pseudo-Dionysianum vulgo dictum,* vol. 2 (Louvain, 1989).

Chronicon ad annum Christi 1234 pertinens. Edited by J.-B. Chabot. Louvain, 1916–20. Latin translation by J.-B. Chabot, 1 (Louvain, 1937). French translation by A. Abouna, 2 (Louvain, 1974). Partial English translation in A. Palmer, *The Seventh Century in the West Syrian Chronicles,* 111–221 (Liverpool, 1993).

Chronicon Pascale. Edited by L. Dindorf. Bonn, 1832.

Cinnamus, John. *Epitome.* Edited by A. Meineke. Bonn, 1836.

Codex Justinianus. Edited by P. Krueger. Berlin, 1877.

Constantine Porphyrogenitus. *De ceremoniis aulae Byzantinae.* Edited by J. J. Reiske. Bonn, 1829–30. Edited and translated by A. Vogt in *Le Livre des cérémonies,* 1: 1–83 (Paris, 1935–39).

Cyril of Scythopolis. *Vita Euthymii.* Edited by E. Schwartz. Leipzig, 1939.

Denha. *History of Maruta.* Edited and translated by F. Nau. *PO* 3.1.63–96.

Digenis Akritis. Edited and translated by E. Jeffreys. Cambridge, 1998.

Documenta ad origines monophysitarum illustrandas. Edited and translated by J.-B. Chabot. Paris, 1907, 1933.

Elias, patriarch of Jerusalem. *De SS. Sergio et Baccho.* In *Analecta Sacra,* ed. J. B. Pitra, 1: 289–91. Paris, 1876.

Ephrem the Syrian. *Carmina nisibena.* Edited and translated by E. Beck. Louvain, 1961–63.

Eusebius. *Historia ecclesiastica.* Edited by E. Schwartz. Leipzig, 1903–9.

———. *Liber de martyribus Palaestinae.* In *Historia ecclesiastica,* ed. E. Schwartz, 2: 907–502. Leipzig, 1908.

Evagrius. *Historia ecclesiastica.* Edited by J. Bidez and L. Parmentier. London, 1898.

George of Cyprus. *Descriptio orbis romani.* Edited by H. Gelzer. Leipzig, 1890.

Gregory of Nazianzus. *Orationes. PG* 35–36.

Gregory of Nyssa. *De sancto Theodoro.* Edited by J. P. Cavarnos. In *Gregorii Nysseni sermones,* ed. G. Heil et al., 2: 61–71. Leiden, 1990.

———. *Hom. in XL martyres* II. Edited by O. Lendle. In *Gregorii Nysseni sermones,* ed. G. Heil et al., 2: 159–69. Leiden, 1990.

Gregory of Tours. *Historia francorum.* Edited by B. Krusch and W. Levison. *MGH, SRM* 1.1.

———Liber in gloriam martyrum.* Edited by B. Krusch. In *MGH, SRM,* 1: 484–561. Berlin, 1885. Translated by R. Van Dam (Liverpool, 1988).

———. *De virtutibus sancti Martini episcopi.* Edited by B. Krusch. In *MGH, SRM,* 1: 584–661. Berlin, 1885. Translated by R. Van Dam in *Saints and Their Miracles in Late Antique Gaul* (Princeton, 1993), 199–303.

———. *Liber vitae patrum.* Edited by B. Krusch. In *MGH, SRM,* 1: 661–744. Berlin, 1885.

al-Harawi, 'Ali. *Kitab al-isharat ila ma'rifat al-ziyarat.* Edited by J. Sourdel-Thomine. Damascus, 1953. Translated by id. under the title *Guide des lieux de pèlerinage* (Damascus, 1957).

al-Harawi, Hassan ibn Thabit. *Diwan.* Edited by W. N. 'Arafat. London, 1971.

History of Ahudemmeh. Edited and translated by F. Nau. *PO* 3.1.7–51.

History of the Patriarchs of Alexandria. Edited and translated by B. Evetts. *PO* 1.2, 1.4, 5.1, 10.5.

Hugeburc. *Life of Willibald.* Edited by O. Holder-Egger. *MGH* 15.1: 86–106. Berlin, 1887.

Ibn Hazm, Abu Muhammad 'Ali ibn Ahmad. *Jamharat ansab al-'arab.* Edited by 'A. Harun. Cairo, 1962.

Ibn Ishaq, Muhammad. *Sirat rasul Allah.* Recension of Abu Muhammad 'Abd al-Malik ibn Hisham. Edited by F. Wüstenfeld. Göttingen, 1858–60. Translated by A. Guillaume under the title *The Life of Muhammad* (London, 1955).

Ibn Shaddad, 'Izz al-Din. *Al-a'laq al-khatira fi dhikr umara'al-Sham wa 'l-Jazira.* Translated by A.-M. Eddé-Terrasse under the title *Description de la Syrie du Nord* (Damascus, 1984).

al-Idrisi, Abu 'Abdallah Muhammad. *Nuzhat al mushtaq fi ikhtiraq al-afaq.* Edited by E. Cerulli et al. In *Opus Geographicum.* Leiden, 1970–84.

al-Isfahani, Abu'l-Faraj. *Kitab al-aghani.* Edited by A. 'A. Muhanna and S. Y. Jabir. Beirut, 1982.

Jacob of Sarug. *Mimra on the Victorious Sergius and Bacchus.* Edited by P. Bedjan. In *AMS*, 6: 650–61. Translated by A. Palmer (unpublished).

———. *Mimra on the Victorious Sergius and Bacchus.* Translated by Andrew Palmer. N.d.

James of Edessa. *The Hymns of Severus of Antioch and Others.* Edited and translated by E. W. Brooks. *PO* 6.1, 7.5.

Jarir and al-Farazdaq. *Naqa'id.* Edited by A. A. Bevan under the title *The Naka'id of Jarir and al-Farazdaq.* Leiden, 1905–12.

John Chrysostom. *Homilia in martyres.* *PG* 50.662–66.

John Diacrinomenus. *Fragmenta.* Edited by G. C. Hansen. In *Theodore Anagnostes, Historia ecclesiastica,* 152–57. 2d ed. Berlin, 1995.

John of Ephesus. *Historia ecclesiastica.* Pars tertia. Edited and translated by E. W. Brooks. Louvain, 1935–36.

———. *Vita sanctorum orientalium.* Edited and translated by E. W. Brooks. *PO* 17.1, 18.4, 19.2.

John of Epiphania. *Fragmenta.* Edited by C. Müller. In *Fragmenta historicorum graecorum,* 4: 273–76. Paris, 1851.

John Lydus. *De magistratibus populi romani.* Edited and translated by A. C. Bandy under the title *On Powers, or, The Magistracies of the Roman State.* Philadelphia, 1983.

John Malalas. *Chronographia.* Edited by L. Dindorf. Bonn, 1831.

John Moschus. *Pratum spirituale.* *PG* 87.2851–3112

John the Persian. *The History of Rabban bar 'Idta.* Metrical version by Abraham of Zabde. Edited and translated by E. A. W. Budge under the title *The Histories of Rabban Hōrmīzd the Persian and Rabban Bar 'Idta* (London, 1902).

Joseph the Scevophylax. *Life of S. John, Abbot of S. Sergius's Monastery.* Edited by K. Kekelidze. In *Etiudebi jveli kartuli literaturis istoriidan,* 3: 260–70. Tbilisi, 1955. Translated by M. van Esbroeck under the title "La Vie de Saint Jean higoumène de Saint Serge par Joseph le Skevophylax," *OC* 80 (1996): 153–66.

Joshua the Stylite. See *Chronicle of Edessa of 506.*

Lactantius. *De mortibus persecutorum.* Edited by J. Moreau. Paris, 1954.

Leontius of Jerusalem. *Contra monophysitas.* *PG* 86.1769–1902.

Malchus. *Fragmenta.* Edited and translated by R. C. Blockley. In *The Fragmentary Classicizing Historians of the Later Roman Empire,* 2: 402–62. Liverpool, 1983.

Mari ibn Sulayman. *Kitab al-mijdal.* Edited by E. Gismondi. *Maris Amri et Slibae de patriarchis nestorianorum commentaria.* Rome, 1896–99.

Μαρτύριον τοῦ ἁγίου μεγαλομάρτυρος Ἀθανασίου τοῦ ἐν τῷ Κλύσματι τῆς Ἐρυθρᾶς Θαλάσσης, Edited by A. Papadopoulos-Kerameus. In *Ἀνάλεκτα Ἱεροσολυμιτικῆς Σταχυολογίας,* 5: 360–67. Saint Petersburg, 1898.

Martyrum Persarum acta. Edited by H. Delehaye. *PO* 2.4.

al-Masʿudi. *Muruj al-dhahab.* Edited and translated by C. Barbier de Meynard and J.-B. Pavet de Courteille under the title *Maçoudi: Les Prairies d'or.* Paris, 1861–77. Revised by C. Pellat. Beirut, 1966–79 (edition). Paris, 1962– (translation).

Menander Protector. *Fragmenta.* Edited and translated by R. C. Blockley under the title *The History of Menander the Guardsman.* Liverpool, 1985.

Michael the Syrian. *Chronicle.* Edited and translated by J.-B. Chabot. Paris, 1899–1910.

Miracula S. Theclae. Edited and translated by G. Dagron in *Vie et miracles de Sainte Thècle*, 284–421. Brussels, 1978.

The Monks of Kūblāi Khān, Emperor of China. Translated by E. A. Budge. London, 1928.

Notitia dignitatum. Edited by O. Seeck. Berlin, 1876.

Olympiodorus. *Fragmenta.* Edited and translated by R. C. Blockley in *The Fragmentary Classicising Historians of the Later Roman Empire*, 2: 152–209. Liverpool, 1983.

Pachymeres, George. *De Michaele et Andronico Paleologis.* Edited by A. Failler. Paris, 1984.

Palladius. *Historia Lausiaca.* Edited by G. J. M. Bartelink. N.p., 1974.

Passio antiquior SS. Sergii et Bacchi. Edited by I. van de Gheyn. *AB* 14 (1895): 371–95. Latin redaction, ed. C. Byeus, *Acta sanctorum Octobris* 3: 863–70. Metaphrastic redaction, ed. C. Byeus, *Acta sanctorum Octobris* 3: 871–82. Syriac redaction, ed. P. Bedjan, *AMS* 3: 283–22.

Patria Konstantinoupoleos. In *Scriptores originum Constantinopolitanarum*, ed. Th. Preger, 1–18. Leipzig 1901–7.

Paulinus of Nola. *Carmina.* Edited by G. de Hartel. *CSEL* 30. Vienna, 1894.

Paulus Silentiarius. *Descriptio Sanctae Sophiae.* Edited by P. Friedländer. Leipzig, 1912.

Photius. *Bibliotheca.* Edited by R. Henry. Paris, 1959–77.

Piacenza Pilgrim. *Itinerarium.* In *Itinera Hierosolymitana saeculi IIII–VII*, ed. P. Geyer. *CSEL* 39. Vienna, 1890.

Procopius. *De aedificiis.* Edited by J. Haury. Revised by G. Wirth. Leipzig, 1964.

———. *De bello persico.* Edited by J. Haury. Revised by G. Wirth. Leipzig, 1962.

Prudentius. *Peristephanon.* Edited by J. Bergman. Vienna, 1926. Translated by H. J. Thomson (Cambridge, Mass., 1953).

Ptolemy. *Geographia.* Edited by C. Müller. Paris, 1883–1901.

Ravenna Geographer. In *Ravennatis Anonymi Cosmographia et Guidonis Geographica.* Edited by M. Pinder and G. Parthey, 1–445. Berlin, 1860.

Sebeos. *Patmut'iwn Sebēosi.* Edited by V. G. Abgarian. Erevan, 1979. Translated by C. Gugerotti under the title Sebēos, *Storia* (Verona, 1990).

Severus of Antioch. *Homiliae cathedrales.* Edited and translated by R. Duval and others. *PO* 4.1, 8.2, 12.1, 16.5, 20.2, 22.2, 23.1, 25.1, 26.3, 29.1, 35.3, 36.1, 36.3.

Scylitzes, John. *Synopsis historiarum.* Edited by H. Thurn. Berlin, 1973.

Socrates Scholasticus. *Historia ecclesiastica.* Edited by G. C. Hansen. Berlin, 1995.

Sophronius. *Miracula Cyri et Ioannis.* Edited by N. F. Marcos. In *Los "thaumata" de Sofronio: Contribucion al estudio de la "incubatio" cristiana.* Madrid, 1975.

Sozomen. *Historia ecclesiastica.* Edited by J. Bidez. Berlin, 1960.

Stephanus of Byzantium. *Ethnica.* Edited by A. Meineke. Berlin, 1849.

Synaxarium ecclesiae Constantinopolitanae. Propylaeum ad Acta Sanctorum Novembris. Edited by H. Delehaye. Brussels, 1902.

Synodicon orientale ou Recueil de synodes nestoriens. Edited and translated by J.-B. Chabot. Paris, 1902.

Syrian Calendar. Edited and translated by F. Nau under the title *Douze ménologues syriaques.* PO 10.1.29–56.

al-Tabari, Abu Ja'far Muhammad ibn Jarir. *Ta'rikh al-rusul wa 'l-muluk.* Edited by

M. J. de Goeje et al. Leiden, 1879–1901. Partial translation by T. Nöldeke under the title *Geschichte der Perser und Araber zur Zeit der Sasaniden: Aus der arabischen Chronik des Tabari* (Leiden 1879). English translation edited by E. Yar-Shater (New York 1985–).

Tabula Peutingeriana. Facsimile edition with commentary by E. Weber. Graz, 1976.

Tarafa ibn al-ʿAbd al-Bakri. *Muʿallaqa.* Edited by ʿA. F. al-Tabbaʿ. In *Diwan Tarafa ibn al-ʿAbd.* Abu Dhabi, n.d. Translated by A. J. Arberry in *The Seven Odes: The First Chapter in Arabic Literature,* 83–89 (London, 1957)

Theodoret. *Graecarum affectionum curatio.* Edited and translated by P. Canivet. Paris, 1958.

———. *Historia religiosa.* Edited and translated by P. Carnivet and A. Leroy-Molinghen under the title *Histoire des moines de Syrie.* Paris, 1977–79.

Theophanes. *Chronographia.* Edited by C. de Boor. Leipzig, 1883.

Theophylact Simocatta. *Historia universalis.* Edited by C. de Boor. Revised by P. Wirth. Stuttgart, 1972. German translation by P. Schreiner (Stuttgart, 1985). English translation by M. and M. Whitby (Oxford, 1986).

Thomas of Marga. *The Book of Governors.* Edited and translated by E. A. Budge. London, 1893.

Translatio reliquiarum [*Anastasii Persae*]. Edited and translated by B. Flusin in *Saint Anastase le Perse,* 1: 97–107. Paris, 1992.

Vita et institutum piisimi patris nostri Alexandri. Edited and translated by E. de Stoop. *PO* 6.5.

Vita Gulanducht. Georgian redaction. Edited and translated by G. Garitte. *AB* 74 (1956): 426–40. Greek redaction by Eustratios presbyteros, Βίος καὶ πολιτεία, ἤγουν ἄθλησις καὶ διὰ Χριστὸν ἀγῶνες τῆς ἁγίας ὁσιομάρτυρος Γολινδούχ, τῆς ἐν τῷ ἁγίῳ βαπτίσματι μετονομασθείσης Μαρίας, ed. A. Papadopoulos-Kerameus, Ἀνάλεκτα Ἱεροσολυμιτικῆς Σταχυολογίας, 4: 149–79 (Saint Petersburg, 1897).

Vita Maruthae. Armenian edition. In *Varkʿ ew Vkayabanoutʿiunkʿ Srboç* (*Vitae et passiones sanctorum*), 2: 17–32. Venice, 1874. Translated by R. Marcus, *HThR* 25 (1932): 47–71.

Vita Maruthae (*BHG* 2265). Edited and translated by J. Noret. *AB* 91 (1973): 80–91.

Vita Maruthae (*BHG* 2266). Edited and translated by J. Noret. *AB* 91 (1973): 80–91.

Vita Petri Iberi. Edited and translated by R. Raabe. Leipzig, 1895.

Vita Simeonis Stylitae (Syriac). Translated by R. Doran. Kalamazoo, Mich., 1992. Based on Vat. Syr. 160 and the edition by S. E. Assemani, *Acta sanctorum martyrum orientalium et occidentalium,* 2: 268–398 (Rome, 1748).

West Syrian Synodicon. Edited and translated by A. Vööbus under the title *The Synodicon in the West Syrian Tradition.* Louvain, 1975–76.

Xanthopoulus, Nicephorus Callistus. *Ecclesiastica historia. PG* 145. 559–147.448.

Yaqut b. ʿAbdallah al-Hamawi. *Muʿjam al-buldan.* Beirut, 1955–57.

Zachariah of Mitylene. *Chronicle.* Edited by E. W. Brooks as *Historia ecclesiastica Zachariae Rhetori vulgo adscripta.* Paris, 1919–21. Translated by F. J. Hamilton and E. W. Brooks under the title *The Syriac Chronicle Known as That of Zachariah of Mitylene* (London, 1899).

Zosimus. *Historia nova.* Edited and translated by F. Paschoud. Paris, 1971–89.

SECONDARY LITERATURE

'Abd al-Ghani, 'A. *Ta'rikh al-Hira fi al-jahiliya wa 'l-islam.* Damascus, 1993.

Aigrain, R. "Sur quelques inscriptions d'églises de l'époque byzantine." *OCP* 13 (1947): 18–27.

al-'Arab, H. *Sadad fi al-ta'rikh.* Damascus, 1995.

Assemani, J. S. *Bibliotheca orientalis.* Rome, 1719–28.

Bakirtzis, Ch., ed. *Ἁγίου Δημητρίου θαύματα. Οἱ συλλογές Ἀρχιεπισκόπου Ἰωάννου καὶ Ἀνωνύμου. Ὁ βίος, τα θαύματα καὶ ἡ Θεσσαλονίκη τοῦ Ἁγίου Δημητρίου.* Athens, 1997.

Balty, J. *Mosaïques antiques de la Syrie.* Brussels, 1977.

Barnes, T. D. *The New Empire of Diocletian and Constantine.* Cambridge, Mass., 1982.

Barnish, S. J. B. "Late Roman Prosopography Reassessed." *JRS* 84 (1994): 171–77.

Baumstark, A. *Geschichte der syrischen Literatur mit Ausschluß der christlich-palästinensischen Texte.* Bonn, 1922.

Baur, P. V. C., and M. I. Rostovtzeff, eds. *The Excavations at Dura-Europos: Preliminary Report of Second Season of Work, October 1928–April 1929.* New Haven, Conn., 1931.

Bauzou, Th. "Épigraphie et toponymie: Le Cas de la Palmyrène du sud-ouest." *Syria* 70 (1993): 27–50.

———. "Routes romaines de Syrie." In *Archéologie et histoire de la Syrie: La Syrie de l'époque achéménide à l'avènement de l'Islam,* ed. J.-M. Dentzer and W. Orthmann, 2: 205–21. Saarbrücken, 1989.

———. "Les Voies de communication dans le Hauran à l'époque romaine." In *Hauran 1: Recherches archéologiques sur la Syrie du sud à l'époque hellénistique et romaine,* ed. J.-M. Dentzer, 137–65. Paris, 1985.

Beard, M. "Writing and Religion: Ancient Literacy and the Function of the Written Word in Roman Religion." In *Literacy in the Roman World,* ed. J. H. Humphrey, 35–58. Ann Arbor, Mich., 1991.

———. "Writing and Ritual: A Study of Diversity and Expansion in the Arval Acta." *PBSR* 53 (1985): 14–62.

Beck, H.-G. *Kirche und theologische Literatur im byzantinischen Reich.* Munich, 1959.

Beck, R. "The Mithras Cult as Association." *Studies in Religion* 21 (1992): 3–13.

Bell, G. *The Churches and Monasteries of the Tur 'Abdin.* Edited and revised by M. Mundell Mango. London, 1982.

Bernbeck, R. *Steppe als Kulturlandschaft. Das 'Ağiğ-Gebiet Ostsyriens vom Neolithikum bis zur islamischen Zeit.* Berlin, 1993.

Bishop, E. *Liturgica historica: Papers on the Liturgy and Religious Life of the Western Church.* Oxford, 1918.

Blair, S. "What Is the Date of the Dome of the Rock?" In *Bayt al-Maqdis: 'Abd al-Malik's Jerusalem,* ed. J. Raby and J. Johns, 1: 59–87. Oxford, 1992.

Blanck, H. *Wiederverwendung alter Statuen als Ehrendenkmäler bei Griechen und Römer.* Rome, 1969.

Blockley, R. C. *East Roman Foreign Policy: Formation and Conduct from Diocletian to Anastasius.* Leeds, 1992.

Blunt, Lady Anne. *Bedouins of the Euphrates.* London, 1879.

Bonner, C. *Studies in Magical Amulets, Chiefly Graeco-Egyptian.* Ann Arbor, Mich., 1950.

Borkowski, Z. *Inscriptions des factions à Alexandrie.* Warsaw, 1981.

Boswell, J. *Same-Sex Unions in Pre-Modern Europe.* New York, 1994.

Boucheman, A. de. *Une Petite Cité caravanière: Suḥné.* Damascus, 1937.

Bowersock, G. W. *Roman Arabia.* Cambridge, Mass., 1983.

———. "Social and Economic History of Syria under the Roman Empire." In *Archéologie et histoire de la Syrie,* vol. 2: *La Syrie de l'époque achéménide à l'avènement de l'Islam,* ed. J.-M. Dentzer and W. Orthmann, 63–80. Saarbrücken, 1989.

———. "Syria under Vespasian." *JRS* 63 (1973): 133–40.

Bowman, G. "Nationalizing the Sacred: Shrines and Shifting Identities in the Israeli-occupied territories." *Man* 28 (1993): 431–60.

Brands, G. "Architektur und Bauornamentik von Resafa-Sergiupolis." Diss., Freie Universität Berlin, 1994. Forthcoming as *Resafa,* vol. 6: *Die Bauornamentik von Resafa-Sergiupolis.*

———. "Die Entstehung einer Stadt—Beobachtungen zur Bauornamentik von Resafa." In *Spätantike und byzantinische Bauskulptur,* ed. U. Peschlow and S. Möllers, 59–74. Stuttgart, 1998.

———. "Martyrion und Bischofskirche—Anmerkungen zur Architektur und Bauornamentik des Zentralbaus von Resafa." In *Akten des 12. Internationalen Kongresses für Christliche Archäologie,* 590–97. Münster, 1995.

———. "Der sogenannte Audienzsaal des al-Mundhir in Resafa." *DaM* 10 (1998): 211–35.

Brière, M. "Introduction générale à toutes les homélies." In *Severus of Antioch, Hom. cath.* CXX–CXXV. *PO* 29.1.5–72.

Brinker, W. "Zur Wasserversorgung von Resafa-Sergiupolis." *DaM* 5 (1991): 119–46.

Brinkmann, A. "Der römische Limes im Orient." *BJ* 99 (1896): 252–57.

Brock, S. "The Syriac Background." In *Archbishop Theodore: Commemorative Studies on His Life and Influence,* ed. M. Lapidge, 30–53. Cambridge, 1995.

———. "Syriac Culture, 337–425." *Cambridge Ancient History,* 13: 708–19. Cambridge, 1998.

Brown, P. *The Cult of the Saints: Its Rise and Function in Latin Christianity.* Chicago, Il., 1981.

———. "The Diffusion of Manichaeism in the Roman Empire." *JRS* 59 (1969): 92–103. Reprinted in *Religion and Society in the Age of Saint Augustine,* 94–118 (London, 1972).

Brünnow, R. E., and A. von Domaszewski. *Die Provincia Arabia.* Strasbourg, 1904–9.

Bryce, J. "Life of Justinian by Theophilus." *EHR* 2 (1887): 657–86.

Bulliet, R. *The Camel and the Wheel.* Cambridge, Mass., 1975. Reprinted with a new preface. New York, 1990.

Butler, H. C. *Early Churches in Syria: Fourth to Seventh Centuries.* Edited by E. Baldwin Smith. Princeton, N.J., 1929.

Cameron, Alan. *Porphyrius the Charioteer.* Oxford, 1973.

Cameron, Averil, "Agathias on the Sassanians." *DOP* 23–24 (1969–70): 67–183.

———. *The Mediterranean World in Late Antiquity, A.D. 395–600.* London, 1993.

Canaan, T. *Mohammedan Saints and Sanctuaries in Palestine.* Jerusalem, n.d. Reprinted from the *Journal of the Palestine Oriental Society,* 1927.

Candea, V., and S. Agémian, eds. *Icones Melkites.* Beirut, 1969.

Candemir, H., and J. Werner. "Christliche Mosaiken in der nördlichen Euphratesia." In *Studien zur Religion und Kultur Kleinasiens: Festschrift für F. K. Dörner*, ed. S. Şahin, E. Schwertheim, and J. Werner, 192–231. Leiden, 1978.

Canivet, M.-T. "Le Reliquaire à huile de la grande église de Ḥuārte (Syrie)." *Syria* 55 (1978): 153–62.

Canivet, P., and M.-T. Canivet. *Ḥuārte: Sanctuaire chrétienne d'Apamène (IVᵉ–VIᵉ s.)* Paris, 1987.

Caquot, A. "Inscriptions judéo-arabes de Ruṣāfa (Sergiopolis)." *Syria* 32 (1955): 70–74.

Caussin de Perceval, A. P. *Essai sur l'histoire des Arabes avant l'Islamisme, pendant l'époque de Mahomet, et jusqu'à la réduction de toutes les tribus sous la loi musulmane.* Paris, 1847–48.

Chabot, J.-B. *Littérature syriaque.* Paris, 1934.

———. "Notes d'épigraphie et d'archéologie orientale." *JA* 16 (1900): 249–88.

Charles, H. *Le Christianisme des Arabes nomades sur le limes et dans le désert syro-mésopotamien aux alentours de l'Hégire.* Paris, 1936.

Chaumont, M.-L. "Où les rois sassanides étaint-ils couronnés?" *JA* 252 (1964): 59–75.

Chesney, F. R. *The Expedition for the Survey of the Rivers Euphrates and Tigris, 1835–37.* London, 1850.

Christensen, A. *L'Iran sous les Sassanides.* 2d ed. Copenhagen 1944.

Ciggar, K. "Description de Constantinople traduite par un pèlerin anglais." *REB* 34 (1976): 211–67.

Clarke, G. W. "Syriac Inscriptions from the Middle Euphrates." *Abr-Nahrain* 23 (1984–85): 73–82.

Conrad, L. "Epidemic Disease in Central Syria in the Late Sixth Century: Some New Insights from the Verse of Ḥassān ibn Thābit." *BMGS* 18 (1994): 12–58.

———. "Historical Evidence and the Archaeology of Early Islam." In *Quest for Understanding: Arabic and Islamic Studies in Memory of Malcom H. Kerr*, ed. S. Seikaly et al., 263–82. Beirut, 1991.

Contenson, H. de. "Quatrième et cinquième campagnes à Tell Ramad, 1967–1968." *AAS* 19 (1969): 25–30.

Contini, R. "Il Hawran preislamico: Ipotesi di storia linguistica." *Felix Ravenna* 4 (1987): 25–79.

Cook, M. "The Heraclian Dynasty in Muslim Eschatology." *al-Qaṭara: Revista de Estudios Arabes* 13 (1992): 3–23.

Creswell, K. A. C. *Early Muslim Architecture.* 2d ed. Vol. 1: *Umayyads.* Oxford, 1969.

Croke, B., and J. Crow. "Procopius and Dara." *JRS* 73 (1983): 143–59.

Cruikshank Dodd, E. "The Monastery of Mar Musa al-Habashi, near Nebek, Syria." *Arte medievale* 1 (1992): 61–130.

Cumont, F. *Études syriennes.* Paris, 1917.

Curtiss, S. I. *Ursemitische Religion im Volksleben des heutigen Orients. Forschungen und Funde aus Syrien und Palästina.* Translated into German by H. Stocks, with additional material by the author. Leipzig, 1903. Originally published as *Primitive Semitic Religion Today: A Record of Researches, Discoveries and Studies in Syria, Palestine and the Sinaitic Peninsula* (Chicago, Il., 1902).

Dagron, G. *Vie et miracles de Sainte Thècle.* Brussels, 1978.

Daumas, F., and A. Guillaumont. *Kellia 1. Kom 219: Fouilles exécutées en 1964 and 1965.* Cairo, 1969.

Dauphin, C. "Encore des judéo-chrétiennes au Golan?" In *Early Christianity in Context: Monuments and Documents,* ed. F. Manns and E. Alliata, 69–84. Jerusalem, 1993.

———. "Golan Survey, 1981–1982." *IEJ* 33 (1983): 112–13.

———. "Golan Survey, 1983." *IEJ* 34 (1984): 268–69.

———. "Golan Survey, 1984–1986." *IEJ* (1986): 273–75.

———. "Paysages antiques du Golan." *Archéologia* 294 (1993): 50–57.

———. "Pèlerinage ghassanide au sanctuaire byzantin de Saint Jean-Baptiste à er-Ramthaniyye en Gaulanitide." In *Akten des XII. internationalen Kongresses für christliche Archäologie,* 667–73. Münster, 1995.

———. "Er-Ramthaniyye: Surveying an Early Bedouin Byzantine Pilgrimage Centre in the Golan Heights." *BA-IAS* 8 (1988–89): 82–84.

———. "Villages désertés juifs et chrétiens du Golan." *Archéologia* 297 (1994): 52–64.

Dauphin, C., S. Brock, R. C. Gregg, and A. F. L. Beeston. "Païens, juifs, judéo-chrétiens, chrétiens, et musulmans en Gaulanitide: Les Inscriptions de Naʿaran, Kafr Naffakh, Farj et er-Ramthaniyye." *P-OChr* 46 (1996): 305–40.

Dauphin, C., and S. Gibson. "Ancient Settlements in Their Landscapes: The Results of Ten Years of Survey on the Golan Heights (1978–1988)." *BA-IAS* 12 (1992–93): 7–31.

———. "Landscape Archeology at er-Ramthaniyye in the Golan Heights." In *Archéologie et espaces: Actes des Xe rencontres internationales d'archéologie et d'histoire d'Antibes, 19–20–21 octobre 1989,* ed. J.-L. Fiches and S. van der Leeuw, 35–45. Juan-les-Pins, 1990.

Degen, R. "Die Inschriften." In T. Ulbert, *Resafa,* vol. 3: *Der Kreuzfahrerzeitliche Silberschatz aus Resafa-Sergiupolis,* 65–76. Mainz, 1990.

Delbrueck, R. *Die Consulardiptychen und verwandte Denkmäler.* Berlin, 1929.

Delehaye, H. *Les Légendes grecques des saints militaires.* Paris, 1909.

———. *Les Légendes hagiographiques.* Brussels, 1927.

———. "Les Martyrs d'Egypte." *AB* 40 (1922): 5–154.

———. *Mélanges d'hagiographie grecque et latine.* Brussels, 1966.

———. *Les Origines du culte des martyrs.* 2d ed. Brussels, 1933.

———. *Les Passions des martyrs et les genres littéraires.* Brussels, 1921.

———. Review of *Die Chronologie der altchristlichen literatur bis Eusebius,* by A. Harnack. *AB* 23 (1904): 476–80.

———, ed. and tr. *Les Versions grecques des actes des martyrs persans sous Sapor II. PO* 2.4.

Delehaye, H., et al., eds. *Propylaeum ad Acta Sanctorum Decembris. Martyrologium romanum ad formam editionis typicae.* Brussels, 1940.

Descoeudres, G. *Die Pastophorien im syro-byzantinischen Osten: Eine Untersuchung zu architektur- und liturgie-geschichtlichen Problemen.* Wiesbaden, 1983.

Devreesse, R. *Le Patriarcat d'Antioche depuis la paix de l'Église jusqu'à la conquête arabe.* Paris, 1945.

Dillemann, L. *Haute Mésopotamie orientale et pays adjacents: Contribution à la géographie historique de la région, du Ve s. avant l'ère chrétienne au VIe de cette ère.* Paris, 1962.

Doe, B. *Monuments of South Arabia.* Naples, 1983.

Donceel-Voûte, P. "La Chapelle des martyrs: Décor, archéologie et liturgie." In J. Noret, "La Société belge d'études byzantines depuis 1990." *Byzantion* 63 (1993): 437–40.

———. *Les Pavements des églises byzantines de Syrie et du Liban: Décor, archéologie et liturgie.* Louvain-la-Neuve, 1988.

———. "Le Rôle des reliquaires dans les pèlerinages." In *Akten des XII. internationalen Kongresses für christliche Archäologie,* 184–205. Münster, 1995.

Donner, F. Mc. *The Early Islamic Conquests.* Princeton, N.J., 1981.

———. "The Role of Nomads in the Near East in Late Antiquity (400–800 C.E.)." In *Tradition and Innovation in Late Antiquity,* ed. F. Clover and S. F. Humphreys, 73–85. Madison, Wis., 1989.

Doughty, C. M. *Travels in Arabia Deserta.* 3d ed. London, 1936.

Downey, G. *A History of Antioch in Syria from Seleucus to the Arab Conquest.* Princeton, N.J., 1961.

Dunand, M. "Nouvelles inscriptions du Djebel Druze et du Hauran." In *Mélanges syriens offerts à Monsieur René Dussaud, par ses amis et ses élèves.* Paris, 1939.

Durliat, J. *Les Dédicaces d'ouvrages de défense dans l'Afrique byzantine.* Rome, 1981.

Dussaud, R. *La Pénétration des Arabes en Syrie avant l'Islam.* Paris, 1955.

———. *Topographie historique de la Syrie antique et médiévale.* Paris, 1927.

Dussaud, R., and M. F. Macler. "Rapport sur une mission scientifique dans les régions désertiques de la Syrie moyenne." *Nouvelles archives des missions scientifiques et littéraires* 10 (1902): 411–744.

Duval, Y. *Loca sanctorum Africae: Le Culte des martyrs en Afrique du IVe au VIIe siècle.* Rome, 1982.

Ebersolt, J., and A. Thiers. *Les Églises de Constantinople.* Paris, 1913.

Esbroeck, M. van. "La Naissance du culte de Saint Barthélémy en Armenie." *REArm* 17 (1983): 171–95.

———. "La Vie de Saint Jean higoumène de Saint Serge par Joseph le Skevophylax." *OC* 80 (1996): 153–66.

Essen, C. van, and M. Vermaseren. *The Excavations in the Mithraeum of the Church of Sta Prisca in Rome.* Leiden, 1965.

Ettinghausen, R., and O. Grabar. *The Art and Architecture of Islam, 650–1250.* Harmondsworth, Middlesex, 1987.

Farès, B. *Vision chrétienne et signes musulmans.* Cairo, 1961.

Farioli Campanati, R. "Per un'introduzione sul Ḥawrān tardoantico." *Felix Ravenna* 141–44 (1991–92): 177–232.

Feissel, D. "Magnus Mégas et les curateurs des 'maisons divines' de Justin II à Maurice." *T&MByz* 9 (1985): 465–76.

———. "Noms de villages de Syrie du nord: Elements grecs et sémitiques." In *Ο Ελληνισμός στην Ανατολή,* 287–302. Athens, 1991.

Feissel, D., and J. Gascou. "Documents d'archives romains inédits du Moyen Euphrate (IIIe siècle après J.-C.)." *CRAI* 1989: 535–61.

Fiey, J. M. *Assyrie chrétienne: Contribution à l'étude de l'histoire et de la géographie ecclésiastiques et monastiques du nord de l'Iraq.* Beirut, 1965.

———. "Identification of Qasr Serej." *Sumer* 14 (1958): 125–27.

————. "Martyropolis syriaque." *Le Muséon* 89 (1976): 5–38.

————. "Maruta de Martyropolis d'après ibn al-Azraq (†1181)." *AB* 94 (1976): 35–45.

————. *Mossoul chrétienne: Essai sur l'histoire, l'archéologie et l'état actuel des monuments chrétiennes de la ville de Mossoul.* Beirut, 1959.

————. "Les Saints Serge de l'Iraq." *AB* 79 (1961): 102–14.

————. "Tagrît: Esquisse d'histoire chrétienne." *L'Orient Syrien* 8 (1963): 289–341.

Flusin, B. *Saint Anastase le Perse et l'histoire de la Palestine au début du VIIe siècle.* Paris, 1992.

Fowden, E. K. "An Arab Building at Rusafa-Sergiupolis." *DaM* 11 (2000).

Fowden, G. "'Desert kites': Ethnography, Archaeology and Art." In *The Roman and Byzantine Near East*, vol. 2, ed. J. Humphrey, 107–36. Portsmouth, R.I., 1999.

————. *Empire to Commonwealth: Consequences of Monotheism in Late Antiquity.* Princeton, N.J., 1993.

Franchi de' Cavalieri, P. "Dei SS. Gioventino e Massimino." In id., *Note agiographiche*, 9: 169–200. *Studi e testi*, 175. Vatican City, 1953.

Frank, R. I. *Scholae palatinae: The Palace Guards of the Late Roman Empire.* Rome, 1969.

French, D. "A Road Problem: Roman or Byzantine?" *IstMit* 43 (1993): 445–54.

Frend, W. H. C. *The Rise of the Monophysite Movement: Chapters in the History of the Church in the Fifth and Sixth Centuries.* Cambridge, 1972. Corrected reprint, 1979.

Freyberger, K. S. "Der Tempel in Slīm: Ein Bericht." *DaM* 5 (1991): 9–38.

————. "Untersuchungen zur Baugeschichte des Jupiter-Heiligtums in Damaskus." *DaM* 4 (1989): 61–86.

Galtier, E. "Contribution à l'étude de la littérature arabe-copte." *BIFAO* 4 (1905): 105–221.

Garitte, G. "La Passion géorgienne de Sainte Golindouch." *AB* 74 (1956): 405–40.

Garsoïan, N. "The Iranian Substratum of the 'Agat'angelos' Cycle." In *East of Byzantium: Syria and Armenia in the Formative Period*, ed. N. Garsoïan, T. Mathews, and R. Thomson, 151–74. Washington, D.C., 1982.

————. "Le Rôle de l'hiérarchie chrétienne dans les relations diplomatiques entre Byzance et les Sassanides." *REArm* 10 (1973–74): 119–38.

Gatier, P.-L. "Inscriptions grecques de Résafa." *DaM* 10 (1998): 237–41.

————. *Inscriptions de la Jordanie*, vol. 2: *Région centrale (Amman, Hesban, Madaba, Main, Dhiban).* Paris, 1986.

————. "Un Moine sur la frontière: Alexandre l'Acémète en Syrie." In *Frontières terrestres, frontières célestes dans l'antiquité*, ed. A. Rousselle, 435–57. Paris, 1995.

————. "Les Traditions de l'histoire du Sinaï du IVe au VIIe siècle." In *L'Arabie préislamique et son environnement historique et culturel*, ed. T. Fahd, 499–523. Leiden, 1989.

Gatier, P.-L., and Th. Ulbert. "Eine Türsturzinschrift aus Resafa-Sergiupolis." *DaM* 5 (1991): 169–82.

Gaube, H. *Ein arabischer Palast in Südsyrien: Hirbet el-Baiḍa.* Beirut, 1974.

Gawlikowski, M. "Palmyra as a Trading Centre." *Iraq* 56 (1994): 27–33.

————. Review of *The Roman Near East, 31 B.C.–A.D. 337*, by F. Millar. *JRS* 84 (1994): 244–46.

Gero, S. "The Legend of the Monk Baḥīrā, the Cult of the Cross and Iconoclasm."

In *La Syrie de Byzance à l'Islam VIIe–VIIIe siècles,* ed. P. Canivet and J.-P. Rey-Coquais, 47–58. Damascus, 1992.

Gessel, W. "Das Öl der Märtyrer: Zur Funktion und Interpretation der Ölsarkophage von Apamea in Syrien." *OC* 72 (1988): 182–202.

Gilles, P. *De topographia Constantinopoleos, et de illius antiquitatibus.* Leiden, 1562.

Gilliot, C. "Une Leçon magistrale d'Orientalisme: L'Opus magnum de J. van Ess." *Arabica* 40 (1993): 345–402.

Gogräfe, R. "Die Datierung des Tempels von Isriye." *DaM* 7 (1993): 45–61.

Goldziher, I. *Muslim Studies.* Edited by S. M. Stern. Translated from the German by C. R. Barber and S. M. Stern. Chicago, Il., 1967–71.

Gordon, R. "Reality, Evocation and Boundary in the Mysteries of Mithras." *JMS* 3 (1980): 19–99.

Grabar, A. *Martyrium: Recherches sur le culte des reliques et l'art chrétien antique.* Paris, 1946.

———. "Recherches sur les sources juives de l'art paléo-chrétien." *CArch* 11 (1960): 40–71.

Grabar, O. *The Formation of Islamic Art.* 2d ed. New Haven, Conn., 1987.

———. *The Shape of the Holy: Early Islamic Jerusalem.* Princeton, N.J., 1996.

Graf, D. "Camels, Roads and Wheels in Late Antiquity." *Electrum* 1 (1997): 43–49.

———. "Rome and the Saracens: Reassessing the Nomadic Menace." In *L'Arabie préislamique et son environnement historique et culturel,* ed. T. Fahd, 341–400. Leiden, 1989.

Graf, G. *Geschichte der christlichen arabischen Literatur. Studi e testi,* 118, 133, 146, 147, 172. Vatican City, 1944–53.

Grant, C. P. *The Syrian Desert: Caravans, Travel and Exploration.* London, 1937.

Gregory, S. *Roman Military Architecture on the Eastern Frontier.* Amsterdam, 1995–97.

Grimme, H. *Palmyrae sive Tadmur urbis fata.* Münster, 1886.

Groom, N. *A Dictionary of Arabic Topography and Place Names.* Beirut, 1983.

Hachili, R. "Late Antique Jewish Art from the Golan." In *The Roman and Byzantine Near East,* Vol. 1, ed. J. Humphrey, 183–212. Ann Arbor, Mich., 1995.

Halkin, F. "Un Second Saint Gordius?" *AB* 79 (1961): 5–15.

———, ed. *Bibliotheca hagiographica graeca.* Brussels, 1957.

Hamilton, R. *Kirbat al Mafjar: An Arabian Mansion in the Jordan Valley.* Oxford, 1959.

———. *Walid and His Friends: An Umayyad Tragedy.* Oxford, 1988.

Hammer[-Purgstall], J. von. *Constantinopolis und der Bosporus, örtlich und geschichtlich beschrieben.* Pesth, 1822.

Harper, P. O. "Thrones and Enthronement Scenes in Sasanian Art." *Iran* 17 (1979): 49–65.

Harrauer, H. "ΣΟΥΒΡΟΜ, Abrasax, Jahwe u.a. aus Syrien." *Tyche* 7 (1992): 39–44.

Harrison, M. Review of *Die Stadtmauer von Resafa in Syrien,* by W. Karnapp. *CR* 34 (1984): 105–6.

Hartmann, M. "Beiträge zur Kenntniss der syrischen Steppe." *ZDPV* 22 (1899): 127–49, 153–77; 23 (1901): 1–77, 97–158.

Harvey, S. A. *Asceticism and Society in Crisis: John of Ephesus and the Lives of the Eastern Saints.* Berkeley, Ca., 1990.

Hasluck, F. W. *Christianity and Islam under the Sultans.* Edited by M. M. Hasluck. Oxford, 1929.

Hatzidakis, M., and E. Drakopoulou. Ἕλληνες ζωγράφοι μετά τήν Ἅλωση. Athens, 1987–97.

Helms, S., with contributions by A. V. G. Betts, W. and F. Lancaster, and C. J. Lentzen. *Early Islamic Architecture of the Desert: A Bedouin Station in Eastern Jordan.* Edinburgh, 1990.

Hendy, M. F. *Studies in the Byzantine Monetary Economy c. 300–1450.* Cambridge, 1985.

Hepper, F. N., and S. Gibson. "Abraham's Oak of Mamre: The Story of a Venerable Tree." *PEQ* 126 (1994): 94–105.

Higgins, M. J. "Chosroes II's Votive Offerings at Sergiopolis." *BZ* 48 (1955): 89–102.

Hill, S. "The 'praetorium' at Mismiya." *DOP* 29 (1975): 347–49.

Høgel, C. "The Redaction of Symeon Metaphrastes: Literary Aspects of the Metaphrastic Martyria." In *Metaphrasis: Redactions and Audiences in Middle Byzantine Hagiography,* ed. C. Høgel, 7–21. Oslo, 1996.

Hoffmann, G. *Auszüge aus syrischen Akten persischer Märtyrer übersetzt und durch Untersuchungen zur historischen Topographie erläutert.* Leipzig, 1880.

Hoffmann, P. *Das spätrömische Bewegungsheer und die Notitia Dignitatum.* Düsseldorf, 1969–70.

Holum, K. "Pulcheria's Crusade, A.D. 421–22, and the Ideology of Imperial Victory." *GRBS* 18 (1977): 153–72.

————. *Theodosian Empresses: Women and Imperial Dominion in Late Antiquity.* Berkeley, Ca., 1982.

Honigmann, E. *Evêques et évêchés monophysites d'Asie antérieure au VIe siècle.* Brussels, 1951.

————. *Die Ostgrenze des byzantinischen Reiches von 363 bis 1071 nach griechischen, arabischen, syrischen und armenischen Quellen.* Brussels, 1935.

————. Review of *Le Patriarcat d'Antioche depuis la paix de l'Église jusqu'a la conquête arabe,* by R. Devreesse. *Traditio* 5 (1947): 135–61.

Horak, U. "Ein amulett aus dem 7. Jahrhundert mit der Darstellung des Hl. Sergius." In *Syrien: Von den Aposteln zu den Khalifen,* ed. E. M. Ruprechtsberger, 194–95. Mainz, 1993.

Howard-Johnston, J. "The Two Great Powers in Late Antiquity: A Comparison." In *The Byzantine and Early Islamic Near East.* Vol. 3: *States, Resources and Armies,* ed. A. Cameron, 157–226. Princeton, N.J., 1995.

Hunt, L.-A. "A Woman's Prayer to St Sergius in Latin Syria." *BMGS* 15 (1991): 96–145.

Hunter, E. C. D. "The Cult of Saints in Syria during the Fifth Century A.D." *Studia Patristica* 25 (1993): 308–12.

————. "Syriac Inscriptions from a Melkite Monastery on the Middle Euphrates." *BSOAS* 52 (1989): 1–17.

Isaac, B. "The Army in the Late Roman East: The Persian Wars and the Defence of the Byzantine Provinces." In *The Byzantine and Early Islamic Near East.* Vol. 3: *States, Resources and Armies,* ed. A. Cameron, 125–55. Princeton, N.J., 1995.

————. *The Limits of Empire: The Roman Army in the East.* Rev. ed. Oxford, 1992.

————. "An Open Frontier." In *Frontières d'empire: Nature et signification des frontières romaines,* ed. P. Brun et al., 105–14. Nemours, 1993.

Jabbur, J. S. *The Bedouins and the Desert: Aspects of Nomadic Life in the Arab East.* Translated by L. Conrad. Albany, N.Y., 1995.

Janin, R. *La Géographie ecclésiastique de l'empire byzantin,* 1: Le Siège de Constantinople et le patriarcat oecumenique, 3: Les Églises et les monastères. 2nd ed. Paris, 1969.

Jireček, C. "Das christliche Element in der topographischen Nomenklatur der Balkanländer." *Sitzungsberichte der kaiserlichen Akademie der Wissenschaften* 136 (1897): 1–98.

Johann Georg, Herzog zu Sachsen. "Sadad, Karjaten und Hawarim." *OC* 2 (1927): 233–42.

Jones, A. *Early Arabic Poetry.* Reading, 1992–96.

Jones, A. H. M. *The Cities of the Eastern Roman Empire.* 2d ed. Oxford, 1971.

———. *The Later Roman Empire, 284–602.* Oxford, 1964.

———. *The Roman Economy.* Oxford, 1974.

Kalla, G. "Das ältere Mosaik des byzantinischen Klosters in Tall Biʿa." *MDOG* 123 (1991): 35–39.

Karnapp, W. "Der Khan in der syrischen Ruinenstadt Resafa." *AA* 1978: 136–50.

———. *Die Stadtmauer von Resafa in Syrien.* Berlin, 1976.

———. "Der Vorplatz vom Zentralbau in Resafa mit den beiden Torbauten." In *Studien zur spätantiken und byzantinischen Kunst Friedrich Wilhelm Deichmann gewidmet,* ed. O. Feld and U. Peschlow, 1: 125–32. Bonn, 1986.

Kaufhold, H. "Notizen über das Moseskloster bei Nabk und das Julianskloster bei Qarytain in Syrien." *OC* 79 (1995): 48–119.

Kazhdan, A. "Post-hoc of two Byzantine miracles." *Byzantion* 52 (1982): 420–22.

Kellner-Heinkele, B. "Ruṣāfa in den arabischen Quellen." In D. Sack, *Resafa,* vol. 4: *Die Grosse Moschee von Resafa-Ruṣāfat Hišām,* 133–54. Mainz, 1996.

Kennedy, H. *The Prophet and the Age of the Caliphates: The Islamic Near East from the Sixth to the Eleventh Century.* Harlow, Essex, 1986.

Khoury, R. G. "Die arabischen Inschriften." In T. Ulbert, *Resafa,* vol. 2: *Die Basilika des Heiligen Kreuzes in Resafa-Sergiupolis,* 179–80. Mainz, 1986.

Kiilerich, B. *Late Fourth Century Classicism in the Plastic Arts: Studies in the So-called Theodosian Renaissance.* Odense, Denmark, 1993.

King, G. R. D. "Islam, Iconoclasm, and the Declaration of Doctrine." *BSOAS* 48 (1985): 267–77.

———. "Some Churches of the Byzantine Period in the Jordanian Hawran." *DaM* 3 (1988): 35–75.

———. "Two Byzantine Churches in Northern Jordan and Their Re-Use in the Islamic Period." *DaM* 1 (1983): 111–36.

Kislinger, E., and J. Diethart, "'Hunnisches' auf einem Wiener Papyrus." *Tyche* 2 (1987): 5–10.

Kleinbauer, W. E. "The Origins and Functions of the Aisled Tetraconch Churches in Syria and Northern Mesopotamia." *DOP* 27 (1973): 89–114.

Knowles, D. *Great Historical Enterprises: Problems in Monastic History.* London, ca. 1962.

Koder, J., and M. Restle. "Die Ära von Sakkaia (Maximianupolis) in Arabia." *JÖB* 42 (1992): 79–81.

Kolb, F. *Diocletian und die erste Tetrarchie. Improvisation oder Experiment in der Organisation monarchischer Herrschaft?* Berlin, 1987.

Kollwitz, J. "Die Grabungen in Resafa." In *Neue Deutsche Ausgrabungen im Mittelmeergebiet und im Vordern Orient,* 45–70. Berlin, 1959.

————. "Die Grabungen in Resafa Frühjahr 1959 und Herbst 1961." *AA* 1963: 329–60.

————. "Die Grabungen in Resafa Herbst 1954 u. Herbst 1956." *AA* 1957: 64–109.

————. "Die Grabungen in Resafa Herbst 1952." *AAS* 4–5 (1954–55): 77–83.

————. "Die Grabungen in Resafa 1952." *AA* 1954: 119–38.

Kollwitz, J., W. Wirth, and W. Karnapp. "Die Grabungen in Resafa: Herbst 1954 und 1956." *AAS* 8–9 (1958–59): 21–54.

Konrad, M. "Flavische und spätantike Bebauung unter der Basilika B von Resafa-Sergiupolis." *DaM* 6 (1992): 313–402.

————. "Frühkaiserzeitliche Befestigungen an der Strata Diocletiana? Neue Kleinfunde des 1. Jahrhunderts n.Chr. aus Nordsyrien." *DaM* 9 (1996): 163–80.

————. *Resafa.* Vol. 5: *Der spätrömische Limes in Syrien. Archäologische Untersuchungen an den Grenzkastellen von Sura, Tetrapyrgium, Cholle, und in Resafa.* Forthcoming.

Koukoules, Ph. Βυζαντινῶν βίος καὶ πολιτισμός. Athens, 1948–55.

Kraemer, C. J. *Excavations at Nessana.* Vol. 3: *Non-Literary Papyri.* Princeton, N.J., 1958.

Kramer, J. *Skulpturen mit Adlerfiguren an Bauten des 5. Jahrhunderts n. Chr. in Konstantinopel.* Cologne, 1968.

Krautheimer, R. "Again Saints Sergius and Bacchus at Constantinople." *JÖB* 23 (1974): 251–53.

Krautheimer, R., with S. Ćurčić. *Early Christian and Byzantine Architecture.* 4th ed. Harmondsworth, Middlesex, 1986.

Krebernik, M. "Schriftfunde aus Tall Biʿa 1990." *MDOG* 123 (1991): 41–70.

Kugener, M. A. "Note sur l'inscription trilingue de Zébed." *JA* 9 (1907): 509–24.

————. "Nouvelle note sur l'inscription trilingue de Zébed." *RSO* 1 (1907): 577–86.

————. "Sur l'emploi en Syrie, au VIe siècle de notre ère, du mot 'barbare' dans le sens de 'arabe.'" *OC* 7 (1907): 408–12.

Labourt, J. *Le Christianisme dans l'empire Perse sous la dynastie Sassanide (224–632).* 2d ed. Paris, 1904.

Lammens, H. "Le Chantre des Omiades: Notes biographiques et littéraires sur la poète arabe chrétien Aḥtal." *JA* 9/4 (1894): 94–176, 193–241, 381–459.

————. *La Syrie: Précis historique.* Beirut, 1921.

Lamy, Th.-J. "Profession de foi adressée par les abbés des couvents de la province d'Arabie à Jacques Baradée." In *Actes du onzième congrès international des orientalistes,* 117–37. Paris, 1898.

Lancaster, W., and F. Lancaster. "Thoughts on the Bedouinisation of Arabia." *Proceedings of the Seminar for Arabian Studies* 18 (1988): 51–62.

Lassus, J. *Sanctuaires chrétiens de Syrie: Essai sur la genèse, la forme et l'usage liturgique des édifices du culte chrétien, en Syrie, du IIIe siècle à la conquête musulmane.* Paris, 1947.

Lauffray, J. *Halabiyya-Zenobia: Place forte du limes oriental et la Haute Mésopotamie au VIe siècle.* Paris, 1983–91.

Lavin, I. "'The house of the Lord': Aspects of the Role of Palace Triclinia in the Architecture of Late Antiquity and the Early Middle Ages." *Art Bulletin* 44 (1962): 1–27.

Lee, A. D. *Information and Frontiers: Roman Foreign Relations in Late Antiquity.* Cambridge, 1993.

LeStrange, G., *Palestine under the Moslems: A Description of Syria and the Holy Land from A.D. 650 to 1500.* Boston, 1890.

Lewis, N. N. *Nomads and Settlers in Syria and Jordan, 1800–1980.* Cambridge, 1987.

Liebeschuetz, J. H. W. G. *Barbarians and Bishops: Army, Church and State in the Age of Arcadius and Chrysostom.* Oxford, 1990.

Ligt, L. de. *Fairs and Markets in the Roman Empire: Economic and Social Aspects of Periodic Trade in a Pre-Industrial Society.* Amsterdam, 1993.

Litsas, F. K. "Choricius of Gaza and His Description of Festivals at Gaza." *JÖB* 32 (1982): 427–36.

Littmann, E. "Die Gemälde der Sergios Kirche in Sadad." *OC* 3–4 (1930): 288–91.

———. "Osservazioni sulle iscrizioni di Ḥarrān e di Zebed." *RSO* 4 (1911): 193–98.

Logar, N. "Kleinfunde aus dem mittelalterlichen Wohnkomplex in Resafa." *DaM* 8 (1995): 269–92.

Lucius, E. *Die Anfänge des Heiligenkults in der christlichen Kirche.* Tübingen, 1904.

Luther, A. *Die syrische Chronik des Josua Stylites.* Berlin, 1997.

Macdonald, M. C. A. "Nomads and the Ḥawrān in the Late Hellenistic and Roman Periods: A Reassessment of the Epigraphic Evidence." *Syria* 70 (1993): 303–413.

———. "The Seasons and Transhumance." *JRAS* 2 (1992): 1–11.

Mackensen, M. "Eine limeszeitliche Scharnierarmfibel aus Resafa, Nordsyrien." *Germania* 61 (1983): 565–78.

MacMullen, R. *Christianity and Paganism in the Fourth to Eighth Centuries.* New Haven, Conn., 1997.

Maffei, F. de'. "Fortificazioni di Giustiniano sul limes orientale: monumenti e fonti." In *The Seventeenth International Byzantine Congress: Major Papers.* New York, 1986.

Magoulias, H. J. "The Lives of the Saints in the Sixth and Seventh Centuries as Sources for the Internal and External Enemies of the Byzantine Empire." Ἐπετηρὶς τῆς Ἑταιρείας Βυζαντινῶν Σπουδῶν 48 (1990–93): 281–316.

Maguire, H. *Earth and Ocean: The Terrestrial World in Early Byzantine Art.* University Park, Pa., 1987.

Majcherek, G., and A. Taha. "A Selection of Roman and Byzantine Pottery from Umm el Tlel (Syria)." *Cahiers de l'Euphrate* 7 (1993): 107–17.

Majeska, G. P. *Russian Travelers to Constantinople in the Fourteenth and Fifteenth Centuries.* Washington, D.C., 1984.

Mango, C. "L'Attitude byzantine à l'égard des antiquités gréco-romaines." In *Byzance et les images,* ed. A. Guillou and J. Durand, 95–120. Paris, 1994.

———. *Byzantine Architecture.* London, 1979.

———. "The Church of Saints Sergius and Bacchus at Constantinople and the Alleged Tradition of Octagonal Palatine Churches." *JÖB* 21 (1972): 189–93.

———. "The Church of Saints Sergius and Bacchus Once Again." *BZ* 68 (1975): 385–92.

———. "Constantine's Mausoleum and the Translation of Relics." *BZ* 83 (1990): 51–61, with addendum 434.

———. "Deux études sur Byzance et la Perse sassanide." *T&MByz* 9 (1985): 91–118.

———. "Discontinuity with the Classical Past in Byzantium." In *Byzantium and the Classical Tradition,* ed. M. Mullett and R. Scott, 48–57. Birmingham, 1981.

Ma'oz, Z. U. "The 'praetorium' at Musmiya, Again." *DOP* 44 (1990): 41–46.

Maraval, P. *Lieux saints et pèlerinages d'Orient: Histoire et géographie des origines à la conquête arabe.* Paris, 1985.

Marcos, N. F. *Los "thaumata" de Sofronio: Contribucion al estudio de la "incubatio" cristiana.* Madrid, 1975.

Marcus, R. "The Armenian Life of Marutha of Maipherkat." *HThR* 25 (1932): 47–71.

Marx, E. "The Ecology and Politics of Nomadic Pastoralists in the Middle East." In *The Nomadic Alternative: Modes and Models of Interaction in the African-Asian Deserts and Steppes,* ed. W. Weissleder, 41–74. The Hague, 1978.

Mathews, T. F. "Architecture et liturgie dans les premières églises palatiales de Constantinople." *Revue de l'art* 24 (1974): 22–29.

Matthews, J. "The Tax Law of Palmyra: Evidence for Economic History in a City of the Roman East." *JRS* 74 (1984): 157–80.

Meimaris, Y., with K. Kritikakou and P. Bougia. *Chronological Systems in Roman-Byzantine Palestine and Arabia: The Evidence of the Dated Greek Inscriptions.* Athens, 1992.

Meischner, J. "Der Hochzeitskameo des Honorius." *AA* 1993: 613–19.

Mercati, S. G. "Epigraphica." *Rendiconti: Atti della pontificia accademia romana di archeologia* 3 (1924–25): 191–214.

Millar, F. *The Emperor in the Roman World, 31 B.C.–A.D. 337.* Corrected reprint. Ithaca, N.Y., 1992.

———. *The Roman Near East, 31 B.C.–A.D. 337.* Cambridge, Mass., 1993.

Miller, E. *Mélanges de philologie et d'épigraphie.* Paris, 1876.

Miller, K. *Itineraria romana: Römische Reisewege an der hand der Tabula Peutingeriana.* Stuttgart, 1916.

Millingen, A. van. *Byzantine Churches in Constantinople: Their History and Architecture.* London, 1912.

Mingana, A. "The Early Spread of Christianity in Central Asia and the Far East: A New Document." *BRL* 9 (1925): 297–371.

Mirzoyan, A. "Les Représentations des saints militaires dans le manuscrit No. 6305 Matenadaran M. Mašto'." *REArm* 20 (1986–87): 441–55.

Mitchell, S. *Anatolia: Land, Men and Gods in Asia Minor.* Oxford, 1993.

———. "Maximus and the Christians in A.D. 312." *JRS* 78 (1988): 105–24.

Mondésert, C. "Inscriptions et objets chrétiens de Syrie et de Palestine." *Syria* 37 (1960): 116–30.

Montgomery, J. E. "The Deserted Encampment in Ancient Arabic Poetry: A Nexus of Topical Comparisons." *JSS* 40 (1995): 283–316.

Morony, M. *Iraq after the Muslim Conquest.* Princeton, N.J., 1984.

Mouterde, R. "Dieux cavaliers de la région d'Alep: Collections Guillaume Poche et François Marcopoli." *MUSJ* 11 (1926): 307–22.

———. Review of *Topographie historique de la Syrie antique et médiévale,* by R. Dussaud. *MUSJ* 12 (1927): 274.

Mouterde, R., and A. Poidebard. *Le Limes de Chalcis: Organisation de la steppe en haute Syrie romaine.* Paris, 1945.

———. See also A. Poidebard.

Moyses (Monachos Agioreites). Ἁγιορείτικες διηγήσεις τοῦ Γέροντος Ἰωακείμ. Thessaloniki, 1989.

Müller, A. "Die Strafjustiz im römischen Heere." *NJKA* 17 (1906) 550–77

Mundell, M. "Monophysite Church Decoration." In *Iconoclasm: Papers Given at the Ninth Spring Symposium of Byzantine Studies*, ed. A. Bryer and J. Herrin, 59–74. Birmingham, 1977.

Mundell Mango, M. *Silver from Early Byzantium: The Kaper Koraon and Related Treasures*. Baltimore, 1986.

Musil, A., et al. *Ḳuṣejr ʿAmra*. Vienna, 1907.

———. *The Manners and Customs of the Rwala Bedouins*. New York, 1928.

———. *The Middle Euphrates: A Topographical Itinerary*. New York, 1927.

———. *Northern Arabia*. New York, 1928.

———. *Palmyrena: A Topographical Itinerary*. New York, 1928.

Naguib, S.-A. "The Martyr as Witness: Coptic and Copto-Arabic Hagiographies as Mediators of Religious Memory." *Numen* 41 (1994): 223–54.

Nau, F. *Les Arabes chrétiens de Mésopotamie et de Syrie du VIIe au VIIIe siècle*. Paris, 1933.

———, ed. and tr. *Un Martyrologe et douze ménologes syriaques*. PO 10.1.

Newby, G. D. *The Making of the Last Prophet: A Reconstruction of the Earliest Biography of Muhammad*. Columbia, S.C., 1989.

Nicholson, O. "The 'pagan churches' of Maximinus Daia and Julian the Apostate." *JEH* 45 (1994): 1–10.

———. "Two Notes on Dara." *AJA* 89 (1985): 663–71.

Nicolle, D. "Arms of the Umayyad Era: Military Technology in a Time of Change." In *War and Society in the Eastern Mediterranean, Seventh through Fifteenth Centuries*, ed. Y. Lev, 9–100. Leiden, 1997.

Nöldeke, Th. *Die Ghâssanischen Fürsten aus dem Hause Gafna's*. Berlin, 1887.

———. "Zur Topographie und Geschichte des damaszenischen Gebiets und der Haurangegend." *ZDMG* 29 (1875): 419–44.

Nogaret, M. "Quelques problèmes archéologiques et topographiques dans la région de Maiyafarikin." *REArm* 18 (1984): 411–33.

Noret, J. "La Vie grecque ancienne de S. Marūtā de Mayferqaṭ." *AB* 91 (1973): 77–103.

Norris, H. T. *Islam in the Balkans: Religion and Society between Europe and the Arab World*. Columbia, S.C., 1993.

Oates, D. *Studies in the Ancient History of Northern Iraq*. London, 1968.

Okada, Y. "Early Christian Architecture in the Iraqi South-Western Desert." *al-Rāfidān* 12 (1991): 71–83.

———. "Reconsideration of Plaque-type Crosses from Ain Sha'ia near Najaf." *al-Rāfidān* 11 (1990): 103–12.

Oliphant, L. "New Discoveries." *PEQ* 1886: 73–81.

Oppenheim, M. F. von. *Die Beduinen*. Leipzig, 1939–1968.

Oppenheim, M. von, and H. Lucas. "Griechische und lateinishe Inschriften aus Syrien, Mesopotamien und Kleinasien." *BZ* 14 (1905): 1–74.

Orselli, A. M. *Santità militare e culto dei santi nell'impero dei Romani (secoli VI–X)*. Bologna, 1993.

Païssios Hagioreitis. Ὁ Ἅγιος Ἀρσένιος ὁ Καππαδόκης. Thessaloniki, 1987.

Palmer, A. "The Messiah and the Mahdi: History Presented as the Writing on the Wall." In *Polyphonia byzantina: Studies in Honour of Willem J. Aerts*, ed. H. Hokwerda et al., 45–84. Groningen, 1993.

———. *Monk and Mason on the Tigris Frontier: The Early History of Tur ʿAbdin*. Cambridge, 1990.

Palmer, A., with S. Brock and R. Hoyland. *The Seventh Century in the West Syrian Chronicles*. Liverpool, 1993.

Paret, R. "Dometianus de Mélitène et la politique religieuse de l'empereur Maurice." *REB* 15 (1957): 42–72.

Pazdernik, C. "'Our most pious consort given us by God': Dissident Reactions to the Partnership of Justinian and Theodora, A.D. 525–548." *CA* 13 (1994): 256–81.

Peeters, P. "Les Ex-Voto de Khosrau Aparwez à Sergiopolis." *AB* 65 (1947): 5–56.

———. "Le Martyrologe de Rabban Sliba." *AB* 27 (1908): 129–200.

———. *L'Oeuvre des Bollandistes*. 2d ed. Brussels, 1961.

———. "La Passion arménienne de S. Serge le Stratélate." In *Recherches d'histoire et de philologie orientales*, 1: 25–36. Brussels, 1951.

———. "La Passion de S. Pierre de Capitolias (†13 Janvier 715)." *AB* 57 (1939): 299–333.

———. "Sainte Golindouch, martyre Perse (†13 Juillet 591)." *AB* 62 (1944): 74–125.

———. *Le Tréfonds oriental de l'hagiographie byzantine*. Brussels, 1950.

———, ed. *Bibliotheca hagiographica orientalis*. Brussels, 1910.

Peters, F. E. "Romans and Bedouin in Southern Syria." *JNES* 37 (1978): 315–26.

Peterson, E. *Εἷς θεός. Epigraphische, formgeschichtliche und religionsgeschichtliche Untersuchungen*. Göttingen, 1926.

Pigulevskaya, N. V. *Byzanz auf den Wegen nach Indien*. Berlin, 1969.

Pinoteau, H. de. "Heraldische Untersuchungen zum Wappenpokal." In T. Ulbert, *Resafa*, vol. 3: *Der Kreuzfahrerzeitliche Silberschatz aus Resafa-Sergiupolis*, 77–86. Mainz, 1990.

Pognon, H. *Inscriptions sémitiques de la Syrie, de la Mésopotamie et de la région de Mossoul*. Paris, 1907.

Poidebard, A. *La Trace de Rome dans le désert de Syrie: Le Limes de Trajan à la conquête arabe. Recherches aériennes (1925–1932)*. Paris, 1934.

Poidebard, A., and R. Mouterde. "À propos de Saint Serge: Aviation et épigraphie." *AB* 67 (1949): 109–16.

Polites, N. G. *"Υβριστικὰ σχήματα'*, *Λαογραφία* 4 (1913–14): 601–69.

Pringle, D. *The Defence of Byzantine Africa from Justinian to the Arab Conquest: An Account of the Military History and Archaeology of the African Provinces in the Sixth and Seventh Centuries*. Oxford, 1981.

Raby, J., and J. Johns, eds. *Bayt al-Maqdis: ʿAbd al-Malik's Jerusalem*. Oxford, 1992–.

Reich, S. *Études sur les villages araméens de l'Anti-Liban*. Damascus, n.d.

Retsö, J. "The Road to Yarmuk: The Arabs and the Fall of the Roman Power in the Middle East." In *Aspects of Late Antiquity and Early Byzantium*, ed. L. Rydén and J. O. Rosenqvist, 31–41. Istanbul, 1993.

Rey-Coquais, J.-P. *Arados et sa pérée aux époques grecque, romaine, et byzantine*. Paris, 1974.

———. "Syrie romaine de Pompée à Dioclétien." *JRS* 68 (1978): 44–73.

Robin, C. "Le Royaume ḥujride, dit 'royaume de Kinda', entre Himyar et Byzance."
    CRAI 1996: 665–702.
Robinson, C. F. "Ibn al-Azraq, His *Taʾrīkh Mayyāfāriqīn* and Early Islam." *JRAS* 6
    (1996): 7–27.
Römer, C. "Die griechischen Graffiti." In T. Ulbert, *Resafa,* vol. 2: *Die Basilika des
    Heiligen Kreuzes in Resafa-Sergiupolis,* 171–77. Mainz, 1986.
Roey, A. van, and P. Allen, eds. and trs. *Monophysite Texts of the Sixth Century.* Leuven,
    1994.
Ronzevalle, P. "Dieu cavalier sur un bas-relief syrien." *CRAI* 1904: 8–12.
Rosen, S. A. "A Roman-period Pastoral Tent Camp in the Negev, Israel." *JFieldArch*
    20 (1993): 441–51.
Rossi, I. B. de, and L. Duchesne, eds. *Martyrologium Hieronymianum.* In *Acta Sancto-
    rum Novembris,* 2, pt. 1: [I–195]. Brussels, 1894.
Rostovtzeff, M. I. "The Caravan Gods of Palmyra." *JRS* 22 (1932): 105–16.
———. "Dura and the Problem of Parthian Art." *YCS* 5 (1935): 157–304.
———. "Graffiti Showing Parthian Warriors." In *The Excavations at Dura-Europos: Pre-
    liminary Report of Second Season of Work, October 1928–April 1929,* ed. P. V. C. Baur
    and M. I. Rostovtzeff, 194–200. New Haven, Conn., 1931.
Rothstein, G. *Die Dynastie der Ḷahmiden in al-Ḥîra: Ein Versuch zur arabisch-persischen
    Geschichte zur Zeit der Sasaniden.* Berlin, 1899.
Roueché, C. "Acclamations in the Later Roman Empire: New Evidence from Aphro-
    disias." *JRS* 74 (1984): 181–99.
Rubin, Z. "Byzantium and Southern Arabia: The Policy of Anastasius." In *The East-
    ern Frontier of the Roman Empire,* ed. D. H. French and C. S. Lightfoot, 383–420.
    Oxford, 1989.
———. "Diplomacy and War in the Relations between Byzantium and the Sassanids
    in the Fifth Century A.D." In *The Defence of the Roman and Byzantine East,* ed.
    P. Freeman and D. Kennedy, 677–95. Oxford, 1986.
———. "The Mediterranean and the Dilemma of the Roman Empire in Late An-
    tiquity." *MHR* 1 (1986): 13–62.
Ruprechtsberger, E. M., ed. *Syrien: Von den Aposteln zu den Khalifen.* Mainz, 1993.
Sack, D. *Damaskus: Entwicklung und Struktur einer orientalisch-islamischen Stadt.* Mainz,
    1989.
———. *Resafa.* Vol. 4: *Die Grosse Moschee von Resafa-Ruṣāfat Hišām.* Mainz, 1996.
Sako, L. *Le Rôle de la hiérarchie syriaque orientale dans les rapports diplomatiques entre la
    Perse et Byzance aux Ve–VIIe siècles.* Paris, 1986,
Sarre, F., and E. Herzfeld. *Archäologische Reise im Euphrat und Tigris Gebiet.* Berlin,
    1911–20.
Sartre, M. "Les Arabes nomades d'Arabie du nord-ouest d'Alexandre au haut-
    empire." In *Le Désert: Image et réalité,* ed. Y. Christie et al., 139–60. Leuven, 1989.
———. *Bostra: Des origines à l'Islam.* Paris, 1985.
———. *Trois études sur l'Arabie romaine et byzantine.* Brussels, 1982.
Sauvaget, J. "Les Ghassanides et Sergiopolis." *Byzantion* 14 (1939): 115–30.
———. *La Mosquée omeyyade de Médine: Étude sur les origines architecturales de la mosquée
    et de la basilique.* Paris, 1947.
Savignac, M. R., and M. Abel. "Chronique." *RB* 2 (1905): 592–606.
Schippmann, K. *Die iranischen Feuerheiligtümer.* Berlin, 1971.

Schlumberger, D. *La Palmyrène du nord-ouest.* Paris, 1951.

Schumacher, G. *The Jaulan.* London, 1888.

Segal, J. B. *Edessa: "The blessed city."* Oxford, 1970.

Serjeant, R. B. "Ḥaram and Ḥawṭah, the Sacred Enclosure in Arabia." In id., *Studies in Arabian History and Civilization,* vol. 3. London, 1981.

———. "Saint Sergius." In id., *Studies in Arabian History and Civilization,* II. London, 1981.

Serjeant, R. B., and R. Lewcock, eds. *Ṣanʿāʾ: An Arabian Islamic City.* London, 1983.

Seyrig, H. "Antiquités syriennes: Les Dieux armés et les Arabes en Syrie." *Syria* 47 (1970): 77–112.

———. "Antiquités syriennes: L'Incorporation de Palmyre à l'empire romaine." *Syria* 13 (1932): 266–77.

———. "Inscriptions grecques." In G. Tchalenko, *Villages antiques de la Syrie du Nord: Le Massif du Bélus à l'époque romaine,* 3: 2–62. Paris, 1958.

Shahîd, I. "The Arabs in the Peace Treaty of A.D. 561." In id. *Byzantium and the Semitic Orient before the Rise of Islam,* VII. London, 1988.

———. *Byzantium and the Arabs in the Fifth Century.* Washington, D.C., 1989.

———. *Byzantium and the Arabs in the Fourth Century.* Washington, D.C., 1984.

———. *Byzantium and the Arabs in the Sixth Century.* Washington, D.C., 1995–.

———. "Ghassān post Ghassān." In *The Islamic World from Classical to Modern Times: Essays in Honor of Bernard Lewis,* ed. C. E. Bosworth et al., 323–36. Princeton, N.J., 1989.

———. *The Martyrs of Najrân. New Documents.* Brussels, 1971.

———. "The Patriciate of Arethas." In id., *Byzantium and the Semitic Orient before the Rise of Islam.* London, 1988.

———. "Procopius and Arethas, Part One." In id. *Byzantium and the Semitic Orient before the Rise of Islam.* London, 1988.

———. "The Restoration of the Ghassanid Dynasty, A.D. 587: Dionysius of Tellmahre." *ARAM* [A Festschrift for Dr. Sebastian P. Brock] 5 (1993): 491–503.

Sinclair, T. A. *Eastern Turkey: An Architectural and Archaeological Survey.* London, 1987–90.

———. "The Site of Tigranocerta.I." *REArm* 25 (1994–95): 183–253.

Sotiriou, G., and M. Sotiriou. *Ἡ βασιλικὴ τοῦ Ἁγίου Δημητρίου.* Athens, 1952.

Spanner, H., and S. Guyer. *Rusafa: Die Wallfahrtsstadt des Heiligen Sergios.* Berlin, 1926.

Speidel, M. P. "Late Roman Military Decorations, I: Neck- and Wristbands." *Antiquité tardive* 4 (1996): 235–43.

———. *Riding for Caesar: The Roman Emperor's Horse Guards.* London, 1994.

Spier, J. "Medieval Byzantine Amulets and their Tradition." *JWI* 56 (1993): 25–62.

Stein, E. *Histoire du bas-empire.* 2d ed. Vol. 1. Paris, 1959. Vol. 2. Paris, 1949.

Stern, H. "Sur quelques pavements paléo-chrétiens du Liban." *CArch* 15 (1965): 21–37.

Stetkevych, J. *The Zephyrs of Najd: The Poetics of Nostalgia in the Classical Arabic* nasīb. Chicago, Il., 1993.

Strommenger, E. "Ausgrabungen in Tall Biʿa 1990." *MDOG* 123 (1991): 7–34.

———. "Die Ausgrabungen in Tall Biʿa 1992." *MDOG* 125 (1993): 5–11.

———. "Die Ausgrabungen in Tall Biʿa 1993." *MDOG* 126 (1994): 11–31.

Syme, R. *Anatolica: Studies in Strabo.* Edited by A. Birley. Oxford, 1995.

———. "Tigranocerta: A Problem Misconceived." In *Armies and Frontiers in Roman and Byzantine Anatolia,* ed. S. Mitchell, 61–70. Oxford, 1983.

Taha, A. "Prospection du site romaine tardif de Juwal (cuvette d'el Kowm, Syrie)." *Cahiers de l'Euphrate* 5–6 (1991): 61–66.

Tardieu, M. *Les Paysages reliques: Routes et haltes syriennes d'Isidore à Simplicius.* Louvain, 1990.

Tate, G. *Les Campagnes de la Syrie du Nord du IIe au VIIe siècle: Un Exemple d'expansion démographique et économique à la fin de l'antiquité.* Paris, 1992–.

Tchalenko, G. *Églises syriennes à bêma.* Paris, 1990.

———. *Villages antiques de la Syrie du Nord: Le Massif du Bélus à l'époque romaine.* Paris, 1953–58.

Teixidor, J. "Deux inscriptions palmyréniennes du Musée de Bagdad." *Syria* 40 (1963): 33–46.

———. "La Palmyrène orientale: Frontière militaire ou zone douanière?" In *Frontières d'empire: Nature et signification des frontières romaines,* ed. P. Brun et al., 95–103. Nemours, 1993.

Thierry, J. M. *Monuments arméniens du Vaspurakan.* Paris, 1989.

Tillemont, L. S. Le Nain de. *Mémoires pour servir a l'histoire ecclésiastique des six premiers siècles.* Venice, 1732. Revision of the second Paris edition.

Trimingham, J. S. *Christianity among the Arabs in Pre-Islamic Times.* London, 1979.

Trombley, F. R. *Hellenic Religion and Christianization, c. 370–529.* Leiden, 1993–94.

———. "War and Society in Rural Syria, c. 502–613 A.D.: Observations on Epigraphy." *BMGS* 21 (1997): 154–209.

Ulbert, T. "Beobachtungen im Westhofbereichen der Großen Basilika von Resafa." *DaM* (1993): 403–16.

———. "Bischof und Kathedrale (4.–7. Jh): Archäologische Zeugnisse in Syrien." In *Actes du XIe congrès international d'archéologie chrétienne,* ed. N. Duval, 1: 429–57. Rome, 1989.

———. "Eine neuentdeckte Inschrift aus Resafa (Syrien)." *AA* 1977: 563–69.

———. *Resafa.* Vol. 2: *Die Basilika des Heiligen Kreuzes in Resafa-Sergiupolis.* Mainz, 1986.

———. *Resafa.* Vol. 3: *Der Kreuzfahrerzeitliche Silberschatz aus Resafa-Sergiupolis.* Mainz, 1990.

———. "Resafa-Sergiupolis 1976–83." *AAS* 33.2 (1983): 69–82.

———. "Resafa-Sergiupolis: Archäologische Forschungen in der Nordsyrischen Pilgerstadt." In *Syrien: Von den Aposteln zu den Khalifen,* ed. E. M. Ruprechtsberger, 112–27. Mainz, 1993.

———. "The Silver Treasures of Resafa / Sergiupolis." In *The Near East in Antiquity,* ed. S. Kerner, 105–10. Amman, 1990.

———. "Ein umaiyadischer Pavillon in Resafa-Ruṣāfat Hišām." *DaM* 7 (1993): 213–31.

———. "Villes et fortifications de l'Euphrate à l'époque paléo-chrétienne." In *Archéologie et histoire de la Syrie,* vol. 2, ed. J.-M. Dentzer and W. Orthmann, 283–96. Saarbrücken, 1989.

———. "Zwei sigmaförmige Mensaplatten aus Syrien." In *Pietas: Festschrift für Bernhard Kötting,* ed. E. Dassmann and K. Suso Frank, 559–65. Münster, 1980.

————. See also P.-L. Gatier.

Van Dam, R. *Saints and Their Miracles in Late Antique Gaul.* Princeton, N.J., 1993.

Velmans, T. "Observations sur quelques peintures murales en Syrie et Palestine et leur composante byzantine orientale." *CArch* 42 (1994): 123–38.

Vikan, G. "Art, Medicine and Magic in Early Byzantium." *DOP* 38 (1984): 65–86.

————. "Two Unpublished Pilgrim Tokens in the Benaki Museum and the Group to Which They Belong." In Θυμίαμα στην μνήμη της Λασκαρίνας Μπούρα, 341–46. Athens, 1994.

Villeneuve, F. "L'Économie rurale et la vie des campagnes dans le Hauran antique" (1er siècle avant J.-C.–VIe siècle après J.-C.) In *Hauran: Recherches archéologiques sur la Syrie du sud a l'époque hellénistique et romaine,* ed. J.-M. Dentzer, 63–136. Paris, 1985–.

Vogüé, M. de, and W. H. Waddington. *La Syrie central: Architecture civile et religieuse du Ier au VIIe siècle.* Paris, 1865.

Wagner, E., Abū Nuwās. *Eine Studie zur arabischen Literatur der frühen 'Abbāsidenzeit.* Wiesbaden, 1965.

Walker, J. T. "'Your heroic deeds give us pleasure!': Culture and Society in the Christian Martyr Legends of Late Antique Iraq." Ph.D. diss., Princeton, 1998.

Walter, C. "The Intaglio of Solomon in the Benaki Museum and the Origins of the Iconography of Warrior Saints." *DCAE* 15 (1989–90): 33–42.

————. "The Origins of the Cult of Saint George." *REB* 53 (1995): 295–326.

————. Review of *Studies on Constantinople,* by C. Mango. *REB* 53 (1995): 374–76.

————. "Some Unpublished Intaglios of Solomon in the British Museum, London." In Θυμίαμα στην μνήμη της Λασκαρίνας Μπούρα, 365–68. Athens, 1994.

————. "The Thracian Horseman: Ancestor of the Warrior Saints." *ByzF* 14 (1989): 1.657–73, with 2.pls 249–55.

Weber, T. "Karawangötter in der Dekapolis." *DaM* 8 (1995): 203–11.

Weigand, E. "Das sogenannte Praetorium von Phaena-Mismije." In *Würzburger Festgabe Heinrich Bulle,* 71–92. Stuttgart, 1938.

Weiss, H. "Archeology in Syria." *AJA* 98 (1994): 101–58.

Weitzmann, K., ed. *Age of Spirituality: Late Antique and Early Christian Art, Third to Seventh Century.* New York, 1979.

————. *The Monastery of Saint Catherine at Mount Sinai: The Icons,* vol. 1: *From the Sixth to the Tenth Century.* Princeton, N.J., 1976.

Wemhoff, M. "Ein mittelalterlicher Wohnkomplex in Resafa." *DaM* 8 (1995): 247–68.

Whitby, M. *The Emperor Maurice and His Historian: Theophylact Simocatta on Persian and Balkan Warfare.* Oxford, 1988.

————. "Procopius and the Development of Roman Defences in Upper Mesopotamia." In *The Defence of the Roman and Byzantine East,* ed. P. Freeman and D. Kennedy, 717–35. Oxford, 1986.

Whittaker, C. R. *Frontiers of the Roman Empire: A Social and Economic Study.* Baltimore, 1994.

Whittow, M. *The Making of Orthodox Byzantium, 600–1025.* London, 1996.

Wiessner, G. "Christlicher Heiligenkult im Umkreis eines sassanidischen Großkönigs." In *Festgabe deutscher Iranisten zur 2500 Jahrfeier Irans,* ed. W. Eilers, 141–55. Stuttgart, 1971.

———. *Christliche Kultbauten im Ṭūr ʿAbdīn.* Wiesbaden, 1982–83.

———. *Zur Märtyrerüberlieferung aus der Christenverfolgung Schapurs II.* Göttingen, 1967.

Wifstrand, A. "Autokrator, Kaisar, Basileus. Bemerkungen zu den griechischen Benennungen der römischen Kaiser." In ΔΡΑΓΜΑ Martino P. Nilsson A.D. IV Id. Iul. anno MCM XXXIX dedicatum, 529–39. N.p., 1939.

Wilkinson, J. "Column capitals in the Ḥaram al-Sharīf." In *Bayt al-Maqdis: ʿAbd al-Malik's Jerusalem,* ed. J. Raby and J. Johns, 125–39. Oxford, 1992–.

———. *Jerusalem Pilgrims before the Crusades.* Warminster, Wilts., 1977.

Will, E. "Damas antique." *Syria* 71 (1994): 1–43.

Wirth, E. *Syrien: Eine geographische Landskunde.* Darmstadt, 1971.

Woods, D. "The Emperor Julian and the Passion of Sergius and Bacchus." *JECS* 5 (1997): 335–67.

Wuthnow, H. *Die semitischen Menschennamen in griechishen Inschriften und Papyri des vorderen Orients.* Leipzig, 1930.

Zacos, G., and A. Veglery. *Byzantine Lead Seals.* Basel, 1972.

Ziegler, R. "Aigeai, der Asklepioskult, das Kaiserhaus der Decier und das Christentum." *Tyche* 9 (1994): 187–212.

INDEX

Text: 10/12 Baskerville
Display: Baskerville
Composition: G & S Typesetters, Inc.
Printing and binding: Thomson-Shore, Inc.
Maps: Bill Nelson Cartography

HIEBERT LIBRARY

3 6877 00166 4142

BR
1720
.S23
F68
1999

DATE DUE

Demco, Inc. 38-293